The World in Brooklyn

The World in Brooklyn

Gentrification, Immigration, and Ethnic Politics in a Global City

Edited by Judith N. DeSena and Timothy Sortell

LEXINGTON BOOKS
Lanham • Boulder • New York • Toronto • Plymouth, UK

Published by Lexington Books
A wholly owned subsidiary of Rowman & Littlefield
4501 Forbes Boulevard, Suite 200, Lanham, Maryland 20706
www.rowman.com

10 Thornbury Road, Plymouth PL6 7PP, United Kingdom

First paperback edition 2014

British Library Cataloguing in Publication Information Available

Library of Congress Cataloging-in-Publication Data
The hardback edition of this book was previously catalogued by the Library of Congress as follows:

The world in Brooklyn : gentrification, immigration, and ethnic politics in a global city / edited by Judith DeSena and Timothy Shortell.
p. cm.
Includes bibliographical references and index.
ISBN 978-0-7391-6670-3 (cloth : alk. paper)—ISBN 978-0-7391-6671-0 (electronic)
1. Gentrification --New York (State) --Brooklyn. 2. Community development --New York (State) --Brooklyn. 3. Brooklyn (New York, N.Y.) --Social conditions. 4. Brooklyn (New York, N.Y.) --Economic conditions. 5. Brooklyn (New York, N.Y.) --Ethnic relations. I. DeSena, Judith N. II. Shortell, Timothy.
HN80.B856 W67 2012
307.3/416097471—dc23

2012006296

ISBN 978-0-7391-6670-3 (cloth : alk. paper)
ISBN 978-0-7391-9063-0 (pbk : alk. paper)
ISBN 978-0-7391-6671-0 (electronic)

™ The paper used in this publication meets the minimum requirements of American National Standard for Information Sciences—Permanence of Paper for Printed Library Materials, ANSI/NISO Z39.48-1992.

Printed in the United States of America

Contents

Figures

Tables

1

Introduction

The World in Brooklyn

Judith N. DeSena and Timothy Shortell

Throughout its history, Brooklyn has been a destination for many. Brooklyn is ranked the 4th largest city in America[1] and a major contributor to New York City's first place ranking. With its Native American roots and pastoral beginnings, to Dutch migrants engaging in commerce and building the environment, and European descendents opening factories to immigrants seeking work, Brooklyn accommodated one and all. Its role in this regard continues. While there has been a shift to a service economy and a change of immigrant and migrant groups, the amenities that Brooklyn offers have kept pace. Brooklyn is a mosaic of diversity comprised of always changing neighborhoods. Brooklyn adjusts and is recycled to meet social needs.

Like other global cities, the story of contemporary Brooklyn is about, in large measure, mobility. As Abrahamson (2004) noted, until quite recently, most of the movement of people and goods occurred within national boundaries rather than between them. In this age of globalization, the ratio has shifted toward global mobility. The number of immigrants to New York City in the 1990s was nearly twice the number from the 1980s (New York City Department of City Planning 2004). In 2009, there were more than 900,000 foreign-born persons in Brooklyn—more than the entire population of any city in Florida, and roughly the size of San Jose, California, the tenth largest city in the U.S. (U.S. Census 2011).

But the global movement of people did not erase or negate other kinds of mobility in Brooklyn. The displacement of lower status communities by higher status populations—also known as gentrification—continues to accelerate. Migration, domestic and global, intersects with social class mobility, of course, and takes place in the context of our long history of race relations. Brooklyn is a place of neighborhoods, and these communities get ascribed with social identities just as people do. So the story of contemporary Brooklyn is a story of immigrant neighborhoods and native-born neighborhoods, of black neighborhoods and white neighborhoods, of poor neighborhoods and rich ones.[2]

Brooklyn's image and reputation has been transformed. Popular representations include iconic places like the Brooklyn Bridge, Coney Island, and Junior's Restaurant with its gritty waterfront and rough neighborhoods inhabited by residents who speak with a vernacular "Brooklyn accent." Present day Brooklyn has a different picture. Reflections are of Brownstone Brooklyn, hip Williamsburg, and enduring poverty in neighborhoods like East New York. For many newcomers, it is with pride that one resides in Brooklyn. But there is no one Brooklyn. Residents have distinct experiences in that Brooklyn's neighborhoods can provide them with dissimilar worlds. What has been constant about Brooklyn is that it has, throughout its development, embraced "the world." Thus, we arrive at this book.

The World in Brooklyn: Gentrification, Immigration, and Ethnic Politics in a Global City, is a collection of scholarly papers which analyze demographic, social, political, and economic trends that are occurring in Brooklyn. Brooklyn, as the context, reflects global forces while also contributing to them. The idea for this volume developed as the editors discovered that there is a group of scholars from different disciplines and various universities studying Brooklyn. Brooklyn has always been legendary and has more recently regained its stature as a much sought after place to live, work, and have fun. Popular folklore has it that most U.S. residents trace their family origins to Brooklyn. It is presently referred to as one of the "hippest" places in New York. Thus, we think a collection of demographic, ethnographic, and comparative studies which focus on urban dynamics in Brooklyn is timely.

This book investigates issues of social class, urban development, immigration, race, ethnicity, and politics within the context of Brooklyn. It begins with a demographic profile of Brooklyn. In "Mapping a Changing Brooklyn, Mapping a Changing World: Gentrification and Immigration, 2000–2008," Lorna Mason, Ed Morlock, and Christina Pisano use Census microdata to uncover four distinct spatial patterns. Northwest Brooklyn, often called "gold coast Brooklyn" is experiencing gentrification by U.S. migrants who are highly educated and mostly white. The outer circle of Brooklyn is composed largely of new and existing immigrant populations. New residents are mostly foreign born, lower income, and ethnically mixed relative to the existing population. Between the gold coast and the outer circle are newcomers who are predominantly white and lower income, and are bringing change to black and Hispanic immigrant neighborhoods. Finally, the most eastern portion of Brooklyn shows little change.

The next chapter, "Forgetting Poverty in Brooklyn and the United States," William DiFazio carries out an analysis of one of the neighborhoods in Brooklyn that has not changed much, but presents persistent poverty. He examines poverty through the "guests" of a soup kitchen in Bedford-Stuyvesant. He shows that poverty in Brooklyn is a reflection of poverty in the larger United States, and that it has become a problem of the middle class as well. According to DiFazio, the global economic crises have worsened conditions for the poor in Brooklyn.

The following section of chapters focus on gentrification and development and in some cases indicates how development is used as an engine of gentrification. Judith N. DeSena discusses "Gentrification in Everyday Life in Brooklyn." With a spotlight on Greenpoint, this chapter analyzes neighborhood change viewing social class as an element of the local culture. It points out how social class differences lead to the creation and maintenance of parallel cultures. This theme is illustrated by exploring the everyday struggles between gentry and working class residents, and the choices made to separate according to social class rather than assimilate and integrate.

Sara Martucci examines an annual event in her chapter on "Williamsburg Walks: Public Space and Community Events in a Gentrified Neighborhood." Through a community event, this article indicates another way that gentrification creates social segregation, and exemplifies DeSena's notion of parallel cultures. Exclusionary practices were used in this event, according to Martucci, to create a new brand for a neighborhood.

Kenneth Gould and Tammy Lewis explore "The Environmental Injustice of Green Gentrification: The Case of Brooklyn's Prospect Park." This chapter reveals how the revitalization of an environmental amenity, in this case Prospect Park, contributes to the displacement of poor and minority residents living in surrounding neighborhoods. The rejuvenation of environmental amenities, according to Gould and Lewis, raises property values which results in pricing-out long-term residents. For Gould and Lewis, this process might be especially discouraging for environmental justice activists to find that success harms the very population they work to protect.

Alessandro Busà studies development in "Rezoning Coney Island: A History of Decline and Revival, of Heroes and Villains at the 'People's Playground.'" Busà analyzes the redevelopment plan for Coney Island under Bloomberg's PlaNYC 2030. He views rezoning as a new tool of production which allows the private market to determine the development plan. In Coney Island, like elsewhere in the city, according to Busà, the redevelopment plan does not address the needs and demands of the local community, and ultimately serves to escalate gentrification.

The following papers investigate the actions of Brooklyn residents regarding polluted waterways and the effects of toxins emanating from them on their neighborhood, namely the Gowanus Canal and the Newtown Creek. In her chapter on "The Gowanus Canal: Local Politics of 'Superfunding' Status," Shanna Farrell examines the contrary plans that were contemplated regarding the future cleanup of the Gowanus Canal. One was through the federal superfunding program and the other was presented by New York City for the purpose of development. These different approaches divided residents of the community. The additional difficulty, according to Farrell, was that the developer working with the city would walk away from the project if the Gowanus Canal became designated a superfund site. In the end, the canal was granted superfund status. Community residents were reunited since they held a common goal of cleaning the canal.

Steve Lang studies "Striving for Sustainability on the Urban Waterfront: The Case of Newtown Creek." He analyzes the community activism of residents of Greenpoint regarding their numerous years of fighting to have the Newtown Creek cleaned up. In many ways, Lang's findings are similar to those by Gould and Lewis in their chapter on Prospect Park. Lang argues that local activism to cleanup the creek has led to green gentrification. Thus, there is the potential for displacement of the very working class and low-income residents who fought the issue for many decades. According to Lang, their voices were not heard until now that there is economic incentive.

The next group of articles focuses on immigration and ethnic politics. Jerome Krase begins this section with his chapter on "Riding the Bus in Brooklyn, New York: Seeing the Spectacle of Everyday Multicultural Life." Krase uses a visual approach along with demographic data and urban journalism to better connect the practices of ordinary people with social theories. Through his riding the B68 bus along Coney Island Avenue, Krase offers a re-presentation of quotidian multiculturalism in Brooklyn.

In a somewhat similar vein, Timothy Shortell, in his chapter on "Brooklyn and Belleville: On the Visual Semiotics of Ethnic Identity in Two Immigrant Neighborhoods," uses the photographic survey in a comparison of immigrant communities in Brooklyn and Paris.

Shortell enlists Jacobson's functions of signs, the expressive, conative, and phatic, to inform his analysis of the spatial semiotics of rapidly changing, multiethnic neighborhoods. Shortell concludes that the global movement of people and their cultural habits result in similar patterns in the global cities.

Immigration and ethnic politics are considered by Mark Treskon in "Constructing an Oppositional Community: Sunset Park and the Politics of

Organizing Across Difference." Treskon traces the debate over rezoning and contends that there is an activism of differences among Latino, Chinese, and young white populations that comprise Sunset Park. A multiethnic coalition developed to oppose what was viewed as the city attempting to gentrify the community and displace existing residents through rezoning. Treskon analyzes the ways that the media and city government portrayed the neighborhood. According to Treskon, the local coalition formed to oppose the ways in which the Latino and Chinese communities were objectified. For Treskon, significant questions regarding the future of Sunset Park and Brooklyn ensue.

Evrick Brown conducts "An Ethnography of Local Politics in a Brooklyn Caribbean Community." Brown investigates East Flatbush and conceptualizes the field work of a local political candidate like that of an ethnographer. In this chapter, Brown elucidates some attributes of public life of the Caribbean community, and indicates ways that they are exploited by candidates for public office. There is also an attempt to draw a methodological and political parallel.

In "The Dual Roles of Brighton Beach: A Local and Global Community," Phyllis Conn traces the history of Brighton Beach from sea resort and post-Soviet era to its present day community. Conn discusses the multiethnic differences between each wave of immigration and the tensions that came with each one. Conn arrives at a contemporary Brighton Beach which is more multicultural than its past, and in that way, more akin to other neighborhoods of Brooklyn.

Noel Anderson's chapter on "Hood Politics: Charter Schools, Race and Gentrification in Fort Greene, Brooklyn" explores the community dynamics around a charter school that is physically located in the same building as a local public school which serves two public housing developments. Consistent with earlier chapters, Anderson views the charter school movement disguised as school reform as an engine of gentrification. Anderson illustrates that gentrification aligns residents by their social class interests which can involve many races.

In the final chapter, "Revising Canarsie: Racial Transition and Neighborhood Stability in Brooklyn," Gregory Smithsimon with his students, Jennifer Candipan, Roberta Cordeau, Mark Peterson, Nicole Riordan, Bengisu Peker, and Danielle Shallow revisited Canarsie, twenty-five years after Jonathan Rieder's study of white resistance to racial change. Although white residents continue to believe that "things just aren't the same," the team of ethnographers contends that things are very much the same. Black in-migrants, mostly Caribbean, have similar occupations, incomes, and attitudes toward the community as the residents Rieder studied. The team of researchers also identifies structural changes to Canarsie which includes racism.

As a whole, this book considers both theoretical and practical urban issues. In most cases the scholarly perspective is on everyday life. With this in mind there are also social justice concerns. Issues of social segregation and attendant homogenization are brought to light. Moreover, social class and race advantages or disadvantages, as part of urban processes, are underscored through critiques of local policy decisions throughout the chapters. A common thread is the assertion by contributors that planning the future of Brooklyn needs to include multiethnic, racial, and economic groups, those very residents who makeup Brooklyn.

The chapters that follow contribute fresh theoretical paradigms to the urban field. The volume is meant to provide contemporary scholarship about Brooklyn. It is also intended to contribute to an ongoing dialogue and to invite further research endeavors about Brooklyn and current urban processes.

NOTES

1. If Brooklyn were counted separately from New York in U.S. Census data, it would rank fourth in the list of American cities, behind Chicago and ahead of Houston (U.S. Census 2011).
2. As the chapters in this book demonstrate, Brooklyn is far more complicated than these binary comparisons suggest. Brooklyn is a place of black, Asian, Hispanic, and white neighborhoods, etc.

REFERENCES

Abrahamson, Mark. 2004. *Global Cities*. New York: Oxford University Press.

New York City Department of City Planning. 2004. "The Newest New Yorkers, 2000." Retrieved August 11, 2011 (www.nyc.gov/html/dcp/html/census/nny.shtml).

U.S. Census. 2011. "Population Estimates: Incorporated Places and Minor Civil Divisions." Retrieved August 11, 2011 (www.census.gov/popest/cities/).

2

Mapping a Changing Brooklyn, Mapping a Changing World

Gentrification and Immigration, 2000–2008

Lorna Mason, Ed Morlock and Christina Pisano

Brooklyn, with a population of 2,567,098, would be the fourth largest city in the United States (U.S. Census Bureau 2009). Let me say that again and let it sink in, 2.5 million people. It has more people than Boston, San Francisco and Detroit combined; and more people than seventeen states including Vermont, New Mexico and Maine (U.S. Census Bureau 2009).

But Brooklyn is much more than its numbers.

Brooklyn . . . say it out loud, to yourself, right now. "Brooklyn." What comes to your mind?

What comes to mind is: hipsters among families, bike riders, pedestrians and drivers, the Park Slope food co-op, struggle and community, diversity amid segregation, stability and change, kindnesses despite great injustices, great compassion amid great greed, communities striving for a better Brooklyn, indeed for a better world.

For every reader different images and stories appear. Think of that times 2.5 million people; each person has his or her own experiences, stories and visions of that untouchable but tangible Brooklyn vibe.

This chapter is meant to present a demographers' perspective, Brooklyn by the numbers. A reminder, that though numbers have their use, they are quite partial. As you read this chapter pause to remember those 2.5 million people living, working and getting by in Brooklyn—children, teens, men and women who are all creating, alone and together, the stories behind the numbers every second of every day in this great flow of life.

The information presented in this chapter is a crucial backdrop to the chapters that follow and serve two functions: to present a spatial overview of the predominant immigrant groups in Brooklyn today; and to demonstrate demographic changes in Brooklyn since 2000. As much as possible the data are mapped to show both the diversity within Brooklyn and the evident spatial patterns contained within the statistics.

Data analyzed for this chapter are taken from the U.S. Census Bureau's 2000 Decennial Census and American Community Survey three year estimates, 2006–2008 (ACS). The ACS is an annual multiphase, mail and CAPI sample survey developed by the U.S. Census Bureau to replace the Decennial Census' Long Form that allows researchers to estimate population changes annually rather than decennially (U.S. Census Bureau 2009a). Most analyses presented here utilize individual-level data called PUMS (Public Use Microdata Series); ACS PUMS samples were derived from the University of Minnesota's Population Center Integrated Public Use Microdata Series (IPUMS). Data for the maps (aggregated Census tract data from the 2000 Census and the American Community Survey Five Year Estimates, 2005–2009) were downloaded from the U.S. Census Bureau website. Throughout the chapter references to Community District characteristics from either 2000 or 2006–2008 utilize the IPUMS data from the University of Minnesota (Ruggles et al. 2010); all other data not from these sources is referenced separately in the text.

Census geographies used in this report include Kings County, NY; PUMAs; and census tracts. Kings County, NY is the same geography as the borough of Brooklyn. PUMAs are Public Use Microdata Areas and while not identical are roughly equivalent to New York City's Community Districts, which are, according to the New York City Charter, service delivery areas.[1] PUMAs must have at least 100,000 people and data are reported annually on the American Community Survey 1-year, 3-year and 5-year estimates for this geography. There are eighteen Community Districts (CDs) in Brooklyn. Figure 2.1 shows the location of many Brooklyn neighborhoods as they relate to Community Districts.[2]

Census tracts are the penultimate smallest census geography. There are 783 census tracts in Brooklyn; the average size of a census tract is 3,242 people, but they range from 9 to 14,000 in persons (fourteen have a population of zero). Data for census tracts are only available from the decennial censuses and the five year ACS estimates.

IMMIGRATION: BROOKLYN'S FOREIGN-BORN

Foreign immigration is and has been a significant component of Brooklyn's population (37.2 percent in 2006/8) since Brooklyn came into existence. Indeed, without immigrant inflow Brooklyn's population would be declining, as each year more people leave Brooklyn than arrive domestically, and births to Brooklyn women do not make up the difference.

Figure 2.1. Brooklyn Neighborhoods within Community Districts. ***Source:*** **Population Division, Department of City Planning, City of New York.**

This section highlights the major immigrant groups in Brooklyn and maps where they live. The maps will be a helpful guide for the following section ("A Changing Brooklyn"), which highlights changes by Brooklyn's Community Districts. While the following section addresses CD change, in this section it is clear that immigrant groups' patterns of settlement move beyond the boundaries of Community Districts.

The maps were created using 2005–2009 American Community Survey five year estimates at the census tract level. The maps do not show the census tract outlines, but dots (representing 100 persons) are placed randomly within the census tract reporting a count of a particular foreign-born group.

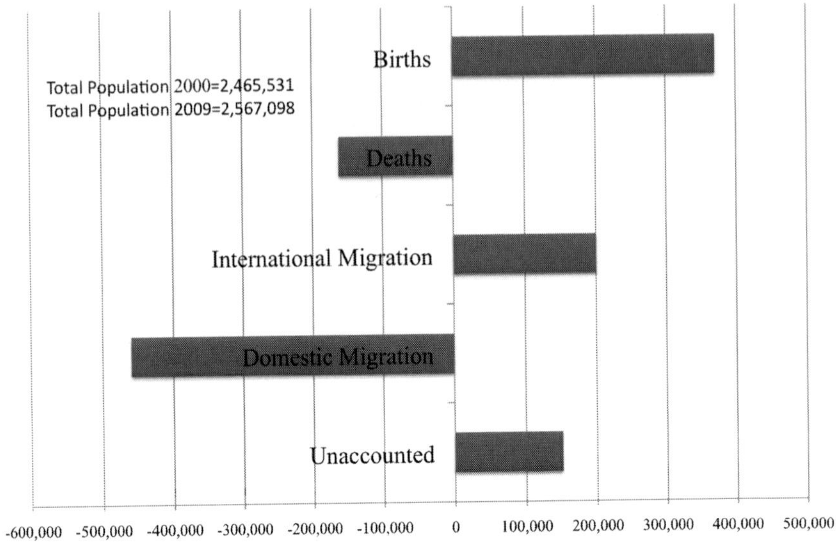

Figure 2.2. Components of Population Change in Brooklyn, 2000–2009. ***Source:*** **Census Population Estimates, 2009.**

The maps do show Community District outlines so that the presentation of foreign-born groups can be correlated with the discussion of changing population patterns in the following section.

The eleven largest foreign-born groups in Brooklyn, in descending order, are: Chinese, Jamaicans, Haitians, Trinidadians, Dominicans, Mexicans, Ukrainians, Russians, Guyanese, Poles and Ecuadorians. Together they comprise 50.4 percent of Brooklyn's foreign-born. If you look at the largest ethnic groups, which include those who are both foreign-born and those which, regardless of place-of-birth, claim an ethnic identity, then the largest groups include in addition to the above: Puerto Ricans, the Jewish population (UJA-Federation of New York 2004), African Americans, Irish and Germans.[3]

The maps show concentrations of a foreign-born population by major world area. It is important to note that this only includes the foreign-born and not counts of an ethnic *community*, which would be larger. For example, according to ACS 2006/8 IPUMS data, Brooklyn's first generation Haitians are an estimated 62,391, but another 23,503 describe themselves as Haitian, despite not being born in Haiti. The maps display only counts of the foreign-born, because combining ethnic and birthplace data is unfortunately not possible at the census tract level. The maps are grouped together by world area of birth in order to show more countries per map. Accompanying each map is a list of countries and an estimated population count within that world area. The areas mapped (Caribbean, Eastern Europe, Eastern Asia, South America, Mexico and Central America, South Central Asia and Western Asia) were chosen because they include the largest immigrant groups in Brooklyn and/or are discussed in other chapters.

Caribbean

Immigrants from Caribbean countries are the largest immigrant group, accounting for over 302,000 of the foreign-born population. The four largest

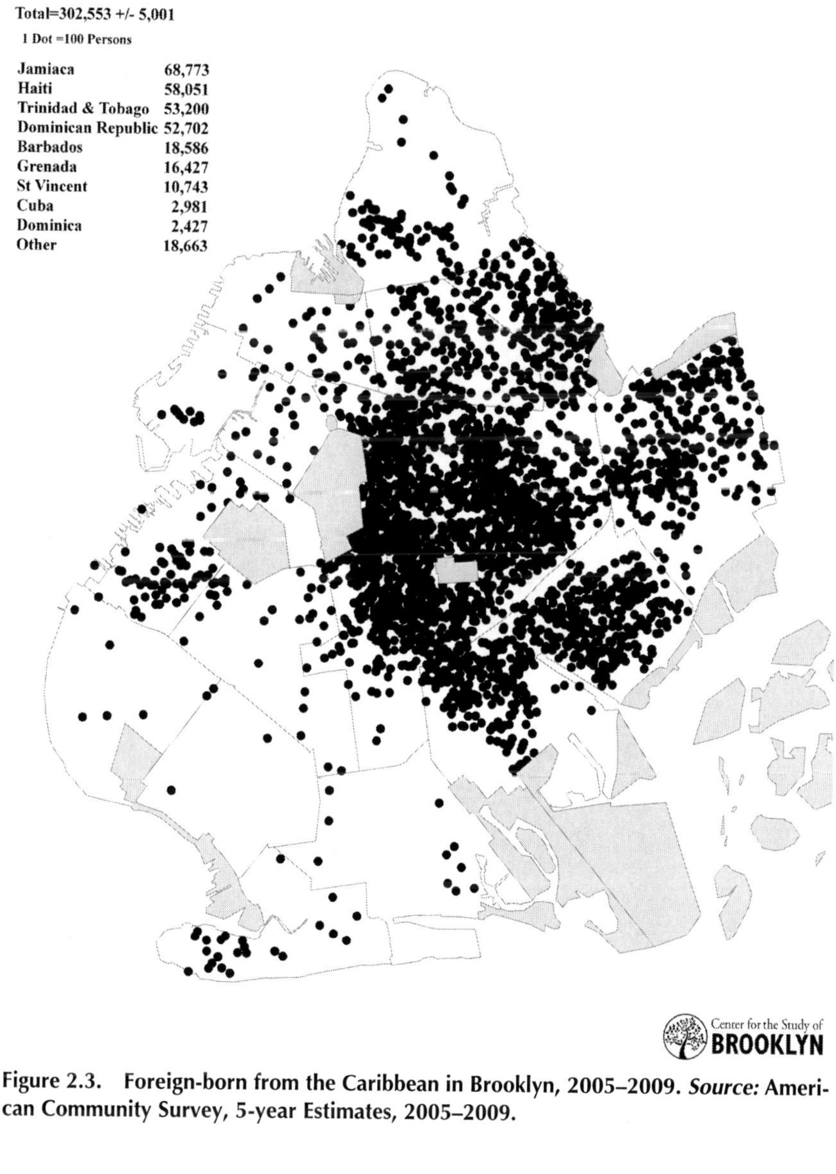

Figure 2.3. Foreign-born from the Caribbean in Brooklyn, 2005–2009. ***Source:*** **American Community Survey, 5-year Estimates, 2005–2009.**

Caribbean populations, each accounting for more than 50,000 persons in Brooklyn, are in descending order: Jamaicans, Haitians, Trinidadians and Dominicans. As seen in figure 2.3 they live predominantly in the central eastern portion of Brooklyn in CDs 4, 8, 9, 17, and 18. While many within the Caribbean population are financially struggling, Canarsie in CD 18 is well known as having a substantial middle class West Indian population.

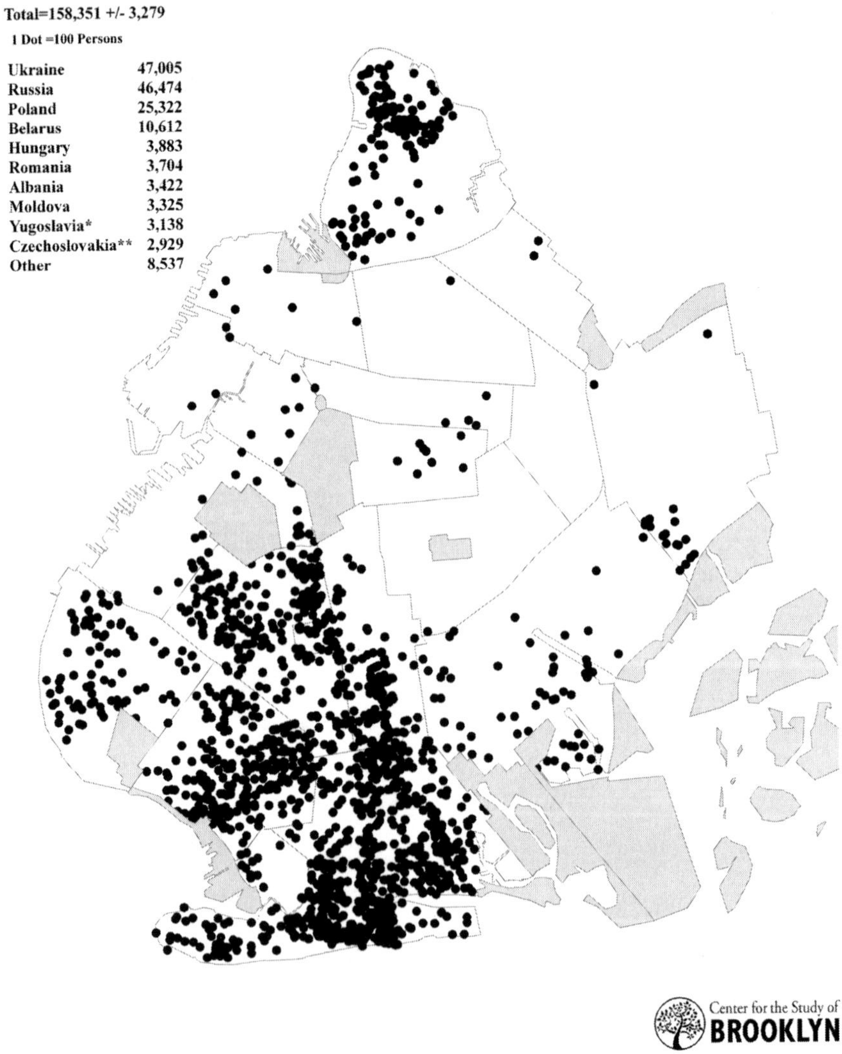

Figure 2.4. Foreign-born from Eastern Europe in Brooklyn, 2005–2009. Note: Asterisk indicates total includes Serbia; double asterisk indicates total includes Czech Republic and Slovakia. *Source:* American Community Survey, 5-year Estimates, 2005–2009.

Eastern Europe

The next largest immigrant group in Brooklyn is from Eastern Europe. This includes Ukrainians and Russians, which rank 7th and 8th for Brooklyn's top immigrant groups. Figure 2.4 shows the location of all Eastern European foreign-born. Eastern Europeans live predominantly in southwestern Brooklyn in CDs 11, 12, 13, 14 and 15, with heavy concentrations of Russians and Ukrainians in CDs 13 and 15. The Eastern Europeans in north Brooklyn

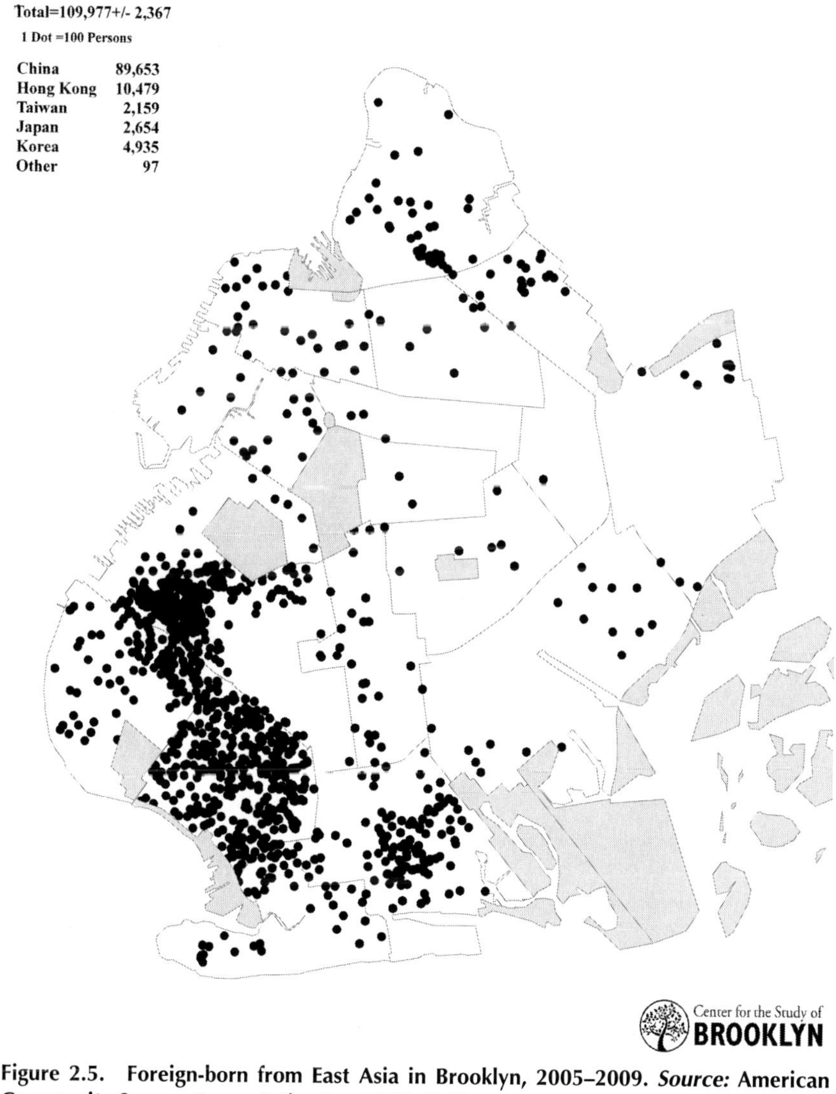

Figure 2.5. Foreign-born from East Asia in Brooklyn, 2005–2009. *Source:* American Community Survey, 5-year Estimates, 2005–2009.

(Greenpoint) are mostly Polish. Many of Brooklyn's Eastern Europeans are also Jewish (UJA-Federation of New York 2004).

Eastern Asia (China)

With over 89,000 immigrants, the Chinese are the largest foreign-born group from a single country. As seen in figure 2.5, the Chinese are heavily concentrated in a band across the southeastern section of Brooklyn that includes

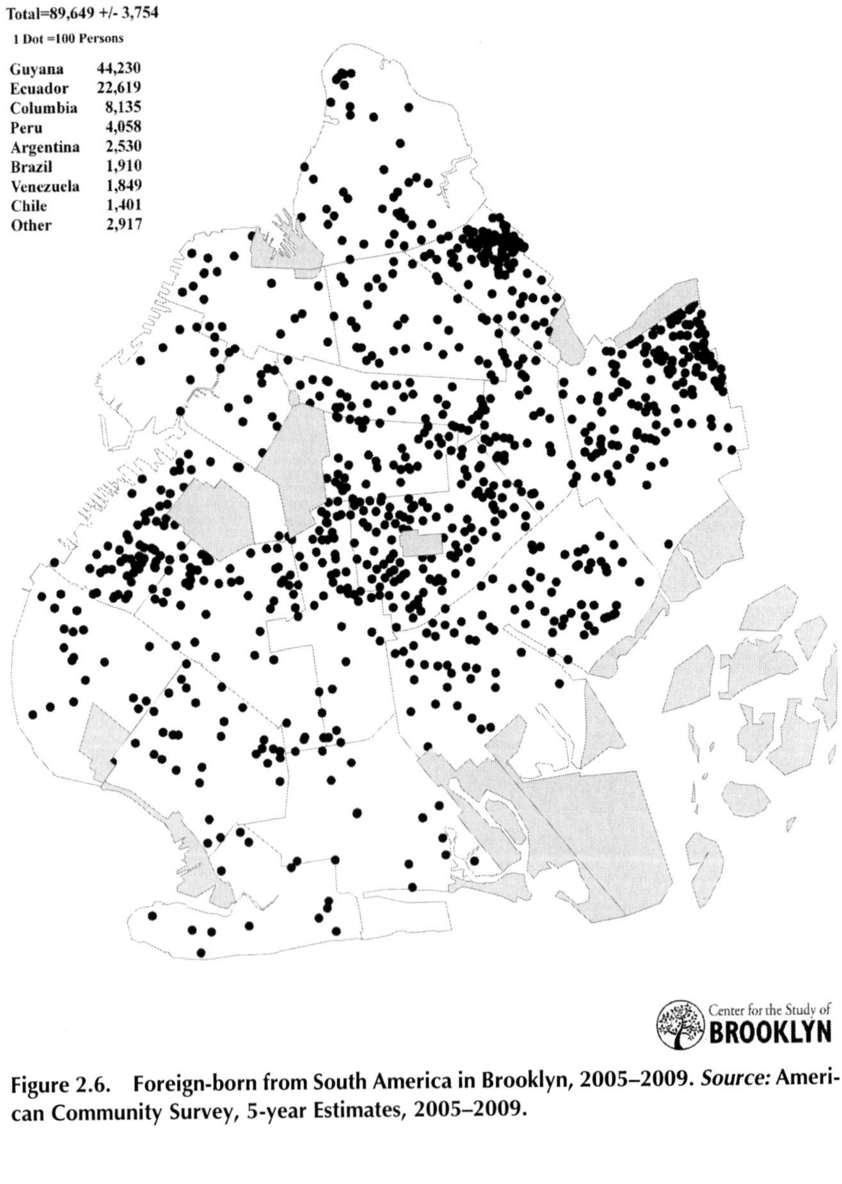

Figure 2.6. Foreign-born from South America in Brooklyn, 2005–2009. *Source:* American Community Survey, 5-year Estimates, 2005–2009.

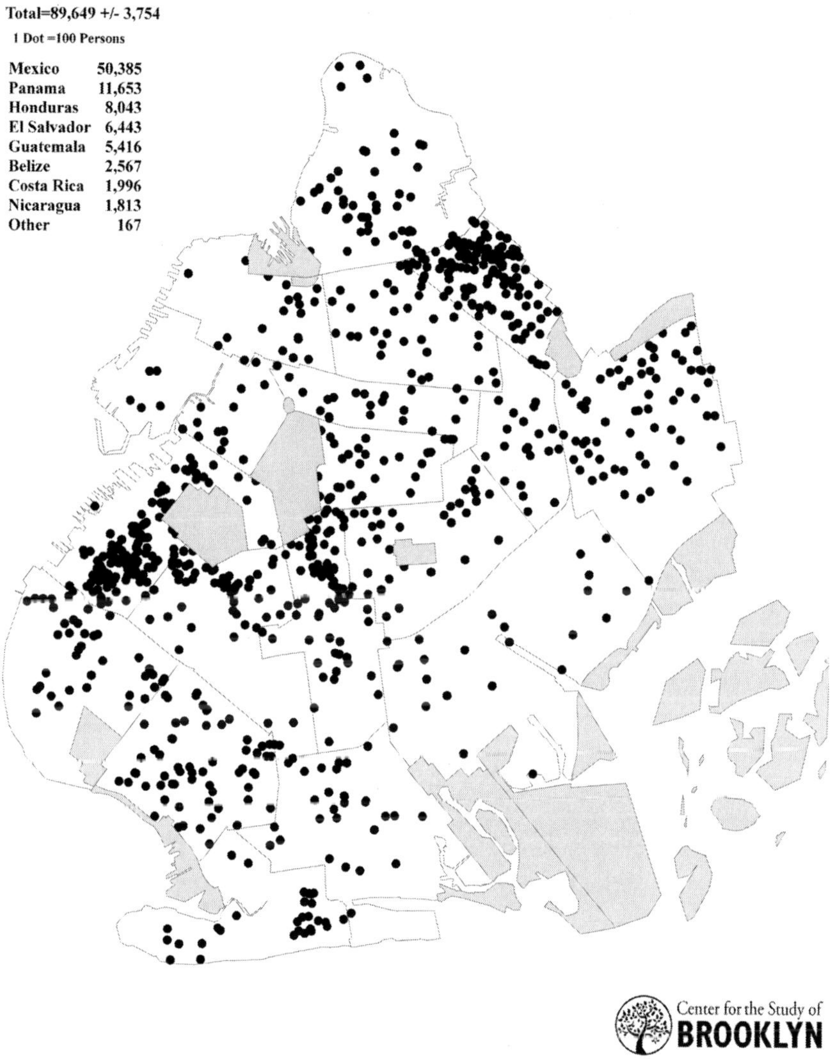

Figure 2.7. Foreign-born from Mexico and Central America in Brooklyn, 2005–2009. *Source:* American Community Survey, 5-year Estimates, 2005–2009.

the eastern portion of Sunset Park (CD 7), the northeastern section of CD 10 (Bayridge), most of CD 11 (Bensonhurst), and into CD 15 in Sheepshead Bay.

South America

Most of the 89,649 South Americans are from just two countries, Guyana and Ecuador. Figure 2.6 shows that South Americans are scattered throughout the borough but are living mostly in the northern half of Brooklyn.

The Guyanese are concentrated more with their other West Indian expatriates in CDs 14, 17, and 9; while Ecuadorians are in both Sunset Park and in the Cypress Hills neighborhood of CD 5 along the extreme eastern border of Brooklyn.

Mexico and Central America

Immigrants from Mexico and Central America number just over 88,000, most of whom are from Mexico (50,385). Mexicans are concentrated in Sunset Park in CD 7 and Bushwick in CD 4, but are otherwise dispersed throughout the borough.

South Central Asia

Immigrants from South Central Asia, mostly from Pakistan, Bangladesh, India and Uzbekistan, are smaller in number (44,117) than other groups, but have affected visible change in the neighborhoods in which they have settled. This is particularly true in the area near Coney Island Avenue, just south of Prospect Park, where South Central Asians are concentrated.

A CHANGING BROOKLYN: POPULATION CHANGES FROM 2002 TO 2008

The term gentrification is often invoked to describe changes in Brooklyn's ethnic, race and class makeup.[4] Only a few areas of Brooklyn, however, could be said to be gentrifying when using a traditional definition of gentrification, i.e., increasing income, increasing educational attainment and concomitant changes in racial/ethnic makeup. While some areas of Brooklyn are experiencing gentrification, it only characterizes a small portion of Brooklyn. Brooklyn is in fact changing in different ways in different regions of the borough. Significant sections of Brooklyn, for example, are seeing new residents who, when compared to the long-term residents, are more likely to be foreign-born and have lower household income; some areas are seeing more native-born whites move in, but whites in this case have lower household income than long-term residents; other sections of Brooklyn are exhibiting little statistically significant change.

In this section a statistical analysis of ACS three year estimates (2006–2008) is combined with a visual presentation of five year estimates (2005–2009) using Census tract data. Individual-level data (microdata) can be obtained for the ACS one and three year estimates, which allows a detailed

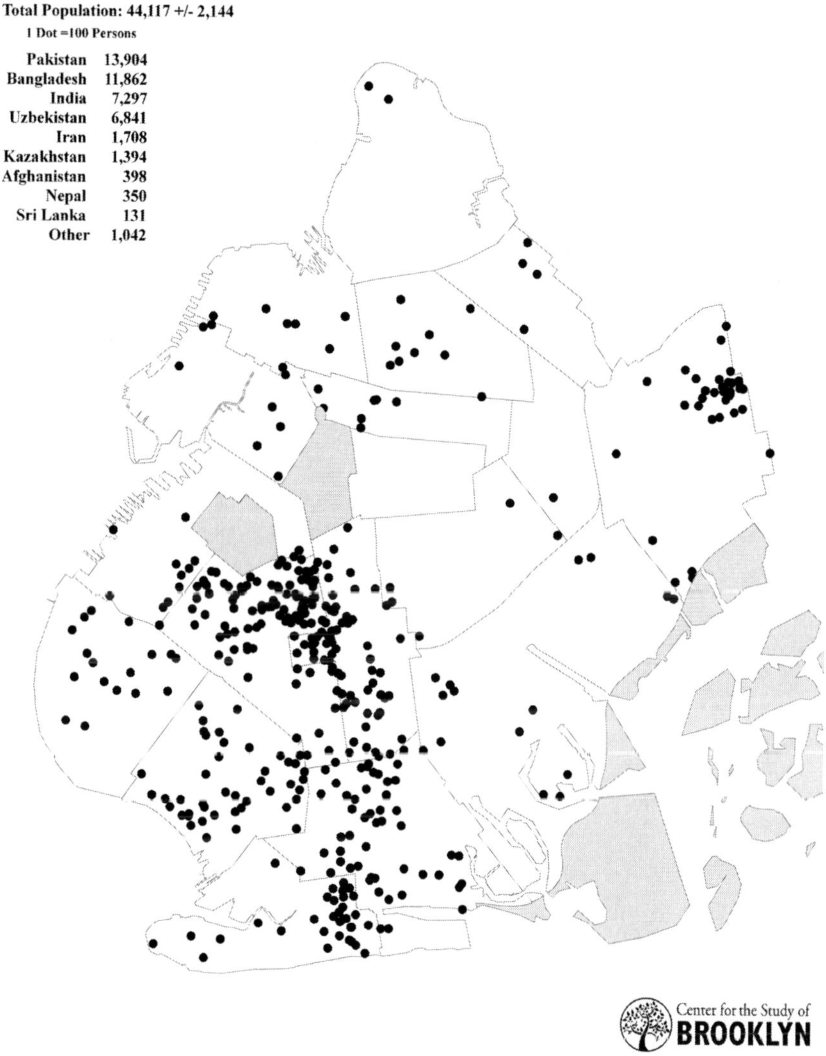

Figure 2.8. Foreign-born from South Central Asia in Brooklyn, 2005–2009. *Source:* American Community Survey, 5-year Estimates, 2005–2009.

analysis that can examine subgroups by various characteristics at the Community District level. Using the three year data, differences between newcomers (householders moving into a Community District between 2002 and 2008) and established residents (householders moving in before 2002)[5] were measured on the basis of four variables: race/ethnicity,[6] educational attainment, median household income and nativity.[7] Because the census data only

Table 2.1. Concepts and Variables used in Newcomer and Established Household Analysis

Concept	*Census Indicator*	*Notes/Categories*
Race/Ethnicity	Race by Hispanic Origin	Non-Hispanic Asian Non-Hispanic Black Latino Non-Hispanic White Other (not reported in chapter as is quite small)
Class	Median Household Income	Median Household Income is adjusted for inflation to 2009 dollars; referred to as Income in tables and text
Class	Educational Attainment	Percent of Adults 24 and Older with a Bachelor's Degree or Above
Nativity	Nativity	Percent Foreign-born; referred to as FB in tables

tracks when a householder (the head of household) moves in and not when each *person* in that household moved in, only households can be analyzed. Throughout the chapter, though, when changes in a particular Community District are discussed, both person (or population) and household data are included. Householder data refers specifically to the analysis between newcomer and established households. This analysis utilizes one dataset (the ACS 2006–2008). On the other hand, any discussion of changes in the *population* of a Community District uses two data sets (Census 2000 and ACS 2000–2008). When the data are discussed, person-based data are referred to as residents or population while any householder-based data has the word "householder" included. In a few cases (3 CDs) there are discrepancies between the analyses of changes by householders versus changes in the population; those discrepancies are discussed in the corresponding sections.

Chi-square tests were run for all nominal variables and t-tests for interval level variables comparing newcomer households to established households. Almost all showed significance when comparing new households to established households; those that did not (across most of the variables) are listed as the "no-change" group. Four patterns of change at the Community District level were evidenced: gentrification-led change, second-order gentrification-led change, immigration-led change and no change. Two Community Districts, CD 13 (Coney Island) and CD 7 (Sunset Park) did not fall cleanly into any of these patterns. Although both CD 7 and 13 were similar to the immigrant-led change CDs, they both had significantly different patterns of racial and ethnic change; they are discussed separately below. The population patterns also have a clear spatial component.

As seen in figure 2.9, Community Districts (CDs) closest to Manhattan and Prospect Park (CD 1, 2, 6 and 8) are gentrifying. Abutting the gentrifying

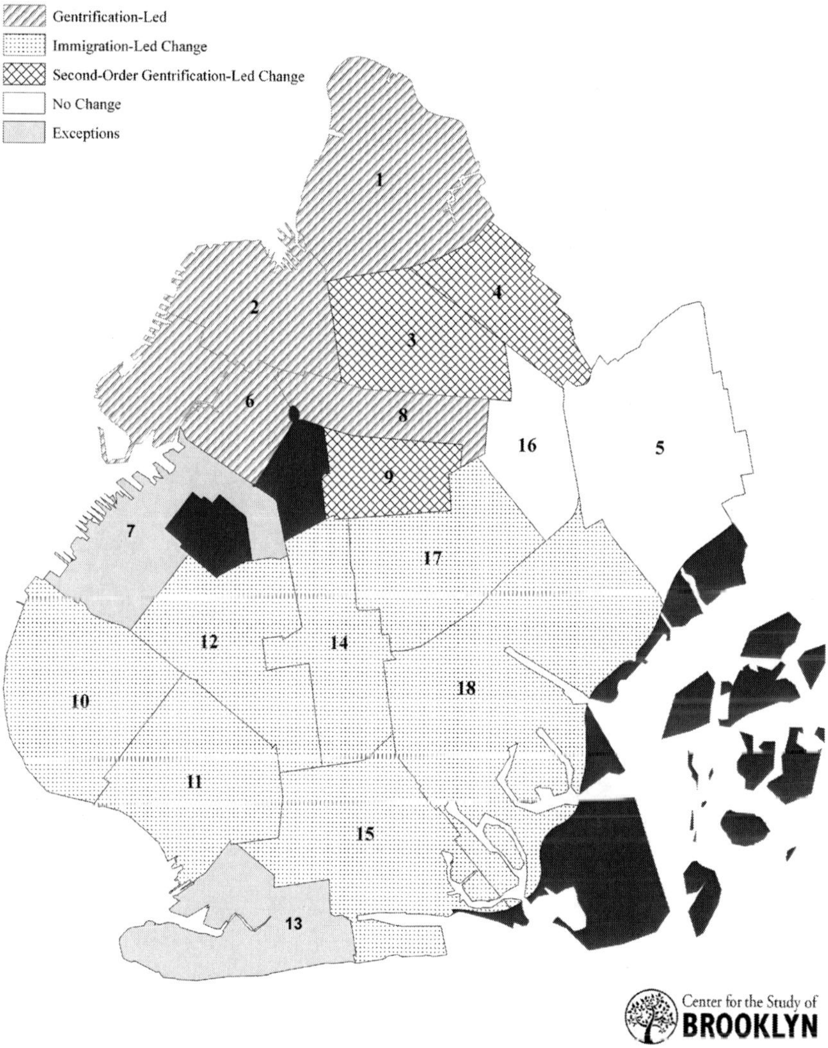

Figure 2.9. Spatial Patterns of Change by Community District in Brooklyn, 2000–2008. ***Source:*** **CSB Analysis of American Community Survey 3-year Estimates, 2006–2008.**

districts are those CDs (3, 4 and 9) to the east that are experiencing second-order gentrification as lower-income whites move into historically black and Latino native and immigrant neighborhoods. The southern half of Brooklyn, comprising 7 CDs (10, 11, 12, 14, 15, 17 and 18) is experiencing strong immigrant growth. Finally, the central eastern section of Brooklyn, CDs 5 and 16, are experiencing little to no population change.

Before discussing specific changes in the Community Districts, there are some important overall trends worthy of discussion regarding ethnic succession, and education as an indicator of gentrification for Brooklyn.

First, in terms of ethnic succession, it is important to note that change is not always dramatic—at least at the Community District level. Comparisons between newcomer and established households by ethnic identity (the Census' ancestry variable) reveal similar qualitative mixtures with quantitative differences. For example, in CD 11, (including the neighborhoods of Bensonhurst and Bath Beach), while Chinese immigration is notable, Italians are the modal ethnic category for both newcomer and established households. Newcomers, however, are only 18.6 percent Italian, while they are 25.9 percent of established households. So it is not that a historically Italian neighborhood is seeing a dramatic change, rather it is a gradual remixing of ethnic populations, where greater numbers of (in the case of CD 11) Puerto Ricans and Chinese alongside various other groups are increasing the ethnic diversity within this particular Community District. Analysis of ethnic change in other Community Districts shows similar patterns: dominant ethnic groups are still moving in, but often in smaller numbers.

Second, Brooklyn's educational attainment between 2000 and 2006/8—for those over the age of twenty-four—increased more rapidly than the national rate. In 2000, Brooklyn was nearly 3 percentage points below the national rate for adults with a bachelor's degree or higher (21.8 percent versus 24.4 percent). In just eight years, that number jumped 6 percentage points to 27.8 percent, which is statistically the same as the national rate (27.4 percent) (Census Bureau 2000; Census Bureau 2008). In gentrification literature increases in educational level are often seen as one sign of gentrification. For Brooklyn, however, we argue education is not a strong indicator, given Brooklyn's considerable rise in educational attainment. As figure 2.10 reveals, most census tracts in Brooklyn show a considerable rise in the percent of the population (over twenty-four) with a bachelor's degree or higher.

For this reason, in the sections below, educational attainment is only occasionally mentioned as an indicator of neighborhood change. Finally, as a note of caution, the strong rise in educational attainment does not diminish the spatial disparity in educational attainment as evidenced in figure 2.11, which displays the 2005–2009 concentrations of adults over twenty-four with a bachelor's degree or higher.

Gentrification-Led Change: Northwest Brooklyn

Northwest Brooklyn, comprising Community District 1 (Greenpoint and Williamsburg), CD 2 (Brooklyn Heights, Clinton Hill, DUMBO and Fort

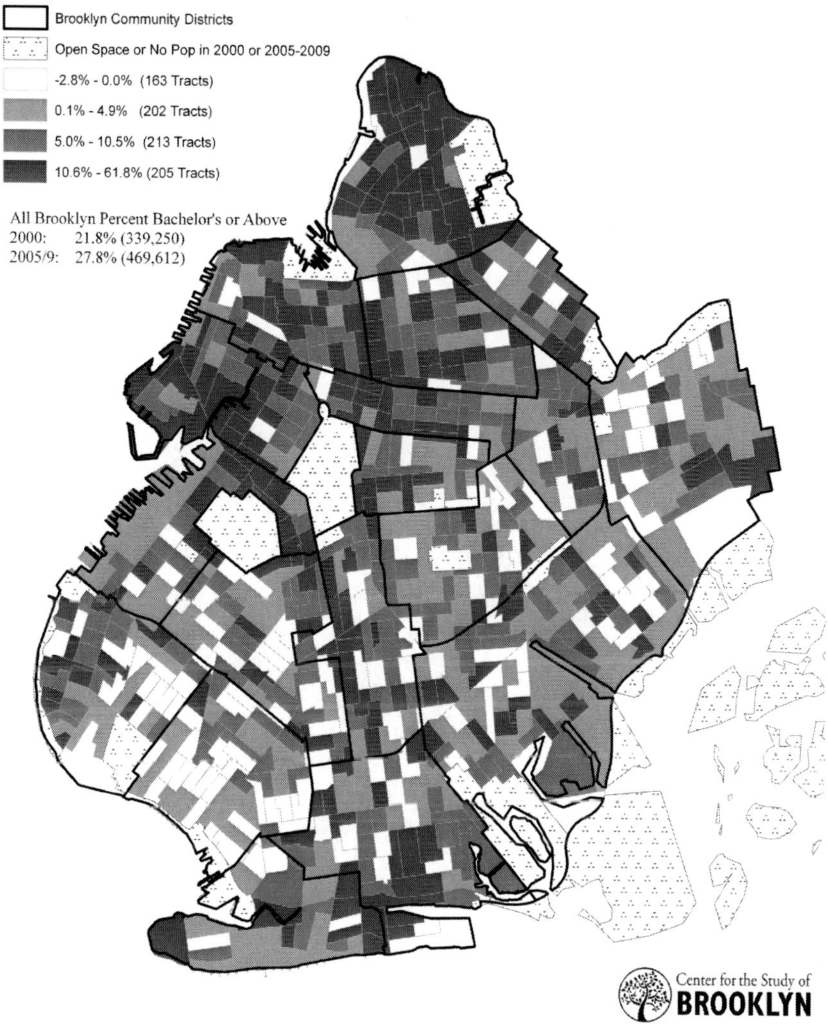

Figure 2.10. Percent Change in Adults over 24 with Bachelor's Degree or Above in Brooklyn, 2000–2009. *Source:* Census 2000 and American Community Survey 5-year Estimates, 2005–2009.

Greene), CD 6 (Carroll Gardens, Cobble Hill, Park Slope and Red Hook) and CD 8 (Crown Heights North, Prospect Heights), was already gentrifying by 2000, and continued to gentrify; in these Community Districts newcomer householders are more likely to be white and Asian, wealthier and more educated than established householders. Likewise, newcomers are less likely to be foreign-born (with one exception noted below) and less likely to be black or Latino than established householders. Table 2.2 compares newcomer and

Figure 2.11. Spatial Disparities in Educational Attainment, Percent of Adults over 24 with Bachelor's Degree or Above in Brooklyn, 2005–2009. *Source:* American Community Survey 5-year Estimates, 2005–2009.

established households based on the number of foreign born (FB); median household income (Income), and racial and ethnic percentages.

While the described pattern is one of traditional gentrification, it is important to note that Community Districts 2 and 6 (containing the neighborhoods of Brooklyn Heights, Park Slope and Carroll Gardens) were, before 2000, already disproportionately whiter and wealthier Community Districts as both ranked in the highest quartile for median household income in Brooklyn for

Table 2.2. Characteristics of Householders in Gentrifying Community Districts

	CD 1		*CD 2*		*CD 6*		*CD 8*	
	NEW	*EST*	*NEW*	*EST*	*NEW*	*EST*	*NEW*	*EST*
FB	27.5%	39.7%	23.2%	17.6%	15.4%	17.2%	37.3%	41.4%
Income	$46,668	$33,398	$75,252	$49,204	$88,771	$71,016	$40,581	$37,030
Latino	21.2%	31.6%	10.7%	18.7%	11.8%	20.2%	10.8%	9.4%
Asian	5.2%	3.6%	7.5%	3.6%	6.7%	4.3%	1.8%	1.1%
Black	2.6%	4.4%	19.7%	41.0%	5.0%	10.4%	60.6%	77.8%
White	69.2%	59.4%	58.4%	34.1%	74.7%	63.3%	24.6%	9.2%

Note: NEW refers to households that moved-in to the Community District between 2002 and 2008, while EST refers to established households that moved in before 2002. Source: American Community Survey 3-year estimates, 2006–2008, IPUMS, University of Minnesota.

2000 and 2006/8. In the case of CDs 2 and 6 then, comparatively well-off Community Districts are becoming better off by traditional measures of class (income and education) and also becoming more racially segregated by becoming whiter, more Asian (to a lesser degree), and less black or Latino.

By contrast, analyses of CDs 1 and 8 reveal a different story (while still exhibiting the same pattern described at the start of this section). CD 8, comprising the neighborhoods of Prospect Heights and Crown Heights North, is a historically black Community District (70.1 percent black in 2006/8 and 78.7 percent black in 2000). Thus white newcomer households are racially different from established residents, and the process of gentrification here means the displacement of black lower-income residents by white higher-income residents. This is most visible by looking at figure 2.12, which visually displays the percentage-point change in the white population from 2000 to 2005/9. The map also shows that white gentrification in CD 8 is strongest in the western part of the CD near Prospect Park. In 2000 only nine Census tracts in CD 8 had more than 150 white residents; by 2005/9 that number had doubled to eighteen Census tracts.

In contrast, CD 1, including the neighborhoods of Williamsburg and Greenpoint, was a predominantly white ethnic immigrant and orthodox Jewish Community District (UJA-Federation of New York 2004). In 2000, 51.6 percent of the CD 1's population was white, while in the same year only 35 percent of Brooklyn's population was white. Predominant groups in 2000, by ethnic identity and place of birth, included Orthodox Jews, Poles, Italians, Hungarians, but also African-Americans, Puerto Ricans and Dominicans. The change since 2000 is most evident by analyzing the top places of birth of newcomer versus established households. As table 2.3 reveals, among the top ten places of birth, more newcomers (as a percent of the top ten and excluding those born in New York) are native born (20.6 percent) as compared to established householders (2.5 percent).

CD 2, including the neighborhoods of Brooklyn Heights, Fort Greene, Downtown Brooklyn and Boerum Hill, is the one exception to the foreign-born trend among the gentrifying Community Districts. Newcomer households are 23.2 percent foreign-born, while established residents are 17.6 percent foreign-born. In this case, though, the percent foreign-born is quite small compared to Brooklyn's newcomers overall (48.3 percent). In addition, the foreign-born coming to CD 2 are very different from many new immigrants groups to Brooklyn; CD 2s newcomer-foreign-born householders had the second highest median household income of any CD at $62,910, or nearly twice the median household income of all newcomer foreign-born households ($38,045). CD 2s foreign-born newcomer households are not from any one

Figure 2.12. Percent Change in Non-Hispanic White Population in Brooklyn, 2000–2009. Note: The ranges are defined so that there are two shades for the declining Census tracts and two shades for the ascending Census tracts. Both declining and ascending tracts were divided as evenly as possible between the two shades. *Source:* Census 2000 and American Community Survey 5-year Estimates, 2005–2009.

Table 2.3. CD 1 Top Ten Places of Birth, Newcomer versus Established Households

Newcomers			*Established*		
Place of Birth	*Count*	*Percent*	*Place of Birth*	*Count*	*Percent*
New York	6,459	32.9	*New York*	12,141	36.9
Poland	1,549	7.9	Puerto Rico	4,180	12.7
Dominican Republic	788	4.0	Poland	4,115	12.5
Puerto Rico	752	3.8	Dominican Republic	2,072	6.3
Massachusetts	632	3.2	Hungary	858	2.6
Michigan	521	2.7	Mexico	802	2.4
California	516	2.6	China	654	2.0
New Jersey	501	2.6	Italy	464	1.4
Mexico	497	2.5	*California*	433	1.3
Ohio	463	2.4	*New Jersey*	402	1.2
Top 10 Totals	12,768	64.5		26,121	79.4
Total N	19,644			32,898	
Domestic Immigrants as a Percent of top 10	2,633	20.6		835	2.5

Note: Italics indicate U.S. places of birth. Source: American Community Survey 3-year estimates, 2006–2008, IPUMS, University of Minnesota.

region or country, but are from varied places. The top five countries/regions are: West Indies, Mexico, United Kingdom, Africa and India.

Second-Order Gentrification: Northern Central Brooklyn

The evidence suggests that change in CD 3 (Bedford Stuyvesant), 4 (Bushwick) and 9 (Crown Heights South and Prospect Lefferts Gardens) is spatially driven. Specifically, white households are displacing black households in the areas closest to gentrifying CDs (1, 2 and 6-if you extend 6 through Prospect Park). The evidence for this is to follow, but first the obvious question to address is why then are these CDs not included in the previous section? CDs 3, 4 and 9 differ in that on average the newcomers (regardless of race) have *lower* median household incomes than established residents.

CDs 3, 4 and 9 are historically black, Latino and immigrant. Community District 3, including the neighborhoods of Bedford Stuyvesant, Stuyvesant Heights and Tompkins Park, is a historically black (74.9 percent black in 2000), and predominantly native-born (81.3 percent) Community District.

Community District 4, Bushwick, is Brooklyn's largest Puerto Rican and Latino immigrant (33.3 percent are foreign-born) community, with 69.4 percent of the residents in 2000 claiming a Latino ethnicity. Crown Heights (South)[8] and Prospect Lefferts Gardens in Community District 9 are historically black (79.6 percent of the CD in 2000) West-Indian immigrant neighborhoods with

Table 2.4. Racial/Ethnic Person Demographics in CD 3, 4 and 9, 2000 and 2006/8

	CD 3		*CD 4*		*CD 9*	
	2000	*2006/8*	*2000*	*2006/8*	*2000*	*2006/8*
Black	90,732 (74.9%)	88,514 (66.2%)	27,961 (24.0%)	26,788 (20.9%)	90,754 (79.6%)	85,855 (77.1%)
White	3,087 (2.6%)	16,896 (12.6%)	3,207 (2.8%)	8,349 (6.5%)	9,499 (8.3%)	14,350 (12.9%)
Latino	23,457 (19.4%)	23,007 (17.2%)	78,302 (67.3%)	87,104 (67.9%)	9,289 (8.1%)	8,535 (7.7%)
Total	121,057	133,689	116,415	128,219	114,012	111,403

Source: American Community Survey 3-year estimates, 2006–2008 and Census 2000 IPUMS, University of Minnesota.

a significantly larger percentage of foreign-born blacks when compared to CD 3 (52.3 percent of blacks are foreign-born, but many of the native-born are second or third generation West Indian). In all cases these CDs had much lower median household income in 2000 than other CDs in the borough (CD 3: $27,003; CD 4: $27,000; CD 9: $37,614; All Brooklyn: $40,549).

Based on the 2006/8 American Community Survey, table 2.5 shows the differences between newcomer (moved in between 2002 and 2008) and established (moved in before 2002) householders by Community District.

In all cases newcomers have lower median household income than established residents, but as median incomes were already quite low, newcomers do not exhibit dramatically lower median incomes. Nativity exhibits varying patterns, but like income, there are small differences. Racial/ethnic differences between newcomer and established households are more prominent, as whites have dramatically increased in these CDs, but the patterns differ by CD. In CD 3, Bedford Stuyvesant, Latinos, as a percent of the households, remain unchanged, but black householders have fallen significantly, while white householders have more than quadrupled. A similar pattern holds in CD 9: black households are falling, while white households are more than doubling, with little change in Latino households. By contrast, in CD 4 both black and Latino households have dropped (as a percent of households), but white households have nearly tripled.

As seen in table 2.4, population counts between 2000 and 2006/8 make it evident that white households are displacing black households. Since 2000 the white population has increased in two CDs (3 and 4), while in both CDs the black population has declined. In CD 9 the population has declined overall, but has increased for whites.[9] The displacement is also spatial. As shown in figure 2.12, whites are increasing more in areas that abut the gentrifying tracts than in other areas.[10]

The title of this section, second-order gentrification, implies that the change exhibited in these Community Districts results from gentrification outcomes, particularly high housing prices, in the gentrifying Community Districts. The change could result from displacement of whites moving from the gentrifying (and mostly predominantly white in the case of 1, 2 and 6) CDs or it could be that newcomer households are moving in—but not necessarily from adjacent gentrifying CDs—to relatively affordable places to live that are still close to the amenities and services of the higher income Community Districts. Census data cannot answer where people are moving from (when they are moving within the borough), but the spatial evidence as well as the fact that white newcomers to CD 3, 4 and 9 are significantly lower in income (see table 2.6) than other newcomer whites, supports the case that whites moving to CD 3, 4 and 9 are significantly different than those moving

Table 2.5. Characteristics of Householders in Second-Order Gentrification-Led Change Community Districts

	CD 3		*CD 4*		*CD 9*	
	NEW	*EST*	*NEW*	*EST*	*NEW*	*EST*
Foreign-born	29.4%	23.3%	50.5%	44.5%	57.1%	62.6%
Income	$31,856	$34,697	$30,436	$32,363	$32,972	$38,552
Latino	17.9%	17.3%	60.2%	66.9%	8.6%	7.1%
Asian	3.3%	0.8%	4.5%	3.1%	1.6%	.5%
Black	60.5%	76.9%	20.3%	23.7%	71.4%	83.1%
White	15.8%	3.4%	14.6%	5.0%	16.2%	7.7%

Source: American Community Survey 3-year estimates, 2006–2008, IPUMS, University of Minnesota.

Table 2.6. Median Household Income of White Newcomer Householders

Geography	*Median Household Income*
CD 3	$32,464
CD 4	$45,654
CD 9	$39,566
All CDs	$55,798

Source: American Community Survey 3-year estimates, 2006–2008, IPUMS, University of Minnesota.

Table 2.7. Newcomer Median Household Income

	CD 3	*CD 4*	*CD 9*
Latino	$20,291	$30,436	$18,261
Black NH	$35,509	$23,638	$32,972
White NH	$32,464	$45,654	$39,566

Source: American Community Survey 3-year estimates, 2006–2008, IPUMS, University of Minnesota.

to CD 1, 2, 6 and 8, and that if they can't live in, they want to live close to the amenities of higher income neighborhoods.

A second implied meaning to "second-order gentrification" is that newcomer white householders coming to CD 3, 4 and 9, while lower income than other white newcomer households in other CDs, may yet be higher income than newcomers to CD 3, 4 and 9. Table 2.7 shows the median household income by racial/ethnic categories for CDs 3, 4 and 9 newcomer households. In the case of CD 4 and 9 (but not 3) white newcomers do have higher median incomes than other newcomer households.

Immigration-Led Change: Southern Brooklyn

Nearly the entire Southern half of Brooklyn, including seven Community Districts (10, 11, 12, 14, 15, 17 and 18), is exhibiting immigrant-led change (see figure 2.9). Newcomer households in these CDs (please see figure 2.1 for neighborhood names), when compared with established households, have lower median household incomes, are more likely to be foreign-born[11] and are less likely to be white. Latino and Asian households are up in all seven of the Community Districts (although in most CDs they are still a small component of all households) while black households show differing trends. Southern Brooklyn has been and remains a stronghold for immigrants.

Figure 2.13 presents the 2005/2009 concentrations of foreign-born throughout the borough and demonstrates the southern concentration of the

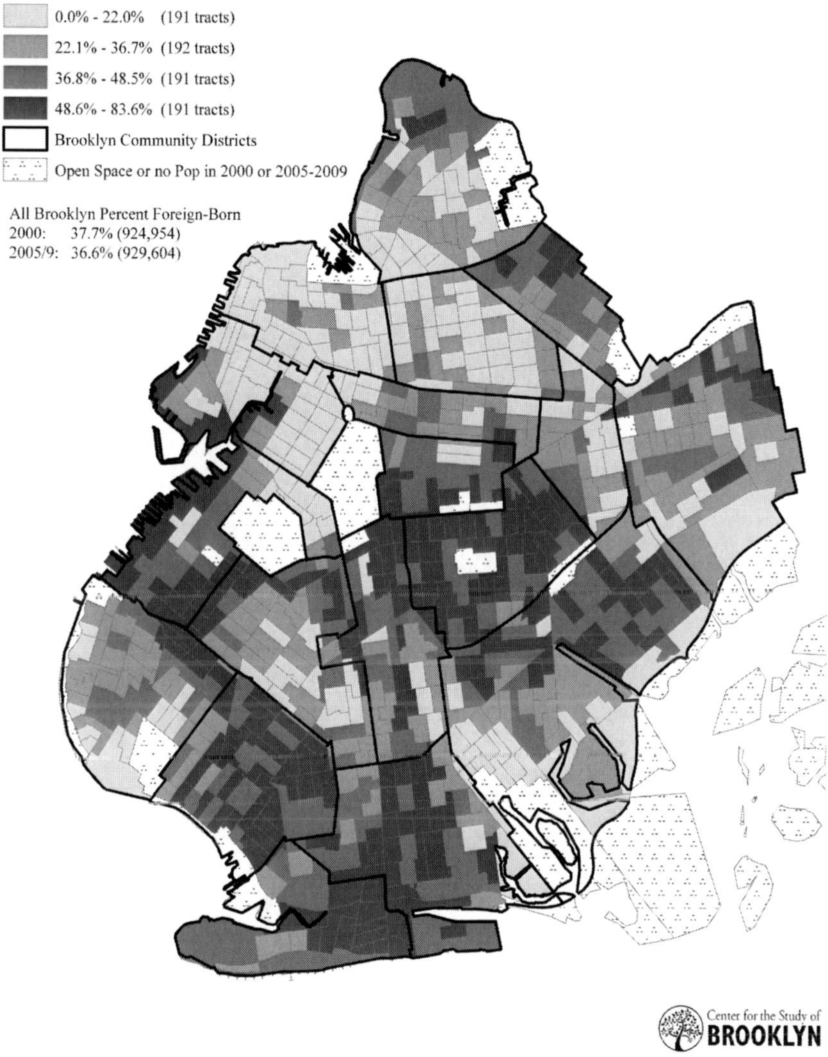

Figure 2.13. Percent Foreign-born in Brooklyn, 2005–2009. *Source:* Census 2000 and American Community Survey 5-year Estimates, 2005–2009.

foreign-born (with the exception of Bushwick in CD 4 and Greenpoint in CD 1, found in northern Brooklyn). In contrast, figure 2.14 shows the change in percent foreign-born between 2000 and 2005/2009.

Figure 2.14 shows there is considerable variation within Community Districts even while these Community Districts remain strong immigrant communities (as shown in figure 2.13). There is, for example, a decrease in the *percent* foreign-born in CD 17, as many blacks and West Indians have

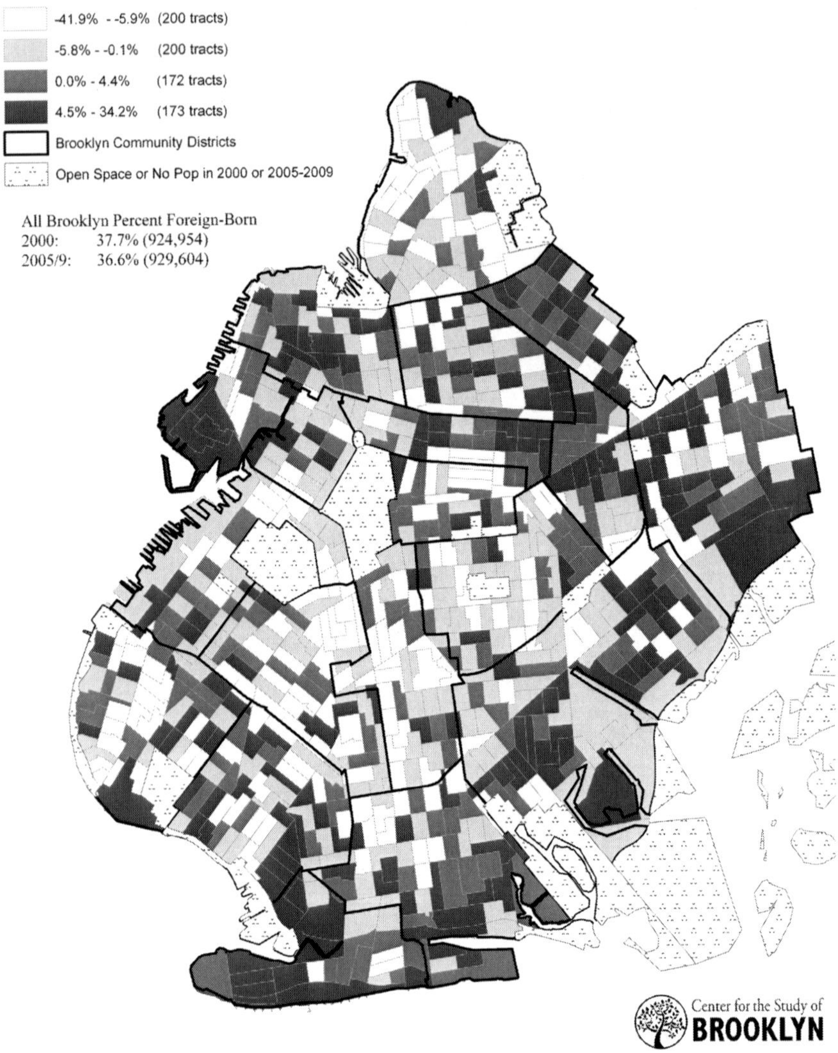

Figure 2.14. Percent Change in Foreign-born in Brooklyn, 2000–2009. Note: The ranges are defined so that there are two shades for the declining Census tracts and two shades for the ascending Census tracts. Both declining and ascending tracts were divided as evenly as possible between the two shades. *Source:* Census 2000 and American Community Survey 5-year Estimates, 2005–2009.

(most likely) moved to Canarsie in CD 18 where there has been significant percentage-point increases in the black and West Indian community. It is still the case, though, (see figure 2.13) that CD 17 is still predominantly immigrant. The discussion below will utilize the two maps to visualize both the change and the consistency as each Community District is reviewed.

For the immigration-led change CDs, ethnic identity is included in the tables as an important aspect of change and to show the diversity of ethnicities within a Community District and thus give a sense of the character of the Community District beyond nativity, income and race. The tables list the top ten ethnicities (a self-reported open-ended question on the census survey) for newcomer and established households. Ethnicities italicized in the tables are unique between both the newcomers and established households.

CD 10 Bay Ridge, Dyker Heights and Fort Hamilton

CD 10, of all the immigrant-led change CDs, has the smallest percentage of foreign-born overall; in 2000, 37.4 percent of the CD 10 residents were foreign-born. Newcomer householders (40.4 percent) were slightly more likely to be foreign-born than established householders (36.8 percent). As seen in figure 2.13, the foreign-born are most heavily concentrated in northeastern section of CD 10, and as seen in figure 2.5, a majority of the foreign-born in this section are from China. Ethnically, the CD is changing slowly, as there is a *similar* mixture of ethnic groups among new and established households. Racially, the CD has been and remains a largely white-ethnic second and

Table 2.8. Characteristics of Householders in Immigration-Led Change in CD 10

	Newcomer Households	*Established Households*
Foreign-born	40.4%	36.8%
Income	$51,537	$53,617
Latino	15.6%	9.7%
Asian	14.3%	10.1%
Black	2.0%	0.9%
White	66.9%	79.0%
Top 10 Ethnicities	Italian (18.6%)	Italian (25.9%)
	Irish (10.1%)	Irish (12.4%)
	Chinese/Cantonese (7.7%)	Chinese/Cantonese (8.0%)
	Puerto Rican (7.2%)	Greek (7.6%)
	Polish (4.1%)	Polish (4.2%)
	Russian (4.1%	Puerto Rican (4.2%)
	English (2.6%)	Religious Responses (3.7%)
	Greek (2.6%)	Russian (2.5%)
	United States (2.2%)	*Norwegian (2.4%)*
	Religious Responses (2.0%)	German (3.4%)
	German (2.0%)	*Lebanese (2.1%)*
Cumulative Percent for top 10 Ethnicities	64.4%	77.3%

Note: Italicized ethnicities indicate unique ethnicities among the top 10. Source: American Community Survey 3-year estimates, 2006–2008, IPUMS, University of Minnesota.

third generation immigrant neighborhood (predominantly Irish and Italian) that is slowly becoming more diverse as the white population declines and all other racial groups increase (while total population increased between 2000 and 2006/8 by 2.1 percent from 122,506 to 125,053). Whites in 2006/8 are 66.2 percent of the population, declining from 69.6 percent in 2000. This pattern follows in the household data as seen in table 2.8, where Latinos, Asians and blacks all account for a greater percent among newcomers than established households.

CD 11 Bensonhurst and Bath Beach

CD 11 has been depicted culturally and is probably best known (at least historically) as an ethnically Italian neighborhood, but even by 2000, while Italians remained dominant at 30.0 percent, immigrants from China (who identified as ethnically Chinese or Cantonese) were a sizable 17.6 percent of the population. Since then many Italians and other white ethnics have left CD 11 to be mostly replaced by a Chinese population. Newcomer Chinese households were the modal ethnic group at 23.1 percent, while Italians were only 13.1 percent of newcomer households. Among established households, however, Italians are the modal group (37.2 percent) followed by the Chinese

Table 2.9. Characteristics of Householders in Immigration-Led Change in CD 11

	Newcomer Households	*Established Households*
Foreign-born	55.7%	51.9%
Income	$35,509	$41,088
Latino	13.5%	11.0%
Asian	14.5%	8.6%
Black	3.8%	2.3%
White	67.8%	77.3%.
Top 10 Ethnicities	Chinese/Cantonese (23.1%)	Italian (37.2%)
	Italian (13.7%)	Chinese/Cantonese (16.6%)
	Russian (9.6%)	Religious Responses (8.8%)
	Religious Responses (7.0%)	Russian (8.5%)
	Ukrainian (4.0%)	Polish (2.4%)
	Polish (3.3%)	Irish (1.9%)
	Spanish (3.2%)	Ukrainian (1.9%)
	Mexican (2.9%)	*Puerto Rican (1.8%)*
	Irish (2.5%)	*Unites States (1.5%)*
	Pakistani (2.4%)	*German (1.2%)*
Cumulative Percent for top 10 Ethnicities	73.6%	84.1%

Note: Italicized ethnicities indicate unique ethnicities among the top 10. Source: American Community Survey 3-year estimates, 2006–2008, IPUMS, University of Minnesota.

(16.6 percent). Indeed, according to the 2006/8 ACS data, the Chinese ethnic population (27.2 percent) exceeded the Italian (23.6 percent). The Chinese are fairly evenly distributed throughout CD 11 (see figure 2.5).

CD 12 Borough Park and Kensington

Overall newcomers to CD 12[12] follow the pattern of immigration-led change: newcomers when compared to established householders are more likely to be foreign-born, Hispanic, black and Asian, have less median household income, and are less likely to be white.

There are, however, differing patterns within CD 12 that merit closer detailing. Borough Park, which consists of most of the western portion of CD 12, was and remains a predominantly Orthodox Jewish neighborhood (UJA-Federation of New York 2004). On the other hand, Kensington was and also remains an eclectic ethnic mix (although predominantly white) with Eastern Europeans most prevalent (see figure 2.4). In the top newcomer foreign-born, but absent among the top established foreign-born households are Bangladeshis, Mexicans, Uzbekistanis and Pakistanis (see figure 2.7 and 2.8). As figure 2.13 shows, the foreign-born are more concentrated in Kensington (the northeastern portion of the CD), even though those concentrations have

Table 2.10. Characteristics of Householders in Immigration-Led Change in CD 12

	Newcomer Households	*Established Households*
Foreign-born	55.7%	51.9%
Income	$35,509	$41,088
Latino	13.5%	11.0%
Asian	14.5%	8.6%
Black	3.8%	2.3%
White	67.8%	77.3%.
Top 10 Ancestries	Religious Responses (15.3%)	Religious Responses (23.1%)
	Russian (7.4%)	*Italian (9.0%)*
	United States (6.8%)	Polish (7.6%)
	Polish (5.9%)	Russian (6.8%)
	Chinese (4.8%)	Hungarian (4.9%)
	Israeli (3.4%)	Chinese (3.6%)
	Hungarian (3.3%)	Puerto Rican (3.2%)
	Mexican (3.1%)	European (2.5%)
	Puerto Rican (3.0%)	*Romanian (1.9%)*
	European (2.7%)	*Irish (1.8%)*
Cumulative Percent for top 10 Ethnicities	60.7%	69.3%

Note: Italicized ethnicities indicate unique ethnicities among the top 10. Source: American Community Survey 3-year estimates, 2006–2008, IPUMS, University of Minnesota.

declined since 2000 as seen in figure 2.14. It also appears based on figures 2.10, 2.12, 2.14 and 2.15 that there is gentrification (more whites, more educated, less foreign-born and higher income) in the Census tracts that are closest to Prospect Park and continuing south along the CDs eastern most border (Coney Island Avenue).

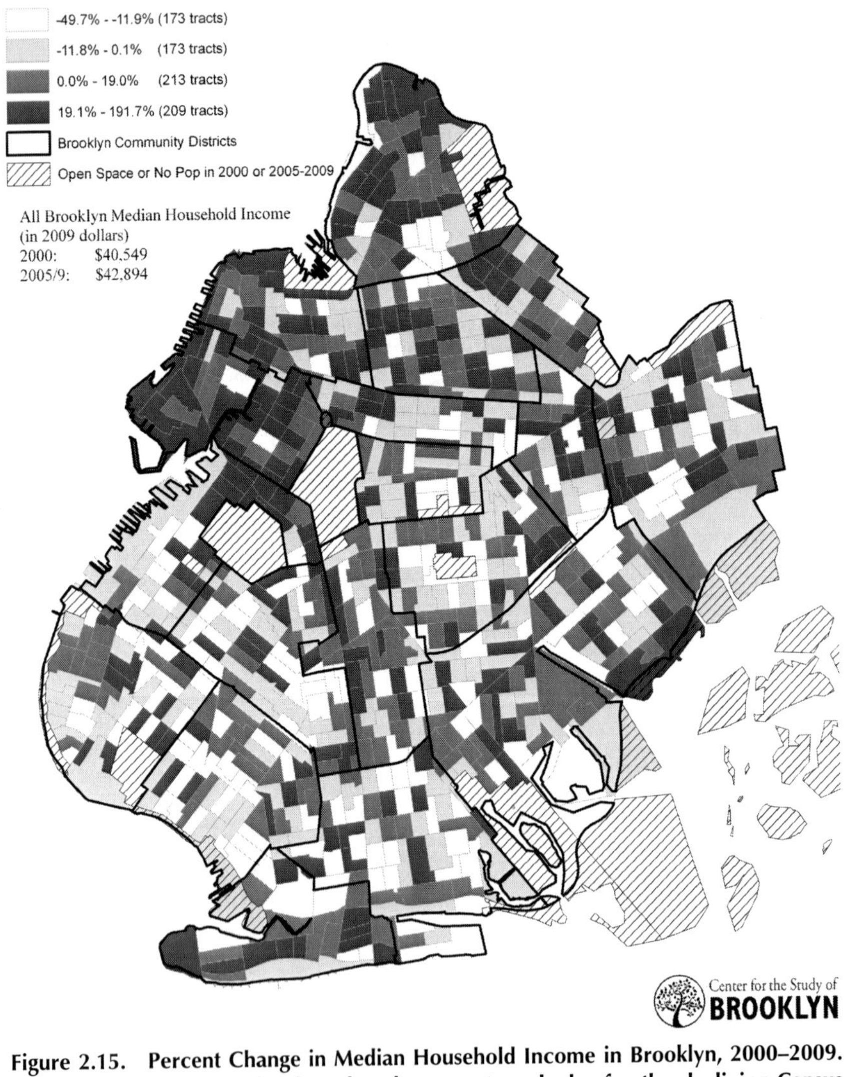

Figure 2.15. Percent Change in Median Household Income in Brooklyn, 2000–2009. Note: The ranges are defined so that there are two shades for the declining Census tracts and two shades for the ascending Census tracts. Both declining and ascending tracts were divided as evenly as possible between the two shades. *Source:* Census 2000 and American Community Survey 5-year Estimates, 2005–2009.

CD 14 Ditmas Park, Flatbush, Manhattan Terrace and Midwood

The data for CD 14 are a bit mixed, but because this CD is home to many of Brooklyn's foreign-born (see figure 2.13), it is included here despite its small decrease (newcomer householders are 59.4 percent foreign-born while established householders are 60.4 percent (see figure 2.14), and because the percent foreign-born in the CD's population is quite high therefore the foreign-born are an important factor of change in the Community District. Other data follow the pattern: newcomer householders are more likely to be Latino and Asian and have less median household income, and are less likely to be white. In this CD blacks are smaller percentage of newcomer householders.

As seen in figure 2.13 concentrations of the foreign-born are found throughout all neighborhoods, although they are denser in the northern section of the CD. Eastern Europeans are dominant in the southern section of the CD (figure 2.4); immigrants from the Caribbean (figure 2.3), Mexico and Central America (figure 2.7) are concentrated in the northern section. Pakistanis, Bangladeshis, and Chinese immigrants are among the newcomers, but absent among established households.[13] As in CD 12, household racial trends for whites and Asians are not in accord with population racial/ethnic trends (see note 11). There are *fewer* white householders among newcomers, but the white population increased between 2000 (61,230; 37.4 percent) and 2006/8

Table 2.11. Characteristics of Householders in Immigration-Led Change in CD 14

	Newcomer Households	*Established Households*
Foreign-born	59.4%	60.4%
Income	$38,754	$43,421
Latino	16.7%	9.4%
Asian	8.3%	4.6%
Black	34.5%	37.5%
White	38.3%	46.7%
Top 10 Ethnicities	Religious Responses (16.8%)	Religious Responses (16.8%)
	African American (8.4%)	Haitian (9.1%)
	Haitian (6.7%)	African American (8.7%)
	Russian (6.0%)	Russian (5.8%)
	Trinidadian (4.0%)	Jamaican (4.1%)
	Jamaican (3.9%)	United States (4.1%)
	Mexican (3.8%)	Trinidadian (3.7%)
	United States (3.4%)	*Italian (3.1%)*
	Puerto Rican (3.0%)	*Polish (2.8%)*
	Chinese (2.7%)	*Irish (2.1%)*
Cumulative Percent for top 10 Ethnicities	58.7%	60.3%

Note: Italicized ethnicities indicate unique ethnicities among the top 10. Source: American Community Survey 3-year estimates, 2006–2008, IPUMS, University of Minnesota.

(68,892; 41.7 percent). There are *more* Asian householders among newcomers, but the Asian population slightly decreased between 2000 (12,882; 7.9 percent) and 2006/8 (11,537; 7.0 percent). Trends for Latino and black households are in accord with population racial/ethnic trends.

CD 15 Homecrest, Gerritsen Beach, Gravesend, Madison, Manhattan Beach, Sheepshead Bay

Overall while CD 15 was and is still a predominantly Jewish (19.6 percent) (UJA-Federation of New York 2004), Russian (12.7 percent), Italian (8.8 percent) and Chinese (8.3 percent). Community District (see figures 2.4 and 2.5), it is seeing small changes in the ethnic mix as some white ethnic householders leave to be replaced by non-white ethnic groups. CD 15 has seen a 4 percent decrease in population between 2000 (150,967) and 2006/8 (144,902). Racially, whites are the only population to decline, but it was and still is a predominantly white (75.5 percent in 2000; 73.7 percent in 2006/8) CD. Sixty-six percent of the newcomer householders are foreign-born (compared to 45.7 percent of established householders).

See table 2.13 for a comparison of new and established householders based on the top ten places of birth. Notable, in table 2.13, is the absence of

Table 2.12. Characteristics of Householders in Immigration-Led Change in CD 15

	Newcomer Households	*Established Households*
Foreign-born	66.1%	45.7%
Income	$45,654	$46,161
Latino	9.4%	4.8%
Asian	10.8%	8.5%
Black	2.8%	3.4%
White	76.1%	82.6%
Top 10 Ethnicities	Russian (20.8%)	Religious Responses (22.5%)
	Religious Responses (18.2%)	Italian (13.0%)
	Ukrainian (7.3%)	Russian (12.9%)
	Chinese/Cantonese (6.1%)	Chinese/Cantonese (6.1%)
	Puerto Rican (5.2%)	Irish (4.7%)
	United States (4.6%)	*Polish (3.9%)*
	Italian (4.6%)	United States (3.9%)
	Irish (2.0%)	Ukrainian (2.6%)
	Syrian (1.7%)	*African American (2.5%)*
	Turkish (1.7%)	Turkish (1.5%)
Cumulative Percent for top 10 Ethnicities	72.2%	73.6%

Note: Italicized ethnicities indicate unique ethnicities among the top 10. Source: American Community Survey 3-year estimates, 2006–2008, IPUMS, University of Minnesota.

Table 2.13. CD 15 Householder Places of Birth in 80th Percentile

Newcomer Households			*Established Households*		
Place of Birth	*Count*	*Percent*	*Place of Birth*	*Count*	*Percent*
New York	4,598	27.7	New York	18,480	48.4
Russia	2,766	16.7	Ukraine	3,448	9.0
Ukraine	2,100	12.6	Russia	2,903	7.6
China	1,013	6.1	China	2,057	5.4
Byelorussia	598	3.6	Italy	828	2.2
Puerto Rico	478	2.9	Byelorussia	735	1.9
Israel	448	2.7	Israel	636	1.7
Turkey	307	1.8	Turkey	523	1.4
Syria	287	1.7	Syria	504	1.3
Uzbekistan	271	1.6	Poland	493	1.3
Mexico	259	1.6			
Pakistan	227	1.4			
Cumulative Total	13,352	80.4		30,607	80.2
Total N	16,610	100.0		38,196	100.0

Source: American Community Survey 3-year estimates, 2006–2008, IPUMS, University of Minnesota.

Italians and Poles among newcomers and the addition of Uzbekistanis, Mexicans, Pakistanis and Puerto Ricans. Also notable is that along with CD 10 and 18, CD 15's median household income is higher than the other CDs in the immigrant-led change CDs, and higher than the median income for all of Brooklyn.

CD 17 East Flatbush, Remsen Village and Rugby

Of all the Community Districts in Brooklyn, CD 17 had and still has the largest proportion of foreign born (2000, 54.2 percent and 2006/8, 54.7 percent). The immigrants here are predominantly West Indian and African (see figure 2.3), and it has the second largest Haitian community in Brooklyn (CD 18 has the largest). While the newcomer householders are slightly less likely to be black, (or white or Asian) the CD still remains racially a predominantly black CD (87.9 percent, 2006/8).

There is a slight increase in Latino householders, and as seen in table 2.14 Puerto Ricans appear on the top ten ethnicities among newcomers but are not among established householders. Newcomer householders are otherwise similar to established householders, with the exceptions of Puerto Ricans among newcomers and Barbadians among established householders. While the total population decreased by 2.4 percent between 2000 (146,623) and 2006/8 (143,031), the foreign-born population increased (74,490–2000; 78,309–2006/8), thus making the foreign born a greater proportion of the CD's residents. Many newcomers face financial hardship as median household income

Table 2.14. Characteristics of Householders in Immigration-Led Change CD 17

	Newcomer Households	*Established Households*
Foreign-born	74.2%	71.4%
Income	$35,509	$48,189
Latino	8.8%	4.1%
Asian	.6%	1.7%
Black	87.6%	90.9%
White	1.0%	1.3%
Top 10 Ethnicities	African (18.4%)	African American (22.7%)
	African American (17.2%)	African (16.7%)
	Haitian (10.4%)	Jamaican (14.1%)
	Jamaican (9.7%)	Haitian (8.7%)
	Trinidadian (8.3%)	Trinidadian (5.9%)
	West Indian (4.0%)	Guyanese (5.4%)
	Guyanese (3.5%)	Grenadian (3.5%)
	Grenadian (3.0%)	West Indian (3.4%)
	United States (3.0%)	*Barbadian (2.9%)*
	Puerto Rican (2.1%)	United States (1.6%)
Cumulative Percent for top 10 Ethnicities	79.6%	84.9%

Note: Italicized ethnicities indicate unique ethnicities among the top 10. Source: American Community Survey 3-year estimates, 2006–2008, IPUMS, University of Minnesota.

among newcomers ($35,509) is considerably less than established households and is well below Brooklyn's (2006/8) median income ($41,392).

CD 18 Canarsie, Flatlands, Georgetown, Marine Park, Mill Basin, Mill Island and Paedergat Basin

CD 18 is unique not only among the immigrant-led change CDs, but also for all of Brooklyn. It has been and remains a predominantly middle and upper class immigrant and native-born black Community District. While median income has fallen since 2000, it still has the third highest median household income (in 2006/8 at $59,857) among all CDs in Brooklyn. Racially and ethnically the CD is becoming increasingly black and more Caribbean. Racially, blacks were the only group to grow between 2000 and 2006/8, and Caribbeans account for 43.1 percent of all newcomer householders. Newcomers, though, are not exclusively black and/or Caribbean, as seen in table 2.15.

Overall, the number of foreign-born residents in CD 18 increased by 16.5 percent between 2000 (68,599) and 2006/8 (79,953); foreign-born population growth outpaced all-population growth in the CD, which grew 7.7 percent over the same period (190,396-2000; 205,115-2006/8).

Table 2.15. Characteristics of Householders in Immigration-Led Change CD 18

	Newcomer Households	*Established Households*
Foreign-born	61.3%	49.9%
Income	$56,814	$60,871
Latino	7.6%	6.3%
Asian	2.5%	2.1%
Black	65.9%	52.6%
White	22.5%	37.4%.
Top 10 Ethnicities	African American (14.0%)	African American (13.3%)
	Haitian (13.1%)	Italian (11.7%)
	Jamaican (12.5%)	Religious Responses (9.0%)
	Religious Responses (7.1%)	Jamaican (8.6%)
	Italian (4.5%)	Haitian (8.3%)
	Guyanese (4.2%)	Irish (4.2%)
	Trinidadian (3.4%)	Trinidadian (3.4%)
	Russian (3.1%)	Puerto Rican (3.4%)
	West Indian (2.9%)	Guyanese (3.2%)
	African (2.7%)	Russian (2.5%)
Cumulative Percent for top 10 Ethnicities	64.6%	67.7%

Source: American Community Survey 3-year estimates, 2006–2008, IPUMS, University of Minnesota.

Little to No Change

In the most eastern section of Brooklyn, in two Community Districts that are predominantly low-income, and black and Latino, there is very little to no difference between newcomer and established households, particularly in terms of race/ethnicity and income. CD 16 contains the neighborhoods of Brownsville and Ocean Hill; East New York, Starrett City and Cypress Hills, among other neighborhoods, are in CD 5.

Residents (2006/8) in CD 5 are predominantly native-born black (47.8 percent) and Latino (39.5 percent) and while CD 5 has increased in population by 10.7 percent, it is included in the no change group because there is little difference between newcomer householders and established householders in terms nativity, median household income and most racial and ethnic categories. There are more people, but they are quite similar to those that are already there. Foreign-born too have increased, but at a similar rate (12.8 percent) as the population increase. In addition proportionally fewer foreign-born (34.1 percent) live in CD 5 than the rest of Brooklyn (37.2 percent).

As seen in table 2.16 though, there are some notable but small differences in the top ten ethnicities. Immigrants from the African continent are coming in greater numbers. Those claiming a Nigerian and African ethnic identity

Table 2.16. Characteristics of Householders in CD 5

	Newcomer Households	*Established Households*
Foreign-born	45.6%	47.1%
Income	$30,436	$29,420
Latino	38.0%	34.2%
Asian	4.2%	3.1%
Black	51.1%	49.7%
White	3.6%	10.4%
Top 10 Ethnicities	African American (30.8%)	African American (30.8%)
	Puerto Rican (15.1%)	Puerto Rican (14.2%)
	Dominican (12.8%)	Dominican (10.4%)
	Guyanese (5.3%)	Guyanese (4.4%)
	Jamaican (4.2%)	Jamaican (3.5%)
	Trinidadian (3.6%)	Trinidadian (2.8%)
	Hispanic (1.9%)	*Italian (2.1%)*
	Nigerian (1.7%)	Ecuadorian (2.0%)
	African (1.5%)	*Haitian (1.5%)*
	Ecuadorian (1.4%)	*Russian (1.5%)*
Cumulative Percent for top 10 Ethnicities	78.3%	73.2%

Note: Italicized ethnicities indicate unique ethnicities among the top 10. Source: American Community Survey 3-year estimates, 2006–2008, IPUMS, University of Minnesota.

(3.2 percent) are absent from the established householders, while Italians, Russians and Haitians, are absent from the newcomer householders top ten.

CD 16 (Ocean Hill and Brownsville), like CD 5, is predominantly native-born (73.7 percent), black (74.3 percent) and Latino (22.5 percent) and has the lowest median household income of all the CDs in Brooklyn ($25,058). While the CD's population has increased 2 percent and the foreign-born 16.6 percent between 2000 and 2006/8, it is classified as a no change CD because its foreign-born population in 2006/8 is relatively small (26.3 percent) and is considerably below the percent foreign-born for Brooklyn. Besides the increase in foreign-born, newcomers are quite similar in terms of race, ethnicity and income.

Exceptions: CD 7 Sunset Park and CD 13 Coney Island

Both CD 7 (Sunset Park and Windsor Terrace) and CD 13 (Brighton Beach, Coney Island, and Seagate) are exhibiting immigration-led change, but unlike the CDs described in the immigrant-led change section, they exhibit differing racial/ethnic and income characteristics.

CD 7 includes the neighborhoods of Sunset Park and Windsor Terrace; the two neighborhoods are dramatically different in terms of race and income,

Table 2.17. Characteristics of Householders in CD 16

	Newcomer Households	*Established Households*
Foreign-born	43.7%	33.1%
Income	$24,856	$25,261
Latino	21.0%	21.0%
Asian	1.0%	.9%
Black	75.4%	75.6%
White	0.7%	0.9%
Top 10 Ethnicities	African American (40.5%)	African American (48.4%)
	Puerto Rican (9.2%)	Puerto Rican (11.3%)
	West Indian (5.8%)	Jamaican (5.2%)
	African (5.1%)	*Dominican (3.6%)*
	Jamaican (5.0%)	Trinidadian (3.6%)
	Trinidadian (3.8%)	Guyanese (3.5%)
	Grenadian (2.5%)	African (2.8%)
	Guyanese (2.2%)	West Indian (2.0%)
	United States (1.6%)	St. Vincent Islander (1.8%)
	St. Vincent Islander (1.5%)	*Panamanian (1.6%)*
Cumulative Percent for top 10 Ethnicities	77.2%	80.2%

Note: Italicized ethnicities indicate unique ethnicities among the top 10. Source: American Community Survey 3-year estimates, 2006–2008, IPUMS, University of Minnesota.

but the overall numbers for CD 7 are dominated by Sunset Park, which comprises most of CD 7's geography and population. In CD 7, while newcomer households are more likely to be foreign-born and have less income (like the immigration-led change CDs) the racial composition of the newcomers is different enough to exclude it from the immigration group.

Blacks and whites show little change, while Latinos are decreasing as a percentage of the population and Asians are increasing. Ethnicity and place of birth are more specific indicators than race, and show just how Sunset Park is changing. Immigrants from China are 14.7 percent of newcomer households, and there are also a considerable number of Japanese immigrants (6.2 percent). Latino newcomer households are most likely to be Mexican (11.1 percent), followed by Puerto Rican (9.8 percent), Dominican (3.8 percent) and Ecuadorian (3.0 percent). While the ethnic mix is similar between newcomers and established households, Puerto Rican households show the greatest amount of change (20.2 percent of established households while only 9.8 percent among newcomer households).

CD 13, including the communities of Brighton Beach, Coney Island, and Sea Gate, has long been and remains a strong Ukrainian, Russian and Jewish community (see figure 4). Total population declined in CD 13 between 2000 (116,574) and 2006/8 (106,400) by 8.7 percent, but at the same time the num-

Table 2.18. Characteristics of Householders in CD 7

	Newcomer Households	*Established Households*
Foreign-born	59.7%	44.4%
Income	$40,581	$45,654
Latino	36.3%	46.6%
Asian	26.7%	16.2%
Black	4.6%	3.9%
White	31.4%	32.0%
Top 10 Ethnicities	Chinese/Cantonese (14.7%)	Puerto Rican (20.2%)
	Mexican (11.1%)	Chinese (10.6%)
	Puerto Rican (9.8%)	Italian (7.4%)
	Japanese (6.2%)	Mexican (7.4%)
	Irish (4.7%)	Irish (6.2%)
	Polish (4.2%)	Dominican (6.0%)
	Dominican (3.8%)	Ecuadorian (4.0%)
	German (3.2%)	*United States (2.7%)*
	Ecuadorian (3.0%)	Japanese (2.3%)
	Italian (2.8%)	*Religious Responses (2.2%)*
Cumulative Percent for top 10 Ethnicities	63.5%	66.8%

Note: Italicized ethnicities indicate unique ethnicities among the top 10. Source: American Community Survey 3-year estimates, 2006–2008, IPUMS, University of Minnesota.

ber of foreign-born remained nearly unchanged, thus the foreign-born became an increasing percent of the total population (47.1 percent in 2000 and 50.7 percent in 2006/8). As seen in figure 2.14, nearly all census tracts in CD 13 had an increase in the concentration of foreign-born. Seventy-one percent of newcomer householders are foreign-born (compared to 57.4 percent of established householders) and 44.2 percent of the newcomer foreign-born householders are from Russia and the Ukraine.

Unlike other CDs with high immigration, newcomers have a *higher* median household income compared to established households, making CD 13 an exception to the other immigrant-led CDs. The increase in income among newcomers, $35,509 (as compared to $28,102 for established households) may not be as important though, as the newcomers' median household income is still relatively quite low and remains below Brooklyn's median household income ($41,392). As in CD 12 and 14, household racial trends are not in accord with population racial trends (see note 11).

Newcomer householders are more likely Latino and less likely white, black or Asian than established householders. Overall though, in terms of population changes, the CD has become proportionally whiter, as the white population has remained the same while Latinos, Asians and blacks have declined in overall numbers.

Table 2.19. Characteristics of Householders in CD 13

	Newcomer Households	*Established Households*
Foreign-born	71.0%	57.4%
Income	$35,509	$28,102
Latino	16.4%	9.0%
Asian	6.1%	6.5 %
Black	8.3%	9.5%
White	68.0%	74.3%
Top 10 Ethnicities	Russian (24.4%)	Religious Responses (31.3%)
	Religious Responses (14.8%)	Russian (13.8%)
	Mexican (7.6%)	Italian (8.5%)
	Ukrainian (7.0%)	African American (7.7%)
	African American (6.3%)	Ukrainian (5.9%)
	Italian (5.2%)	Chinese/Cantonese (4.1%)
	Chinese/Cantonese (4.2%)	Puerto Rican (4.0%)
	United States (3.3%)	*Polish (2.6%)*
	Puerto Rican (3.2%)	United States (1.8%)
	Ecuadorian (1.4%)	*Spanish (1.1%)*
Cumulative Percent for top 10 Ethnicities	77.4%	80.8%

Note: Italicized ethnicities indicate unique ethnicities among the top 10. Source: American Community Survey 3-year estimates, 2006–2008, IPUMS, University of Minnesota.

Table 2.20. Community District 13 Population, 2000–2006/8

	2000	*2006/8*
Latino	15.8% (18,387)	14.3% (15,245)
Asian	8.6% (10,013)	9.6% (10,259)
Black	14.9% (17,337)	11.1% (11,778)
White	57.5% (67,082)	63.6% (67,700)

Source: American Community Survey 3-year estimates, 2006–2008 and Census 2000 IPUMS, University of Minnesota.

CONCLUSION

This chapter has limitations to consider. First it is limited by its quantitative focus, but the chapters that follow will attend to qualitative changes that are taking place amid the quantitative. Second, in order to make space to discuss each of the Community Districts (for they are each unique) necessitated restricting the number of variables under consideration to just four (race, ethnicity, median household income and nativity). Preliminary analysis of comparisons of newcomers and established householders by other variables would be fruitful, particularly by age (newcomer householders in all cases are younger than established); by marital status (those in gentrifying and second-order gentrifying Districts are much more likely to be never married, while those in the rest of the Districts are more likely to be married) and family size (not always significantly different, but has varying patterns worth further research). A third limitation stems from the absence of a discussion about who leaves Brooklyn. According to Census estimates nearly 500,000 people left Brooklyn between 2000 and 2009 (Census 2009b). Early analysis suggests a disturbing pattern as blacks, Latinos and those living at or below poverty are leaving in greater proportions than found in Brooklyn's population.

Despite the chapter's limitation, it is clear Brooklyn is changing, and it is changing in different ways in different places. According to the 2006/8 data, all four major racial/ethnic populations are increasing. Blacks are increasing in number,[14] although they have decreased in proportion, while whites, Asians and Latinos have all increased slightly in both number and proportion. But while Brooklyn's population is growing, newcomers are not randomly distributed across Brooklyn. As seen in the analysis, where a newcomer decides to plant roots has much to do with the economic and sociological factors that influence our lives: income, race/ethnicity, and perhaps more so in Brooklyn than in other places from where we have come, particularly if we are from another country.

The patterns discussed above, we believe, have and will continue as Brooklyn is still a desirable place to live and many more will continue to come and settle based on the patterns discussed. This leads to some disturbing trends. Racially Brooklyn appears to be a very diverse place to live, for in Brooklyn whites account for less than 40 percent of the population. One quick glance at figure 2.12 shows, however, that while at the borough level Brooklyn is indeed diverse, in terms of settlement patterns within Brooklyn we are unfortunately highly segregated, as there are large swaths of Brooklyn where very few blacks live or conversely where whites live.[15] In the gentrifying and second-order gentrifying CDs there is some change in these numbers as whites move in to predominantly black CDs, and the hope would be that segregation would decrease. But what this analysis shows is that blacks are in decline in each of these Community Districts, and that (most likely) they are moving into CD 18 which is becoming increasingly black and less white. Thus Brooklyn is not becoming less segregated but the spatial patterns of segregation are changing. Given also that whites are increasing in the very neighborhoods where black and Latino home ownership is continuing to be hard-hit by the foreclosure crisis, the pattern found in this analysis is, unfortunately, not likely to change.

The foreign-born will continue to be a great engine of change in Brooklyn as over 22,000, (averaged between 2000 and 2009) arrive each year (Census 2009b). Mexicans and Chinese are showing the greatest growth in numbers since 2000 and as global pressures to immigrate show no signs of abating, we see no reason for foreign immigration to slow in Brooklyn for the most prevalent immigrant groups in Brooklyn. Meeting the needs of immigrants in the schools, health system and civically will continue to be of great importance throughout Brooklyn, but particularly in the high-immigrant CDs.

Finally most disturbing are the economic trends, as income inequality seems to be growing, even as median household income for the borough remains unchanged between 2000 and 2006/8. There is a growing disparity both within Community Districts and within Brooklyn between those who have plenty and those who continue to struggle. The Community Districts that are relatively wealthy in terms of median household income have merely increased their wealth, while the poorest CDs have seen little change in their median household income. And while poverty has decreased overall (probably because many are of the poorest are leaving), signs of struggles abound as the use of emergency food pantries is increasing as is the number of families seeking help from New York City's Department of Homeless Services (NYCDHS 2010). The trends leading toward more segregation, hunger and homelessness are certainly not hopeful and can lead to racial, ethnic and class tensions that have plagued Brooklyn in the past. Let us hope we all work, along with those already doing so, to take responsibility for amending extant inequalities, whether those inequalities befall those who are new arrivals or those that are established Brooklynites.

ACKNOWLEDGMENTS

The authors would like to thank and acknowledge Gretchen Maneval, the Director of the Center for the Study of Brooklyn, for both institutional and editorial support. The Center's support of Brooklyn research is invaluable and without it this chapter would remain merely an idea rattling in the brain. Additional thanks are due to Lennese Semple, research assistant at the Center for the Study of Brooklyn, for her comments on an early draft.

NOTES

1. Community Districts are governed by Community Boards, which are one vehicle through which citizens can redress issues with the city's varied services. Community

Boards have 50 members all of whom are appointed by the respective borough President. Boards serve an advisory role to elected officials to address land use and zoning, budget and other community issues (NYC Office of the Mayor 2011).

2. Full-size maps in this chapter are available from the first author at lmason@brooklyn.cuny.edu.

3. Unfortunately, the very significant Jewish population cannot be adequately counted using Census data. The Census Bureau is by law not allowed to ask questions regarding religion. Based on a survey conducted in 2002 the United Jewish Federation estimates the Brooklyn Jewish population to be 516,600 (21 percent of Brooklyn's population). A 37 percent described themselves as Orthodox, the largest concentration of Orthodox Jews in NYC. Predominant Jewish neighborhoods include Williamsburg, Borough Park, Coney Island, Brighton Beach, Sheepshead Bay, Flatbush, Midwood, Kensington, Kingsbay, Madison, Besonhurst and Gravesend (UJA-Federation of New York 2004).

4. 2002 rather than 2000 is the beginning date because, unfortunately due to the coding for the IPUMS variable, MOVEDIN, 2002 is the closest year to 2000 by which the data set can be split into newcomer households and established households. MOVEDIN is an ordinal household variable that measures the amount of time that a householder has lived at their current residence. 2008 is the end date because at the time of the writing 2008 American Community Survey data was the latest available.

5. There is an important limitation in the data. Newcomers, as delineated for this analysis, are those who have moved into their household since 2002. The ACS data, however, does not measure from where the householder moved. The householder could have moved from anywhere including the same Community District. If they moved within the same CD the householder may not be a newcomer; it is however, impossible to know if this is the case.

6. Four racial/ethnic categories are adapted from the Census Bureau American Community Survey's Race and Hispanic variables. For textual flow purposes, within the text, non-Hispanic Asians are "Asian," non-Hispanic blacks are "black," Hispanics of any race are "Latino" and non-Hispanic whites are "white."

7. Microdata are, unfortunately, not available at the census tract level, thus the analysis conducted here can only be accomplished at the Community District level.

8. A significant portion of Crown Heights South is a Jewish (predominantly Hassidic) community, and a large portion of the whites that lived in CD 9 in 2000 (8.3 percent) lived within Crown Heights South.

9. It is important to note that overall in Brooklyn, at least using the 2006/2008 ACS data, the black population has not decreased. There is an increase in the black population in the CDs east and south of CD 3, 4 and 9.

10. Please note that the census tract maps do not show newcomers versus established residents; they only show changes since 2000 to the census tract population as a whole. For example, increases in median household income at the census tract level could be due to newcomers and/or to changes within established households; characteristics like place of birth and race/ethnicity are less likely to change at the household level, thus those maps are more closely aligned with the newcomer/established household analysis conducted at the Community District level for this paper.

11. CD 14 is the one exception to this, as newcomers are slightly less likely to be foreign-born (59.4 percent 60.4 percent). CD 14 does, however, have a high foreign-born population as part of its newcomers and otherwise follows the trends in the rest of the CDs characterized by immigrant-led change.

12. In CD 12, when exploring population (rather than household) changes from 2000 to 2006/8 using decennial Census and ACS 2006–2008, the data show the foreign-born population *decreasing*. So it is curious that in the case of CD 12 household data shows more foreign born householders while population data shows the total foreign born decreasing. It is also true for racial data; there are less white householders when comparing newcomers to established households but there are more whites in the population (comparing 2000 and 2006/8), conversely there are more blacks among newcomer households, but fewer blacks in the population. The full exploration of this is beyond the scope of this chapter, but initial data exploration suggests a few possibilities:

I. Data noise. The data are from different samples. The newcomer versus established household analysis relies on one data sample (ACS 2006/8) while the population data are from the 2000 decennial Census and the 2006/8 ACS. In addition the householder analysis divides newcomers into those that arrived between 2002 and 2008, and does not go all the way back to 2000.
II. White and native born households have more people in their households compared to foreign-born, thus driving population totals higher for those groups;
III. the householder is foreign-born but other household members are native-born;
IV. and finally (but less likely) there could be many mixed-race and mixed-ethnic households so that a householder may be of one race and ethnicity but others in the household are of different races and ethnicities.

13. This is based on place of birth data, not ethnic (ancestry) data, which is found in the tables.

14. The 2010 Decennial Census has the black population declining since 2000, but that data is now being contested by New York City, and for now is not considered in this analysis.

15. There are of course blocks, neighborhoods, public schools and other spaces in Brooklyn where there is great diversity, but overall the pattern is one of segregation.

REFERENCES

Census Bureau. 2000. Decennial Census, Summary File 3.

Census Bureau. 2008. American Community Survey, 3-Year Estimates, 2006–2008.

Census Bureau. 2009. American Community Survey Single-Year Estimates, 2009.

Census Bureau. 2009a. *Design and Methodology American Community Survey*. U.S. Government Printing Office: Washington, DC.

Census Bureau. Population Estimates 2000–2009.

NYC Department of Homeless Services. 2010. *Critical Activities Reports* 2002–2010. Retrieved on April 2, 2011 (www.nyc.gov/html/dhs/html/about/car.shtml).

NYC Office of the Mayor. 2011. "Community Boards and City Government." Mayor's Community Affairs Unit. Retrieved on April 2, 2011 (www.nyc.gov/html/cau/html/cb/place_in_gov.shtml).

Ruggles, Steven J., Trent Alexander, Katie Genadek, Ronald Goeken, Matthew B. Schroeder, and Matthew Sobek. 2010. "Integrated Public Use Microdata Series: Version 5.0" [Machine-readable database]. Minneapolis: University of Minnesota.

UJA-Federation of New York. 2004. *Jewish Community Study of New York: 2002.* New York: New York.

3

Forgetting Poverty in Brooklyn and the United States

William DiFazio

Global poverty is increasing during the world recession. The United States as part of a global system has poverty increasing as well. The United Nations pledged to half extreme poverty families that are living on less than $2 a day by the year 2015 but the global recession has increased poverty in the world to three billion people. The poverty threshold for a family of four is $22,000 (U.S. Bureau of the Census 2009). In Brooklyn alone 24 percent of the population—over 600,000 people—live below the poverty threshold (City-Data.com 2011). The United States and state governments have not increased welfare grants to the poor even though poverty is increasing as unemployment increases, job training for welfare participants is being slashed, Wall Street and the wealthy are not paying their fair share of taxes and the homeless crisis has now included formerly middle class people because of the foreclosure explosion caused by the banks and the mortgage industry. The conditions of the poor increasingly resemble Engels' description of the working class in England in 1844 (Engels [1845] 2009). If President Bush's tax cuts for the wealthy at 1 percent and the trillions of dollars spent on war were stopped we would have no budget crisis in this country, but budget cuts are the theme of the day and the poor are disproportionately hurt by these cuts (Stiglitz 2010).

The following description of life in a Brooklyn soup kitchen in one of the largest poor neighborhoods, Bedford-Stuyvesant, is based on research from 1988 to 2008 where poverty still resonates today after President Clinton's welfare reform and even though Obama is now president little has changed except the names of the programs and that less support is available for those in need. Ultimately the nature of the reform is that there isn't any change. Everything is worse for the poor in Brooklyn and misery is increasing steadily. This reflects a general tendency throughout the United States.

I describe two ethnographic scenes, the first at a large soup kitchen in Bedford-Stuyvesant Brooklyn. The soup kitchen study gave me access to large numbers of poor people for a period of twenty years, 1988 to 2008. In contrast, the second scene is at a Passover Seder in Brooklyn where I observed a moment in the lives of middle class Americans in which I describe their separation from the lives of the poor and their forgetting of the simple fact that poverty is increasing. To the people at the Seder poverty is something that only happens in underdeveloped countries. This chapter is about the contradiction between these two Brooklyn scenes and their possible resolution.

SCENES OF POVERTY IN BROOKLYN

October 11, 1989

We are averaging 1200 guests for lunch. I am late today and instead of serving the soup, Sr. Bernadette assigns me to serving juice with Louella. Kate walks up for some water and says hello. She is a white woman in her thirties; she has sores on her face. When she first started to come to the soup kitchen she weighed thirty pounds more than she does now. I assume she has AIDS.

"Bill, can I have seconds on the Kool-Aid." I give her more Kool-Aid and I ask her if she has a sore-throat. "I have a bad throat. I can't get rid of it. Living on the streets, it's cold and you can't get warm. Now I'm living on the subway platform (Myrtle Ave. and Broadway). Sometimes I ride the trains but they chase you."

"My counselor wants me to go to the shelter in South Harlem. I tell her that if she's so hot on the shelter, why don't you go there. It's not safe. Everyone is always fighting. They fight over the sheets, over beds, over food; everyone has a bad attitude. I hate the shelters everyone is always fighting." Her coughing is increasing. Not knowing what to say, I tell her that she has to find a way to keep warm.

"I won't go to the shelter. The subway's bad, but not as bad as the shelter. The other day some kids attacked me on the subway. One of them whacked me with a 2 by 4. I thought he broke my back. It's still killing me. They didn't try to rob me or anything. The fucking bastards thought it was funny to whack me with a 2 by 4." A male friend walks over and says they have to go. She says goodbye and leaves.

December 1, 1989

The soup kitchen is getting more crowded even though it's check day. It's cold, people are huddling together on the line that winds down Willoughby

Street. Everyone is waiting for the soup kitchen to open. As I wait on line, a man goes through the line asking, "You want good dope, good dope?" No one is buying.

Bill, who works the door, allows some people to wait inside where it's warm. People are irritable. They begin to yell at Bill to let them in. Richard, a soup kitchen volunteer, is standing next to Bill. A woman seeing Richard starts to yell at him, "No wonder the line is moving so slowly, they have the dwarf at the door." The woman has two broad (a quarter-inch wide and three inches long) scars on her face.

Most of the talk on line is everyday talk about the ordinary trivialities of their lives. In this way their lives are like everyone's. They trade information or anecdotes about social services, or they exchange neighborhood gossip, or they engage in good-natured fooling around, or they complain about the weather. They are used to waiting in line at welfare offices, shelters, emergency rooms, supermarkets and even here at the soup kitchen. The man standing next to me tells me he's feeling sick. "I changed my methadone program because I'm working part-time now. I'm sick but I want to eat. If I don't eat now when am I going to eat? Oh, I just went in yesterday, but my hours are different. I'm all screwed up." He's on a take-home program. He gets three bottles of methadone, one a day. This reduces the amount of time necessary for him to go to the clinic." I ask, "Do you have your bottle?" He answers, "Yeah, yeah, I got to go." He leaves. If he doesn't have his bottle, the nurse doesn't have to medicate him. He'll return to the clinic and give the nurse his bottle, demonstrating that he hasn't sold his bottle. She'll make him drink a bottle in front of her and supply him with the bottles until Monday. The nurse's surveillance function seems to be more important than her pain relieving function for her patient.

Another man standing next to me is also on methadone. "I haven't worked in years. I could never be on a take-home program. I've got dirty urine. I take Valium; it relieves the pressure, especially since I'm detox now. I hate it. I'm going back on methadone. Since I detoxed I have no energy. I functioned better. When I took methadone I never cheated. I never took other drugs, except Valium. I was an intravenous drug user for twenty-five years. I can't function without it. I'm too old. The methadone saved my life. I plan to be on methadone for the rest of my life."

We finally get into the kitchen. Bill asks me what am I doing on line, "too lazy to work today?" He laughs; I tell him that I'll work later. I sit down with Jose. I know that he's a single man on public assistance and that I would like to ask him some questions about welfare. He also jokes with me about working today. I laugh and ask him to explain check day. I want Jose to explain to me the daily life of insecurity and the sense of always living on the edge of the poor people who come to the kitchen through his own experiences.

"Well, today is SSI (Supplemental Security Income) check day. You get SSI on the first of the month. That's why there are fewer people here than usually. On Tuesday, it's emergency food stamps. On Thursday, a lot of people will be getting welfare checks and regular food stamps. But it's all different, even the days are different. But SSI always comes on the first of the month.

I ask him, "What are your benefits?"

Jose responds: "I get $100 every two weeks, that's welfare. I don't get SSI. I get $90 once a month, food stamps. I get a housing check, a rent check. I endorse it and give it to the superintendent, he deposits it. I can't cash it. Only the landlord can cash it. I think the maximum rent that they'll give for a single man is $215, not much. But different people get different amounts. My buddy here gets $111 in food stamps but no welfare, everyone is different. I try to eat here as much as possible and save $30 a month of my food stamps. All the bodegas around here will buy them. They give you $7 cash for $10 of food stamps. It gives me some freedom. Yeah some buy drugs and alcohol, but you don't really make enough and you need necessities, a shirt, cigarettes, go to a movie. I also use them to go to restaurants. Get bacon and eggs for breakfast. I love that. And then I save them so that at the end of the month, I always save at least $30; I can go to the A&P and pig out, cake and chocolate milk, some luxuries."

Grinker (1989) tells us that "13.5 percent of all people living in the United States were poor as compared to 23.2 percent of those living in New York City. The city's poverty rate for children was 37.9 percent as compared to the national average of 20.6 percent. . . . The effectiveness of federal food stamp programs decreased dramatically between 1980 and 1987. Food stamp participation rates dropped nationally by almost one million people; during the same period, the number of people in poverty rose by two million. In this same period, the number of soup kitchens and food pantries rose from 30 in 1981 to 603 in 1987. These six hundred programs feed approximately 570,000 people per month" (p. v–vi).

As we see here there is an inverse relationship between aid and the number of poor people; that is, as poverty and hunger increased from the 1980's to 2011, there is less help from the federal, state and local governments. Thus, too many go hungry, and because of this many people are forced to cheat and sell their food stamps for other "luxuries." It is thus that I argue in this chapter that only a guaranteed adequate standard of living for all citizens will end the need for welfare and prevent the selling of food stamps in the underground economy.

I sit down with Bea. She lives in the Roosevelt Houses across the street from the soup kitchen. She has lived there all of her life. Even though there's crime and it's dangerous at night, she says, "Everyone knows me and I feel safe there." In general, the "projects" are the best housing that the area offers. There are some well-kept and more expensive homes where middle class and working class people live but the projects are better than most of the housing in the neighborhood.

Bea says: "We have a five-and-a-half-room apartment in the projects. There are four of us, my sister and her son and my son. I get $48.50 in public assistance every two weeks. My son gets SSI because he's disabled; he's blind. The rent is $217 per month and we get $196 food stamps per month. That's hard, things are expensive. I baby-sit and I clean house and I make about $75 more a week. (This is not allowed and technically she is a welfare cheat. Almost everyone who receives aid works odds and ends jobs, off the book jobs because the welfare grants are insufficient to live on.) That helps, but what we really live on is really nothing."

I ask her about selling food stamps. She answers: "I don't think the system is fair. They don't give you enough to live on. But I think it's wrong to trade them in and not buy food. That's unfair. Food stamps is how I survive. They're like gold to me. I may have no money, but I always have food. Like now it's the first of the month. I'm going to buy my meat. I buy a case of chicken, a loin of pork chops, big shell steak, chopped meat, rice, and noodles. We'll have enough food for a month, and I'll eat my lunches here at least a few days a week. And I get to see my friends and talk. And Sister Bernadette is just beautiful. But again, I think it's wrong to sell food stamps, to buy cigarettes, clothes, crack or OTB (off-track betting). Even though it's not much money and we don't have much, it's wrong."

Bea is typical of the women who come to the soup kitchen and of the poor women who raise children without the aid of men. Female-headed families did not cause poverty but were caused by poverty and race and gender discrimination. Bea and Jose both died in 2006 of heart attacks. Hard lives and bad diets—the cheapest foods have the highest amount of calories. Life is hard for everyone but poverty makes the ordinary hardships of life worse. The poor do not have the economic resources to dull life's misery and everything that results is just increased. Still the poor, in general, conform to society's rules and regulations. The soup kitchen is most of the time a peaceful and safe place. We don't have social change here; we have a lot of people trying to survive as best they can. Poverty is not the result of overgenerous welfare programs as the conservative's claim. First most poor people do not receive welfare and second the programs are not generous, they maintain people at close to subsistence. Somehow inequality must be ended to end poverty and a real democratization of the USA is required. A real democracy cannot just include political rights but economic guarantees as well. A real democracy is both political and economic but our current democracy is just political and insufficient in meeting real human needs. This has been forgotten as has poverty as the basis of human suffering has also been forgotten. The following ethnographic anecdote may be helpful to understand why poverty and democracy are forgotten.

SCENE FROM A SEDER

At a Passover Seder in Brooklyn one of the guests at the table said how lucky we were to live in a country where there was no longer any poverty and hunger. But poverty is increasing and is 5 percent higher in 2009 then it was in 1999 (Eckholm 2010). He took his privilege for granted. This was a very privileged upper middle-class white group of both Jews and non-Jews. I mention this only to give a sense of what it must be like to be poor and live in a world where you are continually judged by the non-poor in almost all of your situations, from welfare to work and housing to education. This very privileged and well-meaning guest was up on his political correctness and, thus, knew the right things to say on issues of sexism, racism and nutrition but really had no sense of both hunger and poverty. This at first seemed shocking, since the Seder deals with the misery of the powerless Hebrews and their decision to flee in the face of overwhelming power. But, here and now for the poor in the United States, there is no possibility of flight and nowhere to go, and furthermore, only the privileged can afford to flee. Ironically, the well-meaning guest seems to know all the details of the Seder but misses its point. Thus, Elijah is still waiting outside the door, still without anyone to listen to his prophecy of the coming of the Messiah. The well-meaning guest is like current-day economists and businessmen who talk about all the new opportunities of global capitalism but forget that global capitalism still forces billions of people in the world to live on less than two dollars a day (The World Bank 2011).

Currently, economists believe that all economic problems can be resolved by just reducing the involvement of government in the free market. They believe that the private interest of global capitalism is the same as the general interest. They believe that the seemingly political and social problems only need technical economic remedies. But are these economists forgetting that democracy is not necessarily beneficial for the specific, individual interests of corporate capitalism? The economists also forget that armed with his science he can still never answer a simple question about the United States labor force. That is why can't the capitalist economy produce middle class jobs for over half of the population in the United States? These "dismal" scientists ignore the class hardships for an enormous number of working people and continue to produce optimistic economic forecasts for the few whom can take advantage of them. Are economists just ignorant of the lives of the majority of Americans or do they just believe that "trickle down economics," will really make "all boats float"? Are they purposely ignorant or has their fetishism of their mathematical models made them blind to the real hardships of ordinary people?

Of course poverty in Brooklyn is further mirrored in the United Sates. Poverty has been both racialized and feminized but it is also about class. This means that it's about the resources that are required to live a normal life in the society—what Weber called "life chances"—that is, the opportunities for jobs, wages, education, health care, housing and the access to culture. The ignoring of these class issues has spread in this society. This seems to be true of those in power in general. To say it succinctly, it is that "the oppressors cannot see the impact of their oppression on the oppressed." The powerful are unable to see the poor and the powerless through their own eyes, thus the poor are just seen as incompetent and/or mentally challenged, i.e., constitutionally lazy. Their poverty is their own fault, even though fully half of the population lives below the median family income and about 60 percent is living in hardship as a result of the costs of maintaining their lifestyle and are forced to live in significant debt (Samuelson 2003: A25).

This willful ignorance about the hardships of life is seen at almost every point in the society. Thus, economists parade their statistics as if they are unaware of at least two of their failures. First, they fail to understand the actual human relations that lie behind their statistics. They are cynical about the actual description of the daily lives of the have-nots by ethnographers and journalists who spend enormous amounts of time studying the lower classes and instead these positivists call these descriptions anecdotal. Second, they fail to understand that their statistics are not absolutes but representations. Like all representations they are approximations of reality; they allow for heuristic understanding and suffer from the crisis of representation and what Whitehead called the "fallacy of misplaced concreteness," that is "mistaking the abstract for the concrete" ([1925] 1953: 51).

Here I retell the Seder story as just a way to get to the key question for this chapter which is how the privileged guest was ignorant of tens of millions of poor people who live in the United States of America. This is typical in a society in which everyone is assumed to be middle class and in which the poor are treated like Sudnow's (1967) terminal patients for whom the doctors treat as dead before they are dead. Still the poor are forgotten, ignored and as some say, they are invisible.

EVERYDAY LIFE AND FORGETTING POVERTY

It is in the space and time of everyday life that movements of freedom and oppression coexist. Though separate from the workplace, which has its own everyday life, it is in everyday life where alienation and exploitation are lived out. It is here that the moments, banalities, trivialities, repetitions, pleasures of family, church, shopping, love-making, TV watching, shopping, eating and all of the various aspects of personal life happen. It is a personal life overwhelmed by class contradiction and endless moments of struggle. We pay bills, argue with our children, study for tests, wake-up to go to work, have appointments, vote for president and never have enough time for all of the obligations that we have to fulfill. Too many obligations without forgetting we couldn't survive. We all have our own insecurities; we cannot deal with the misery of poverty so we forget it exists or blame the poor for their poverty.

Still, it is in everyday life that the cement of society is fixed but never absolutely and where change must and does occur if a revolution is to be possible. There is no revolution in everyday life currently but change is always happening, often very slowly. Though the political economy is separate it infiltrates everyday life and is experienced not only externally and internally in the lives of people, it is the space and time of class contradictions. It is in daily life that commodities are fetishized, that advertisements, news, movies, books are read and watched. It is the space and time of ideology and of going beyond ideology. It is the space and time in which change must occur and freedom is possible. It is in daily life that both domination and imagination are ongoing. They exist in contradiction with each other in the ordinary interactions of people. How this works out is never over-determined, it is always fluid and fragile and in transformation, however slowly. The world-historical events are translated in this world never separated from a non-reified totality. Totality and everyday life coexist but never as absolutes and they are redefined in a multiplicity of ways. Even freedom is understood in daily life but not in the ways that philosophers understand. Freedom is never just an abstraction, has its limits and will last only to the extent that the concept is still sensible within the lives of people. As Lefebvre has told us, "Everyday life can be defined as a level of social practice within totality. . . . It is where the basic question is not the Kantian, "How do we know what we know," but "How do men live as they are living and How do they accept it" (2007: 30–31). And, more how can we go beyond it and develop a daily life that is no longer programmed by global capitalism and the state, and against this the possibility of a utopian time and space of freedom. It is in terms of the ideology of freedom that the current class contradictions are both maintained and possibly upset in everyday life. Here ordinary people can redefine freedom and possibly end poverty.

THE COMMON SENSE FREEDOM OF EVERYDAY LIFE

In the United States, there is no possibility of overcoming poverty without overcoming the hardships of middle class life. These hardships are most visible in everyday life where both economic and political power, rule their bodies and freedom has been debased. The middle class has less and less access to good jobs and more of them live at the edge of poverty.

In the United States, freedom has been constructed and redefined by ordinary people because they have so little access to real freedom. First, freedom as mobility in space, mainly the auto and the interstate highway system allows people to move around. Second, part and just as important is homeownership which enables personal freedom in your life when you are finished with your daily labor. For Americans work is a place of un-freedom and the supposedly automatic conditions of the free market over which they have no control. Fewer and fewer Americans understand the powerful interests of the free market and are almost unaware of the intensification of economic, political and social inequality that the capitalist free market generates. The third part is consumer choice their common sense notion of freedom of choice for a public good, that is shopping keeps the economy viable. Consumers are the current notion of a citizenship that is that you vote for products and for shopping at expensive or cheaper malls. The shopping mall is a degraded public sphere which is the center of civil society in global capitalism. Americans have lost their sense of community and live in planned isolation in urban condos and suburban gated subdivisions. They have participated in dividing and conquering their own lives and there purposeful ignorance of this allows the current class war against them by global capital to continue. At the same time that there is this purposeful ignorance the current crises undermines the three major freedoms that Americans are truly concerned with owning their own home, driving their cars and shopping wherever they want. They don't see the increase in poverty as their homes are foreclosed and they are forced to get food at soup kitchens.

In the United States, the lack of freedom in the workplace has not been translated into class struggle even for the small percentage of unionized workers. For a small minority of people they have avoided alienated labor by taking the risks of small business. This has allowed them a modicum of freedom, but at the same time the expansiveness and the control of global markets by big business and big landlords has made small business a major victim of the transnational regimes. They believe that small business is the heart of American capitalism but it is not; in fact small business gets in the way of global, corporate development. As costs and rents double and triple small businesses close and only chain stores can afford to stay in business. The diversity and personal service that small business once provided has given way to the impersonal, homogenized super stores like Wal-Mart, Home Depot and Barnes and Noble. It is true that stores like Wal-Mart have allowed Americans to continue to shop at affordable prices but at the tremendous expense of lower and lower wages, i.e., the rush to the bottom. Somehow when we shop it has no relationship to the wages that we worked for. Somehow we complain about high taxes but not high prices?

It goes almost unnoticed that our wages have been falling for thirty-five years. In the 1970s more workers were working for better wages at companies like U.S. Steel and General Motors. Now we work for lower wages at non-union jobs at McDonalds, or at temporary service companies like Man Power, Labor Ready and Kelly Services. The Bureau of Labor Statistics tells us that these three temp-employment services are three of the five biggest employers in the United States (Aronowitz and DiFazio 2010). We live in a world where it goes unnoticed, even by philosophers, that there cannot be political freedom separate from economic equality. And how can this be rectified when jobs with good wages and benefits continue to disappear? Our three commonsense freedoms are central for Americans' sense of freedom but now they are threatened by the housing, oil and credit crises. Can the global capitalism deliver the goods for most Americans? No, it cannot, but will the left provide the alternative messages and strategies for another way of living in the United States? This chapter is an attempt at this in the first major crises of the twenty-first century.

For Americans, freedom is not the abstract freedom of political philosophy. It is not freedom of choice and freedom of action, nor does freedom of choice really have a relationship to a higher good. We have unaffordable housing and medical care and a notion of democracy that has nothing to do with citizens participating in governance. Citizenship has been reduced to voting once a year. The lives of the poor are becoming common for the lower middle classes.

And worse, the true antidemocratic impulse of many Americans is that government should be run like a business; for too many there is no longer a concern with the "will of the people." Most Americans do not realize that businesses aren't democratic institutions. The "higher good," is the very determined freedom of shopping in the store of your choice, though you no longer have any credit, or home ownership, though homes are heavily mortgaged, and the freedom to drive your SUV or pickup truck even though you have to go into immense debt to drive your $30,000 vehicle at $4+ a gallon. Still this is what Americans mean by individual freedom, though it has nothing to do with the enlightenment freedom of the founders. These freedoms have been earned through their hard work and have been maintained through increasing debt. It has put Americans on an endless stress filled treadmill of longer hours of work and never ending debt. It has made time the central condition of their daily lives that is that there is never enough time because Americans are working longer and harder. The time constraints have become overwhelming as we work more hours and spend less time with friends and family. Everyone is now on a tight schedule and even families must schedule their diminished personal time together.

Currently the joint energy and housing crises have increased the stress and strain upon most Americans as well as undermining the illusion of the "American Dream." The American Dream was never for everyone, the lower classes were always exempt from it; the middle classes rarely managed the mobility that the dream promised but now that has almost totally disappeared. We have been disempowered and this disempowerment has added to our personal problems. But, once again, Americans cannot relate these personal problems to the public issues of our time, nor do they understand that their individual freedoms are dependent on social, collective action. We do not understand the limits of individual action because the achievement of individuals is glorified in the media. The central message that we are sold is of the heroism of a man or woman making it on their own. Instead of the critique of the bourgeoisie as oppressor they have become the models for our children. The myth of the individual entrepreneur, like Donald Trump making his billions of dollars on his own, although the truth is that almost all of his money is inherited. The important function of this myth of the successful individual isn't just the maintaining of control over the population by making collective action more difficult and undesirable but of telling the masses that if they aren't successful that they have only themselves to blame. The myth of the individual provides a message that failure is always personal. It can never be the failure of capitalist society and its individualized entrepreneurial vision. Americans blame themselves for society's failures. If they lose their homes or their cars or become bankrupt because they cannot pay their "world historic" personal debt it is their failure.

This is the universal message of both liberals and conservatives and there aren't any alternative messages. Thus, it is the bumper sticker on many cross country trucks, "stop crying." You must cope with your personal failure; you must bear the brunt of your personal misery silently. America can't be at fault; it is "the greatest country in the history of the world" and it is best in everything. Americans are in a bind in the current crises, they are trapped between their narrowly defined American Dream and their inability to afford it, even through an enormous personal debt. They can no longer depend on the common sense freedom's, the price of gas has quadrupled in the last five years and they cannot afford their SUVs and they can no longer afford their homes or use the equity as an ATM and thus consumer choice as shoppers has come down to the bare necessities. What are they to do? They can no longer afford personal freedom. At the same time they still cannot understand the relationship of public issues to their personal problems and neither, the media, the Republicans or the Democrats, nor Palin or Obama provides them with any real solutions. They are in "bad faith" they act as if they have no personal responsibility and thus they do not take political action. Their freedoms were shallow and participating as citizens in a democracy was not part of their lives.

Wilhelm Reich in *The Mass Psychology of Fascism* asked a crucial question; "what has to be explained is not the fact that the man who is hungry steals or the fact that the man who is exploited strikes, but why the majority of those who are hungry don't steal and why the majority of those who are exploited don't strike" (1982: 13).

We need an alternative message that connects individual freedom to collective struggle and personal problems to public issues. The stresses and strains of everyday life are the pathological result of disempowerment. They can only be resolved through a new empowerment. They can only be resolved when the alienated and exploited are willing to do more than strike, and to create new alternative institutions that guarantee their freedom and power. The middle class must understand that they are connected to the poor and a better life for all is connected to making a long struggle in which poverty is ended. We must understand that the local and the global are connected, with the local dependent on the global. Thus, Brooklyn is part of New York City, and New York State, and the United States, and the globe and a world recession is very hard to solve at the local level unless the global crisis is solved as well. The global crisis has made poverty in Brooklyn worse and there seems to be "no bottom to the bottom."

REFERENCES

Aronowitz, Stanley and William DiFazio. 2010. *The Jobless Future*, second edition, Minneapolis, MN: University of Minnesota Press.

City-Data.com. 2011. "Brooklyn, New York (NY) Poverty Rate Data—Information about poor and low income residents." Retrieved on August 28, 2011 (www.city-data.com/poverty/poverty-Brooklyn-New-York.html).

Eckholm, Erik. 2010. "Recession Raises Poverty Rate to a 15 Year High." *New York Times*, September 16.

Engels, Friedrich. [1845] 2009. *Conditions of the Working Class in England.* Oxford, UK: Oxford University Press.

Grinker, W. J. 1989. *Unfinished_Business: Report on the Insurgency Task Force on Food and Hunger.* New York, NY: Human Resources Administration.

Lefebvre, Henri. 2007. *The Critique of Every Day Life, Vol. II,* New York, NY: Verso.

Reich, Wilheim. 1982. *The Mass Psychology of Fascism.* New York: Farrar, Strauss and Giroux.

Samuelson, Robert J. 2003. "A Sixty Year Credit Binge." *Washington Post*, August 27, p. A25.

Stiglitz, Joseph E. 2010. *Freefall: America, Free Markets and the Sinking of the World Economy.* New York: W.W. Norton and Company.

Sudnow, David. 1967. *Passing On: The Social Organization of Dying.* Englewood Cliffs, NJ: Prentice-Hall.

The World Bank. 2011. "Poverty Reduction and Equity, Overview" Retrieved on August 28, 2011 (http://go.worldbank.org/77LE4ON4V0).

U.S. Bureau of the Census. 2009. "Poverty Thresholds." Retrieved on August 28, 2011 (www.census.gov/hhes/www/poverty/data/threshld/thresh09.html).

Whitehead, Alfred North. [1925] 1953. *Science and the Modern World.* New York: The Free Press.

4

Gentrification in Everyday Life in Brooklyn

Judith N. DeSena

This chapter is about the process of gentrification in a Brooklyn neighborhood in New York. It focuses on the arrangement of groups, of gentry and working class residents within the community. Gentrification represents another cycle of neighborhood change. The neighborhood of Greenpoint, the focus of this study, has for most of its existence been a working class community inhabited by immigrants and later generations of those immigrants' families. It is now experiencing an influx of more formally educated and affluent residents relative to the long-term, sometimes life-long population. This chapter ultimately highlights the central theme of social class distinctions in a changing community.

With a multitude of ethnic groups, several religions, and now a mixture of social classes, on an everyday basis, Greenpoint is generally an orderly place within one of America's oldest and largest cities. On most days, nothing very much out of the ordinary happens. People carry out their daily lives racing to and from work, moving children around, frequenting local retail establishments and recreational facilities. Even within the context of difference, both cultural and social class, people appear to get along. There is rarely physical violence between groups. In a community such as Greenpoint people engage in "parallel play," interacting next to each other while focused on their own group and activities. In his study of Boston, Daniel Monti states,

> It is not immediately apparent how all these different persons residing in the same place figure out that they can work together or at least do not have to fight all the time . . . Kindergarten teachers call it "parallel play" . . . Parallel play operates in a similar way in cities where different and sometimes quarrelsome groups must stumble into a state of mutual regard . . . When one set of them

> puts together groups of their own or watches how other persons do it, this is how they learn about each other. It is also how they come to see the possibility and necessity of working together at least part of the time . . . Cities are really big parallel playpens" (Monti 1999: 206).

Supporting Monti's contention about parallel play is a remark made by a Greenpoint resident and mother as she observed people gathering while waiting for children to be dismissed from school. She said,

> You see it in the schoolyard as we pick the kids up. There's groups. There's us, the old neighborhood, the YUPPIES, the immigrants. The YUPPIES say, "we're integrating." They're not integrating! They don't want to integrate. They want to be their own group.

The groups she described are engaged in parallel play.

In Greenpoint, for example, McCarren Park is a large complex of three parks serving the communities of Greenpoint and Williamsburg, and marks a boundary between these neighborhoods. On weekends and holidays, the parks are crowded with residents of all ages speaking numerous languages engaged in various activities. Particularly in the summer, some families' barbecue, couples picnic drinking wine from festive glasses, and immigrant youths play soccer and cricket. They operate individually in unison. In addition, in another park in the community during the summer months, a variety of films have been shown on Friday nights. There too is a mixing of groups of gentry, working class, and immigrant residents who gather in the park to cool off, while also being accompanied by some entertainment. On one such occasion, a working class man commented, "I watched my neighbors come here with trays of hors d'oeuvres!"

Neighborhoods like Greenpoint are the places in cities in which tensions and disagreements are negotiated and people learn to work things out to some conclusion. In neighborhoods residents cannot avoid each other. They can either escape for a time, move, or engage in some level of dialogue. This is also a way that neighbors who are different from each other learn about each other, learn from each other, and become somewhat like each other, while at the same time possibly remaining unequal. Brooklyn and New York City's folklore claims to have a resident from every country around the world. Historically and presently, it is in Brooklyn's many diverse neighborhoods that people from different cultures with different languages and religions learn about each other's ways of life and also become acculturated, integrating habits of another group into their own lives. For example, in Greenpoint, a resident explained that as a young man he was often asked by a rabbi to turn on the lights of a synagogue on his street during Jewish holidays. After obliging, the rabbi would offer him a "shot" of liquor in gratitude. The man was Catholic and through his assistance he learned a bit more about Jewish religious customs. And historically, white Anglo-Saxon Protestant groups learned about peasant immigrants from their migration to neighborhoods of Brooklyn. In this way we are all social observers, studying one another, taking from each other, and integrating new ways as our ways.

It has been argued that a common American culture and American cities developed in this way based on these multicultural interactions. In sociology, the urban culturalist perspective presents this view (Borer 2006). According to this perspective, there is a relationship between culture and places in which shared meanings get constructed, negotiated, and reworked. For urban culturalists, neighborhoods are places in which ways of life are constantly negotiated and continually changing. "Culture is never a matter of pure consensus . . . What matters are the shared meanings that can create connections between individuals, groups, and something larger and more lasting than both" (Borer 2006: 192). American culture and life in cities are created in this way. Culture is created in everyday life. Greenpoint's local cultures could be analyzed using this framework.

MAKING ACCOMMODATIONS

Residents of Greenpoint, with all their differences, arrive at a level of accommodation in which they are able to live together in a neighborhood. In many ways, the mere density and attendant physical proximity of residents in a neighborhood in Brooklyn forces a dialogue among people regardless of their dissimilar social characteristics. Since they cannot completely avoid each other perhaps people become more alike than they will ever be equal. There is a process of homogenization that seems to occur.

In everyday life in Greenpoint, there are instances in which "bridges" are built connecting individuals from different social classes. It is not uncommon for gentry and working class renters and homeowners to bid each other "good morning" or to gesture "hello" with a nod or a wave of the hand. Working class and gentry neighbors will stop and chat with each other about their respective vacations. Such a conversation occurred in which two neighbors of different cultural backgrounds and social classes discussed time that each spent in Milan, Italy. Homeowners will also collaborate on solving a problem common to their individual houses. For example, as residents face somewhat changing weather patterns and encounter torrential rains which on one occasion a few summers ago, paralyzed the subway system from flooding, many homes in Greenpoint were met with sewer backflow into their basements.

Gentry, working class, and immigrant homeowners would stop each other on the street and talk about what they may have learned from various sources in hope of resolving the problem. They shared information and also shared individual decisions made for each home.

As working class and immigrant homeowners living in the neighborhood's historic district confront the need for a permit from the Landmarks Preservation Commission in order to renovate their building's facade, such as replacing windows or exterior doors and shingle, they will often employ the services of local, gentry architects to navigate through the process. Gentry residents, including tenants, have introduced the "stoop sale" to the neighborhood. These are a city version of the suburban garage sale in which a household's used items are displayed on the street, in front of their residence and sold to passersby. On any given day posters are hung from street poles and sidewalks are marked in chalk announcing the date, time, and place of an upcoming stoop sale. Working class residents can be seen mimicking this practice and holding stoop sales, an example of becoming alike. Gentry residents have also brought with them the practice of bicycling to Greenpoint on a much larger scale than had existed prior to their residence. New York City's government supports this alternative transportation habit as part of its "green" campaign, and has drawn bike lanes on local streets and provided bike racks outside parks and some subway stations. Working class and immigrant inhabitants are riding bicycles more often and can also be found participating in the global biking phenomenon.

Greenpoint's long-term, working class and immigrant, resident homeowners accommodate gentry newcomers because of the higher rents and higher home sale prices that they are willing and able to pay relative to the working class. Thus, long-term residents have come to tolerate a gentry renter's trumpet playing out his apartment window, or another gentry renter spending the day sitting on a front stoop sketching nearby buildings and photographing local scenes, or yet another having a party in which guests arrive by bicycle and lock them to poles, trees, and gates nearby the host's apartment.

Much accommodation takes place around children, especially between mothers with a focus on children. In the spring, mothers of young children will see each other on the street and exchange information and opinions about schools they have toured for their child's kindergarten enrollment. One morning a woman was rushing past and remarked, "I'm going to another tour. PS 110."

Both gentry and working class mothers whose children have started preschool or to a lesser extent, kindergarten will stop and ask each other how their child is doing making the transition during the first few weeks of school. Observers will hear, "She cried for an hour! My heart was broken. I called later that morning and [the teacher] told me she was fine. She stopped crying after I left." On other occasions, gentry and working class mothers will chat about which extracurricular activities their child will enroll in. "Is she taking ballet? Class starts Saturday," which was answered, "I think we'll be doing soccer." And for older children, gentry and working class mothers will discuss the middle school and high school application process, their opinions about schools they have visited and ultimately, their final admission and placement.

Gentry and working class mothers and their children also interact at children's birthday parties. Children's closest friends from school are often invited to a celebration, or at times, an entire school class is invited. Just recently, a boy's second grade class was invited by his gentry parents to an amusement park to celebrate his birthday. In the past, preschool classes were invited to a local restaurant owned by the parents of children enrolled. It is during these occasions that mothers in particular share and disseminate information. In these instances, mothering appears to transcend social class.

This chapter focuses on gentrification in Greenpoint, Brooklyn. It is an analysis of neighborhood change with a focus on social class as an element of the local culture. It highlights how social class differences lead to the creation and maintenance of parallel cultures which include different norms and expectations producing accommodation, negotiation, tension, and conflict within the neighborhood. The following analysis looks to examine the process of gentrification by examining the power dynamics that exist in this neighborhood as gentrifiers develop into the dominant group of a previously stable, working class community, and Greenpoint moves toward a complete transition by social class. This theme is illustrated by exploring the everyday struggles between gentry and working class residents, and the choices made to separate according to social class rather than assimilate and integrate.

The subsequent portrait highlights social class as a primary component of the development of culture. The intent of this work is to contribute to a discourse about social class and its part in changing vernacular space and working class community.

THE SOCIOLOGICAL CONTEXT

The concept of gentrification is being defined as "the conversion of socially marginal and working class areas of the central city to middle-class [and elite] residential use" (Zukin 1987: 129). Although the literature refers to gentrifiers as middle class, this analysis considers them upper middle class with more money and job security than the traditional middle class. Research on gentrification focuses primarily on the causes and consequences of this urban process.

Analyses fall into two major theoretical perspectives, ecological theory and critical theory (Wittberg 1992). The ecologists examine the needs, tastes, and desires of populations, which are responsible for precipitating neighborhood change in the form of gentrification (Friedenfels 1992; Laska and Spain 1980). Included are studies that examine the strategies used by the middle class to create and produce gentrification in specific neighborhoods (Kasinitz 1988; Krase 1982). Critical theorists, on the other hand, view the causes of gentrification as manufactured by actions taken by the political economy, namely the investments of capital and the policies of the state (Abu-Lughod 1994; Fitch 1993; Smith 1996; Zukin 1982, 1987).

Some scholars discuss a change in the process of gentrification in the 1990s. Smith (1996) contends that due to the 1987 stock market crash and ensuing recession, degentrification has occurred. For Smith, upper middle class and elite gentrifiers found themselves with lowered property values and forced interactions with minority groups, immigrants, and women as they competed for the urban terrain. Hackworth's (2002) study of three gentrifying neighborhoods in New York City argues that a major change in gentrification is that the state is investing in the process more directly than in the past. In addition, corporate developers are the initial migrants prior to gentrifiers more so than before when they followed pioneers. Moreover, the actions by ordinary people against gentrification have been marginalized in that their concerns are dismissed by those in power.

The discourse on gentrification documents the benefits and costs of this process on the local community. The literature profiles most gentrifiers as affluent, young, single, urban professionals, and young, married couples who are both wage earners and have no children, or small families. This segment of the population is credited with revitalizing older, city neighborhoods, and by extension, the city itself through housing improvements and loft conversions, service upgrades, and an expansion of the local economy with the introduction of new restaurants and retail establishments. Studies dealing with the consequences of gentrification on neighborhoods examine primarily housing, and present increasing housing costs and displacement of existing populations as outcomes (Cybriwsky 1978; LeGates and Hartman 1986; Marcuse 1986). Thus, in general, the major consequence of gentrification documented in the literature is the displacement or "replacement" (Freeman and Braconi 2004) of ordinary people and small businesses to more affluent groups, sometimes elites, as well as the transition of "mom and pop" businesses to retail chains and boutiques. Another outcome is that ordinary people have fewer choices regarding places of residence, since affordable neighborhoods are diminished by gentrification.

The dynamics of gentrification in a neighborhood and the way it affects community life, and the everyday lives of residents beyond housing, is an under-represented area of scholarship. This study of Greenpoint attempts to address the void by examining the process of gentrification, the period of time prior to complete neighborhood change, and investigates the interactions of ordinary people and gentrifiers in a neighborhood for which they compete.

THE NEIGHBORHOOD

Greenpoint is a peninsula at the northernmost tip of Brooklyn. Greenpoint lies across the river from Manhattan. The Citicorp building on Manhattan's east side is visible from the tip of Greenpoint's major commercial center, looming far above the low scale buildings in the community. Greenpoint is also connected to neighborhoods in Queens (Long Island City, Sunnyside, and Maspeth) by the Pulaski, the Greenpoint Avenue and the Kosciusko Bridges. The Kosciusko Bridge also links the Brooklyn-Queens Expressway with the Long Island Expressway.

Adjacent to Greenpoint in Brooklyn, lying just across its southern boundary is Williamsburg. Greenpoint and Williamsburg share the administration of many municipal services, and together, they make up Brooklyn's Community Board 1, an extension of New York City government in the community.

GENTRIFYING GREENPOINT

In 2000, along with trends in the City and the borough of Brooklyn, the total population of Greenpoint increased to 47,881 since 1980 (U.S. Bureau of the Census 2000). In contrast to New York City as a whole and the Borough of Brooklyn, there were few changes in the racial profile of the neighborhood since 1980. In 2000, 74 percent of the population was white, 2 percent was black, 4 percent was Asian, and 20 percent was Hispanic/Latino. Since 1980, there was a 1 percent decrease in whites, a 1.5 percent increase in blacks, a 1.5 percent increase in Asians, and a 1 percent decrease in Hispanic/Latinos. In contrast, both New York City and the borough of Brooklyn lost more significant amounts of white, non-Hispanics between 1990 and 2000 than Greenpoint (New York City Department of City Planning nd). In terms of the formal education of Greenpoint's residents, in 2000 those with bachelor's degrees or higher amounted to 31 percent of the population. This is a dramatic increase since 1980. In 1999, the median household income in Greenpoint was $35,435. In terms of occupation, in 2000, managers and professionals constituted the largest group (34 percent), followed by sales and office occupations (19 percent). This is in contrast to 1980 when the largest occupational group was in technical and sales followed by operators and laborers. The persistence of a mostly white community, coupled with an increase of formal education and income among the population, and a shift to significantly more professionals and less laborers than in the past are indicators supporting the growth of a gentrifying neighborhood (Mason 2011).

In terms of housing in 2000, 81 percent of households in Greenpoint are renters, and about a quarter of these are not rent regulated (Scott 2003). Furthermore, "The percentage of affordable housing in Greenpoint is dropping faster than it is in New York City as a whole. The percentage of rental units in the most expensive category is skyrocketing" (Scott 2003: 7). The notion of affordability is defined as being no more than 30 percent of a household's income going toward rental costs. In Greenpoint in 2000, "about 40 percent of households paid more than 30 percent of their income on rent" (Scott 2003: 9). The median contract rent in 2000 was $629 compared to $140 in 1980. Market rate rents for a two bedroom apartment in Greenpoint in 2002 ranged from $1500 to $1900 (Scott 2003: 160). This represents a 50 percent increase since 1997. Additional indicators of gentrification within the housing sector are featured in articles in the local newspapers discussing "skyrocketing rents," and "loft regulations urged" (Greenline 2001). Houses are selling for $600,000 and upwards.

Greenpoint has been a community envied. It was historically white, stable, affordable, physically well kept, with high occupancy rates, low crime, high levels of social capital, and a high degree of neighboring relative to other neighborhoods in Brooklyn. Ironically, these very characteristics attracted gentrifiers. Its low scale, small town charm, and relative affordability were appealing to gentrifiers as a place of residence. At the same time, gentrifiers in Greenpoint, do not participate in the predominate life of the community. They do not involve themselves in the very aspects of the community that attracted them to it in the first place. Instead, they segregate themselves from other working class and immigrant residents, and socialize and create community with other residents like themselves. As described by one resident gentrifier, "We liked that it was a neighborhood with other creative people like ourselves."

Furthermore, gentrifiers in Greenpoint impose their lifestyle and public practices on long-term residents instead of adapting to local, established ways. In general, what has developed is a clash of lifestyles and social norms between ordinary, working class and immigrant residents and upper middle class gentrifiers. Gentrifiers, once attracted to the physical neatness of the housing stock, are now critical of its aluminum siding and instead support restoration to a building's original (historical) façade. Thus, among other things, there is a clash of people's sense of aesthetics. Subsequently, a parallel culture for each group develops and ensues. The working class (and immigrants) continue to engage in traditional, local institutions (church, ethnic organizations, PTA), while gentrifiers create new social milieus (bars with sidewalk seating, art galleries, new community organizations). These differences of lifestyle and conflicting social norms are played out in the course of everyday life.

PERFORMING THE STUDY

This is a qualitative study of gentrification in Greenpoint. Years have been spent engaged in various community settings with both gentrifiers and ordinary residents. This investigation was carried out through participant observation and content analysis. One moved around playgrounds and playgroups within the neighborhood with children and became familiar with many (mostly) mothers and children who were relatively new residents, and did not have the social ties or attachments of long-term residents. Their professional and technical status quickly became obvious as topics discussed included work, experiences in college and graduate school, residential history, and aspirations for children's education. The research style was unobtrusive in that I listened closely to the daily conversations among mothers and asking questions of them as a neighbor and "new" mother were the main approaches. Furthermore, time was spent with, life-long working class residents, and relatively newer, upper middle class residents, an approach which allowed for the examination of both groups. This was accomplished by moving in and out of various local settings which also allowed opportunities for comparison. Data collection on gentrification is ongoing.

GENTRIFICATION IN EVERYDAY LIFE

Everyday life is embedded in the field of sociology. The concept of everyday life is used to elucidate our taken for granted interactions and the social life in which we engage. The investigations of contemporary theorists such as Robert Park, Erving Goffman and Dorothy Smith are grounded in everyday life.

As head of the Sociology Department, Park's (1925) vision for the Chicago School was to study the everyday life of various groups and people in the city. Goffman (1959) viewed our actions in everyday life in one sense as theatre, in which we are front stage or backstage engaging in public or private behavior. Public behavior is for an audience, which involves more formality and "standing on ceremony," while private behavior involves being oneself.

Goffman also discusses the "face work" that we do in order to "save face." It involves the work of deference for the purpose of impression management, adjusting one's behavior in order to control the impression one makes on others.

Smith's (1987) standpoint theory focuses on the everyday life of women. Unlike Smith, gentrification in everyday life in Greenpoint does not focus exclusively on women. The accounts of everyday life in Greenpoint lead to an analysis of social class from the standpoint of the working class, including women, who serve as the subordinate group.

This paper focuses on the interactions of everyday life between ordinary, working class people who are established, long-term (even life-long) residents and new gentrifiers. Haywoode (1991), in her work on working class feminism, adds another dimension to Goffman's analysis; that is community. Haywoode argues that community is located between public and private. Community serves as a middle ground in which the private home and public world meet and social expectations are negotiated. Using Haywoode's (1987) conception of community, my focus on everyday life investigates the informal interactions among neighbors and residents of the community that take place on the street.

This chapter documents various clashing social norms between ordinary residents and gentrifiers that get manifested while living together sharing a neighborhood. The aspects of everyday life examined include bicycle parking, housing prices, and aesthetics, reactions to noise, and dog walking. This paper indicates that as newcomers to the community, gentrifiers exhibit a lack of deference toward established ways of life which creates tension and conflict culminating in a "contested terrain" (Krase 2009).

Bicycles

With an increase in gentrifiers comes an increase in bicycle use as a means of transportation within the community and the city. Gentrifiers use bicycles far more than other groups in Greenpoint. One observes gentrifiers riding all types of bicycles, in various sizes (some with decorative baskets), with or without protective helmets, moving in tow with vehicular traffic. Car drivers and pedestrians need to exercise more caution since bicyclists ride both ways on one way streets. In fact, on one street corner in Greenpoint stands a "ghost bike," a white painted bicycle chained to a pole. This white bike signifies that a cyclist was killed on that street. A plaque attached tells the story of a young woman killed by a truck. Negotiation is required for all moving, transport vehicles, and pedestrians. One life-long resident said as she crossed the street and was almost hit by a moving bicycle, "These bicycles, they're so arrogant!" The creation of bicycle lanes throughout neighborhoods in Brooklyn has ignited much debate within some of the more organized communities. As a result of calls from residents to enforce the laws regarding bicycling, the New York Police Department announced that it will issue violations.

The parking and storing of bicycles by gentrifiers also ignites a clash of social norms in Greenpoint. Bicycles are often parked by attaching them to a pole by a chain and lock and left that way on someone else's property. Long-term homeowners often leave notes on these bicycles asking that they be removed and not parked there again. When the bicyclist does not respond to the request of a homeowner, the local police are sometimes called to remove the bicycles. The police are able to intervene in these matters because

Figure 4.1. "Don't lock bikes to fence!!!" Photograph by the author.

the bicycles are usually chained to a pole indicating parking regulations, so the bikes obstruct public property. In this vein, one can observe signs on the entrance to subway stations indicating that chaining bicycles to the subway structure violates the law. The police are reluctant to intervene, however. As one desk sergeant at the local precinct remarked, "Someone in City Hall likes bikes!"

The clash exists because long-term residents keep sidewalks clear, and do not act in the same way. For them, bicycles, including those belonging to children, are stored inside one's home, apartment, or some other place on one's own property. Long-term, resident homeowners are not happy to have bicycles, which do not belong to anyone in their building, parked on their property. As one person said, "If someone trips over it, you're responsible. You'll be sued!" Homeowners perceive these acts as a violation of existing practices, social norms, and basic respect for another's property. The following accounts illustrate the conflict between long-term, resident homeowners and gentrifiers over bicycles. An elderly woman who is a resident homeowner explained,

> I came out the other morning and there was a bicycle chained to my pole. My son was over when the owner came back. My son told him not to park the bicycle there anymore. The man started yelling that he could put his bike anywhere he wanted to and said he was reporting us to the police for harassment. He left to go to the police station. When he came back, he apologized and told me that the police said I was right, he couldn't leave his bike near my house.

This account illustrates the conflict that erupts when homeowners make requests regarding local practices and local law. In another instance, a resident homeowner said,

> A few times there have been bicycles chained to the pole in front of our house. They're sometimes there for days. The first time, we thought it was being parked for the winter! My neighbors told me to clip the chain and throw the bike away, but I wasn't comfortable doing that. So I called the Community Relations Officer at the precinct that I knew, and asked if I could get rid of the bike. He told me not to touch it. He took my address and put me on a list at the precinct to have it removed. The police will [eventually] confiscate them. Another time, there were two bikes left. My wife put a note on one saying that if they weren't removed, we will have the police take them. A couple of days later, my neighbor told me that late at night a car pulled up, two people got out and unlocked the bikes. One read the note and started cursing like crazy. They put the bikes in the trunk of the car and drove away.

Embodied in this narrative is the depiction of clashing cultures stemming from class struggle. Ordinary residents attempt to preserve their way of life, while gentrifiers seek to change those ways to suit their own lifestyle.

The following exchange occurred between a resident homeowner and a resident member of a local synagogue. The synagogue was located across the street from where the homeowner lived. The congregant said "I was thinking about putting up a sign saying people can lock bikes on the synagogue gate." To which the homeowner replied "That's good because I don't want them in front of my house!"

The member of the synagogue is a gentrifier who joined the congregation upon moving to Greenpoint. His position on bicycle parking differs from that of long-term homeowners since he sides with those more like himself. Besides, the synagogue is not his personal property, so his decision does not affect him directly.

Noise

Greenpoint is usually a relatively quiet place, but it is also part of "the city that never sleeps." Thus, on occasion, there is street noise: people shouting, loud parties and music, car horns and alarms blaring, fireworks, bottles smashing on the ground, and the sirens of emergency vehicles. For the most part, these events are treated as background noise. Sometimes, residents will respond to the noise to see if anything extraordinary is happening. The focus here is not on these extremely loud street noises, but on noise associated with everyday life, such as people talking, spending time outdoors, babies crying; noises which are generally perceived as "normal." With the mixing of gentrifiers and ordinary people, there are different perceptions and levels of tolerance for the clamor of everyday life.

One reaction to noise involves a young, working class woman who grew up in Greenpoint, and resided in her childhood home with her husband and young children. The house next to her was purchased by new gentrifiers who were childless. She shared the following account,

> When [my son] was a baby, he went through a period of night tremors and screamed all night. My neighbors left a nasty note saying that his screaming disturbed their sleep and maybe we should move his room away from [the common wall near] their house.

A baby crying, in the middle of the night, disturbs everyone. This account, however, indicates an arrogance of sorts with a focus on one's own needs, while also exhibiting a lack of understanding for the baby and his family.

Another occurrence involved an exchange between a working class resident and a new gentrifier. This one concerned a car alarm.

> My husband leaves for work early and he accidentally set off his car alarm. A neighbor came out yelling, "What are you crazy!" My husband thought he was

> yelling, [because he was] thinking that someone was breaking into our car. So my husband yelled, "It's fine." But he continued to scream, "Are you crazy, we're trying to sleep!"

Street noises like car alarms disturb everyone. They are part of the soundtrack of city life. The interesting part of the last quotation is that, from a working class perspective, it was initially believed that the neighbor's yelling was about protecting another's property, and not a matter of noise control required by neighbors of neighbors where mistakes are not tolerated.

Filmmakers

Greenpoint has become a popular place in Brooklyn for filming movies and television shows. In addition to commercially produced films, independent filmmakers are also found. Commercial filmmakers are required to secure permits and post notices in the community of their forthcoming work in order to reserve parking on local streets for their equipment. Independent filmmakers are smaller operations with fewer people and often impose themselves on the ordinary landscape. The following was conveyed,

> One resident was visiting his mother who also lived in Greenpoint. He was talking to neighbors as they went by. At the same time, a film was being shot at a house nearby and the man was asked, "Please be quiet while we're shooting." The man responded with sarcasm, "You mean when you're done we can resume our normal lives?"

This interaction indicates the tension that exists on the street in everyday life between ordinary people and the new "hipsters" in Greenpoint.

In a similar exchange, gentry impose on gentry. A gentry couple explained how they were barbecuing in their backyard and their neighbors, another gentry couple, asked them to please be quiet while they were filming. They described the situation in a sarcastic and humorous manner while at the same time asking, "Can you believe this?"

All these cases bring to light the different meanings attached to living in a neighborhood by social class. Working class residents live in a community, which requires cooperation and negotiation, and the reward is mutual obligation, loyalty, concern, and reliance among neighbors. New gentrifiers expect accommodation for their lifestyle, and seek to impose their desired lifestyle upon the existing community. New gentrifiers do not look to "fit in" to Greenpoint, but instead, they attempt to change it to meet their own needs while disregarding the local history and culture.

Figure 4.2. "No Parking. Film Shoot." Photograph by the author.

Dog Walking

Dogs have a prominent place in Greenpoint. They serve as family pets as well as security systems for homes in lieu of alarms. Dog walking is very much a part of the neighborhood culture. Residents are required by city law to keep dogs on a leash, "curb your dog," and "pick up after your dog," or face fines.

Dog walking is another area of everyday life in which new gentrifiers expect accommodation, and convey that the law and the rights of others do not apply to them. Gentry residents walk their dogs on the sidewalk instead of in the street, and allow their pets to urinate on trees and the iron gates outlining people's homes, as well as drop their "poop" on the sidewalk. They do not "curb their dog" as is customary in the neighborhood, and often do not "clean up" after the dog. In some cases, homeowners have installed fencing around trees to discourage dogs and their owners. When abuses are witnessed, long-term homeowners confront violating dog walkers and articulate the local practice as well as the City's law. The actions of new gentrifiers suggest that neither, local practice nor City law applies to them.

Resident school personnel, who greet children and parents each morning at a local school, have also expressed concern about the dog walking style of gentrifiers. The relatively few gentry children who attend this particular public school in Greenpoint are often accompanied by a parent and a dog to the school's entrance. One school aide said, "I told the principal about these dogs. God forbid a kid is bitten. You never know, they're animals!" In addition, there are notices taped around light posts outside the school indicating City laws regarding dogs. The first reminds the public that dogs must be on a leash and the second states the "pooper scooper" ordinance in which there is a fine for not cleaning up after your dog. The location of these notices on school property is a deliberate reminder to parents with dogs and dog walkers in general.

The everyday life of ordinary residents in Greenpoint has been disrupted by increasing gentrification and the subsequent lack of gentry-adaptation to sharing a community with others.

Housing

Among Greenpoint residents, it is common to hear and participate in conversations regarding housing. The topic will cover a wide range of inquiries from who has new tenants, is renovating and/or selling, to the condition of houses and apartments, the price of market rents, what house sold and for what price. In the course of these conversations, the dissimilar interests of working class residents and new gentrifiers emerge. One illustration is a conversation between a life-long resident homeowner and a gentry resident homeowner who live on the same street. They were discussing a house that was being sold with an asking price of $1.4 million. The gentry homeowner remarked, "I can't believe it's only $1.4 million." The life-long resident responded, "I can't believe the price either!" The interest of the gentry homeowner is for booming real estate prices, giving her investment more worth. The comment by the life-long resident was a statement that she could not believe a house in Greenpoint would ever cost that much money.

Another area in which differences surface is with regard to an aesthetic view of the built environment. The local practice has been to maintain houses in practical ways using materials that are effective and cost efficient, but not always artistic or creative. The gentry are more interested in the aesthetic quality of the built environment and support the idea of historic preservation through restoration to original façade. The following dialogue highlights this point:

> A couple stopped to examine and admire the wood shingle of a newly restored home in the historic district. The owner noticed them and came out. They talked for a while about the renovation and the owner remarked, "You don't live in the historic district, so that's good." To which the response was, "Why is that good?"

This exchange presents a number of things. It indicates support by gentrifiers for the visual presentation achieved through historic preservation and restoration. There is also an acknowledgement that there is more social status and economic value in places designated "historic." It is the preferred place of residence of the gentry. For the resident homeowner, living outside the historic district gives one more options regarding renovation and its cost. In historic districts, rules designated by the N.Y.C. Landmarks Commission limit one's choice of building materials, color of the building's exterior, and stipulates an approved architectural plan and a permit. Approved restoration is a relatively costly endeavor. Once again, the different standpoints regarding housing costs, location, and appearance is brought to light and provides an additional layer to the meaning of gentrification in everyday life.

Everyday life in Greenpoint involving the ordinary, working class and gentrifiers defies Goffman's contention that we look to manage the impressions that others have of us. It is logical to expect that gentry newcomers would attempt to make "a good impression" on long-term residents. Instead, gentrifiers assert themselves in order to create "a definition of the situation" in an attempt to colonize working class life. Gentrifiers do impression management with each other, and proceed to make their ways of everyday life dominant in the community.

CONCLUSIONS

This chapter suggests that the impact of social class on the creation and practice of culture is critical in the lives of ordinary people. The analysis demonstrates that culture, by itself, lacks depth and the very essence of a sociological analysis. It examines everyday interactions of civility in which residents of cities engage for social order and functionality. Borer includes Gans' (1962) book *The Urban Villagers* as part of the urban culturalist genre.

Gans disagrees with Borer's categorization and explains that during his study of the West End, the city of Boston had bigger plans which West Enders did not fit into (Gans 2007a). Gans explains that West Enders lacked the necessary political, economic, and social power to be of any concern to the city of Boston, since the city needed the urban renewal funds for its coffers flowing from the federal government. In fact, Gans goes on to say,

> culture per se is not a useful explanatory tool because it is generally devoid of agency and can quickly turn into an Uncaused Cause. As a descriptive tool, culture runs the danger of restating already well-known observations in technical language, thus giving ammunition to those claiming sociology to be unnecessary (2007b, p. 159–60).

Being unequal makes us different, even if we appear to act the same and to get along. That is precisely the point of the life's work of many sociologists. Being unequal creates power relations and power dynamics which involve tensions and disagreements over resources and amenities. In fact, Marx and Engels contend, "Political power, properly so called, is merely the organized power of one class for oppressing another" (2002, p. 244). "[And] culturalism cannot explain power" (Gans 2007b: 159).

Borer himself admits, "And even though communities are collective accomplishments, not everyone plays an equal role in making these decisions or practices them exactly the same way" (2006, p. 186). Thus, power, inequality, and difference are implicit in community building, and community maintenance, and creating culture.

In a discussion about ethnic groups in *The American City: A Social and Cultural History*, Monti writes,

> Success came with a price. There have been many occasions when representatives of more established groups tried to encourage newcomers to think and act more like the old-timers or actively punished the newcomers for being different. To a great extent the newcomers actually did become a whole lot more like the persons who already were here. However, they also managed to retain some important ideas and practices that were connected to their native cultures or early experiences in a new land (1999, p. 379).

The newcomers in Greenpoint too are holding on to their ideas and practices that are tied to their social class. As Krase (1993) states, "Humans . . . carry ideas for designing their home environments from places where they lived in the past and adapt them to the resources and opportunities in new locales" (p. 46). The gentry create a parallel culture that coexists with the established local culture of immigrant and working class residents.

This chapter indicates various activities of the gentry and working class exhibited side by side, sometimes conflicting because each group's social practices stem from social class differences. Their parallel play, in the final analysis, is about dominance and the eventual colonization of the neighborhood by the gentry class. This change evolves over time, but ultimately, the working class and immigrants lose out.

Unlike the relationship described by Monti between old-timers and newcomers, gentrifiers in Greenpoint, who are the newcomers, are not assimilating in the same way. Gentrifiers spend time among their own. According to Monti and Borer this is how people learn from each other, however "parallel play" in Greenpoint is segregation by social class between the gentry and the working class, which serves to perpetuate social inequality.

The parallel cultures that presently exist in Greenpoint respectively composed of the working class and gentrifiers, developed because of social class differences. Social class is a driving force, at times more dominant than race and gender, and at other times operating in confluence with race, gender or other social characteristics. Together, they create culture. Gentrification and the ways in which social class differences are revealed in a neighborhood reproduces social inequality and maintains the current system of social stratification.

With economic restructuring in the United States comes gentrification, while also occurring globally. In fact, a recent image-based analysis examined gentrification in both Greenpoint and Krakow (Krase 2005). Gentrification is now a tool of global capitalism in which working class communities are replaced by the affluent and elite. "Mom and Pop" retail establishments, which are part of the social fabric of a community, earn a living owning and operating small businesses that were in some cases inherited from their parents, are replaced by large chain stores, such as Starbucks, Rite Aid, and Staples. Housing, both rental and homeownership, becomes out of reach for ordinary people. And the creation of rental housing in particular is replaced by privatized condominiums. "The more recent and still ongoing privatized urban renewal [is] called gentrification . . ." (Gans 2007c: 232). These changes occur locally within the context of economic restructuring in which the gentry fare better economically in the job market, and ordinary people struggle to earn a living wage and avoid catastrophe, and attempt to "hang on" to a standard of life with the hope that they will raise their children to have a relatively better life. This is particularly difficult in Brooklyn, and conditions may be still worse for their children.

Thus is the course of Greenpoint as depicted by this analysis. Greenpoint is experiencing the imposition of global capitalism, a process which cannot be completely stopped by the community. Residents bid farewell and extend warm wishes to the owners of some of their favorite stores who seemed forever embedded in the neighborhood landscape. These retailers can no longer compete locally with trendy boutiques, organic food, and health food stores, thrift shops, "stoop sales," and farmer's markets. These establishments sell goods that are often too expensive for ordinary people. In the view of working class culture, thrift shops, and stoop sales were often reserved for poor people no matter how "retro" and "vintage" items may be, and from a working class perspective, they remained used or second hand, a sign of poverty. In contrast, the gentry frequent them and purchase items from them. On a larger scale, megastores like Best Buy, Target, Toys"R"Us, and online shopping also hurt long-term merchants.

For the neighborhood of Greenpoint, there are negative consequences. Greenpoint finds itself divided by social class. As neighborhood issues develop, as with rezoning the waterfront from manufacturing to residential use, which requires community input, many self-interested voices were heard. For the most part, the working class and immigrant groups with their respective local institutions unite for neighborhood preservation, while the gentry, as a group, present concerns such as aesthetics, recreational spaces, and property values, under the guise of community support. The policies of the Bloomberg administration favor new privatized development over honoring working class and ethnic neighborhoods. The private sector, often made-up of commercial developers, is turned to as investors and builders. There is a boom of new housing that will not cater to the needs of ordinary residents but hopes to attract more gentry. Ordinary people cannot afford this housing. These are privatized condominiums, a type of "urban spectacle" (Kern and Wekerle 2008) which stand out of place among the nineteenth- and early-twentieth-century buildings. As Kern and Wekerle point out in their study of Toronto, condominiums, as a new form of built environment foster social space in which residents turn inward to amenities within the development. They contribute to gentrification and the maintenance of parallel cultures in Greenpoint, and social inequality in America between long-term, ordinary residents, and newer gentrifiers.

Social segregation by the gentry and the maintenance of their own community within the neighborhood does not create diversity in their community, but rather homogeneity. These actions produce a rather insular group. As a group, the political and social rhetoric of the gentry is a contradiction given the everyday life they create and experience in Greenpoint. On the one hand their political open-mindedness places them in a position to favor human diversity. Their neighborhood of residence, Greenpoint, is both culturally and economically diverse, but they choose to rebuff it. The actions of the gentry suggest that they remain cautious about social integration with working class and immigrant residents and are unwilling to fully engage in the community with them. Paradoxically, ethnic, working class residents, and their everyday lives make-up the same working class culture that the gentry initially found attractive. Ordinary residents provide a mixing of race, class, and ethnicity. As the gentry move forward in colonizing Greenpoint, the neighborhood's composition will be primarily white and affluent. Thus, in the final analysis, gentrification also leads to racial and ethnic segregation as well as segregation by social class.

This brings us to the case of Daniel. Daniel was a young man who grew up in Greenpoint with two brothers like his parents before him. Daniel became a member of the New York City Fire Department and died in an accident at a small fire in Williamsburg. Daniel lived and worked to sustain Brooklyn everyday by the proverbial sweat of his brow. Daniel lost his life; the working class has lost too. The younger children of Greenpoint families have forever lost their working class neighborhood. Daniel's younger brother, who followed in his footsteps as a firefighter, and their friends are doing everything that is socially right. They are following the prescription to acquire the American Dream, but most will not have the ability to buy or even rent in Greenpoint like their parents. The underlying class struggle that is symbolized and underscored by this tragic event begs the questions: Where will ordinary people and the working class locate in Brooklyn? Where will they find a place? Will they be directed toward cheaper and poorer areas, which are also diminishing, or will they be supported through urban policy designed to preserve working class communities?

To look to global capitalism with resignation as a completely unstoppable force reduces humanity to pawns on a chess board waiting to be overtaken. In Brooklyn, gentrification, rezoning, and development continue to occur. The gentry blame developers and capitalists for neighborhoods becoming ever increasingly upscale but fail to recognize their role in the process. This point was illustrated during a live music event at a local bar in which a musician opened her set by criticizing gentrification through a comment about the displacement of artists. Her remarks were met by a reply shouted by a working class patron, "You mean like you've done to us?" As gentry reside in the city while attending school, for short-term fun, or as a long-term living arrangement, they change the very character of working class neighborhoods. The hope is that with each economic crisis comes greater class consciousness for ordinary people. They must continue their activism, their use of traditional institutions as vehicles for social change, their efforts to reach out and build coalitions, and their constant push for greater participatory democracy. As Piven so aptly affirms in *Challenging Authority: How Ordinary People Change America*, "My point in this book is not to lay out a blueprint for the future, but to show that all of our past experience argues that the mobilization of collective defiance and the disruption it causes have always been essential to the preservation of democracy" (2006, p. 146). Local communities can mediate and mitigate structural and global forces on behalf of ordinary people. What seems imperative for a racially, culturally, and economically diverse city is urban policy that is socially just and even-handed and considers everyone equitably. We need an urban policy that appreciates the contribution of working class citizens to the larger society, as they literally build, repair, and protect, while also creating culturally diverse and economically stable neighborhoods and cities. To choose, instead to celebrate massive development by the rich for the young, affluent class and others like them will result in the obliteration of the working class. Urban policy that is socially fair-minded and responsible for all citizens knows that these are deliberate choices to be made, and understands the value of preserving working class neighborhoods and communities. It is only then that we will have the opportunity to truly consider the future of Brooklyn.

REFERENCES

Abu-Lughod, J. L. 1994. *From Urban Village to East Village: The Battle for New York's Lower East Side*. Cambridge, MA: Blackwell.

Borer, M. I. 2006. The Location of Culture: The Urban Culturalist Perspective. *City & Community* 5(2):173–97.

Cybriwsky, R. 1978. "Social Aspects of Neighborhood Change." *Annals of the Association of American Geographers* 68:17–33.

Fitch, R. 1993. *The Assassination of New York*. New York: Verso.

Freeman, L. and F. Braconi. 2004. "Gentrification and Displacement: New York City in the 1990s." *Journal of the American Planning Association* 70:39–52.

Freeman, L. 2006. *There Goes the Hood*. Philadelphia, PA: Temple University Press.

Friedenfels, R. 1992. "Gentrification in Large American Cities from 1970–1980." Pp. 63–93 in *Research in Urban Sociology: Gentrification and Urban Change, Volume 2*, edited by R. Hutchison. Greenwich, CT: JAI Press.

Gans, H. J. 1962. *The Urban Villagers*. New York: The Free Press.

Gans, H. J. 2007a. "A Comment on Borer's 'Cultural Turn.'" *City & Community* 6(2):157.

Gans, H. J. 2007b. "But Culturalism Cannot Explain Power: A Reply to Borer." *City & Community* 6(2):159–60.

Gans, H. J. 2007c. "Remembering *The Urban Villagers* and Its Location in Intellectual Time: A Response to Zukin." *City & Community*, 6(3):231–36.

Goffman, E. 1959. *The Presentation of Self in Everyday Life*. Edinburgh, UK: University of Edinburgh Social Sciences Research Centre.

Hackworth, J. 2002. "Postrecession Gentrification in New York City." *Urban Affairs Review* 37:815–43.

Haywoode, T. L. 1991. "Working class feminism: Creating a politics of community, connection, and concern." Ph.D. diss., The City University of New York, New York.

Kasinitz, P. 1988. "The Gentrification of 'Boerum Hill': Neighborhood Change and Conflict over Definitions." *Qualitative Sociology* 11(3):163–82.

Kern, L. and G. Wekerle. 2008. "Gendered Spaces of Redevelopment: Gendered Politics of City Building." Pp. 233–262 in *Gender in an Urban World, Research in Urban Sociology, Volume 9,* edited by J. N. DeSena. Bingley, UK: Emerald Group Publishing.

Krase, J. 1982. *Self and Community in the City*. Washington, DC: University Press of America.

———. 1993. "Traces of Home." *Places: A Quarterly Journal of Environmental Design* 8(4):46–55.

———. 2005. "Poland and Polonia: Gentrification as Ethnic Aesthetic Practice and Migratory Process." Pp. 185–208 in *Gentrification in Global Perspective,* edited by R. Atkinson and G. Bridges. London, UK: Routledge.

———. 2009. "Contested Terrains: Visualizing Globalization in Global Cities." Pp. 65–73 in *Home, Migration, and the City: Spatial Forms and Practices in a Globalising World*, edited by A. Datta. Newcastle, UK: Open House International.

Laska, S. and D. Spain. eds. (1980). *Back to the City. Issues in Neighborhood Renovation*. New York: Pergamon Press.

LeGates, R.T. and C. Hartman. 1986. "The Anatomy of Displacement in the United States." Pp. 178–203 in *Gentrification of the City* edited by N. Smith and P. Williams. London, UK: Allen and Unwin, Inc.

Loft Regulations Urged. 2001. *Greenline*. March 2001, p. 1.

Marcuse, P. 1986. "Abandonment, Gentrification, and Displacement: The Linkages in New York City." Pp.153–57 in *Gentrification of the City* edited by N. Smith and P. Williams. London, UK: Allen and Unwin, Inc.

Marx, K., and F. Engels. 2002. *The Communist Manifesto,* edited by Gareth Stedman Jones. New York, NY: Penguin Classics.

Mason, L. 2011. "Mapping a Changing Brooklyn, Mapping a Changing World: Gentrification and Immigration, 2000–2008. Pp. ###-### in *Gentrification, Immigration, and Ethnic Politics in a Global City*, edited by Judith N. DeSena and Timothy Shortell. Lanham, MD: Lexington Books.

Mead, G. H. 1934. *Mind, Self, and Society*. Chicago, IL: University of Chicago Press.

Monti, D. J. 1999. *The American City: A Social and Cultural History*. Cambridge, MA: Blackwell Publishers.

New York City Department of City Planning. nd. Population: 1990 Census Summary.

New York City Department of City Planning. nd. Population: 2000 Census Summary.

Park, R. 1925. *The City: Suggestions for the Study of Human Nature in the Urban Environment.* Chicago, IL: University of Chicago Press.

Piven, F. F. 2006. *Challenging Authority: How Ordinary People Change America.*
Plymouth, UK: Rowman and Littlefield Publishers, Inc.

Robinson, T. 1995. "Gentrification and Grassroots Resistance in San Francisco's Tenderloin." *Urban Affairs Review* 30(4):483–513.

Scott, R. 2003. *Inclusionary Zoning: A Proposal for North Brooklyn and New York City*. Unpublished report.

Skyrocketing Rents. 2001. *Greenline*. March 2001, p. 1.

Smith, D. E. 1987. *The Everyday World as Problematic: A Feminist Sociology*. Boston, MA: Northeastern University Press.

Smith, N. 1996. *The Urban Frontier: Gentrification and Revanchist City*. New York, NY: Routledge Press.

U.S. Bureau of the Census. 1980. *Census of population and housing: Summary tape file 3*. Retrieved on January 30, 2007 (http://factfinder.census.gov).

U.S. Bureau of the Census. 2000. *Census of population and housing: Summary tape file 3A*. Retrieved on June 6, 2007 (http://factfinder.census.gov).

Wittberg, P. 1992. "Perspectives on Gentrification: A Comparative Review of the Literature." Pp. 17–46 in *Research in Urban Sociology: Gentrification and Urban Change*, edited by R. Hutchison. Greenwich, CT: JAI Press.

Zukin, S. 1982. *Loft Living*. Baltimore, MD: Johns Hopkins University Press.

———. 1987. "Gentrification: Culture and Capital in the Urban Core." *Annual Review of Sociology* 13:129–47.

5

"Williamsburg Walks"

Public Space and Community Events in a Gentrified Neighborhood

Sara Martucci

It's one of the first hot days of the season and I'm walking towards Bedford Avenue, the main commercial street of my Brooklyn neighborhood. As I walk I notice that several of the front stoops are occupied by groups of elderly Polish and Ukrainian women—a sure sign of summer. Turning onto Bedford the squeals of young children playing at an opened fire hydrant nearly drown out a woman singing opera on a nearby corner; but the sound of car traffic is noticeably missing. I walk into the middle of the street, watching for cars out of habit, and my neighbor beckons to me. Wearing a starched floral dress and a strand of pearls she hands me a glass of lemonade and begins chatting about our neighbors, some of whom are sitting on her Astroturf lawn. Except this is not her lawn, it is the middle of a busy Brooklyn street and she is not my neighbor but Emily, from another part of the borough. Her 1950s-style "lawn" is part of an art competition that was organized by Williamsburg Walks, a community street closure event initiated by the Department of Transportation (DOT). Nearby Emily's "Garden Party" exhibit there's a blanket with a board game and a few twenty-somethings gathered around it. Up the block, members of a yoga studio are giving demonstrations and the garden design center "Jungle" has set up a patch of grass and plants in the street.

Williamsburg Walks is part of a broader initiative proposed by the Department of Transportation and the City of New York. Because other cities are experimenting with similar projects[1] it is important to understand how these events are planned and what effects they might have on diverse, gentrifying neighborhoods. This event, which urges residents to "rethink" their public space, has become an annual summer occurrence in Williamsburg since its inception in 2008. On chosen weekends in June, July, or August the main shopping and transportation street, Bedford Avenue, is closed to car traffic

Figure 5.1. "Garden Party" Exhibit. Photograph by the author.

between noon and dusk. Residents and visitors are then encouraged to use the street as they wish, but not all residents use the space. As the event aims to create more public space and "a celebration of neighborhood," it simultaneously exposes divisions among residents. The event is overwhelmingly homogenous, mostly comprised of white twenty-somethings and their older, professional counterparts who bring their toddlers to Williamsburg Walks. Although the neighborhood has significant Hispanic and Polish populations as well as older adults, these groups rarely attend the event. This chapter examines how the exclusion of some and inclusion of others at Williamsburg Walks reflects broader class and ethnic tensions common to many gentrifying neighborhoods.

CHANGE IN NORTH WILLIAMSBURG

This research focuses on Williamsburg's "Northside," where the Walks event takes place. The neighborhood is bounded by the Polish community of Greenpoint to the north, Hasidic and Hispanic communities to the south, an Expressway overpass to the east, and New York's East River on the west. The Northside has been the site of much of Williamsburg's change over the past

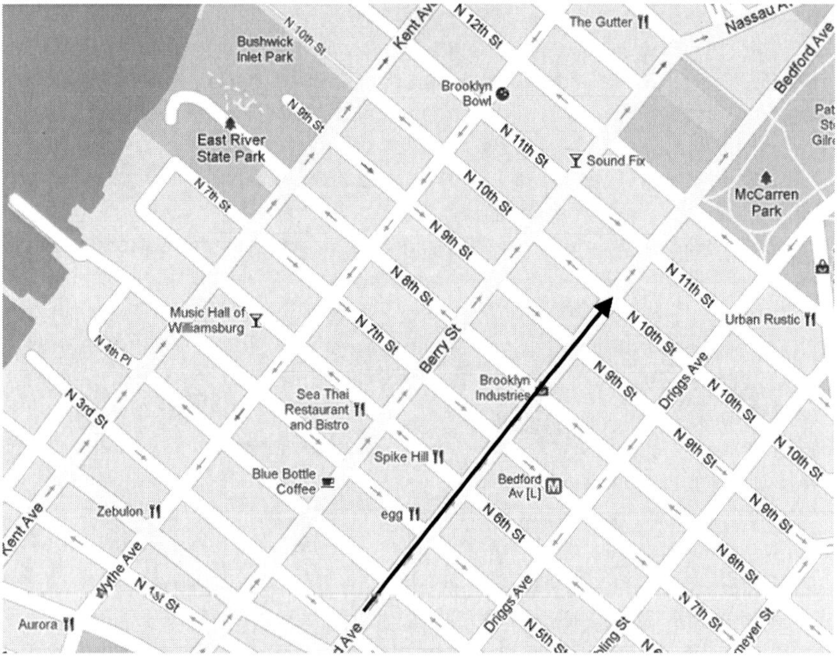

Figure 5.2. Map of Williamsburg's Northside. *Source:* Image from Google Maps.

two decades. The main shopping street, Bedford Avenue, is a transportation hub with a subway station (only one stop from Manhattan) and a bus route that heads North into Greenpoint and Queens.

Williamsburg has become synonymous with the process of gentrification, and is prominent in academic literature on the subject (Patch 2004; Zukin 2009; Krase 2009). Formerly a working-class community with an abundance of manufacturing firms, the post-industrial landscape of the neighborhood was gritty and disinvested (Curran 2003; Zukin 2010). The urban scene attracted artists and later students who had been priced out of Lower East Side apartments. Lofts, galleries, cafés, and clubs began to populate the neighborhood in the late 1990s, and Williamsburg's cool factor skyrocketed.

In the process, Williamsburg's Northside has experienced dramatic changes in the economic and social makeup of the population. When it was still a manufacturing center, the area was primarily home to working class families and residents who were often immigrants from Italy and Eastern Europe. The artists and students who later moved into the neighborhood may not have had more economic capital than their working-class neighbors, but they did have a different set of cultural capital (Bourdieu 1984). Their interests in art, music, and bohemian culture directed them towards different tastes than many of their working class neighbors. Soon indicators of this taste—cafés, trendy thrift stores, and vegetarian restaurants—began to dot Bedford Avenue and the surrounding streets (Lloyd 2010). Eventually these amenities gave the neighborhood a hip reputation, and as popularity increased, Williamsburg started to attract not just young bohemians, but professionals as well. In the real estate bubble of the 2000s, rents in Williamsburg quickly rose, and as still wealthier residents moved into the neighborhood new retail choices were created to meet their needs and desires.

The change in economic and social demographics is reflected in census data.[2] In 1980, 17 percent of the population was still employed in manufacturing, but by 2000 only 7 percent were. When accounting for health, education, and professional services, 6 percent of residents were employed in such fields in 1980; by 2000, it had risen to 14 percent. In 1980, 38 percent of people were between the ages of 20 and 40. By 2000, 46 percent of the residents were in this age group—inconsistent with the population for the rest of Brooklyn or New York City.

More tangibly, the change in tastes, produced by these differences in income and age, are physically manifested in the retail options of the Northside. Pierre Bourdieu described taste as "a systematic expression of a particular class of conditions of existence" (1984: 175). In Williamsburg one can see how this change has physically taken place. Many stores that once catered to the necessities and leisure activities of working class residents were either adapted to the tastes of the hip and then wealthy newcomers or were replaced by new stores.

SPATIAL EXCLUSION OF LONG-TERM RESIDENTS

In order to understand the physical and aesthetic change in the neighborhood's public spaces I employ the visual method of repeat photography to compare the commercial options available on Bedford in 2003 and 2011 (Rieger 1996). A sample of businesses along Bedford provides a clear picture of how merchants and storeowners have adapted to the changing tastes in Williamsburg. Because the event takes place on the Northside of the neighborhood most of these examples relate to the loss of Polish presence on the street, the Hispanic residents live primarily on the Southside.

The hardware store that used to sit on the northwest corner of North 8th Street and Bedford was replaced by "Brooklyn Industries." The locally based boutique chain sells clothing designed with a creative lifestyle in mind (their mantra is "Live, Work, Create."). The graffiti that tagged the wall space of the hardware store was painted over with a mural by Brooklyn Industries, which in turn has received some tagging. Across the street a laundromat, a former hangout for many of the neighborhood's older residents, is now

Figure 5.3. "North Star Hardware." Photograph by Jerry Krase.

Figure 5.4. "Brooklyn Industries Boutique." Photograph by the author.

Figure 5.5. Laundromat. Photograph by Jerry Krase.

"Saints Alp" a bubble tea café. Two Polish butchers "B&B Meat Products" and "Polska-Masarnia" have both been given way to convenient take out options. On North 6th Street the "Ristorante Italiano," with its neon sign and homey appearance was replaced by "Chai," a sleek Thai restaurant with posh décor.

Figure 5.6. "Saints Alp Tea." Photograph by the author.

Some local businesses have been able to keep up with the neighborhood change by adapting their images and the products they sell. "Red Pearl" a lingerie and gift shop used to cater to a different population. When the current manager, Amina, started working at "Red Pearl" in 2005 the clothing was geared towards an older clientele. She mentioned that they used to have a lot of Polish women as customers, but "they don't really come in anymore." The inventory of the shop changed to reach a different niche in the Williamsburg market, and as a result the customer base shifted to a younger, wealthier crowd.

"S&B," a Polish restaurant, also changed their image to keep up with the neighborhood. In 2003, the building's awning was red and white, the colors of the Polish national flag, and included the Polish word for restaurant "Restauracja." By 2011, the restaurant's image had changed to fit in with modern restaurants in the area. Like many of the newer eateries in Williamsburg, the name "S&B" is now missing from the minimalist décor; only a neon "Zywiec" beer sign and a pierogi menu in the window indicate the cuisine being

Figure 5.7. The old "S&B." Photograph by Jerry Krase.

Figure 5.8. Keeping up with the change. Photograph by the author.

served. While the menu still lists inexpensive Polish dishes, Polish words are now absent from the storefront.

"Vittoria" had been an Italian bakery on Bedford since the 1960s. It closed in September of 2010 but reopened a few months later as a café. Gone were the linoleum floors and the big plastic cookie trays, the walls are now exposed brick, the floor is polished wood, and an antique scale sits on top of the counter next to an espresso machine. In the past older women would meet for a coffee inside, but the owner told me that with the new image, "we're going for more of a café than a bakery—hoping to catch the younger people."

As the socioeconomic demographics of a neighborhood change, so too do the tastes of the services and retail options available to that community. The stores on Bedford Avenue and the surrounding streets have adapted to fit the hip reputation that Williamsburg has garnered. While some establishments, like the former "L Café" and "Galapagos" nightclub helped launch Williamsburg's initial popularity, many more establishments open or change to tap into the new market niche. Establishments focused on necessity give way to those based on luxury consumption—clothing boutiques, organic food stores, and trendy bars and restaurants (Krase 2009).

The public space of Bedford Avenue has been transformed as business owners continue to accommodate the needs and desires of the hip and newer professional classes of Williamsburg. Former sites of necessity for the working class and immigrant population—the Laundromat, butchers, and hardware store are gone. Even the leisure space of the neighborhood bakery has changed into a different aesthetic, geared towards a younger hip crowd. This narrative is similar to many other instances of gentrification: a neighborhood's stores and aesthetics change, reflecting a shift in demographics and attracting still newer residents at once (Carpenter 1995; Levine 2004; Lloyd 2005; Zukin 2009; Levy and Cybriwsky 2010).

Beyond their immediate functions, these former establishments also provided meeting spaces for residents—particularly older men and women (Lofland 1998). Long-term residents now have few reasons to use Bedford Avenue because of the transformation of these neighborhood establishments. Although they have not been physically displaced from Williamsburg, the gentrification of stores and public spaces has changed who uses the street leading to social exclusion of long-term residents (Smith 1996; Freeman 2006; Deener 2007; Gotham 2010).

By focusing on the planning and evolution of one community event I hope to contribute a new perspective for understanding the processes of gentrification and exclusion in residential neighborhoods. Combining fieldwork observations from Williamsburg Walks and interviews with various actors, this case study provides a deeper understanding of the symbolic meaning of community events in gentrifying neighborhoods. This research illustrates how such events can be interpreted in the context of neighborhood branding—discussed in the next section—and how they can perpetuate common symptoms of gentrification like exclusion of long-term residents, ethnic/class tensions, and luxury consumption.

BRANDING CHANGE IN WILLIAMSBURG

Williamsburg's past as an industrial center made it appealing to the hip artists and students who began moving there at the end of the twentieth century (Zukin 2010). The grit of urban decay and low rents were inviting for a bohemian lifestyle—and so the idea did not need to be "sold" to newcomers. In order for modern Williamsburg to transition from its recent past as a mecca of hip youth culture into a luxury neighborhood replete with expensive condos and Manhattan style amenities, some convincing *is* necessary. This is carried out through a careful rebranding of the neighborhood, playing down the industrial past in order to promote it as a site for consumption and entertainment.

Through aesthetics, retail options and community events Williamsburg is becoming branded as a consumption destination for the upper classes. These facets of public life "conceal a highly unequal socioeconomic reality" (Greenberg 2008: 10). The working class and long-term residents often do not participate in the new entertainment and luxury services that are made available, and community events like Williamsburg Walks support the exclusionary characteristic of neighborhood change (Judd and Fainstein 1999, Holcomb 1999).

Andrew Deener (2007) explores this theme of branding at Venice Beach in Los Angeles where merchants and real estate developers collaborated to shift the image of the district. "Local actors," as Deener refers to them, created an image of Venice that focused on the artistic history and effectively erased previous images that the neighborhood was associated with. This changed the main shopping strip into a manufactured experience, a destination for tourists at the exclusion of many long time residents. A similar process is now occurring in Williamsburg. Bedford Avenue features expensive restaurants and cafes, boutiques and bars to satisfy luxury condo dwellers, "such local institutions both drive the neighborhood identity and reflect it" (Lloyd 2010:185). The public and commercial spaces of the neighborhood predominantly cater to wealthier newcomers, at the exclusion of working-class residents. Williamsburg Walks can be understood as both a method and outcome of this branding process.

INITIATING WILLIAMSBURG WALKS

Williamsburg Walks was a forerunner of NYC's Summer Streets[3] program. Initially proposed in 2007 by the New York City Department of Transportation (DOT), it was designed to be "a celebration of the Williamsburg community, centered around a pedestrian-only Bedford Avenue" (Colvin 2008: 4). Although Williamsburg Walks is promoted by city initiatives, nearly all the funding must be organized by local community groups.

The event has taken place for the past three consecutive summers, occurring on various weekends. For the first event the street was closed to car traffic for four Saturdays, the 2009 edition was extended to six, and in 2010 the street was closed for only one weekend in June. Each time, part of Bedford Avenue was transformed from a busy thoroughfare into a venue for picnics, sports, and neighborly interaction.

While the event has changed over the past three years, the slogan "rethink your public space" has remained constant. With this mantra the organizers (several of them urban planning students from New York University and the City University of New York) hoped to communicate that the event is about community: it's about neighbors getting out to know one another and using the newfound public space for just about anything noncommercial. Flyers remind residents and visitors that the event is not a street fair "there will be no funnel cake and no cheap tube socks . . . we simply want the community

(YOU) to come out and enjoy the public space" (Colvin 2008: 47). The emphasis for Williamsburg Walks, at least how it has been marketed, is that it is a social experiment—a new way of building community.

DOT began the planning process by contacting Brooklyn's Community Board 1 and the transportation committee chair, Maggie Anderson. Maggie had previously worked with business owners a few years prior when the L train was out of service for several weekends; she knew how important it was that the businesses support this change in vehicle transportation. She said of the L train situation, "the businesses were really impacted at that time" so it was vital that local business owners understood "how DOT's idea would differ from a street fair, [there would be] no sidewalk competition for the businesses."[4] The Williamsburg Walks' website and literature stresses that the event is about members of the community using public space, but the DOT website states "Local merchants' associations, community groups, and business improvement districts host these Weekend Walks to provide a fun new way to highlight local businesses and cultural institutions" (Weekend Walks 2010:np).

The role of businesses in Williamsburg Walks is contentious. Some planners claimed that business owners had nothing to do with the concept, one organizer said the goal was to "build community instead of capital." While others, like Maggie, acknowledge the need for their support. A few owners on Bedford Avenue have fought against the Walks initiative claiming it hurt their businesses, while other owners support the event in hopes that solidarity among local proprietors will facilitate the creation of a Business Improvement District (BID). Michael Parsons, owner of an artisanal cheese shop and a café, included a discussion of the Walks event in a recent grant application for the Northside Merchants Association. Whatever the capacity business owners play in the production of Williamsburg Walks, their opinions do matter. Complaints about lost profits and competition from street vendors resulted in fewer Walks for 2010 and strict policing of street vendors.

2008: A PUBLIC SPACE EXPERIMENT

The inaugural event was primarily organized by Transportation Alternatives, Community Board 1 of Brooklyn, local businesses and a community group, Neighbors Allied for Good Growth (NAG). I was not present at any of the planning meetings for the first year of Williamsburg Walks, and so must rely on post-event interviews with organizers and the end report produced by Michael Parsons' company, Mixer. According to the end report, the goal of Williamsburg Walks was to create a social experiment where people come out and use temporary public space however they would like, the original planners did not want to fill the street with activities, but encourage people to use their imaginations.

> Not a street festival or street fair, this was an experimental temporary pedestrian street closure intended to promote the enjoyment of Northside Brooklyn, both on Bedford Avenue and beyond, by encouraging the community to come together to shop, stroll, and socialize in an area unobstructed by traffic" (Colvin 2008: 4).

This goal was perhaps only realized for the 2008 edition, after which the event did become more programmed.

The community organizers I spoke with insisted that the event had no explicit benefits for businesses, maintaining that it was by and for the community with just some local business sponsorship. However, in an interview with Michael, he stated that when writing a grant for the merchants association, he portrayed the event as a merchants' initiative. His web company, Mixer, was also the biggest sponsor of Williamsburg Walks. Mixer produced an end report for the event, which included meetings about BID formation and a brochure that presented Walks as a "collaborative" effort between the merchants association and the aforementioned planning groups.

The planners knew that they need cooperation from the businesses in order to make the event a success, but Bedford Avenue merchants seemed to have the expectation that Williamsburg Walks should improve their sales or at least be used as a unifying force among storeowners. After the scheduled Walks, business owners were polled about their experiences. The comments and concerns that came out of this poll had a significant effect on how future Williamsburg Walks would be organized—relating to length of the event and the precarious place of street vendors during the event.

The original event was not well advertised, a critique shared by planners, storeowners, and residents. There were a few posters on Bedford Avenue and surrounding blocks in the weeks leading up to Walks, but they were ambiguous and many people did not know what to expect. The end report mentioned that English and Spanish language brochures were passed out to residents and merchants a few weeks before the event, but it is unclear how widespread the distribution was. Translation issues prevented the circulation of a Polish language brochure. Other than these methods the event was primarily advertised by blog or website posts, a Facebook page, and word of mouth. As a result a relatively small number of people knew about the event before hand, but despite a lack of funding and publicity Williamsburg Walks kicked off at noon on July 19, 2008.

That morning volunteers set up barricades along Bedford Avenue from Metropolitan to North 9th Streets. Businesses on Bedford were allowed to

Figure 5.9. View of Williamsburg Walks 2008. Photograph by Michael Freedman-Schnapp.

use the sidewalks in front of their buildings as extensions of their restaurants or boutiques, and individuals were encouraged to enjoy and creatively use the street. Some people made use of the DOT tables and chairs that were set up in the street and others even sat down to read or suntan, but the majority of people just walked down the street as if it were the sidewalk.

Maggie, one of the central planners, acknowledged this in her interview, "we wanted so much to distinguish it from a street fair—the whole point is to open up the environment; but that's a very lofty concept and people weren't understanding that." Activity on the street was fairly limited, as was diversity. From both my observations at the event and photographs that were later posted on the Mixer site, the event was demographically homogenous. Most people taking part in the event were young and white. There were a few families on the street, but the older residents were almost completely absent. Oddly the Mixer end report noted, "locals welcomed Williamsburg Walks as an opportunity to unite the community's diverse, and sometimes divided, collection of residents" (Colvin 2008, 21). This is in direct contrast to what I observed at the event, and it is unclear how this information was gathered. When I asked one of the planners about the lack of diversity at Williamsburg Walks he said that the event "just kind of reflects who was at Bedford Avenue anyway." Walks demonstrated the usual exclusion of certain groups from the neighborhood's public spaces.

After the first few Saturdays a number of people began to sell food, art, and yard sale items on the street. Williamsburg already has a rich sidewalk vending culture—which contributes to its reputation as a hip/urban locale. There are several licensed vendors who regularly sell books, jewelry and other wares on the Bedford Avenue sidewalk. For the 2008 Walks event these legal vendors were allowed to continue their regular business, but the unauthorized people who set up in the street were not. Many of these new vendors were Hispanic women selling horchata or mango slices. Although there is a large Puerto Rican community on the South side of Williamsburg, virtually the only Latino/a presence I saw were those who came as vendors. Something that the planners did not anticipate was that for many people, amateur entrepreneurialism was how they would use their public space. The merchants complained that the commercial activities taking place on the street were detracting from their businesses, and the planners worried that the tents and tables clashed with the "not a street fair" aesthetic. These notions had an important impact on how future Walks would be organized.

2009: GROWTH AND CHANGE FOR WILLIAMSBURG WALKS

After 2008 the community group NAG took over most of the planning for Williamsburg Walks; this was spearheaded by two urban planning students, Alex and Christian. Alex had volunteered for the event in 2008, and he and Christian organized a planning meeting for the 2009 edition that April. The meeting was held several blocks away from the Walks site at the "Swinging Sixties Senior Center."

Aside from the two planners and myself, there were seven people at the meeting, all but one of whom were White. Three of the people in attendance identified themselves as business owners, and one young man was a writer for *L* magazine, a cosponsor of Williamsburg Walks. The aim of this meeting was to brainstorm about how to make Walks more engaging. Mixer's survey had made it clear that in order for it to be more popular, some activities needed to be provided. While commerce was a concern, the foci of the 2009 planning meeting were how to bring more programming to the street and how to better promote Williamsburg Walks. Those present at the meeting decided to arrange activities oriented towards "art, music, community organization, local food [and] family activities" (Williamsburg Walks 2009–2010 Report: 8).

Initially the Walks were supposed to take place every Saturday in June and July, but after protest from the merchants and a lack of funding, they were cut down to six days from eight. The 2009 Walks were better attended as a result of programming. More of the restaurants and cafes on the street had extended their services onto the sidewalks and a few of the boutiques placed clothing racks or merchandise outside of their stores. The legal sidewalk vendors set up their tables, and the street was generally more active than the previous year.

The northern most part of Bedford was designated the "Children's block." A giant roll of paper was unfurled down the middle of the street and dozens of children were busily working with crayons and markers. One of the five "interconnected purposes" of Walks was to "encourage a dialogue between old timers/new comers/insiders/outsiders" (Williamsburg Walks 2009–2010 Report: 1) This goal was attempted by the creation of a "civic block" which provided a space for community organizations like the YMCA and NAG to promote their work. On the last day the international group Project for Public Spaces (PPS) joined the Civic block. Representatives from PPS played a primary role in the 2010 planning. The local CSA (Community Supported Agriculture) organized several food themed activities on one block and on another there were intermittent performances—some planned, some spontaneous.

Although non-permit vending was prohibited, there were still some people selling food. Once again, most of the people I saw doing this vending were Latinas and this was still the main Hispanic presence on the street.

Figure 5.10. Street Performance, 2009. *Source:* Photograph from Williamsburg Walks 2009 (https://picasaweb.google.com/lh/photo/NpA_baIysFwLEJcsvb0PIQ).

The issue of vending was addressed in the 2009 planning meeting, but it became a central focus for the 2010 meeting. The summary document at the end of 2009 stated that the activities needed to be "monitored" more closely in future Walks.

The 2009 events seemed closer to the idea DOT had initially proposed. People were doing more with their public space than just walking up and down the street. There were enough activities to engage residents and visitors; and the broad themes of art, community, food and family that were mentioned in the planning meeting were actualized at the events. Once again, the event was overwhelmingly young and White, although the "children's block" did help to offset this by bringing out dozens of families.

Walks organizers produced a summary document for 2009, based on post–Walks meetings. One concern in the document was as follows: "several people at the wrap up session complained that too many activities were taking place reinforcing the feeling of Bedford Ave as a 'permanent Mardi Gras' and diverting people from shopping" (Williamsburg Walks 2009–2010 Report: 8). The wrap up session was mostly comprised of business owners, presumably the only people who would really be concerned with diversions from shopping. The activities they referred to had encouraged more people to use the street, the initial purpose of Williamsburg Walks. Aside from a few unauthorized vendors, there was nothing for sale on the street—the goal of "building community not capital"—but the owners still felt that Williamsburg Walks was detrimental to their businesses. As a result organizers stated, "working with merchants will be among the top priorities this year [2010]" (Williamsburg Walks 2009–2010 Report: 6).

This indicates that by 2010 the purpose of Williamsburg Walks had shifted from being a "social experiment" to a street closure that was limited by the whims of business owners. This was also signaled by the fact that the number of Walks was cut once again—because of owner protests and a lack of city funding. At the post-event meeting planners scheduled the 2010 Walks for three weekends (Saturdays and Sundays for a total of 6 days) in June and July. However the 2010, Williamsburg Walks only took place on the last weekend in June.

2010: RESTRICTIONS

On April 21 the 2010 "Williamsburg Walks Community Brain Storming Session" was held at "Teddy's" a restaurant off Bedford Avenue on the Northside. This gathering was much larger than the planning meeting for 2009. In addition to several planners from NAG and PPS there were about twenty business owners and residents present. Even though the group was larger there was less variation in age than the previous year, nearly everyone was White and there was roughly an equal proportion of men to women. Representatives from PPS gave a presentation on the mission of this years' event: celebrate the neighborhood, relax, shop at local stores, rethink public spaces. Most of the themes from the 2009 meeting were also set in place for the next Walks: food, family, art and community. In 2010 there would also be two additions: an art competition to facilitate the rethinking of public space, and a significant police presence.

Illegal vending was a major concern at the 2009 wrap up session where it was decided that, "all 'unplanned/spontaneous activities' should be controlled more drastically—vending as well as music or performances" (Williamsburg Walks 2009–2010 Report: 8). The organizers stated that over the past two years they had realized the importance of enforcing a "no vending" rule, and that vending would be policed for 2010. As a result of pressure from local businesses, the organizers agreed to have a considerable police presence at the event. They maintained that vendors who were normally on the street would be allowed to continue selling, but no new vendors would be permitted. One resident asked why vending was such a concern. Christian, a 2009 planner, replied that the extra vendors made it "too crowded," and they were trying to promote the established businesses. While promoting local business is one of the many benefits of Williamsburg Walks, it was clear from this meeting that it had become a primary goal. As the brainstorming continued people gave ideas about how to get Walkers to visit stores—ideas like a scavenger hunt that leads you through the stores or a booth where you could sew your own bag to use while shopping were proposed. One organizer said he wanted any ideas "that connect[ed] the programming with the merchants."

After about an hour, the meeting broke up into subcommittees, one being for merchants. The group came up with several ideas of how to focus Williamsburg Walks on stores and shopping. One of the goals stated in the 2009 summary report was to connect long-term residents and newcomers, but at this meeting the emphasis was on shopping. This was more in line with Williamsburg's new reputation as a site of luxury consumption—something that long-term residents are usually excluded from because of differences in tastes and income.

The 2010 Williamsburg Walks lasted for one weekend—noon to dusk on June 26 and 27. This was the most programmed version of Walks to date and it approached the "street fair" aesthetic that planners in earlier years had tried to avoid. However this led to a high level of engagement among residents and visitors, and was successful enough to ensure that the event would continue in 2011.

The "Children's block," renamed "Kid's Island," returned with an outdoor gymnasium and crafts for children. Hundreds of kids played in the street throughout the weekend, and many of the parents were long-term members of the Williamsburg community. The rest of the blocks were dedicated to "Skill Sharing" in the form of crafts and information, a huge picnic area, and public art throughout the blocks. There was not as much civic activity as there had been in 2009, aside from a "Williamsburg Walks" info table, a NAG presence, and representatives from "The Brooklyn Torch"—a small organization that promoted the use of a special currency to increase local spending. The CSA had sponsored a "local cuisine" cooking competition, and this was the only time that Polish or Hispanic culture was explicitly referred to during Williamsburg Walks. Only one young woman, Meghan, entered the competition—so she sold the food she had brought and then left. Although this type of vending was not permitted at Walks, no one stopped her.

An art competition was featured on several blocks, with installations (and usually artists to explain them) positioned throughout Bedford Avenue. Using the "Rethink your Public Space" slogan, Walks planners sent out a call to artists asking them to contribute any art form that could help facilitate this reimagining of space. The result was about a dozen pieces which ranged from sculptures, furniture, shrines inspired by Plato's dialogues, and interactive pieces like Emily's "Garden Party" described above. Emily, who studied urban issues as an undergrad, felt that the art competition was an important contribution to Walks because there is "this idea that commerce drives pedestrian activity" but she felt it was also important to just be "able to sit and watch people and engage in other types of activities, and art is fundamentally noncommercial."

The art competition provided the opportunity for people to "rethink their public space" in an environment where nothing was being "sold" either directly or indirectly through advertising. It was one of the few activities at the 2010 Walks that was completely not for profit. One thing that changed drastically between the 2009 and 2010 events was the sudden presence of businesses in the street. Bedford Avenue businesses had always been allowed to use the sidewalks in front of their stores, but in 2010 businesses who did not have storefronts on Bedford were allowed to program in the street as well. In the planning meeting back in April Christian had stressed that there were "no commercial intentions" for Williamsburg Walks. Later in an interview he explained the presence of local businesses on the street, "When you simply pedestrianize the street it's not enough, people didn't see the point of it—we felt that if the festival would survive we had to make people happier about closing the streets." Walks has never been well funded, so Christian saw

Figure 5.11. Timaeus. Photograph by the author.

existing businesses as one of the few options to make the event engaging. He reached out to local businesses and if they could provide some service or activity during the event, then they could take up space on the street.

As a result of this there were a lot of free programs available for people to participate in; but nearly every activity was a means of advertising and promotion for a business. The boutique "Peachfrog" set up a table where they handed out flyers for their store and as previously mentioned a garden supply store, set up a green oasis at one end of the event. A yoga studio provided demonstrations and nutritional information, and nearly everything on the "Kid's Island" was provided by for-profit businesses.

"Brooklyn Brainery" and "Green Mountain Energy"[5] both had booths set up in the street, although the former is based out of downtown Brooklyn and the latter has nothing to do with Brooklyn at all. The Brainery hosted a perfume-making workshop, which required a nominal 'donation'; and representatives from Green Mountain stopped people on the street to tell them about their company's residential energy plans. Even though these business were not neighborhood institutions, they fit in with the themes of Williamsburg Walks—like skill sharing and sustainable resources. These businesses also fit in with the image of Williamsburg as a neighborhood where people can spend income on perfume-making lessons and alternative energy sources.

Figure 5.12. Aaron's "Street Boutique." Photograph by the author.

Someone who did not fit in with this image was Aaron. Aaron was selling jewelry at the corner of a side street. His NYC permit was clearly displayed but he was not located on Bedford Avenue. I was surprised at this since he was clearly an authorized vendor, and at the planning meeting organizers confirmed that the usual vendors would be permitted.

Aaron showed me a letter he received from Williamsburg Walks planners stating that there would be no street vending allowed and police action would be taken if he set up his booth on Bedford Avenue. Aaron is a regular presence on Bedford Avenue, and has been for a few years. He said he appreciated what Williamsburg Walks did for the community, but was very upset that he was suddenly not allowed to sell in his usual spot—he considers himself part of the community too. In our interview Christian mentioned that the reason for this no-vendor decision was because the planners deemed it too difficult to distinguish between legal and illegal vending. Unfortunately for Aaron and many other legal vendors, this decision led to their exclusion from Bedford Avenue on Williamsburg Walks days.

The explicit exclusion of all street vendors is closely related to the implicit exclusion of Hispanics and older adults from Bedford Avenue, during Williamsburg Walks and the rest of the year. Images that do not fit in with the new luxury brand of Williamsburg—Polish and Spanish languages, bodegas, butchers, elderly people, and street vendors—are less and less a part of daily life on Bedford Avenue.

While 2010 was very successful at attracting families it was still not representative of the diverse community. It is important to note here how the nature of advertising and outreach for Walks affects who actually comes to the event. Williamsburg Walks has its own website where it hosts pictures and videos of previous Walks, FAQs, and a map of the planned activities. Blogs like "free Williamsburg" and "Greenpointers" also advertise the event in great detail. However the signs that go up in the physical spaces of Williamsburg are deliberately vague, and for many people in the neighborhood this would be their only way of finding out about the event. Thus certain people are more likely to have prior knowledge about the event—people who speak English and are young and/or have regular Internet access. They can plan ahead to visit or avoid Williamsburg Walks, and if they do choose to come they know roughly what to expect. The lack of outreach to the Polish and Hispanic communities in the neighborhood inhibits their participation. They might come to Bedford Avenue while the event is going on, but from my observations this only results in confusion.

I met Lilian and Stan, a middle-aged Ukranian and Polish couple, sitting on chairs on the sidewalk at the very end of the event on Sunday. I asked if they had participated in any way "There's nothing here for us," Lilian replied. This spoke not only to age and taste divisions, but also to a lack of knowledge about the event. Gladys, a Puerto Rican woman, was studying the activities map with her husband and daughter when I approached them. It was around 6:00 p.m. on Saturday and the event was packing up for the day. I asked if they had participated in any of the festivities and Gladys replied that they had just wandered over because they were wondering why the street was closed.

The lack of outreach to the working-class and long-time residents coupled with the increasing focus on boutiques and restaurants reflects broader themes in Williamsburg. The community event can be understood as part of a process to brand Williamsburg for the upper classes that are recently moving in. This results in the inclusion and promotion of consumption activities and the exclusion of less wealthy residents from the physical spaces—an issue that is not only a problem for Williamsburg, but many gentrifying neighborhoods.

CONCLUSIONS: EVALUATING WILLIAMSBURG WALKS

Williamsburg Walks provides many benefits to the neighborhood. Having a car free street gives everyone (theoretically) an opportunity to enjoy public space. The children's block gave guardians the opportunity to socialize, possibly leading to the creation of various networks among parents. Residents and visitors were able to use the street to share food, play games, and make crafts—undoubtedly leading to a stronger, if temporary, sense of 'community' among participants.

Still, there are serious problems with the execution of Williamsburg Walks. The event has come to reflect the branding of Williamsburg as a site of luxury consumption; leading to the privileged inclusion of some and the exclusion of others. As a free community event, Williamsburg Walks has the opportunity to unite neighborhood residents of different socioeconomic backgrounds. However, by failing to engage elderly and working-class residents and by relying on local business to program events, Williamsburg Walks also has the potential to perpetuate the gentrifying patterns of exclusion and consumption. When I asked an organizer about the lack of Polish and Hispanic visitors at the 2008 Williamsburg Walks he replied that the flyers were not translated into Polish and Spanish early enough for the first event. These groups were also absent from years two and three, indicating that the problem lies not in timely translation but rather an overall lack of outreach.

These groups do not fit into the gentrified brand of Williamsburg as a site of luxury and convenience. The everyday indicators of Polish and Hispanic culture are disappearing in favor of upscale restaurants and boutiques. As an experiment in public space, planners at Williamsburg Walks should make a more concerted effort to engage these populations who are increasingly absent from Bedford Avenue.

Although well intentioned, the current state of Williamsburg Walks reflects the processes of exclusion and inclusion that go on throughout the neighborhood as it gets branded as a site for luxury. The original purpose of Walks was to utilize temporary public space, but at the 2010 event nearly everything one could do on the street (aside from viewing the art competition) served as advertising for local businesses. With a focus on consumption, less wealthy residents were not engaged in the activities. Certain companies—like the "Children's Gym," "Jungle" nursery, and "Brooklyn Brainery," were allowed to sell or advertise on the street. This was an opportunity that was not afforded to the book vendors and the Hispanic food stands that are a daily fixture on Bedford Avenue and certainly contribute to the everyday public space of the neighborhood. These remnants of hip and/or working class Williamsburg do not fit into the new brand of the neighborhood because they do not cater to upper class tastes. By excluding these businesses from Williamsburg Walks and failing to engage disadvantaged populations, the planners have contributed to the preference of certain groups and businesses in the new face of the neighborhood.

NOTES

1. Such as, Project for Public Spaces (www.pps.org).

2. All census data comes from infoshare.org, information from the 1980 and 2000 census was produced for tract 553 in Brooklyn.

3. The Summer Streets program started in 2008, Williamsburg Walks was the first of these public space "experiments." The original goal of the project entailed closing the street to car traffic and encouraging people to use the space as they will (www.nyc.gov/html/dot/summerstreets/html/home/home.shtml).

4. This quote, and any others that do not have citations, are from my interviews with organizers, storeowners, and participants.

5. Brooklyn Brainery is a creative DIY "school" where people sign up to take classes, topics ranging from cooking or crafts to American Sign Language.

REFERENCES

Bourdieu, Pierre. 1984. *Distinction: A Social critique of the judgment of taste*, translated by Richard Nice. Cambridge, MA: Harvard University Press.

Carpenter, Juliet and Loretta Lees. 1995. "Gentrification in New York, London and Paris: An International comparison." *International Journal of Urban and Regional Research* 19(2):286–303.

Colvin, Connie, Dana Feingold and Alex Sweet. 2008. "Williamsburg Walks 2008 End Report." Blenderbox, Brooklyn, New York. Unpublished report.

Curran, Winifred. 2003. "Gentrification and the nature of work: Exploring the links in Williamsburg, Brooklyn." *Environment and Planning A* 36:1243–58.

Deener, Andrew. 2007. "Commerce as the structure and symbol of neighborhood life: Reshaping the meaning of community in Venice, California." *City & Community* 6(4):291–312.

Freeman, L. 2006. *There Goes the 'hood: Views of gentrification from the ground up.* Philadelphia, PA: Temple University Press.

Gotham, Kevin Fox. 2010. "Tourism gentrification: The Case of New Orleans' Vieux Carre (French Quarter)." Pp. 145–65 in *The Gentrification debates*, edited by Japonica Brown-Saracino. New York: Routledge.

Greenberg, Miriam. 2008. *Branding New York: How a city in crisis was sold to the world.* New York: Routledge.

Holcomb, Briavel. 1999. "Marketing cities for tourism" Pp. 54–70 in *The Tourist city,* edited by Dennis R. Judd and Susan S. Fainstein. New Haven, CT: Yale University Press.

Judd, Dennis R. and Susan S. Fainstein. 1999. "Global forces, local strategies, and urban tourism" Pp. 1–17 in *The Tourist city,* edited by Dennis R. Judd and Susan S. Fainstein. New Haven, CT: Yale University Press.

Krase, Jerome. 2009. "Gentrifying Poland and Polonia." Retrieved April 24, 2009 (www.brooklynsoc.org/blog/docs/Krase_PolandPolonia.html).

Lees, Loretta. 2003. "Super-gentrification: The Case of Brooklyn Heights, New York City." *Urban Studies* 40(12):2487–509.

Levine, Myron A. 2004. "Government policy, the local state, and gentrification: The Case of Prenzlauer Berg (Berlin), Germany." *Journal of Urban Affairs* 26(1):89–108.

Levy, Paul R. and Roman A. Cybriwsky. 2010. "The Hidden dimensions of culture and class: Philadelphia." Pp. 285–93 in *The gentrification debates*, edited by Japonica Brown-Saracino. New York: Routledge.

Lloyd, Richard. 2005. *Neo-Bohemia: Art and commerce in the post-industrial city.* New York: Routledge.

Lloyd, Richard. 2010. "Living Like an Artist." Pp. 185–93 in *The Gentrification Debates*, edited by Japonica Brown-Saracino. New York: Routledge.

Lofland, Lyn. 1998. *The Public realm: Exploring the city's quintessential social territory.* New York: Walter de Gruyter Inc.

Patch, Jason. 2004. "The Embedded landscape of gentrification." *Visual Studies* 19:169–186.

Rieger, Jon. 1996. "Photographing social change." *Visual Sociology* 11:5–49.

Smith, Neil. 1996. *The New urban frontier: Gentrification and the revanchist city.* New York: Routledge.

"Weekend Walks 2010" 2010. Accessed December 5, 2010 (www.nyc.gov/html/dot/weekendwalks/html/home/home.shtml).

"Williamsburg Walks 2009–2010 Report" 2010. Private correspondence, November 29, 2010.

Zukin, Sharon, Valerie Trujillo, Peter Frase, Danielle Jackson, Tim Recuber and Abraham Walker. 2009. "New retail capital and neighborhood change: Boutiques and gentrification in New York City." *City & Community* 8(1):47–64.

Zukin, Sharon. 2010. *Naked City: The Death and life of authentic urban places.* New York: Oxford University Press.

6

The Environmental Injustice of Green Gentrification

The Case of Brooklyn's Prospect Park

Kenneth A. Gould and Tammy L. Lewis

How are environmental "goods" distributed? This chapter takes a twist on environmental injustice by examining the allocation of environmental goods, rather than environmental bads. Traditionally, the literature on environmental justice has largely focused on who gets the environmental "bads" of society—toxic waste, hazardous facilities, and poor air quality, to name a few. As movements shift from pointing out environmental injustices to seeking environmental justice and what Agyeman (2005) calls "just sustainability," we need to ask, who gets the environmental amenities? Parks? Water cleanup? Access to affordable public transportation? Resources for environmental improvements? Which communities get the "goods" to improve their quality of life?

By looking to goods as well as bads, this chapter attempts to shift the conversation to a broader understanding of environmental inequality, one that looks to the full spectrum of distribution (Lewis 2011). An analogy can be made to income inequality. We cannot understand income inequality only by studying poor people.[1] Likewise, we cannot understand environmental inequality only by studying contaminated communities. While it is not the task of this chapter, by considering the range of distribution, we can devise environmental measures similar to those used to assess income inequality. We might ask, at what levels of environmental equality do we recognize just sustainability?

If we could quantify environmental "goods" and environmental "bads," a distribution score, like the GINI coefficient (a measure of inequality of income distribution), could provide indicators for whether the distribution of environmental goods and bads was getting more or less equal. This inequality has real consequences for responses to environmental change. Greater inequality in the distribution of environmental goods removes those at the top of the distribution from negative environmental feedback loops (Gould 2006). Thus, those with the most political, social, and economic power are also those least likely to recognize environmental problems or have incentives to address them.

Historically, environmentally poor groups led movements for environmental justice based on threats to their communities, and environmentally rich groups sought further environmental amenities, such as bike paths, brownfield cleanups, farmers markets, and waterfront improvements. If environmental distributions proceed along "environmental class" lines much like income, we would expect the environmentally rich to get richer, and the environmentally poor to get poorer. Agyeman (2005) argues that groups for environmental justice and for environmental sustainability have the potential to blend frames to work for "just sustainability." However, this may be increasingly difficult if those at the top are seeking environmental goods and those at the bottom are trying to avoid environmental bads. The two ends do not see the same "environment."

This chapter attempts to move the study of environmental distributions forward by focusing on a specific form of environmental good: ecological restoration of urban environmental amenities. The chapter asks, how do real estate markets, organizations, and institutions respond to the transformation of an environmental bad (or neutral) into an environmental good? What are the consequences for nearby residents? How does ecological restoration impact social inequality and the distribution of environmental goods? We propose that, due to the operation of markets and actors that form the urban growth machine (Logan and Molotch 1987), the creation or restoration of an in situ environmental good will increase environmental inequality, as the amenity drives up property values, physically displaces those at the lower end of the stratification pyramid, and attracts new residents at the higher end. The benefits of the environmental good are thus distributed away from those who lived near it, and upward to those who can afford to be attracted to it. Therefore, without clearly focused public policy intervention, in situ environmental improvements will tend to increase racial and class inequality, and decrease environmental justice, a process we refer to as "green gentrification."

In this chapter we explore the distributional dynamics of green gentrification in Brooklyn using the restoration of Prospect Park as a case. The research and analysis presented here is drawn from a larger project that is analyzing the distributional consequences of a number of environmental amenity projects in Brooklyn. The projects vary in terms of the degree to which they have been completed and the policy interventions that have or have not been made. The case presented here, that of Prospect Park, is the example that has the longest history, with the remediation intervention beginning in 1980, and one that proceeded without policy intervention to address distributional outcomes. To fully understand the unique role that environmental amenity restoration plays in the redistribution of urban quality of life in general, and the distributional impacts of Prospect Park restoration in particular, it is first necessary to examine the housing market dynamics that underlie the distribution of environmental goods and bads by race and class.

THE RACE AND CLASS LANDSCAPE OF RESIDENTIAL INEQUALITY

Much of the literature addressing issues of environmental justice focuses primarily on the role of institutional, cultural, and individual racism in directing environmental and public health hazards toward politically disenfranchised racial and ethnic groups (Bryant and Mohai 1992; Bullard 1990, 1993, 1994; Bryant 1995; Roberts and Toffolon-Weiss 2001; Pellow 2002; Sze 2006; Taylor 2009). The term "environmental racism" originated to specifically describe race-based discrimination in the siting of hazardous facilities and the remediation of environmental hazards in the United States. Numerous studies have indicated that in the United States, race is a predictor of where environmentally hazardous facilities will be located (Bryant and Mohai 1992; Bullard 1994; Mohai and Saha 2007). This can only occur because of racial segregation in housing. Various manifestations of racism in environmental policy, real estate markets, lending institutions, and employment generate extreme levels of racial segregation in residential patterns (Massey and Denton 1993). Well-documented social phenomena such as "white flight" allow real estate companies to "block bust" and "flip" entire neighborhoods. Race-based differences in access to credit due to lending discrimination in mortgage and home improvement loans, and lending institution red-lining of neighborhoods restrict housing markets for people of color, and slate neighborhoods for decay and devaluation. Real estate companies similarly redline neighborhoods to use racial animosity and unease to manipulate the relative value of housing stock in order to maximize profits on sales and investments. The reliance of public education funding on property values in many cases (and local parent-teacher associations in urban neighborhoods) reinforces such inequalities by slating neighborhoods of color for lower quality education (Kozol 1992), thus reducing long-term purchasing power and credit worthiness, and restricting access to more expensive and extensive housing options and locations. All of this feeds into larger sociocultural and social structural patterns of racial discrimination in employment and promotion, again limiting access to the income, wealth, and credit that facilitates better and wider housing horizons for people of color.

These multifaceted systems of racial inequality produce the landscape of "residential apartheid" that is a key factor in allowing the owners of and investors in production and disposal facilities to target communities of color for a disproportionate share of the environmental and public health costs of production (Bullard, Grigsby and Lee 1994). At the same time, the existence of racially segregated housing patterns allows for the environmental protection of white communities, who reap a greater share of the economic benefits of production while shifting the ecological and health costs to communities of color. Underlying the race-based systems of housing distribution is an economic structure that routinely and regularly distributes environmental hazards socioeconomically downward, and environmental amenities socioeconomically upward.

The distribution of environmental hazards by social class is a normal outcome for capitalist economies. Markets, left to function on their own without state intervention, will normally distribute goods and services on the basis of wealth. The treadmill of production generates both economic benefits and environmental hazards (Schnaiberg 1980; Schnaiberg and Gould 2000; Gould, Pellow and Schnaiberg 2008). The economic benefits of production tend to be distributed up in the stratification system. Owners, managers and investors reap a greater share of the economic benefits generated by the production of goods and services than do workers. Conversely, the environmental hazards generated by the production of goods and services tend to be distributed down in the stratification system (Gould et al. 2008). The contamination of water, land, and air by toxic industrial effluents, and their consequent negative impacts on human health disproportionately impact workers and the unemployed, while owners, managers and investors are able to use the wealth gained from production to purchase housing in environmentally safe areas. Those whom cannot afford to move to such areas are forced to live with environmental hazards. In this way, each round of economic growth tends to increase the gap between rich and poor, as well as increase the gap between environmentally safe and environmentally hazardous residential spaces (Schnaiberg and Gould 2000).[2]

What makes it possible to distribute environmental hazards to workers and the poor is the segregation of housing locations. By segregating the working-class and the poor into specific residential locations away from those of the wealthy, the owners, managers, and investors are able to direct environmental contamination toward the lower socioeconomic classes and away from themselves. Were residential patterns not segregated by class, environmental hazards and their negative public health impacts would by necessity tend to be distributed more evenly across the stratification system. Similarly, without class-based residential segregation, access to neighborhood environmental amenities could not be easily reserved for the wealthy.

The class-based segregation of housing is a normal outcome of the functioning of a capitalist economy in which housing is distributed on the basis of wealth. Housing costs tend be lower in areas in close proximity to environmentally hazardous facilities such as industrial plants, waste dumps, and sewage treatment plants. In general, the higher the known and obvious environmental risks in an area, the lower the cost of housing. Housing costs in relatively environmentally safe areas at greater distances from hazardous facilities tend to command a higher price in housing markets. Housing abutting environmental amenities such as well-maintained parks, greenways, and clean waterfronts come at a premium, especially in congested urban areas. As a result, the poor and working-class are quite constrained in their choice of housing location and restricted to living in those areas with greater environmental and health risks and lower access to environmental amenities. Those earning higher wages or receiving their income from investments have greater freedom to choose among more and less desirable housing locations. With the option to do so, wealthy individuals will tend to choose to live where environmental risks are lower, and environmental amenities are greater. If an area previously believed to offer low risk of exposure to environmental hazards is later found to be contaminated, those with greater wealth will be able to move to a less hazardous location. Those with less wealth will be forced to remain in the contaminated area (Szasz 1994). In this way the structure of housing markets functions to continually reinforce and deepen the class-based distribution of exposure to environmental hazards as the wealthy exercise an exposure "exit option" that is unavailable to the lower classes (see figure 6.1). Conversely, if environmental amenities are created or restored in a previously poor or working-class community, the value of that real estate is necessarily increased, as the environmental amenity makes the location more attractive to a larger market. As demand for housing with easy access to an environmental amenity increases, real estate and rental prices are pushed upward. Existing residents without the means to increase the share of their incomes spent on rent are forced to abandon their neighborhoods to make room for new, wealthier residents. Additionally, as the market values of homes near a restored environmental amenity rise, incentive for existing homeowners to sell increases, further increasing the likelihood that houses and neighborhoods will be "flipped." Market forces in general, and real estate markets in particular, therefore tend to respond to ecological restoration by redistributing access to previously degraded environmental amenities away from existing poor, working-class, and middle-class residents to wealthier in-migrants able to afford the inflated housing costs that environmental improvements have generated (see figure 6.2).

As noted above, a combination of racial discrimination in lending and real estate practices (rooted in exploiting racism to boost profitability) limits

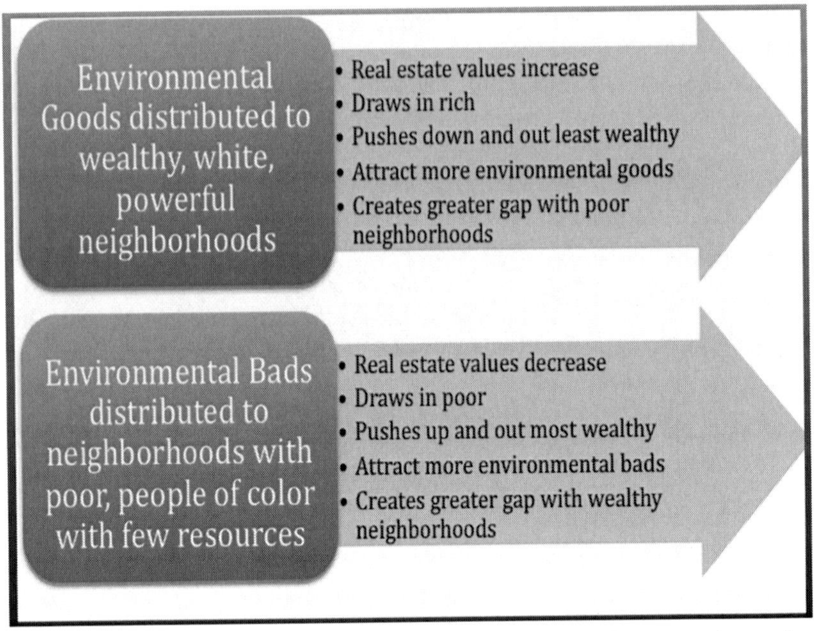

Figure 6.1. Distribution of mobile environmental goods/bads creates increasing gap between affluent and poor neighborhoods.

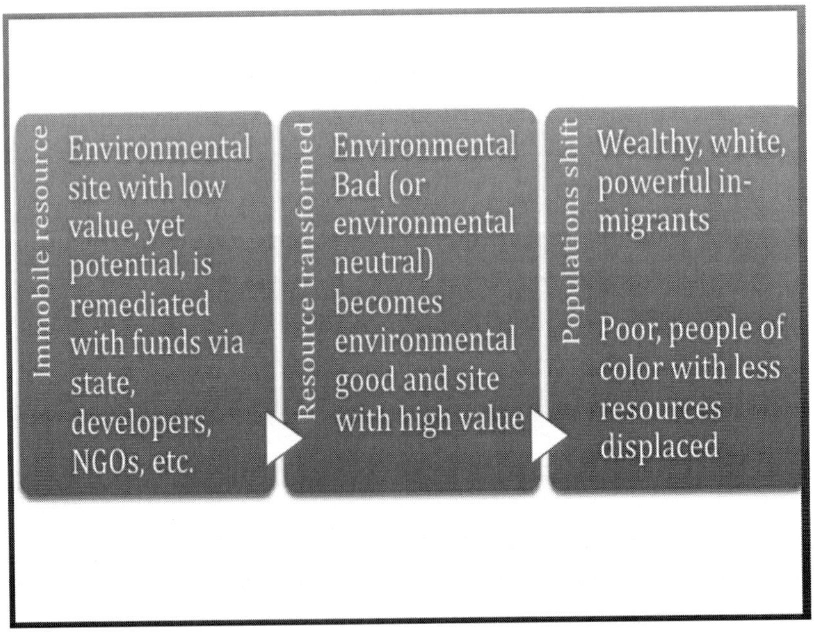

Figure 6.2. Changes in distribution of benefits of immobile environmental resource when it changes from an environmental bad (or environmental neutral) to an environmental good via remediation/restoration.

the housing market for people of color. The structure of the economy limits the ability of the poor and working-class to avoid exposure to environmental hazards, and institutional and cultural racism serves to limit the ability of people of color to avoid exposure to environmental hazards. Since poor people of color experience both forms of restriction both independently and synergistically (in terms of racism reducing access to the means by which to increase class status, most notably education, employment, and credit), it is they who have the least capacity to avoid exposure to environmental hazards, and the least capacity to exercise an "exit option" when hazards are identified. Conversely, these same synergistic and independent processes of racial and class discrimination in housing options make it less possible for people of color, especially poor, working-class, and middle-class people of color to move into neighborhoods which offer easy access to environmental amenities, or to remain in neighborhoods in which environmental amenities have been added or restored. Ecological remediation of potential environmental amenities is therefore likely not only to redistribute access to the amenity through residential access to those with greater wealth, but in doing so (and independently) such environmental improvements are likely to redistribute access to the amenity and surrounding residential spaces from people of color to white in-migrants.[3]

THE SOCIAL GEOGRAPHY OF POWER

In capitalist societies, wealth is a primary component of power. Those with greater economic power have a greater ability to influence the state, even in ostensibly democratic political systems (Domhoff 1998). Power to control patterns of capital investment, to control the creation and distribution of employment, to finance electoral campaigns, and to purchase mass media time and space provides the wealthy with greater access to, and influence over public policy decision-makers. While greater political power accrues to those with greater wealth, greater wealth also accrues to those with greater political power. Residential segregation concentrates the politically powerful in specific communities (Domhoff 1998), while simultaneously concentrating the politically less powerful in other communities. The distribution of political power and the distribution of housing location synergistically generate a spatial distribution of power. In theory, it should be possible to map this distribution as a social geography of political power.

The distribution of distinct spatial locations of political power within and between various neighborhoods is a normal outgrowth of the functioning of a market economy. This result produces neighborhoods with limited capacities to reject the imposition of environmental hazards and to affect the restoration of environmental amenities, while simultaneously creating neighborhoods with enormous capacity to control their own environmental trajectories. The more powerful neighborhoods will be home to politicians, lawyers, doctors, real estate developers, and other professionals who may be mobilized as a political resource in efforts to repel the siting of locally unwanted land uses (LULU) or to initiate the remediation of degraded environmental resources. The less powerful less wealthy neighborhoods are less likely to have such human capital resources immediately at their disposal (Pastor, Sadd and Hipp 2001). This lack of professional human capital resources makes those neighborhoods more vulnerable to state and industry efforts to site LULUs in close proximity to their residential locations. This unequal spatial distribution of power may operate in two ways. First, those seeking to locate a hazardous facility may apply their sense of the spatial geography of power to choose siting locations where low levels of effective political resistance are likely (Cerrell Associates and Powell 1984). In this way, the existence of potentially mobilizeable power is sufficient to keep environmental hazards out of wealthier neighborhoods. The environmental trajectory of gentrified urban neighborhoods is therefore "greener." Poorer, less powerful neighborhoods are, conversely, more likely to be targeted for hazardous facility siting as decision-makers anticipate the political resistance of more powerful neighborhoods (Lake 1996, Pulido 1996). The neighborhoods to which those displaced by gentrification are forced to relocate are therefore likely to have "browner" environmental trajectories. Second, more powerful neighborhoods, if chosen as the preferred location for the siting of such a facility may mobilize their economic and political resources to effectively defeat the siting effort. Less powerful poor communities, lacking the economic resources, political connections, and professional human capital resources which may bolster an effort to prevent a facility siting, will be less able to mount a successful rejection campaign. The outcome of the unequal spatial distribution of political power is a further reinforcement of the economic tendency to distribute environmental and public health risks to poor and working-class populations.

Less wealthy and less powerful communities of color will clearly find it difficult to effectively fight for the ecological restoration of environmental amenities in their urban neighborhoods. Poor and working-class communities of color possess limited resources, and greater policy attention will be focused on the environmental demands of wealthier neighborhoods. Additionally, policymakers have incentive to retain the important functions that environmentally degraded neighborhoods play in the greater metropolis as spaces to where the environmental risks that are unwanted by wealthier communities may be distributed. Therefore, community-based, grassroots struggles for green-space or waterfront restoration in poor neighborhoods face a daunting uphill battle. Environmentally motivated community activists from wealthier neighborhoods may be enlisted to join the battle to restore urban environments, but arguments resting on purely ecological and quality of life grounds may fall short in a policy arena that responds to power, profit, and economic growth. However, with the potential profit to be realized from environmental restoration for real estate investors and developers, efforts for the rehabilitation of environmental amenities may attract other external allies. Ecological remediation can make entire neighborhoods more attractive and more valuable, thus holding out the promise for fusing economic growth priorities with environmental values. However, from its conception, the social trajectory of such ecological renewal is to combine the improvement of the environment with the dislocation of the urban residents who inhabit it. Neighborhoods may be environmentally rehabilitated, but for newcomers with resources, not for those who currently live with the degraded amenity.

GREEN GENTRIFICATION

We use the term "green gentrification" to describe urban gentrification processes that are facilitated in large part by the creation or restoration of an environmental amenity. Rather than cases in which already gentrified neighborhoods develop constituencies for local environmental amenities (where gentrification leads to greening), our focus is primarily on cases in which a significant "greening event" leads to gentrification. In cases in which the gentrification process *may* be in the earliest stage, it is often difficult to tease out the causal direction (i.e., whether gentrification leads to greening or greening to gentrification.) We do not doubt that gentrification can lead to greening. In the 1980s, the Park Slope neighborhood adjacent to Prospect Park showed early signs of gentrification (in terms of shifting constituencies) at the same time the City and a nonprofit organization were starting to raise funds for redevelopment of Prospect Park. The neighborhood gentrification and the park redevelopment contributed to each other; i.e., the nascent gentrification created a demand for greening and the greening increased the gentrification, though it is not clear which came first. In addition to this iterative growth process, we argue that greening has an independent and direct effect on gentrification. In other words, a "greening event," on its own, can create gentrification.[4] Nevertheless, both causal directions have distributional implications. They both have the effect of providing greater access to environmental amenities to richer, more powerful groups. In green gentrification, existing and potential environmental amenities price out the current group of residents and draw in a wealthier group, with the displaced becoming a new form of "environmental refugees" forced to flee from enhanced environmental improvements, which increase quality of life and property values. In many instances, such green-led redevelopment is intentional, as investors and public officials create new or renewed green spaces as a means to raise property values and tax revenues. For example, as we discuss later, the original idea for Prospect Park emerged as a gentrification scheme in which the establishment of a green amenity would attract wealthy residents and boost real estate values in Brooklyn. The success of the park generated high quality housing stock that would later provide the infrastructure for waves of gentrification. Clearly, there are many causes of gentrification. Historical architecture, proximity to transportation, and cycles of investment are some of these (see Zukin 1987 and Smith 1996). Our purpose here is to show the impacts and implications of "greening" as an element of gentrification.

The concept of "green gentrification" builds on the idea of "gentrification." There are numerous ways that gentrification has been described. A definition we find useful for its emphasis on the distributional impacts is the one Tom Angotti uses in his book about New York City real estate processes, *New York for Sale.* Angotti explains gentrification:

> Throughout the city's history, working people without wealth have been shunted from one city tenement to another, especially after they make improvements to their housing and neighborhood. As tenants and small business owners invest their time and money to gradually upgrade their neighborhoods, real estate investors become attracted to these areas and anxious to capitalize on the improvements. As investors large and small move in, they effectively appropriate the value generated by others. This is the essence of what is now known as *gentrification.* It is not simply a change in demographics. It is *the appropriation of economic value by one class from another* (2008: 108).

"Green" gentrification is different than the gentrification that Angotti describes in that the "greening" of the amenity is not necessarily due to the actions of "tenants and small business owners," rather the "greening" comes primarily from outside investors (public and private) who appropriate the value of an [unrevitalized] environmental resource. In this sense it is the *appropriation of the economic values of an environmental resource by one class from another*. As we will illustrate with the case of Prospect Park, calls for environmental restoration draw state resources aimed at producing an urban environmental amenity that are then appropriated by extra-local capital interests (both developers and in-migrants).[5]

RACE, CLASS, AND ENVIRONMENTAL CHANGE IN BROOKLYN

Brooklyn is the most populous of New York City's five boroughs, and has been a site of constant, often dramatic, economic, and demographic change throughout its history. In the post-World War II era, Brooklyn experienced steady and dramatic deindustrialization, lead by the shifting of port facilities to New Jersey and the closing of the Brooklyn Navy Yards. Most older Brooklynites mark the end of a romanticized era by the defection of the Brooklyn Dodgers to Los Angeles in 1957. Throughout the 1960s and 1970s the borough experienced a steady population decline, fueled by reduced economic opportunities, and white flight. Many of Brooklyn's white ethnic residents moved to the expanding suburbs of Long Island and New Jersey, or relocated to the borough of Staten Island, facilitated by the opening of the Verrazano Narrows Bridge in 1964. By 1981 Brooklyn's population began to rebound, largely due to a wave of immigration from the Caribbean that would eventually give Brooklyn the largest Caribbean population outside of the Caribbean itself.

As higher wage manufacturing jobs gave way to lower wage service employment, the demographic profile of Brooklyn became poorer and less white. The well-known cycle of urban decay proceeded, with steady disinvestment following New York City's economic crisis of the 1970s, and steady increases in crime and aid dependency. The perception of most public officials was that Brooklyn was in "decline." That decline took its toll on Brooklyn's substantial environmental amenities as well, such as Prospect Park.

Of course, economic decline can be parlayed into economic opportunity, and gentrifiers were able to claim some of Brooklyn's high quality housing stock at relatively low costs while in disrepair. However, major reinvestment in Brooklyn did not emerge until the 1990's, marked by the downtown construction of the Metrotech center (in the corner of Brooklyn closest to Manhattan's financial district). Efforts to reinvigorate Brooklyn's economy and attract investment were not limited to office parks. Investment in Brooklyn's premiere nature park was also part of the redevelopment push in an era in which urban environmental amenities were increasingly recognized as valuable. As real estate prices in Manhattan pushed wealthy whites over the bridges into Brooklyn, and the attacks of 9/11 made lower Manhattan even less attractive, a wave of gentrification in Brooklyn ensued. By 2002 there were sufficient push and pull factors in place to set off a major wave of real estate investment and a major redistribution of housing. In the first half of the first decade of the new century, unemployment in Brooklyn fell, the number of jobs increased, and so did wages (Brooklyn Chamber of Commerce 2006). Not only was existing housing stock increasingly colonized by in-migrants into formerly less wealthy neighborhoods, but also some of that housing stock was purchased by developers for a wave of new construction. The number of new residential building permits issued for Brooklyn doubled from 2001 to 2005 (Brooklyn Chamber of Commerce 2006). By 2005, Brooklyn had more new residential units permitted for construction than Manhattan (Brooklyn Chamber of Commerce 2006).

Brooklyn clearly manifests the geography of racial and class residential segregation, despite its remarkable diversity. While market forces in Brooklyn real estate serve to generate residential class segregation, overt and covert racism in the real estate industry serve to generate greater residential racial segregation. The wave of gentrification and residential redevelopment in Brooklyn has redistributed housing location along racial lines, and often quite intentionally. For example, from 2003 to 2006, the National Fair Housing Alliance (NFHA) conducted a study of housing segregation and racial discrimination in twelve cities. The NFHA found one of the largest real estate firms operating in Brooklyn to be engaged in "discriminatory real estate sales practices, including limited service, lack of follow-up, and withholding of housing information" in regard to its African-American clients (NFHA 2006: 4).

> In Brooklyn, NFHA's testing of the Corcoran Group Real Estate, a member of NRT, Inc., revealed that real estate agents steered home buyers by race and denied basic services to African-Americans. Throughout NFHA's investigations, NRT, Inc. has proven time and time again that it maintains a pattern and practice of discrimination based on race (NFHA 2006: 4).

In the midst of Brooklyn's wave of gentrification, one of its largest real estate firms was found to be deeply engaged in the intentional racial restructuring of the borough. Corcoran's red-lined map (discovered by NFHA in a sting operation) clearly marks neighborhoods adjacent to recently restored environmental amenities such as a rehabilitated Prospect Park, and green-space redesignated piers (Brooklyn Bridge Park) as places to which white in-migrants should be resettled (Cohen 2006). Corcoran's racial steering illustrates the spatial relationship between redeveloped urban environmental amenities and the redevelopment of urban neighborhoods for new, white, residents.

PROSPECT PARK

The idea of Prospect Park was conceived in the 1850s and construction began in 1866.[6] At the time, Brooklyn was a separate city from Manhattan, and leaders in the two cities competed on all fronts. A builder and railroad constructor (a.k.a., early developer), James Stranahan, wanted Brooklyn to have a park that rivaled Manhattan's new Central Park, to draw the wealthy and to increase property values. He wanted the park to "hold out strong inducements to the affluent to remain in our city, who are now too often induced to change their residences by the seductive influences of the New York [Central] park" (Berenson and deMause 2001). The original motivation for the park was clearly tied to creating wealth in Brooklyn via housing distribution.

By the time of Prospect Park's 100th anniversary, the Park's infrastructure had been neglected and as a result, visits to the Park dropped in the late 1970s to the lowest in its history (less than 2 million visitors per year). The Park had developed a reputation as a crime-ridden home to drug dealing and homeless encampments, a dangerous place to be avoided. In the 1970s and 80s, reportage on the park was distinctly negative. Local papers routinely reported on murders, bicycle thefts, muggings, and purse snatching in the park, deepening the park's image as a social hazard rather than an environmental amenity. In October of 1980, the New York Times ran a series of articles addressing the decay of New York's parks, bemoaning the fact that "these once glorious urban oases are now unsightly and dangerous dumps" (*New York Times* 1980: A30).

In response to concerns raised by local citizens, the City, under Mayor Ed Koch, committed $10 million for restoration projects. The New York Times announced that start of Prospect Park restoration with the headline "For Prospect Park, $10 Million to Recapture What It Was" (Quindlen 1980: B1). According to the Prospect Park Alliance (PPA), a nonprofit organization formed in 1987, this is when the Park's renaissance officially began. By 1985, police had established antigraffiti stakeouts in Prospect Park to thwart highly visible signs of neglect and decay (Carmody 1985: B3), nearly thirteen years after Mayor Lindsay had publicly denounced graffiti in a speech at the Prospect Park boathouse (*New York Times* 1972: 30). Throughout the 1980s and 1990s, ecological restoration of the park picked up steam.

Since that time, the park has been restored as an environmental amenity. The ecological restoration of the park has included a meticulous reconstruction of Olmsted and Vaux's original design specifications, increased focus on restoring native species and controlling invasive and nonnative species, reducing soil compaction by limiting visitor's off-path access to forested areas, and restoring understory and herbaceous plants (again by limiting visitor's off-path access). The ecological and social renewal and redirection of the park have come hand in hand. "Prospect Park has successfully overcome its 1970s reputation as an unsavory place. Today more than eight million annual visitors enjoy a variety of activities and destinations, from in-line skating to nature walks, from baseball games to zoo visits, and from picnicking to volunteer projects." (www.prospectpark.org). Park programming also seeks ways to embrace the cultural diversity of Brooklyn's residents. Numerous racial and ethnic groups use the park for a variety of activities (Low et al. 2005). Today, the park is operated by the Prospect Park Alliance, a private organization in partnership with New York City. The Park reached its low point in the late 1970s, and since that time, has been transformed from an in situ socio-environmental bad with potential, to an important socio-environmental amenity.

The ecological restoration of Prospect Park helped transform the image of the park from an urban liability to an urban amenity. Park features such as the Third Street Playground became attractions for white, wealthy parents and their children (see figure 6.3), who in an earlier era, would have avoided the park. The late twentieth century image of the park as a social liability contrasts starkly with the image of the park presented by Brooklyn's booming real estate industry in the early twenty-first century. The Corcoran Group now uses proximity to Prospect Park to move real estate in Park Slope, Prospect Heights, and Prospect Park South, listing the park as one of the neighborhoods "most wonderful amenities" (Corcoran Group 2010). Fillmore Real Estate proclaims the virtues of the park's "majestic 585 acres" noting that it "includes a forest, [and] a meadow," to move real estate in the Crown Heights and Lefferts Gardens neighborhoods (Fillmore Real Estate 2010). Other real estate agencies describe Windsor Terrace as "tucked between the rolling hills and vast green spaces of Prospect Park and Greenwood Cemetery," and Prospect Park as "home to green lawns, lakes, a tennis center and endless recreational opportunities," an "urban oasis" (Prudential Douglas Elliman Real Estate 2010; Rapid Realty 2010). And Corcoran sells the new Richard Meier building as "the borough's premier address, gracing the heart of Brooklyn at

Figure 6.3. Prospect Park's Third Street Playground, Park Slope. Photograph by Ken Gould.

One Grand Army Plaza. Steps away from over 500 acres of natural parkland" (Corcoran Group 2010).

Indeed, Prospect Park has been transformed. Meticulous restoration to much of its original beauty has proceeded effectively, and continues with the construction of new skating facilities to replace those that blighted Olmstead and Vaux's original design. No longer perceived as a place one goes to get mugged, the park is vibrant with runners, bikers, skaters, baby strollers, picnickers, and others. Park users can be seen sporting thousands of dollars worth of outdoor recreation equipment seemingly without serious security concerns (see figure 6.4). Clearly, it is not the 1970s in the park anymore.

As Prospect Park was transformed from a perceived social hazard into a quality of life enhancing environmental amenity, it attracted both urban gentrifiers, and those who would profit from them. In her book, *Landscapes of Power*, Sharon Zukin notes small-scale real estate developers as a primary category of gentrifiers. She quotes one such gentrifier in Brooklyn who explains the strategy: "You find it [a building to upscale] in a neighborhood that still has problems but is close to a park . . . something that will bring in the middle class. And almost by the time you are through other buildings around it will have started to be fixed up" (Zukin, 1991: 193). In addition to rehabilitating existing structures, the restoration of the park set off a wave of new

Figure 6.4. Riders and runners in Prospect Park. Photograph by Ken Gould.

Table 6.1. Building permits issued for new residential construction by community district

Community District	*1997*	*2002*
6	2	228
7	9	165
8	0	149
9	6	41
14	18	70
Total	35	653

Source: Community District Profiles (http://www.nyc.gov/html/dcp/html/lucds/cdstart.shtml).

construction. Brooklyn's new housing construction boom was, and is, focused on a number of specific neighborhoods. The social re-taming, and ecological re-wilding of Prospect Park made many of the neighborhoods surrounding it prime targets for developers. Table 6.1 captures the onset of the new construction boom in the five community districts that border Prospect Park, illustrating a greater than 1,800 percent increase in new residential construction building permits (Brooklyn Community District Profiles 2009). As the purchase and rental costs of new construction in Brooklyn have approached those of Manhattan, the class and racial profile of the neighborhoods into which such construction has been thrust has necessarily shifted up the stratification scale.

CENSUS DATA-BASED EVALUATION OF "GREEN GENTRIFICATION"

To evaluate the degree to which green gentrification is occurring around Prospect Park, we use census data to examine three propositions. If green gentrification is occurring we expect that over time: 1) minorities will be displaced from the area surrounding the park (*greening whitens hypothesis*), 2) poor people will be displaced (*greening richens hypothesis*), and 3) rents and property values will rise (*greening raises rents hypothesis*).

We analyze census data for the five neighborhoods surrounding the park (see figure 6.5 and tables 6.2–6.7). These neighborhoods include Park Slope, Prospect Heights, Lefferts Gardens, Prospect Park South, and Windsor Terrace. Neighborhood boundaries are fluid, and shift according to the desirability of the neighborhood. For instance, as Park Slope, the gentrified neighborhood on the west side of Prospect Park, has commanded higher and higher rents and sales prices, its real estate borders have grown westward and southward. In this context, it can be tricky to define the borders of the neigh-

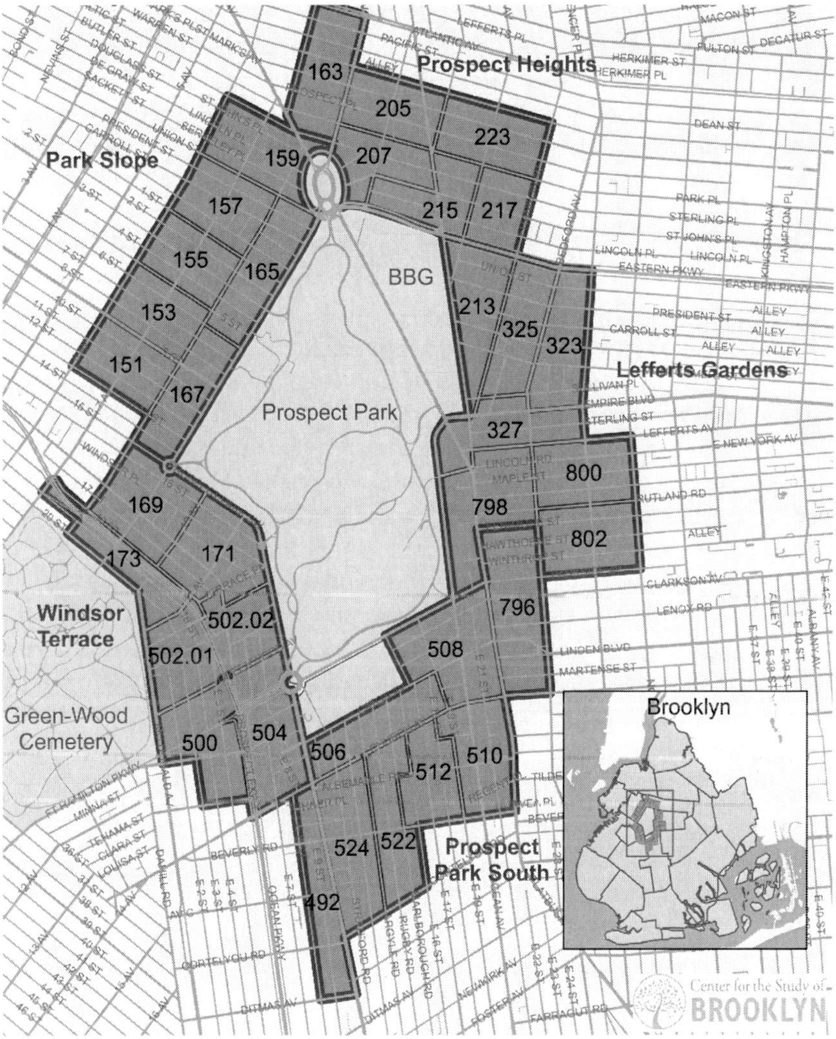

Figure 6.5. Census Tracts Adjacent to Prospect Park. ***Source:*** **Center for the Study of Brooklyn.**

borhoods around the park. In order to define the neighborhoods, we used five types of sources: 1) maps in print and on-line (see, for example, Jackson 1998), 2) real estate borders, 3) geographic boundaries, 4) census tracts, and 5) residents' self-identification. As figure 6.5 illustrates, this resulted in an examination of the area around the park within about two census tracts from the park The proximity of these neighborhoods make them most likely to experience a "park effect."

We evaluate the demographic changes from 1990 until present to see if "greening" the park also "gentrified" the neighborhoods by way of "whitening," "richening," and raising rents. We compiled census data from the U.S. Census Bureau with regard to race, class, social power, and housing for each neighborhood (see tables 6.3–6.7) to evaluate these trends. We also consider how Brooklyn changed over the same period (table 6.2) to tease out broader borough-wide changes from local changes.

Before discussing the quantitative changes, it is worth providing some background for each of these neighborhoods. Park Slope, to the west of the park, is currently one of the most sought after places to live in Brooklyn. It features restored brownstones, trendy coffee shops, Brooklyn's oldest natural food co-op, and numerous children's clothing boutiques. The park is its most important amenity, with multiple entrances to the neighborhood along Prospect Park West. This side of the park has three renovated playgrounds, the Bandshell (which houses free summer concerts), the Picnic House, a New York City landmark (Litchfield's Villa), in addition to being close to Grand Army Plaza, the focal point of the park.

Prospect Heights (the highest elevation of the park) sits at the north end of the park surrounding Grand Army Plaza, where the weekly farmers market draws thousands of visitors to buy local produce, just across from the main branch of the Brooklyn Public Library. Though there are multiple entrances around the park this is the "main" entry into the park's famous "long meadow." The entry at Grand Army Plaza also serves as the venue for community events, such as Brooklyn's New Year's eve party, where elected officials speak, local bands play, and families gather to watch the fireworks on the long meadow. Real estate agents have been aggressively expanding the boundaries of the neighborhood east, to associate more housing stock with the park.

Lefferts Gardens runs along the east side of the park. There are numerous attractions along this side of the park, such as the Carousel, the Prospect Park Zoo, and the historic Lefferts House, however, access to the park from Lefferts Gardens is limited in two ways. First, on the northeast end, the park and the neighborhood are separated by an approximately block wide swath of greenspace that contains the Brooklyn Botanic Garden (BBG). While the BBG is certainly a green amenity, it is fenced in and charges an entry fee. Residents of Lefferts Gardens north cannot walk across the BBG to enter the park, they must walk to the north, to Grand Army Plaza, or to the south, to the entry located in the center of the west side, near the Carousel. Secondly, if residents were able to cross the BBG, they would find that when they do reach the border of the park, because of the location of the Zoo, this area of the park is fenced. Thus, despite the proximity of Lefferts Gardens residents to the park, access is difficult.

Prospect Park South abuts the park at the narrow south end. The Parade Grounds, which include soccer and football fields, and the tennis center, are in Prospect Park South. The Park's lake is at the south end, and in the south east corner is the "Drummer's Grove." According to the Prospect Park website, "In 1968, the Congo Square Drummers began gathering here informally. Since then, the circle has expanded to include an ever-evolving mix of musicians, dancers, and vendors. The growing popularity of this area as a site for a weekly drumming circle inspired the Prospect Park Alliance to add seating and officially name the site. Anyone is free to bring their drums and participate, or just stop and listen while passing by on the East Drive. The Drummer's Grove was a part of a $1 million renovation of the Parkside Avenue/Ocean Avenue entrance to the Park that occurred in 1997" (www.prospectpark.org/visit/places/drummers).

Finally, Windsor Terrace sits to the south west of the park, between Prospect Park South and Park Slope, and is nearest the park's ballfields. Green-Wood Cemetery, Brooklyn's second largest green space borders the other side of Windsor Terrace. At its northern corner, is a large entryway to the park with subway access. Windsor Terrace has a reputation as a residential neighborhood where houses never go on the market because homes are bought among family members, neighbors, and friends.

The five neighborhoods adjoining Prospect Park each responded to the restoration of the green space as an environmental amenity. The extent to which greening whitened, richened, and raised rents in Prospect Park neighborhoods varied, in part, due to the variations in ease of park access and pre-existing demographics.

Does greening whiten? In the period from the 1990 Census until the American Community Survey estimates in 2005/9, the population of Brooklyn increased by about ten percent. The populations of three of the park neighborhoods grew; Park Slope, Prospect Heights, and Windsor Terrace all grew by around 8 percent.

Racially, Brooklyn became less "White" and less "Black." In 1990 almost 47 percent of the Brooklyn population was white and the most recent figure is 44 percent. For blacks, the percentages are 38 percent and 35 percent, respectively. These figures probably reflect changes in the data collection method, since now respondents must respond "white only" and "black only" in an effort to identify the increasing biracial population. Also, the Hispanic and Asian populations of Brooklyn increased during this time. Despite the borough-wide decreases in whites (a 5 percent drop over time), around the Park the percentage of whites increased in three of the five neighborhoods (Prospect Heights, Lefferts Gardens, and Prospect Park South). The population of whites in these neighborhoods increased by 109 percent, 98 percent,

Table 6.2. Demographic Changes in Brooklyn, 1970–2005/9

	Brooklyn	*1970*	*1980*	*1990*	*2000*	*2005/9*	*% Change 1990–2005/9*
	Population	2,602,012	2,230,936	2,300,664	2,465,326	2,538,140	10.3%
Race	White	73.8%	56.0%	46.90%	41.2%	44.4%	–5.3%
	Black	25.2%	32.4%	37.9%	36.4%	34.7%	–8.4%
Class	Median household income (1999 $)	$25,000–49,999	$27,414	$34,508	$32,135	$33,310	–3.5%
	Families below poverty line	13.9%	15.5%	19.5%	22.0%	18.6%	–4.6%
Social Power	Bachelors degree or higher	27%	11.6%	16.5%	21.9%	28.3%	71.5%
Housing	Owner occupied housing units	24%	23.4%	26.1%	27.1%	30.8%	18.0%
	Median gross rent (1999 $)	$300 or more	$460–$573	$608	$650	$759	24.8%
	Median single family owner occupied home value	$50,000 or more	not available	$248,052	$229,200	$424,931	71.3%

Notes: There are some differences among the years: For 1970, the college rate is inflated. The category reported here is for percentage "college," which could include only some college. For other years, it is BA or higher. For 1970, median family income is calculated from aggregated data, thus only a range is available. For 1980, the Bachelors degree or higher is based on those responding that they had completed "4 or more years" college. For 1990, the median value is for "specified owner occupied housing." This excludes "housing units in multi-unit buildings" and therefore is probably a higher report. For 2000 and 2005/9, white = "white alone" and black = "black alone."
Sources: Social Explorer, 1980, 1990, 2000, and 2005/9 (American Community Survey).

Table 6.3. Demographic Changes in Park Slope, 1970–2005/9

	Park Slope	*1970*	*1980*	*1990*	*2000*	*2005/9*	*% Change 1990–2005/9*
	Population	37,068	29,255	28,767	28,272	30,960	7.6%
Race	White	86.8%	79.5%	81.9%	79.5%	81.6%	–0.4%
	Black	10.9%	11.0%	9.2%	7.5%	6.4%	–30.4%
Class	Median household income (1999 $)	$25,000–49,999	$37,829	$60,311	$68,580	$83,566	38.6%
	Families below poverty line	11.8%	6.7%	4.6%	2.6%	2.5%	–45.7%
Social Power	Bachelors degree or higher	51.9%	43.4%	63%	73.5%	79.4%	25.2%
Housing	Owner occupied housing units	17.1%	19.6%	35.2%	37.9%	49.0%	39.2%
	Median gross rent (1999 $)			$840	$1,006	$1,274	51.7%
	Median single family owner occupied home value	$50,000 or more	not available	$584,997	$387,344	$696,152	19.0%

Notes: There are some differences among the years: For 1970, the college rate is inflated. The category reported here is for percentage "college," which could include only some college. For other years, it is BA or higher. For 1970, median family income is calculated from aggregated data, thus only a range is available. For 1980, the Bachelors degree or higher is based on those responding that they had completed "4 or more years" college. For 1990, the median value is for "specified owner occupied housing." This excludes "housing units in multi-unit buildings" and therefore is probably a higher report. For 2000 and 2005/9, white = "white alone" and black = "black alone."
Sources: Social Explorer, 1980, 1990, 2000, and 2005/9 (American Community Survey).

Table 6.4. Demographic Changes in Prospect Heights, 1970–2005/9

	Prospect Heights	*1970*	*1980*	*1990*	*2000*	*2005/9*	*% Change 1990–2005/9*
	Population	29,740	24,246	23,779	23,734	25,597	7.6%
Race	White	36.3%	16.0%	18%	21.3%	37.9%	109.4%
	Black	61.1%	76.9%	74.3%	64.2%	46.5%	−37.4%
Class	Median household income (1999 $)	$25,000–49,999	$22,916	$38,252	$41,618	$47,458	24.1%
	Families below poverty line	17.1%	25.6%	18.3%	16.3%	12.9%	−29.5%
Social Power	Bachelors degree or higher	35.5%	13.3%	29.6%	38.8%	49.4%	66.9%
Housing	Owner occupied housing units	6.9%	8.6%	18.0%	18.6%	27.1%	50.6%
	Median gross rent (1999 $)			$614	$730	$865	40.9%
	Median single family owner occupied home value	$50,000 or more	not available	$399,969	$237,962	$419,436	4.9%

Notes: There are some differences among the years: For 1970, the college rate is inflated. The category reported here is for percentage "college," which could include only some college. For other years, it is BA or higher. For 1970, median family income is calculated from aggregated data, thus only a range is available. For 1980, the Bachelors degree or higher is based on those responding that they had completed "4 or more years" college. For 1990, the median value is for "specified owner occupied housing." This excludes "housing units in multi-unit buildings" and therefore is probably a higher report. For 2000 and 2005/9, white = "white alone" and black = "black alone."
Sources: Social Explorer, 1980, 1990, 2000, and 2005/9 (American Community Survey).

Table 6.5. Demographic Changes in Lefferts Gardens, 1970–2005/9

	Lefferts Gardens	*1970*	*1980*	*1990*	*2000*	*2005/9*	*% Change 1990–2005/9*
	Population	35,172	34,758	39,368	36,842	36,119	−8.3%
Race	White	41.9%	6.9%	3.7%	3.6%	8.3%	97.8%
	Black	56.1%	87.4%	92.3%	89.3%	83.5%	−9.5%
Class	Median household income (1999 $)	$25,000–49,999	$27,540	$37,326	$30,709	$32,195	−13.7%
	Families below poverty line	9.9%	4.9%	15.7%	20.9%	15.5%	−1.3%
Social Power	Bachelors degree or higher	44.4%	11.5%	16.2%	15.7%	24.5%	51.2%
Housing	Owner occupied housing units	11.2%	11.4%	13.5%	13.5%	10.9%	−19.3%
	Median gross rent (1999 $)			$614	$632	$737	20.0%
	Median single family owner occupied home value	$50,000 or more	not available	$260,029	$224,634	$525,835	102.2%

Notes: There are some differences among the years: For 1970, the college rate is inflated. The category reported here is for percentage "college," which could include only some college. For other years, it is BA or higher. For 1970, median family income is calculated from aggregated data, thus only a range is available. For 1980, the Bachelors degree or higher is based on those responding that they had completed "4 or more years" college. For 1990, the median value is for "specified owner occupied housing." This excludes "housing units in multi-unit buildings" and therefore is probably a higher report. For 2000 and 2005/9, white = "white alone" and black = "black alone."
Sources: Social Explorer, 1980, 1990, 2000, and 2005/9 (American Community Survey).

Table 6.6. Demographic Changes in Prospect Park South, 1970–2005/9

	Prospect Park South	*1970*	*1980*	*1990*	*2000*	*2005/9*	*% Change 1990–2005/9*
	Population	40,828	44,856	55,775	53,352	51,236	−8.1%
Race	White	92.1%	24.0%	13.6%	11.2%	17.9%	31.6%
	Black	56.1%	59.6%	74.5%	70.6%	65.3%	−12.3%
Class	Median household income (1999 $)	$25,000–49,999	$26,355	$35,656	$28,540	$32,288	−9.4%
	Families below poverty line	7.3%	21.7%	18.0%	26.1%	21.9%	21.7%
Social Power	Bachelors degree or higher	46.9%	13.6%	15.4%	13.1%	22.5%	46.1%
Housing	Owner occupied housing units	6.9%	6.7%	8.70%	8.4%	10.3%	18.4%
	Median gross rent (1999 $)			$650	$673	$767	18.0%
	Median single family owner occupied home value	$50,000 or more	not available	$309,667	$242,374	$433,556	40.0%

Notes: There are some differences among the years: For 1970, the college rate is inflated. The category reported here is for percentage "college," which could include only some college. For other years, it is BA or higher. For 1970, median family income is calculated from aggregated data, thus only a range is available. For 1980, the Bachelors degree or higher is based on those responding that they had completed "4 or more years" college. For 1990, the median value is for "specified owner occupied housing." This excludes "housing units in multi-unit buildings" and therefore is probably a higher report. For 2000 and 2005/9, white = "white alone" and black = "black alone."
Sources: Social Explorer, 1980, 1990, 2000, and 2005/9 (American Community Survey).

Table 6.7. Demographic Changes in Windsor Terrace, 1970–2005/9

	Windsor Terrace	*1970*	*1980*	*1990*	*2000*	*2005/9*	*% Change 1990–2005/9*
	Population	22,890	20,522	19,743	20,545	23,571	19.4%
Race	White	99%	86.0%	80.2%	69.6%	74.3%	–7.4%
	Black	0.7%	5.1%	8.90%	8.8%	6.3%	–29.2%
Class	Median household income (1999 $)	$25,000–49,999	$33,418	$44,884	$48,052	$55,577	23.8%
	Families below poverty line	6.6%	11.4%	6.7%	7.7%	10.3%	53.7%
Social Power	Bachelors degree or higher	33.4%	14%	29.3%	40.7%	52.0%	77.5%
Housing	Owner occupied housing units	27.1%	27.1%	35.7%	35.2%	49.2%	37.8%
	Median gross rent (1999 $)			$682	$788	$889	30.4%
	Median single family owner occupied home value	$50,000 or more	not available	$237,969	$227,076	$477,276	100.6%

Notes: There are some differences among the years: For 1970, the college rate is inflated. The category reported here is for percentage "college," which could include only some college. For other years, it is BA or higher. For 1970, median family income is calculated from aggregated data, thus only a range is available. For 1980, the Bachelors degree or higher is based on those responding that they had completed "4 or more years" college. For 1990, the median value is for "specified owner occupied housing." This excludes "housing units in multi-unit buildings" and therefore is probably a higher report. For 2000 and 2005/9, white = "white alone" and black = "black alone."
Sources: Social Explorer, 1980, 1990, 2000, and 2005/9 (American Community Survey).

and 32 percent respectively. These neighborhoods had relatively small percentages of whites in 1990 (18 percent, 4 percent, and 14 percent). The two neighborhoods whose white population percentage decreased (Park Slope and Windsor Terrace) already had high percentages of whites in 1990 (82 percent and 80 percent). The decline was very small for Park Slope (from 81.9 percent to 81.6 percent), but larger for Windsor Terrace (from 80 to 74 percent). In short, the overwhelmingly white neighborhoods around the park became slightly less white between 1990 and 2005, while the nonwhite neighborhoods became substantially more white. The whitening of Prospect Heights was particularly dramatic in this period.

In terms of the change in black population around the park, all of the five neighborhoods showed losses. The percentage decrease in black population in the borough overall was 8 percent; all of the neighborhoods surrounding Prospect Park had a higher percentage decrease. The three blackest neighborhoods in 1990 decreased by large percentages. Prospect Heights was 74 percent black in 1990 and by 2005/09 this percentage had decreased to 46 percent, a percentage change of 37 percent. Lefferts Gardens went from 92 percent black to 83 percent black, almost a ten percent decrease. Prospect Park South's black population also declined: from 74 percent to 65 percent, a 12 percent decline from 1990. The very white neighborhoods (Park Slope and Windsor Terrace), which already had small percentages of blacks, both had around 30 percent decreases in the percentage of blacks. In sum, even though the percentage of blacks declined in the borough, the neighborhoods around Prospect Park lost blacks at a far greater rate. By the end of the period of major Prospect Park restoration, Prospect Heights was no longer a majority black neighborhood. In the case of the restoration of Prospect Park as an urban environmental amenity, the census data support the claim that greening whitens.

Does greening richen? Income levels on tables 6.2–6.7 are adjusted for inflation and reported in 1999 dollars. In Brooklyn, median household income declined from $34,000 to $33,000 over the 1990 to 2005/9 period. We see a pattern emerge around the park. The two whitest neighborhoods (Park Slope and Windsor Terrace) and the neighborhood experiencing the greatest "whitening" (Prospect Heights) have income increases, while the two blackest neighborhoods show income decreases (Lefferts Gardens and Prospect Park South). The median incomes of Lefferts Gardens and Prospect Park South are very close to that of Brooklyn's overall. Park Slope, which started with the highest median income ($60,000) had the highest percentage increase (39 percent) and the highest ending income in 2005/9 ($83,000). Windsor Terrace, which started with the second highest median income (around $45,000), increased 24 percent to almost $56,000. Prospect Heights and Lefferts Gardens started similarly (around $37–$38,000), but they diverged over this period: Prospect Heights increased 24 percent to end at $47 thousand (well above Brooklyn's median), but Lefferts Gardens dropped 14 percent to end just below the borough median. Prospect Park South also declined by 9 percent over the period. This pattern of median income change reflects growing inequality and a declining middle class nationally. The richest neighborhoods became richer, the poorest neighborhoods became poorer, and the neighborhood experiencing the most dramatic whitening also became much wealthier. In terms of poverty, Brooklyn had almost 19 percent of families below the poverty line in 2005/9. With the exception of Prospect Park South (22 percent below poverty), all of the neighborhoods are below that rate, with Park Slope having the lowest level (2.5 percent).

Greening appears to have richened three of the neighborhoods: Park Slope, Windsor Terrace, and Prospect Heights. It did not richen Lefferts Gardens or Prospect Park South. Prospect Heights is an interesting case to explore. Why did it richen while Lefferts Gardens and Prospect Park South did not? Here the relationship between race and class would appear to be quite evident. Of the three majority black neighborhoods, the one that most dramatically lost black population (Prospect Heights), leaving it no longer majority black at the end of the 1990–2005/9 period, became substantially richer. The neighborhood adjacent to Prospect Park that experienced the smallest percentage of decrease in black population, Lefferts Gardens, had the largest decrease in median income in the same period.

Does greening raise rents (and home values)? The impact of urban environmental amenities on the trajectory of home values and rents is a primary engine of redistribution of environmental goods. Across the borough, controlling for inflation, median home values increased by 71 percent from 1990 to 2005/9. Values also increased around the park. The largest percentage gains were in Lefferts Gardens and Windsor Terrace, which outpaced the increases in Brooklyn, both at least doubling the median value. Lefferts Gardens exceeds Brooklyn's median value by over $100,000 and Park Slope exceeds it by over a quarter million dollars (although the percentage of owner occupied homes in Lefferts Gardens is only 11 percent compared to Park Slope's 49 percent). Windsor Terrace exceeds the borough median by $50,000 and Prospect Heights and Prospect Park South were around Brooklyn's median. The percentage of owner occupied housing units in Brooklyn increased over the period from 27 percent to 31 percent. All of the park neighborhoods also increased in percentage of owner occupied housing, with very high ownership rates in Park Slope and Windsor Terrace (both 49 percent). Lefferts Gardens and Prospect Park South were well below the Brooklyn average (11 percent and 10 percent respectively).

Another important indicator of housing value is median rent. In Brooklyn rents increased 25 percent over the 1990–2005/9 period. Lefferts Gardens and Prospect Park South track closely to Brooklyn's changes in median gross rent in terms of both actual dollar amounts and changes over time. Bigger increases and higher rents are seen in Windsor Terrace (30 percent increase), Prospect Heights (41 percent increase) and Park Slope (52 percent increase). In 2005/9, the median rent in Park Slope is $1274. In the case of Prospect Park restoration, urban greening appears to have raised rents.

During the period of major Prospect Park restoration as an urban environmental amenity, access to housing near that amenity became increasingly restricted to those situated higher on the socioeconomic stratification pyramid. Although increases in median gross rent in Lefferts Gardens tracked below the increase for Brooklyn as a whole (20 percent versus 25 percent), the simultaneous decline in income in the blackest neighborhood surrounding Prospect Park during the same period indicates that it became increasingly difficult for Lefferts Gardens residents to remain in their neighborhood (as rising rents ate larger and larger shares of declining incomes).

CONCLUSIONS

As our model of green gentrification would predict, many former near-Prospect Park residents experienced reduced access to Brooklyn's premier green space as a result of park renewal efforts. As working-class and minority residents are progressively priced further back from environmental amenities, it becomes evident that urban greening and the reclaiming and renewal of urban environmental amenities are broadly negatively redistributive policies. If not by intent, then by effect, urban greening tends to increase environmental inequality, reduce the access of poor and working class communities and communities of color to environmental amenities, and dissolve communities to make way for new, wealthier residents. The combination of market-forces in urban real estate, institutional and cultural racism, and urban environmental policy can be a powerful tool of urban renewal and urban removal, with the "greening" of urban areas becoming code for the "whitening" of neighborhoods. This is not to say that outcomes could not be different with appropriate policy interventions.

As calls for environmental justice expand from the focus on the distribution of environmental hazards to include demands for more equitable distribution of environmental amenities, processes of green gentrification have clear implications for community-based urban environmental justice groups seeking to generate more local environmental goods. The success of activists in poor and working-class communities of color in achieving remediation of parks, waterfronts, or other local environmental amenities, or in gaining the establishment of new green-spaces in urban environments, is likely to be followed by the green gentrification processes examined here. Efforts at achieving community quality of life improvements may thus be converted into community disintegration, as urban growth machines seize upon greening as an opportunity for profit. Under such conditions, the restoration of urban environmental amenities might be properly viewed as an environmental bad, posing a greater threat to community stability than the siting of some LULUs. Environmental justice activists will therefore need to be vigilant to prevent green gentrification processes from turning their efforts on their heads.

Policy that responds to public intervention can make a difference in the outcomes of green gentrification. In 2005, the Williamsburg-Greenpoint development on the northeast Brooklyn waterfront was approved by the Zoning Commission (see DeSena 2009). It is an important case to follow because "The zoning text change adopted by the Commission and the City Council includes a groundbreaking Inclusionary Housing program, reflecting recommendations made during the public review process. The program promotes affordable units in both rental and condominium developments, encourages preservation of existing affordable units, and targets affordable housing to a range of income levels" (New York City Department of Public Planning).[7]

Unfortunately, no such policy interventions were put in place in regard to the restoration of Prospect Park, and the trajectory of near-park neighborhoods indicates that affordable housing near Brooklyn's largest environmental amenity is rapidly waning. The renewal of Prospect Park, which used public and private funds, involved no redesignation of existing land uses (i.e., from industrial to residential or to public green space). As an existing island of newly attractive green space, the restoration project was less available to public intervention to preserve existing patterns of distribution of access to the amenity, and the fate of surrounding neighborhoods was left to real estate market forces. Although the park is under the jurisdiction of the city's Parks and Recreation Department, it is managed by the Prospect Park Alliance, which can make decisions about the park without public input (O'Neill 2011). One can only hope that the lessons from the distributional consequences of the restoration of Prospect Park will be utilized by other communities (such as Gowanus), as environmental restoration plans are proposed and implemented in their neighborhoods. Alternatively, the real estate profitability consequences of the restoration of Prospect Park will serve as a model of, and incentive for, residential displacement and upward distribution of access to urban environmental amenities, illustrating the viability of using urban greening as a method of attack on the urban poor, working-class, and communities of color.

Often presented to the public as urban sustainability projects, the restoration of urban environmental amenities may in effect, be just the opposite. The concept of sustainability rest on the three pillars of ecological integrity, economic development, and social equity. If urban greening initiatives tend to decrease social equity, then they may be properly conceived as antithetical to the pursuit of urban sustainability. As the case of Prospect Park restoration illustrates, urban greening may whiten and richen as it redistributes environmental amenities upward, but it may not enhance urban sustainability from a social equity perspective.

ACKNOWLEDGMENTS

The authors thank Dr. Lorna Mason and Ed Morlock of the Center for the Study of Brooklyn, Mike Jolley, Martyna Cieniewicz, and Alina Pavlova for essential data collection and support. The authors also thank Dr. Setha Low and her Public Space Working Group at the CUNY Graduate Center for their comments.

NOTES

1. There have been some studies that address aspects of environmental amenities. For instance, this line of thinking can be found in Robert Bullard's (1990) classic book, *Dumping in Dixie*. Though Bullard focused primarily on the distribution of "bads," he also writes that getting an area declared a Superfund Site is positive. Though ironic, being able to get this designation for a site ensures some commitment to cleanup. Bullard showed that Superfund sites were disproportionately listed in white communities. Similarly, the Environmental Protection Agency charged higher fines for polluters in white neighborhoods.

2. Similarly, the best jobs in the production process tend to be awarded to the already wealthier individuals, while the dirtiest and most hazardous jobs are reserved for the poor and people of color (Hurley 1995; Pellow 2002). The poor and working-class therefore find themselves at the greatest environmental risk both on the job and at home, while the wealthy remain relatively protected in both locations (Szasz 1994). Managers tend to live at some distance from potentially hazardous production facilities, and usually upwind and upstream from industrial effluent flows. Workers tend to live close to production facilities, and downwind and down stream from effluent flows (Mumford 1934). Workers and their families are thereby exposed to carcinogens and other toxins resulting from production, while managers, owners and investors are not.

3. In terms of the siting of new potentially hazardous facilities, similar processes operate. Production facilities will tend to locate where land values are lowest in order to reduce construction costs. Lower land values will be found in precisely those locations where the poor and working-class can afford to live. Higher land values will be found where the upper and upper middle-class can afford to live in relatively environmentally sound locations. New environmental hazards are therefore likely to be placed in close proximity to the residential areas inhabited by those near the bottom of the stratification system. Those areas that are attractive as residential locations for those with the wealth to avoid environmental hazards are likely to be the least attractive locations for installation of new production facilities that are associated with increased environmental and public health costs. So, as environmental restoration proceeds, it shifts people of color and the poor and middle class out, draws wealthier whites in, then serves as a bulwark to protect the new residents from exposure to potential future environmental risks. The same real estate value-based processes that fuel urban gentrification of an environmentally restored neighborhood, act to distribute future environmental hazards away from the gentrified area and toward those locations where the less wealthy and people of color live.

The poor and working-class are concentrated in areas typified by high levels of environmental risk and low levels of wealth, and people of color are disproportionately represented among this socioeconomic group. Poor communities face limited economic options in terms of type of employment and remuneration from that employment. Concentrating the unemployed and underemployed in specific locations creates communities of economic desperation. Under such condition, poor and working-class communities are structurally coerced into accepting any economic development initiative promising an increase in local employment (Pellow 2002). As a result, poor communities are less free to reject specific proposals for the siting of production or disposal facilities within their communities than are wealthier communities where new employment opportunities are a less pressing concern. The less wealthy a community, the more likely it is to be accepting of new environmental hazards where those hazards come with the promise of economic benefit (Pellow 2002). It is not that poor communities are less concerned about the protection of their health and environment, but rather that they have less structural freedom to act on their environmental and health concerns when faced with the consequences of absolute poverty. Conversely, wealthy communities are no more environmental or health conscious than poor communities, but with little need for additional local economic development, they are more structurally free to prioritize their environmental and health values under conditions where their basic needs are already being met. Segregated residential housing patterns generate a spatial distribution of economic development need. Environmentally hazardous facilities will be most attractive to communities with the highest level of economic desperation (Gould 1991; Pellow 2002). The ability of wealthy communities to reject hazardous facilities due to low economic need (and greater political resources), combined with the desperation of poor communities for any increase in employment opportunity, reinforces both the downward distribution of environmental hazards, and the upward distribution of environmental amenities, increasing both the environmental protection of the rich and the environmental degradation of the poor.

4. On a microlevel, the creation of community gardens have been shown to increase neighborhood property values in New York City by as much as 9.4 percent within five years (Voicu and Been 2008), although the implications for subsequent neighborhood stability have not been systematically explored.

5. This process has been documented in environmental justice struggles elsewhere in New York City (Sze 2006).

6. This brief history is compiled from *The Complete Illustrated Guidebook to Prospect Park and the Brooklyn Botanic Garden,* 2001, New York: Silver Lining Books and the Prospect Park Alliance's website (www.prospectpark.org).

7. The New York City Department of Housing guidelines defined low-income housing (in 2005) as a maximum income of $37,675 for a one-bedroom apartment, at a rent of $877 per month. To qualify for a one-bedroom moderate-income unit, the maximum income is $58,875, with a rent of $1,407 per month.

REFERENCES

Agyeman, J. 2005. *Sustainable communities and the challenge of environmental justice*. New York: NYU Press.

Angotti, T. 2008. *New York For Sale: Community Planning Confronts Global Real Estate*. Cambridge, MA: MIT Press.

Berenson, R. J., and N. deMause. 2001. *The Complete Illustrated Guidebook to Prospect Park and the Brooklyn Botanic Garden.* New York: Silver Lining Books.

Brooklyn Chamber of Commerce. 2006. *Brooklyn labor market review, Spring 2006.*

Brooklyn, NY: Brooklyn Chamber of Commerce.

Brooklyn Community District Profiles. 2009. Retrieved December 12, 2009 (http://home2.nyc.gov/html/acs/downloads/pdf/cd_snapshots/brooklyn_cd6.pdf).

Bryant, B. ed. 1995. *Environmental justice: Issues, policies and solutions*. Washington, DC: Island Press.

Bryant, B. and P. Mohai. eds. 1992. *Race and the incidence of environmental hazards: A time for discourse*. San Francisco, CA: Westview Press.

Bullard, R. D. 1990. *Dumping in Dixie: Race, class and environmental quality*. San Francisco, CA: Westview Press.

———. ed. 1993. *Confronting environmental racism: Voices from the grassroots.* Boston, MA: South End Press.

———. ed. 1994. *Unequal protection: Environmental justice and communities of color*. San Francisco, CA: Sierra Club Books.

Bullard, R. D., J. E. Grigsby and C. Lee. eds. 1994. *Residential apartheid: The American legacy*. Los Angeles, CA: CASS Publications.

Carmody, Deirdre. 1985. "Staking Out Parks to Stop Graffiti." *New York Times*, February 18, p. B3.

Cerrell Associates and J. S. Powell. 1984. *Political difficulties facing waste-to-energy conversion plant siting*. Sacramento, CA: California Waste Management Board.

Cohen, Ariella. 2006. "Corcoran Group Charged with Selling 'White' Nabes." *The Brooklyn Paper*, October 14. Retrieved on January 15, 2011 (www.brooklynpaper.com/stories/29/40/29_40corcoran.html).

Corcoran Group. 2010. Retrieved October 10, 2010 (http://www.corcoran.com/neighborhoods/index.aspx?page=BrooklynDescription&N=ProspectParkSouth).

DeMause, N. and R. J. Berenson. 2001. *The Complete Illustrated Guidebook to Prospect Park and the Brooklyn Botanic Garden.* New York, NY: Silver Lining Books.

DeSena, J. 2009. *Gentrification and Inequality in Brooklyn: The New Kids on the Block*, Lanham, MD: Lexington Books.

Domhoff, G. W. 1998. *Who rules America?: Power and politics in the year 2000.* Mountain View, CA: Mayfield Publishing Company.

Fillmore Real Estate. 2010. Retrieved October 20, 2010 (www.fillmore.com/neighborhoods/crown-heights).

Gould, K. A. 1991. "The sweet smell of money: Economic dependency and local environmental political mobilization." *Society and Natural Resources: An International Journal* 4(2):133-150.

———. 2006. "Promoting Sustainability." Pp. 213–229 in *Public sociologies reader*, edited by Judith Blau and Keri Iyall Smith. Lanham, MD: Rowman and Littlefield.

Gould, K. A., D. N. Pellow and A. Schnaiberg. 2008. *The treadmill of production: Injustice and unsustainability in a global economy.* Boulder, CO: Paradigm Press.

Gould, K. A., A. Schnaiberg and A. S. Weinberg. 1996. *Local environmental struggles: Citizen activism in the treadmill of production.* Cambridge, MA: Cambridge University Press.

Hurley, A. 1995. *Environmental inequalities: Race, class, and industrial pollution in Gary, Indiana, 1945–1980.* Chapel Hill, NC: University of North Carolina Press.

Jackson, Kenneth T. 1998. *The Neighborhoods of Brooklyn, 2nd edition.* New Haven, CT: Yale University Press.

Kozol, J. 1992. *Savage inequalities: Children in America's schools.* New York, NY: Harper Perennial.

Lake, R. W. 1996. "Volunteers, NIMBYs, and environmental justice: Dilemmas of democratic practice." *Antipode* 28(2): 160–74.

Lewis, T. L. 2011. "Global Civil Society and the Distribution of Environmental Goods: Funding for Environmental NGOs in Ecuador." Pp. 87–104 in *Environmental Justice Beyond Borders: Local Perspectives on Global Inequities*, edited by Julian Agyeman and JoAnn Carmin. Cambridge, MA: MIT Press.

Logan, J. R. and H. L. Molotch. 1987. *Urban fortunes: The political economy of place.* Berkeley, CA: University of California Press.

Low, S., D. Taplin and S. Scheld. 2005. *Rethinking Urban Parks: Public Space and Cultural Diversity.* Austin, TX: University of Texas Press.

Massey, D. S. and N. A. Denton. 1993. *American apartheid: Segregation and the making of the underclass.* Cambridge, MA: Harvard University Press.

Mohai, P. and R. Saha. 2007. "Racial inequality in the distribution of hazardous waste: A national-level reassessment." *Social Problems* (54)3:343–70.

Mumford, L. 1934. *Technics and civilization.* New York, NY: Harcourt Brace Jovanovich.

National Fair Housing Alliance. 2006. *Housing segregation background report: Brooklyn, NY*. Washington, DC: NFHA.

New York City Department of City Planning. 2011. Retrieved on March 6, 2011 (www.nyc.gov/html/dcp/html/greenpointwill/greenoverview.shtml).

New York Times. 1972. "Lindsay Assails Graffiti Vandals." August 25, p. 30.

———. 1980. "Losing Ground in the Parks." October 15, p. A30.

O'Neill, N. 2011. "Prospect Park Alliance slashes budget, killing Macy's contest and other programs." The Brooklyn Paper. May 25. Retrieved January 15, 2011 (http://brooklynpaper.com/stories/34/21/dtg_parkbudgetcuts_2011_5_27_bk.html).

Pastor, M., J. Sadd and J. Hipp. 2001. "Which came first? Toxic facilities, minority move-in, and environmental justice." *Journal of Urban Affairs* 23:1–21.

Pellow, D. N. 2002. *Garbage Wars: The Struggle for Environmental Justice In Chicago*. Cambridge, MA: MIT Press.

Prospect Park Alliance. 2010. Retrieved October 30, 2010. (www.prospectpark.org/visit/places/drummers).

Prudential Douglas Elliman Real Estate. 2010. Retrieved October 10, 2010 (www.elliman.com/new-york-city/brooklyn/windsor-terrace/2-92).

Pulido, L. 1996. "A critical review of the methodology of environmental racism research." *Antipode* 28:142-159.

Quindlen, Anna. 1980. "For Prospect Park, $10 Million to Recapture What It Was." *New York Times*. January 4, B1.

Rapid Realty. 2010. Retrieved October 10, 2010 (http://www.rapidnyc.com/living/neighborhood/35/Windsor-Terrace-Brooklyn-Neighborhood-Information).

Roberts, J. T. and M. Toffolon-Weiss. 2001. *Chronicles from the environmental justice frontline*. Cambridge, MA: Cambridge University Press.

Schnaiberg, A. 1980. *The environment: From surplus to scarcity*. New York, NY: Oxford University Press.

Schnaiberg, A. and K. A. Gould. 2000. *Environment and society: The enduring conflict*. Caldwell, NJ: Blackburn Press.

Smith, N. 1996. *The New Urban Frontier: Gentrification and the Revanchist City*. New York, NY: Routledge.

Szasz, A. 1994. *EcoPopulism: Toxic waste and the movement for environmental justice*. Minneapolis, MN: University of Minnesota Press.

Sze, J. 2006. *Noxious New York: The racial politics of urban health and environmental justice*. Cambridge, MA: MIT Press.

Taylor, D. E. 2009. *The Environment and the People in American Cities, 1600s–1900s: Disorder, Inequality, and Social Change*. Durham, NC: Duke University Press.

Voicu, I. and V. Been. 2008. "The Effect of Community Gardens on Neighboring Property Values" *Real Estate Economics* 36(2):241-283.

Zukin, S. 1987. "Gentrification: Culture and Capital in the Urban Core." *Annual Review of Sociology* 13:129–47.

———. 1991. *Landscapes of Power: From Detroit to Disney World*. Berkeley, CA: University of California Press.

7

Rezoning Coney Island

A History of Decline and Revival, of Heroes and Villains at the "People's Playground"

Alessandro Busà

Facing the Atlantic Ocean on the southern tip of the Brooklyn shore, the peninsula of Coney Island developed over the nineteenth and early twentieth centuries from a seaside resort of Victorian hotels and private beaches to a popular midway of vaudeville theaters, bathhouses, arcades dance halls and thrill rides, which attracted New Yorkers, immigrants and visitors alike (Denson 2004: 9–31). At the turn of the century, Coney became a popular display of magnificent architectures, artificial paradises and never before seen technological innovations: electric lights, impressive machineries, roller coasters and even baby incubators were all pioneered here. Kasson (1978: 8) described Coney Island as the utopian laboratory of modern mass culture, while Koolhaas (1978: 29) saw it as best representing the Zeitgeist of New York City in the industrial age.

Coney's first glorious amusement parks were strongly indebted to the City Beautiful Movement and particularly to Burnham's "White City," a model for an idealized, utopian, harmonious urban environment unknown to most American city dwellers of the time. Dreamland and Luna Park featured monumental buildings and slender towers, all generously decorated and orderly articulated among green spaces, wide canals, reflective pools and picturesque lagoons. The pioneering steel structures that characterized Coney Island in the 40s—the vertiginous Parachute Jump, the Wonder Wheel and the many roller coasters—emulated the World's Fairs' quest for a revolutionary technological utopia.

Coney Island was renamed "The nickel Empire," and "The People's Playground," because it provided accessible recreation for the working classes of New York City[1] and of the entire world. In 1925, Cautela wrote "When you bathe at Coney Island, you bathe in the American Jordan. It is holy water.

Figure 7.1. Luna Park and Surf Avenue, 1912. Photo courtesy of the Library of Congress, Bain News Service publisher.

Figure 7.2. Coney Island, in Luna Park (Irving Underhill, between ca. 1910 and ca. 1915). Photo courtesy of the Brooklyn Museum.

Figure 7.3. The Coney Island waterfront, 2008. Photo by Nicholas Breslow.

Nowhere else in the United States will you see so many races mingle in a common purpose for a common good [...]" (1925: 283).

A prototype for the artificial, light-fed, congested consumer landscape that would forge Manhattan in the following years, Coney Island was the creature of visionary ambitions as much as the product of unscrupulous entrepreneurship.[2] Yet the very ruthless development that had given birth to Coney's glory at the turn of the Century was to become its worst foe after World War II, when the peninsula became the bloody battlefield of conflicting redevelopment utopias, social unrests, political ambitions and greedy speculations. Throughout all these years, both city planning and private development have waged a ferocious war against Coney Island, a war that is still unfolding.

This history of decline begins in 1938, when Robert Moses assumed control of the area as City Park Commissioner; in 1941 he widened the boardwalk inland, erasing dozens of arcade amusements and vernacular architectures, including the municipal bathhouse and the ruins of the legendary Dreamland Park, which had opened in 1904 and had been destroyed by fire seven years later (Denson 2004: 67). By making extensive use of eminent domain, Moses later razed down several blocks of amusements at the site of the Dreamland's fairground to clear land for new venues: the New York Aquarium (1957), a scarcely attended enclosed venue (Caro 1975: 687), and the Abe Stark ice skating rink, "a dark brown prison covered in barbed wires" (Matassa 2006: 56). Both were surrounded by vastly unused parking lots, as it was common practice in the era of modernist urban planning.

Later in 1953, while running the City's Slum Clearance Committee, Moses had again huge swaths of land rezoned to make room for high-rise public housing projects: the Coney Island Houses, completed in 1956, were the result of a major land grab that favored large developers and destroyed more lots of amusements and hundreds of private houses (Denson 2004: 75). After the urban renewal plans took place and older middle class houses were replaced with high-rise public housing projects, the local crime rate soared, giving rise to episodes of gang violence and racial conflicts which culminated in the 1960s and 1970s. In these dark years, fewer people ventured into Coney Island. The advent of the automobile, which provided access to the less crowded and more appealing beaches of Long Island and to other state parks, forced many amusement owners to abandon their properties, while repeated episodes of arson obliterated much of the remaining structures in the amusement area. Coney's heyday was coming to an end.

In 1964, Coney's last remaining large theme park, Steeplechase[3], which had opened in 1897 and had thrived since then, was shut down. The property was sold to Fred Trump, who envisioned luxury condominiums on the ocean waterfront, and spent several years battling in court to get the property rezoned to residential uses. But Trump's plans were opposed by the Lindsay administration, which instead was pushing for "a combination of Disney and Tivoli Gardens" (Tuccille 1985: 59) at Coney's waterfront. Realizing that there was a chance that the City might landmark the celebrated Steeplechase Pavillion (built in 1907), Trump rushed to have it demolished: in the summer of 1966 he organized a "funeral party for the amusement industry" (Denson 2007: 138), where bikini-clad girls handed out stones which Trump invited the press to toss through the stained-glass pavilion; weeks later, he had it bulldozed.

In the early 1970s, Coney experienced modest signs of revival as Norman Kaufman, an amusement operator who had leased the property from Trump, created a little amusement park on the site and publicly disclosed plans to eventually resurrect the historic Steeplechase. In 1979, however, the City purchased the lot and proceeded to harass Kaufmann with lengthy legal battles (Denson 2007: 205–10). In 1981, the small park was eventually evicted, and the property remained vacant for another two decades.

In the late 1970s, the Koch administration came up with yet another plan to revitalize Coney Island—this time by bringing in gambling and casinos, as had been done with success in Atlantic City. The plan created a frenzy of land speculations in which property was bought up in stock while the few remaining rides were cleared in preparation of reselling. However, gambling eventually was never legalized at Coney Island, and the land ended up again with even more vacant lots.

In the mid 1980s, businessman Horace Bullard revealed plans for a vintage theme park based on the original Steeplechase; this time, the plan was approved by the city in 1986, but the park failed to materialize. The deal was finally broken when Mayor Giuliani took office in 1994 and decided to build a baseball stadium on its site. Bullard, now no longer rebuilding Steeplechase, wanted to restore the once glorious Thunderbolt roller coaster, which had been prominently featured in Woody Allen's "Annie Hall" (1977), as part of a scaled-down amusement park. But in an unpredictable turn of events, in November 2000, Giuliani ordered an early-morning raid on the derelict Thunderbolt, claiming that the coaster was in immediate danger of collapse, and illegally[4] ordered it bulldozed.

The demolition of the Thunderbolt, which had been seen by historic preservationists and Coney enthusiasts as a monument to survival, was the climax of a decades-long struggle of city planning against the livelihood of Coney Island. In fact, history of development at Coney Island in the past seventy years has been the history of its progressive obliteration: unimaginative city planning, private profit and political opportunism have reduced Coney island to a wasteland over the years, with a rush to its complete disintegration during the second Bloomberg term—and with new, unexpected twists and turns in the latest years.

Figure 7.4. A family having fun at Coney Island, 2008. Photo by Alessandro Busà.

CONEY ISLAND TODAY: LOVE IT OR HATE IT

Through the recent years, a negative public perception of Coney Island has been reinforced by alarming press and TV reports, and by frightening representations in the movies, which have popularized the image of an "urban dystopia, a marginal space inhabited by the underbelly of the city where urban problems are endemic and untreatable ("The Warriors," 1979; "Requiem for a Dream," 2000)" (Matassa 2006: 3). Still today, Coney Island is to some New Yorkers nothing but an infamous, impoverished and crime-ridden neighborhood which "retains the notorious reputation it acquired during past decades" (Rivero 2004: 16–17). For others, however, Coney Island holds a special role as the legendary birthplace of American mass culture, and as a beloved, unconventional amusement park district. Despite its current dilapidated condition and the loss of many of its open-air rides, Coney Island has managed to survive ebbs and flows, thanks to attractions that continue to draw millions of visitors and locals: its beach and boardwalk, the legendary Cyclone roller coaster, the Wonder Wheel, the open-frame steel relic of the Parachute Jump, Nathan's Famous hot dogs and dozens of arcade houses. Signs of Coney's cultural legacy are still alive in today's burlesque and freak shows, in the parades and the music festivals on the beach, and in its very democratic sense of place. Like the haven and playground of the immigrants and working-class New Yorkers in past decades, Coney's boardwalk is still today a beloved place for people of all colors, ages and incomes.

Coney Island is a mixed community composed of long-time residents who occupy the older housing stock and more recent households concentrated in the public housing units. As of the 2000 census, there were 51,574 people living in Coney Island: 59.6 percent were White, 32.4 percent were Black or African American, 17.9 percent were Hispanic, and 4.5 percent were Asian (SocioWiki NYC 2011). The figures also show a predominantly low-income neighborhood, with a median household income of $21,654 as of 2009 (SocioWiki NYC 2011) as opposed to an average $55,980 for New York City in 2008 (U.S. Census Bureau 2011). As of the 2000 census, 32.9 percent of all households were below poverty level, with a 12.9 percent unemployment rate (U.S. Census Bureau 2011).

Coney Island today attracts a predominantly native tourism from Brooklyn and the New York metropolitan area. If it's true that the district's tourism activity is in part "driven by nostalgia and by the few remaining vestiges of its storied past" (Rivero 2004: 17), Coney Island serves above all as the public beach and amusement area for thousands of native New Yorkers who just can't afford to go elsewhere. A mix of White, Hispanic and African American low- and middle-income families here can linger along the boardwalk, bathe in the ocean or join the free street parades and music shows for the price of a subway ride and of a hot dog.

Coney Island is not a corporate theme park but a mosaic of small, fragmented amusements. Traditionally, the amusement area has been managed by a number of small business owners with longtime connections to the neighborhood. It has been the clustering of many independent operators that has given the place its unique character:

Coney Island's amusement area is one of the few in the country that is not centrally owned, is ungated and requires no general admission, allowing visitors to wander freely among the rides and concessions. These freedoms are unique with regard to many of New York City's other public spaces, most notably city parks, which nowadays impose strict curfews and limit access through fences and gates (Matassa 2006: 57).

The social and ethnic diversity of its population and the anarchic palimpsest of its derelict urban fabric, coupled with the relative lack of privatized and controlled spaces, allow for a very peculiar form of tourism at Coney Island, one that eludes common notions of voyeurism and consumerism (Matassa 2006: 33): to many visitors, Coney Island represents a safe retreat from the homogeneity of the controlled and commodified inner city: "a heterogeneous tourist space that offers possibilities for less officially scripted experiences of tourism" (Matassa 2006: 25).

THE BLOOMBERG YEARS: REZONING CONEY ISLAND

Amid turbulent ups and downs, the "People's Playground" has somehow managed to survive over seventy years of relentless attacks by city planning and private development. However, the summer of 2009 has marked a turning point for Coney Island, one that was destined to effect its future development for good. On July 29, 2009, the New York City Council approved a plan that promised to "bring this beloved icon back to life, renewing Coney Island's legacy for generations to come" (Burden 2009: np). But the plan was controversial: it envisioned the radical de-mapping of over sixty-one acres formerly zoned for outdoor amusements and their reduction to about twelve acres.[5] Despite dozens of heated public hearings, and the overall negative responses from amusement advocates, Coney Island enthusiasts and historic preservationists, the plan was hastily approved without any significant changes from its original layout.

The preparatory process for the rezoning had started in September 2003, when the Mayor, the City Council and the Brooklyn Borough President formed the Coney Island Development Corporation (CIDC) to articulate an economic development strategy for the area. The CIDC was born as a subsidiary department of the New York City Economic Development Corporation (NYCEDC), a nonprofit local development corporation that is owned and financed by the city, and is fully controlled by the mayor (Angotti 2009).[6] The City's primary intention was to revitalize Coney Island as a potential site for the 2012 Olympics. However, when the bid for the Olympics was lost, the CIDC came up with a rezoning scheme that solicited the conversion of several lots to residential uses, in order to lure high-end development into the area. This draft was later integrated into a comprehensive plan developed by the Department of City Planning (DCP) in partnership with the Department of Parks and Recreation and the Department of Housing Preservation and Development, and that was named "Coney Island Comprehensive Rezoning Plan." According to a statement by City Planning Commissioner Amanda Burden in 2009, the plan:

> will preserve amusements in their historic location in perpetuity as Mayor Bloomberg promised. In addition to creating a year-round 27-acre amusement and entertainment district, the plan will also make possible the much needed and long awaited revitalization of the surrounding neighborhood. The plan will reestablish the area as South Brooklyn's economic engine, bringing new jobs, retail services and affordable housing to the Coney Island community (Burden 2009: np).

The renderings released by the Department of City Planning in 2009 depicted a landscape dense with spectacular rides and attractions—with just a hint, far away in the horizon, of what seemed to look like a cluster of condominium towers. Yet, aside from such jubilant representations, the plan

Figure 7.5. A rezoned beach, boardwalk and amusement area at Coney Island. Rendering courtesy of Department of City Planning New York.

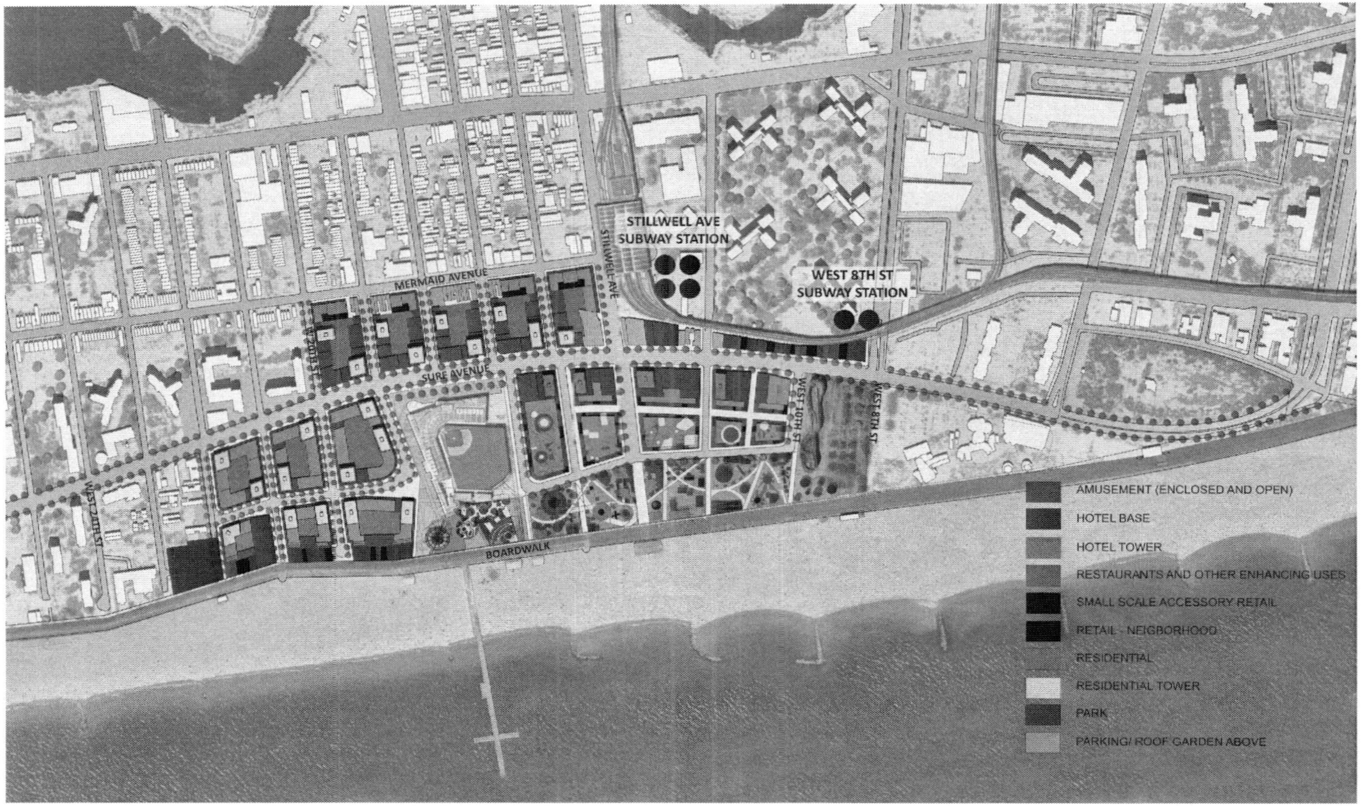

Figure 7.6. Zoning map. Courtesy of Department of City Planning New York.

dictated a substantial inflation of the residential destination of the area—a use that many see as incompatible with the livelihood of the amusement district[7]—and a radical reduction of its amusement component. While before 2009 over sixty-one acres were zoned for open-air amusements, the plan has permanently shrunk the outdoor parkland to about 12 acres (Save Coney Island 2009a): according to Treiman (2009: np), "Mayor Bloomberg appears to be finally on the cusp of completing the work of Moses and Trump."

The rezoning covers nineteen blocks bounded by the New York Aquarium to the east, West 24th Street to the west, Mermaid Avenue to the north and the Riegelmann Boardwalk to the south. It prescribes the demapping of 9.30 acres of currently zoned parkland at KeySpan Park, which is to be replaced by the mapping of two parks along the Riegelmann Boardwalk: a 9.39 acre park that would be developed as the amusement area, and a 1.41 acre "neighborhood park." In the immediate surroundings of the amusement area, the plan foresees hotel towers, indoor amusements, retail and restaurants. To the north and west of the amusement area, the plans fosters the redevelopment of vacant or underutilized land by rezoning it to a mix of residential, service and retail uses, with the aim of generating 4,500 new units of housing and roughly 500,000 square feet of new retail. Around twenty-five high-rise buildings will be scattered throughout the area; to serve them, car parking will be accommodated in multilevel above grade garages that will have to be wrapped by active uses on visible street frontages.

The proposal establishes a new special zoning district, the "Special Coney Island District," which encompasses seventeen blocks located between the Aquarium, the Riegelmann Boardwalk, Mermaid Avenue and West 22nd Street. This special district includes use, density, bulk and parking regulations to guide development of the amusement and entertainment area as well as the residential developments surrounding it. The special district is comprised of three subdistricts, each with its own special zoning regulations:

Coney East (what today remains of the amusement area). Here, rezoning will broaden the range of allowed uses, including hotels, enclosed entertainment venues, retail restaurants, and service uses. High-rise hotels will be allowed on Surf Avenue, in front of the main subway station. The tower height will range from 150 feet closer to the Wonder Wheel to 270 feet (Parachute Jump height) closer to KeySpan Park.

Coney West (now mainly vacant) will be rezoned to allow for residential uses with ground-floor retail along Surf Avenue and new uses along the Boardwalk. On Surf Avenue, commercial ground floor uses will be mandatory, and 20 percent of the frontages will have to be dedicated to entertainment-related uses. High-rise residential buildings will be allowed, with the highest tower placed at the corner of Surf Avenue and the intersecting streets.

For developments that participate in the inclusionary housing program, towers will be able to rise to 270 feet.

Coney North/Mermaid Avenue will be rezoned to allow for residential uses with ground-floor retail along Surf Avenue and Mermaid Avenue.

The rezoning introduces new uses to Coney Island, including new retail and amenities which will benefit a district whose retail supply is currently inadequate. However, the plan may bring burdens as well as benefits to Coney residents: it allows for the development of more than 1,750 housing units in Coney North, adjacent to existing residential areas, and roughly 2,700 residential units west of KeySpan Park. But very few of these housing units may be affordable to Coney residents: the "inclusionary zoning" bonus integrated in the plan is likely to prove of little use, as similar programs adopted in other parts of the city haven't been utilized by developers in sufficient numbers to create a significant number of affordable units.[8]

The plan is fostering new constructions as much as it encourages the demolition of existing structures: it allows developers to obliterate Coney Island's handful of surviving historic buildings, as it has promptly occurred in the fall of 2010. The loss of much of historic Coney, coupled with the plans for brand new condominium towers, will forever transform a skyline currently defined by historic landmarks like the Wonder Wheel and the Parachute Jump. What will remain of the amusement area, overshadowed by soaring high-rises, "will be too small to accommodate new, iconic rides and would not leave much space for future generations of visionaries to carry forward Coney Island's traditions of inventiveness and artistry" (Treiman 2009: np). The plan also entirely redefines the role of the amusement industry at Coney Island. Coney has always been primarily an open-air seasonal destination, yet the plan proposes to transform it into a year-round destination by accommodating indoor entertainments, hotels and residences. Coney Island has always been run by multiple independent operators, yet the City is now privileging a new management carried by a single major operator, thus penalizing the few remaining local businesses.

THE LIMBO OF CONEY ISLAND

Shortly before the CIDC Strategic Plan was released in September 2005, Joseph J. Sitt—a politically connected tycoon[9] and CEO of real estate development firm Thor Equities—purchased the 168,000-square-foot Washington Bath House lot west of the current amusement area for $13 million dollars. Owning property that was now potentially earmarked for rezoning to residential uses, Sitt flipped it the same year to Taconic Investment Partners for $90 million—a $77 million profit (Fung 2009). Today, Taconic controls about 10 acres at Coney Island, where it plans to build around 2,000 apartments (Taconic 2011). Between 2003 and 2006, Thor Equities proceeded purchasing almost every piece of property (about 10 acres) inside the traditional amusement area: in the winter of 2007 and then again in 2008, the developer evicted dozens of small businesses and ride operators, and purchased the largest remaining amusement park at Coney Island, Astroland. The park, which had opened in 1962, closed at the end of 2008: a few weeks later, all rides were dismantled and sold.[10]

Thor Equities' real plans for Coney have always been unclear, largely because they have changed significantly from year to year. In 2005, when the economy was booming, dazzling renderings of a resort area sporting luxury high-rise condo towers were released with the promise to bring a Vegas-style development to South Brooklyn (Sargen 2005). Four years later, in the midst of the 2009 recession, Thor presented other vague designs which included what seemed to be a small gated amusement park, featuring high rise hotels and large retail stores. Thor Equities' requests to the City to boost the maximum retail size limit in the rezoning plan from 2,500 to 10,000 square feet led many critics to assume that the developer intended to turn the area into a charmless mega-mall on the ocean. In reality, Thor Equities' intentions of actually building anything at Coney Island have always been severely biased by its bad reputation of acquiring property, requiring zoning changes and then flipping the land to other developers for a profit. This is exactly what Thor had done during the first Bloomberg administration with the Albee Square Mall site in downtown Brooklyn, which was purchased for $25 million in 2001, and resold in 2007 to Arcadia Realty Trust for five times the amount (Fung 2009).

In November 2008, the City eventually started negotiations with Joe Sitt, offering the developer $110 million for the land required for its plans of a nine-acre outdoor amusement district. Sitt declined, and demanded more than double the amount (Miller 2009). The City silenced the possibility of using eminent domain to seize the land, even though the Environmental Impact Statement states that land "could be acquired through condemnation, as necessary" (Calder 2009: np). After lengthy negotiations, in November 2009 the City finally managed to buy from Thor Equities the 6.9 acres of land located in the core of the amusement district, including the site of the former Astroland Park, for an astounding 95.6 million dollar deal: "While Mr. Sitt got much less than the $140 million he had wanted for 10.5 of the 12.5 acres he owned, the $95.6 million for 6.9 acres came to more than $300 a square foot—a huge amount in the current market" (Bagli 2009a: np).

After the land was finally purchased in December 2009, the City issued a request for proposals for an interim amusement operator (on a ten year lease) to run a temporary park on the now city-owned property: the bid was won by Italian group Zamperla (Povoledo 2010), which also operates Victorian Gardens in Central Park. NYEDC offered this international company far more favorable leasing conditions than any other locally owned business in Coney Island had ever enjoyed[11] (Amusing the Zillions 2010a).

In the summer of 2010, four giant pinwheel and crescent moons reminiscent of the long-gone Luna Park were put into place on the front gate of a brand new amusement park, whose nineteen rides, although state-of-the-art, have a nostalgic allure to them. The cheerful opening of "Luna Park" on Memorial Day 2010 was such an overwhelming success (Pearson 2010) that Central Amusement International (of which Zamperla is majority shareholder) promptly scheduled to open another 137,000-square-foot park in the adjacent lots before the summer of 2011. But good times were not to last: just a few weeks after the opening of the new park, Thor Equities started to demolish most of the remaining historical buildings in Coney Island's amusement zone: the Henderson's Music Hall (built in the late 1880s, it had been renovated in 2004 and was the last surviving example of the music halls that thrived at Coney Island at the turn of the century); the Bank of Coney Island (a 1923 neoclassical revival building that testified to Coney's past prosperity) and the Shore Hotel (built in 1903 and Coney Island's last operational hotel), were all razed down in a matter of weeks (Amusing the Zillions 2010b). Thor Equities' *tabula rasa* started a few months after the New York State Office of Parks, Recreation and Historic Preservation had issued a determination that Coney Island's amusement district meets the criteria for inclusion on the State and National Register of Historic Places, naming each of these endangered structures as the district's "key buildings."[12] However, the City's Landmarks Preservation Commission denied them landmark designation, and refused the creation of a historic district at Coney Island.[13] The commission, whose chair is directly appointed by the mayor, has always played a long waiting game at Coney Island, and didn't calendar any of the buildings until 2010,[14] long after the lots had been rezoned.[15] Aside from the Cyclone Roller Coaster,[16] the Wonder Wheel[17] and the Parachute Jump,[18] only one significant building outside of the amusement area has survived the wrecking ball: the Shore Theater, a neo-Renaissance building built in 1924 and boarded up since the late 1970s, which was given landmark status in December 2010.

Thor Equities' rush to demolition was part of a strategy that has become routine in Bloomberg's New York: in order to head off the lengthy landmarking process and take full advantage of the potential that comes with

Figure 7.7. A boarded-up Henderson building sporting Thor Equities' "Stores for Lease" signs, 2009. Photo by Heather Dunsmoor.

the rezoning (in this case, the plan allows for 30-story high-rise hotels), small-scale historical buildings are gladly sacrificed to the dragon of development. In Bloomberg's New York, thousands of historical buildings are being demolished each year—most of the time right before, or right after rezoning plans get final approval (Pincus 2008).[19]

In a TV interview on NY1,[20] Thor Equities CEO Joe Sitt declared: "Every one of these buildings is just horrible, rundown relics with nothing exciting about them."[21] In reality, all of these buildings were open for business before Thor Equities' acquisition led to the eviction of the former tenants and businesses in 2008 and 2009. After demolition, the developer promptly released appalling renderings of one-story retail boxes, reminiscent of a suburban strip mall, that would replace the old buildings. The *New York Observer* noted that Thor's renderings were "almost designed to inspire distaste," and that they highlighted "the potential for fast food, slapping a Burger King-like joint on the corner, next to a taco restaurant with signage highly suggestive of Taco Bell" (Brown 2010: np).

"This is a tale of two Coney Islands," claimed advocacy group Save Coney Island: "Luna Park is laying the groundwork for an exciting summer, while a block away Thor is planning to lay waste to Coney Island's heritage, threatening to ruin all at once the area's past, present and future. The Bloomberg administration needs to decide: Will this summer be remembered as the beginning of Coney Island's rebirth? Or will be remembered as the summer that the City allowed an opportunistic developer to demolish Coney Island's history?" (Save Coney Island 2010a: np).

But as Thor Equities' desecration of property in Coney Island continued unchallenged, worse was yet to come: on the day after the 2010 season ended, almost all remaining boardwalk businesses, some of which were in place since over forty years, received immediate eviction notices, this time from the executives of CAI/Zamperla (Amusing the Zillions 2010c)—the alleged heroes who had given Coney Island a second chance: "They didn't have the vision that we have for the Boardwalk [. . .] It's a business decision," said Zamperla CEO (Amusing the Zillions 2010c: np). Local businesses like Ruby's, Cha Cha's, Paul's Daughter, Grill House, Gyro Corner, Shoot the Freak, Beer Island, Pio Pio Riko and Coney Island Souvenir Shop all had two weeks to vacate the premises they had occupied for decades. Some of them united in a lengthy legal battle in order to have their leases renewed at least for one more year. Meanwhile, at the corner of Surf Avenue and 10th Street, Zamperla is scheduling to open a $1.4 million restaurant with view of the Cyclone Roller Coaster, which will replace the defunct forty-year-old Gregory & Paul's diner (Amusing the Zillions 2010d). The restaurant will be run by French multinational Sodexo, one of the largest and most loathed[22] food and facilities management companies in the world, and a novel partner of NYCEDC. Just in June 2010, Attorney General Andrew M. Cuomo had announced a $20 million settlement with Sodexo for overcharging twenty-one New York school districts as well as the State University of New York (Attorney General 2010).

KILLING VIA URBAN PLANNING

The story of Coney's decline and marginalization by the city disappears from the books but rises again in the built landscape. As I wander present day Coney, I am faced with a more recent urban history of racism, economic inequality, institutionalized poverty and social injustice, left in pockmarks on the lunar landscape, in vacant lots and towering housing projects. The word "preservation" seems ironic in a neighborhood which has experienced so much demolition (Matassa 2003: 79).

It was the very city-initiated planning process for Coney Island that sparked the frenzy of land speculation that has ravaged the amusement district and most of its historical landmarks. Once it appeared that the zoning status quo would change, the land has been cleared to make it ripe for more profitable development: between 2007 and 2010, most of the remaining historical buildings at Coney Island had been obliterated, while the old amusement district has been reduced to a fraction of its former size.[23]

Ironically, the City's plan has eventually rewarded Thor Equities' notorious record of land-flipping by upzoning the developer's land, increasing its value and allowing him to get rid of anything (former tenants and businesses, buildings) that could prevent him from an easy resale. According to Save Coney Island:

> it was irresponsible and tactically stupid for the city to make zoning concessions before being close to a deal to acquire property. The city could have easily played hardball with Thor Equities and used the line they use with everyone else—this or nothing. Instead, they blinked, and ended up with a plan that, by upzoning Thor's land, made the realization of amusement-related goals far more expensive.[24]

The difference between what the city would have paid for the land pre-rezoning and what it had to pay post-rezoning has been absorbed by the public: "the rezoning, in other words, has been a form of 'sponsored speculator subsidy program' that has benefited a private developer whose history in Coney Island has been that of systematically trying to destroy it."[25] But, while Thor has been massively responsible for the blighting of present-day Coney Island, according to Treiman (2009: np)

It is the city's plan that poses the greatest danger to the amusement district's future. Coney Island's amusement district has survived the pressures of the New York City real estate market thanks to its special C7—amusement-only zoning. Land that is rezoned to allow for other uses, however, will be lost to amusements forever.

As of today, the remaining outdoor amusements at Coney Island occupy around three acres. Before the plan's approval, over sixty-one acres were still zoned for outdoor amusements, while the legendary Coney Island of the past had over one hundred acres of parkland, including rides, arcades, bathhouses, hotels, houses and retail. The approved rezoning plan shrinks the amusement area *in perpetuum*. Today, many at Coney Island are convinced that by granting Thor Equities the dirty job of harassments, evictions and demolitions in the amusement area, the City has managed to keep its hands clean in the public eye, and even to eventually stage itself as the *deus ex machina*, the last-minute savior of the agonizing amusement park.

REZONING AND THE CRISIS OF URBAN PLANNING IN BLOOMBERG'S NEW YORK

The struggles for development at Coney Island, which featured the City of New York and a private developer fighting for land for whose state of demise both have been responsible, and culminated with a net transfer of public money into private pockets, casts a light on the failure of the Bloomberg administration's urban planning schemes, and more broadly on the crisis of "entrepreneurial" urban management strategies that the Bloomberg agenda has espoused.

Under the label of urban entrepreneurialism, Brenner (2004: 177) describes a "reorientation of urban governance from the managerial, welfarist mode of the Fordist-Keynesan period to an entrepreneurial, growth-oriented framework." Harvey (1989b) sees this reorientation as a response to the structural change in the world economy following the crisis of Fordism in the early 70s, when the devolution of federal responsibilities to local levels of government increased cities' dependence on own-source revenues (mainly property tax revenues), which in turn made them more dependent on investments in real estate. Weber (2002) summarizes the major shift that the "entrepreneurial" framework brought about: the aim of local governments shifted from the provision of welfare in order to sustain consumption, to the pursuit of growth in the form of profitable returns in real estate investment. In the "entrepreneurial" era, policies and practices of local governments are committed to make land profitable to private investment: "rather than retreat from policymaking, the last two decades have witnessed a proliferation of municipal regimes increasingly active in creating landscapes amenable to the quick excavation of value" (Weber 2002: 531).

This shift to entrepreneurial forms of local governance has brought about significant changes to spatial planning strategies. In order to become more responsive to the demands of an increasingly flexible real estate market, urban planning has shifted to less rigorous and less centralized forms of land-use zoning; while the private market has been fully integrated in the decision-making over land use and development in general, the role of the state has limited its scope to the production of fragmentary blueprints for flexible development (Butler 2003).

In the specific case of New York City under Bloomberg, the extensive use of rezoning has led to a full reformulation of old-style managerial urban planning standards that were embodied in the obsolete zoning code of 1961. In recent years, fragmentary overhauls of zoning regulations have become the substitute for comprehensive planning frameworks (Angotti 2008).[26] Bloomberg's ambitious *PlaNYC 2030* is a blueprint for a fragmentary development at the discretion of private market forces—the plan sets broad guidelines towards green development, rezoning and housing production in the city, but generally lets the private market decide upon what kind of development will be carried forward and where. Rezoning schemes have been flexibly implemented in response to developers' pressure or to citizen groups' demands: in some cases they have taken the form of "upzoning," allowing for increasing residential density and mixed-use development in marginalized neighborhoods; in other cases of "downzoning," limiting bulk and scale of new developments, usually in more affluent districts, in order to preserve neighborhood character. According to Bloomberg, already in 2007 the City had secured approval for the rezoning of 6000 city blocks: "More rezoning in the past six years than the ones achieved since 1961 under the past six Mayors combined" (Bloomberg 2007). Between 2003 and 2009, over 30 percent of the city's land has been rezoned, totaling almost 100 rezoning plans approved as of September 2009, leading to the most sweeping revision of land-use regulations throughout the city's five boroughs in the last fifty years.

The extensive use of rezoning, which generally aims at increasing density by promoting mixed-use and transit-oriented development, urban-infill, and a set of policy tools aimed at favoring a functional mix and a visual sense of "diversity," has become the primary device of production of a new physical and social space, at the same time as it has created new geographies of consumption within the city. By providing flexible opportunities for land development, rezoning has proven appealing to large business groups and to the real estate business. According to Angotti (2008: 159), "zoning as a tool of land-use control offers maximum flexibility for the real estate industry, which can use its influence at City Hall to get zoning changes when and where they need them."

Rezoning has proven to be a perfect device for the engineering of new outlets for the "extraction of value" (Weber 2002: 531), but only at the cost of a relentless erasure of former cultural and socioeconomic local assets. The City's "routinized" approach to rezoning generally envisions a comprehensive upgrading of the commercial and residential units, mostly by allowing taller or bulkier buildings in place of existing ones, regardless—except for a few "cosmetic" prescriptions—of the distinctive economic, social and historical character of the district. So far, the private market has overwhelmingly responded with the production of luxury residential developments and large retail outlets in formerly disadvantaged neighborhoods, and with the wholesale reinvention of former manufacturing areas and Brownfield sites, thus escalating a process of generalized gentrification of inner city working-class and ethnic districts (Newman and Wyly 2006). By superimposing a routine-package of development in diverse neighborhoods scattered all over the metropolitan area from Queens to East Brooklyn, rezoning has been leading to their progressive social and spatial homogenization.

PROMISES NOT KEPT

The plan has been presented as the City's response to Coney Island's chronic decline. By accommodating new housing, retail and entertainments, and by bringing in new jobs, the plan promises to "ensure that future generations can enjoy an open, affordable, urban twenty-first century Coney Island that does justice to its illustrious history and enduring appeal" (Burden 2009: np). However, as the following points clarify in detail, the plan has failed to address the demands of local residents and businesses, and to recognize Coney Island's key-potential as a large-scale, diversified amusement district that generates local jobs. While opening up the doors to injections of external capital may generate new employment opportunities for locals in the hotel and amusement industry, the ripple effects of market-rate development in an overwhelmingly impoverished community may represent a serious threat to the livelihood of local residents and businesses.

Participation

"The plan [. . .] is the product of over 300 public meetings with numerous stakeholders, ranging from elected officials, residents, property and business owners, to Coney Island enthusiasts from New York City and beyond" (Burden 2009: np).

The plan has been presented as the result of an intensive public outreach process. In reality, many residents, grassroots organizations and advocacy groups claim that their voices and proposals haven't been heard in the making of the plans. For instance, activist groups Save Coney Island and Coney Island USA, *The New York Times* and the Municipal Art Society in many occasions urged the City to expand the amusement area and to remove four high-rise towers from the heart of the amusement district; Coney Island's Community Board 13 also recommended the relocation of the hotel towers, while the New York Landmarks Conservancy and the Historic Districts Council pushed for the preservation of some of Coney's historical buildings. All of their requests remained unanswered: despite dozens of public hearings, none of the several civic coalitions opposing the rezoning or asking for amendments has been able to substantially affect the plan.

In New York City, representative bodies that serve as advocates for local residents and communities (Community boards) have only an advisory role in all major land-use resolutions: the final decisions on all these matters belong to the City Planning Commission (whose seven of thirteen members are appointed by the mayor) and the City Council. The City Council, which has final say on each rezoning plan, is often seen as siding closely with the City Planning Commission, so that as of 2008, "the City Council has approved every one of the 84 rezonings that have gone through the uniform land use review procedure […] since 2002" (Gross 2008: np).

The Role of the Amusement Park

> The plan seeks to [. . .] facilitate the development of a vibrant year round, 27-acre urban amusement and entertainment district by catalyzing a variety of new indoor and outdoor amusement, entertainment, and complimentary uses, and laying the groundwork for the development of a 12-acre urban amusement park preserving and expanding amusement uses in their historic boardwalk location in perpetuity (Burden 2009: np).

The twentieth-century leisure phenomenon that is the theme park industry has one of its most legendary progenitors at Coney Island. Still today, hundreds of parks around the world are inspired by the former magnificence of Coney. Luna Park, in Melbourne, features a giant entrance gate inspired by the iconic face of George C. Tylou, who founded Steeplechase Park in 1897; "Coney Island Park" in the Cincinnati Area features a range of classic rides which pay tribute to the legend of Coney Island. Full-size replicas of the Wonder Wheel stand in Disney's California Adventure Park, and Yokahama Park in Japan. According to Save Coney Island spokesman Juan Rivero: "There are numerous places around the globe that have built glorious parks that pay tribute to Coney Island. Here, where we have the original, the city has been all too happy to shrink it out of existence" (Save Coney Island 2009a: np).

A series of initiatives[27] launched by the Municipal Art Society[28] in 2007 tried to emphasize the potential of Coney's amusement industry as a crucial engine for growth in the area. In a testimony for the City Planning Commission in May 2009, MAS highlighted several key points for a sustainable development at Coney Island. These included: capitalizing on the amusements industry as an economic engine that generates employment opportunities for local residents; expanding[29] the amusement area, and retaining the existing C7 (amusement only) zoning code to allow for future growth; safeguarding Coney Island's architectural heritage through aggressive preservation of historical buildings; keeping large-scale, general retail out of the amusement district through specific zoning regulations.

MAS's recommendations were in support of a different, more imaginative approach to redevelopment, one that focused on the amusement area as an economic engine for the area and as a provider of quality jobs[30]. Unfortunately, the City rejected[31] the call for a larger amusement area. MAS's testimony emphasizes the underlying contradictions of a plan that claims to capitalize on the "brand" of Coney Island, while at the same time it radically scales down its primal vocation as an amusement park.

Housing

"The plan will reestablish the area as South Brooklyn's economic engine, bringing new jobs, retail services and affordable housing to the Coney Island community" (Burden 2009: np).

Usually, developers who chose to build in New York City can take advantage of a broad range of tax exemption programs. Most newly-constructed housing developments in New York City are currently eligible for a ten-to-twenty-five year exemption from property taxes under the City's "421-a" program,[32] which traditionally has been used to subsidize luxury development at a cost to the city of hundreds of millions in foregone tax revenues each year.[33] In rezoned districts, developers are generally granted extra bonuses (in the form of additional height and extra residential floor area) if they set a percentage (20 percent) of residential units as "affordable" through the City's "inclusionary zoning" program. Through the implementation of the "inclusionary zoning" tool, the Department of City Planning maintains that through March 2009, the building of 85,089 units of affordable housing has been started under Bloomberg's "New York Housing Marketplace" plan.[34] However, the few units under construction are simply unable to keep pace with the larger number of those lost: a May 2005 report conducted by the Furman Center for Real Estate and Urban Policy at New York University stated that only between 2002 and 2005, nearly 205,000 housing units affordable to families at 80 percent or below the city's median income level were lost, due to expiring rent stabilizations programs or increasing rents. Moreover, since the "inclusionary zoning" tool is non-mandatory, in booming times few developers have profited from it, while most have focused on the development of market-rate housing for an ever increasing demand set by a rising class of affluent urbanites (Pratt Institute Center for Community and Environmental Development 2004). A proper number of affordable units would be generated by mandating developers to build a proportion of moderate-priced housing, instead of establishing a voluntary incentive (Pratt Institute Center for Community and Environmental Development 2004).

To make matters worse, the very standards in use to define "affordable housing" in New York City are highly contested: the term is generally used to describe dwelling units whose total monthly costs don't exceed a third of a family's monthly income; eligibility is based on the Area Median Income (AMI, a federal index of average incomes for the metropolitan area). In the specific case, the plan provides incentives to developers who set off 20 percent of the units as "affordable" to households making up to 80 percent of the AMI (in New York City, the AMI for a family of four is $70,900). However, the median household income in Coney Island ($22,315 as of 2009[35]) is significantly lower than that of the whole metropolitan area: as a result, the rezoning may at best produce very few units affordable to Coney households. Of the 4,500 housing units proposed, about 900 units (20 percent) would be designated as "affordable." As the inclusionary zoning tool is based on voluntary programs, it is questionable how many of these "affordable" units will ever be built. The first private beachfront condominiums to be built on the Coney Island Boardwalk are currently under construction at West 32nd Street, and are expected to be completed before the summer of 2011: sales prices range from $685,000 for a one-bedroom apartment to $1.55 million for a penthouse.

Historic Preservation

"The plan seeks to [...] recognize and support Coney Island's unique character, culture and needs through the creation of the Special Coney Island District" (Burden 2009: np).

The plan promises to strengthen Coney Island's "unique character" and culture. Contrary to this claim, it has encouraged property owners to demolish small-scale historical buildings in order to build more profitable, taller ones in the core of the "Special District." As clarified in the previous chapters, the frenzy of speculations bred by the rezoning process has led to the obliteration of both historical architectures and amusements, and has escalated the eviction of dozens of small businesses in the amusement area.

Local Jobs

"Through the development of year-round uses and job opportunities for the residents, [the plan seeks to] facilitate the economic revitalization of the peninsula" (Burden 2009: np).

The NYCEDC has helped run job fairs to hire employees in the new "Luna Park" operated by Zamperla, and in the upcoming restaurant run by Sodexo. Both operators have stipulated specific clauses that give hiring precedence to people from the neighborhood, however most of these jobs are entry level positions that pay very low wages. Furthermore, the plan doesn't include a comprehensive strategy aimed at preserving or encouraging locally-owned retail or avoiding the forced relocation of local businesses. As these get evicted, most of the new tenants are likely to be large companies that can afford higher rents.

The character of New York City is being eroded by the increasing proliferation of chain retail and franchising outlets that pay minimum-wages and do not generate lively street life (Center for an Urban Future 2008); but the Bloomberg administration's recent opposition to Councilman Jackson's proposed "Small Business Survival Act,"[36] shows that the City's commitment to the cause of small local businesses ends where the interests of large companies begin. The toll of rezoning on local businesses is among the most unanimously contested aspects of Bloomberg's "pro-growth" policies (Center for an Urban Future 2009). With the Coney Island Rezoning, the City has replicated a development model that encourages large companies but undermines existing local economies.[37]

Street Activity

"The plan seeks to [. . .] create a vibrant pedestrian environment, with Surf Avenue serving as the reinvigorated retail and entertainment spine of the district" (Burden 2009: np).

The rezoning adopts specific requirements and restrictions aimed at fostering an active street life: "To promote a vibrant active district [. . .], new developments [. . .] would be required to have amusements occupying half of the total street frontage, and the ground floor level of hotels would be required to have active uses such as restaurants, retail and entertainment venues" (DCP Plan 2009: np). Such creative devices, however, if not combined with a comprehensive scheme aimed at retaining and encouraging a locally based, diversified retail, will fail to deliver what they promise.

At the commemoration of his mother Jane Jacobs in 2009,[38] Ned Jacobs said he was "appalled" by the City's plan:

> This rezoning plan does not appear to reflect the urban values and planning principles my mother espoused. These include sensitivity and integration with the scale, character and performance of existing neighborhoods and their established uses; the need to retain aged but serviceable buildings for the sake of economic diversity and continuity, as well as for their history and charm; the benefits of planning and redevelopment based on organic, iterative change, and the inherent dangers of top-down urban renewal-type schemes, propelled by cataclysmic money. (Save Coney Island 2009b: np)

THE STRUGGLE BETWEEN "ABSTRACT SPACE" AND "DAILY PRACTICES" AT CONEY ISLAND

The reengineering of inner-city land through infill developments, the conversion of manufacturing districts into residential areas, and the development of brand new waterfront residential enclaves, are all different facets of rezoning in Bloomberg's New York. In cases such as that of Coney Island, by targeting unproductive areas and reengineering them in order to cater to more affluent residents or larger businesses, rezoning acts both as a design tool and as a socioeconomic upgrading device: obsolete housing markets make room for new, more profitable ones, while local economies are supplanted by external injections of capital.

The empirical analysis provided in this paper has investigated the role that rezoning plays in the production of a distinct social space; it has explained how rezoning commodifies and produces the space over which it exercises jurisdiction. By applying Lefebvre's theory of space, in this conclusive chapter I theorize that the use of rezoning plans in New York City contributes to the reproduction of a spatial form which Lefebvre refers to as *abstract* space—a space that is simultaneously fragmented, homogeneous and hierarchically organized (Butler 2003). In producing the physical and social space of the city, rezoning plans embody specific "representations of space" (Lefebvre 1991: 38). These are official discourses of city representatives, visions of city planners and dominant models of urbanity propagated through the media. They are abstract in themselves, but have the ability to permeate social and political practices, and thus exert a concrete impact on the physical and social space of the city. Therefore, according to Lefebvre, they represent the "dominant space" in any society: under capitalism, specific "representations of space" facilitate the manipulation of 'representational spaces'" (Lefebvre 1991: 39)—that is, the space as it is lived and appropriated by the city inhabitants and users. "Dominant space" in this case can hence be seen as a superimposed hegemonic model of urban living that, on one hand, responds to the demands of capital accumulation and consumption, while on the other instructs the way people make use of space, influences and prescribes certain "spatial practices" while excluding others.

According to Lefebvre (1991: 50), "dominant space" is a space that informs, instructs and flattens distinctiveness: "it has nothing of a 'subject' about it, yet it acts like a subject in that it transports and maintains specific social relations, dissolves others and stands opposed to yet others."

The rezoning plan for Coney Island devises a form of "dominant space": through the creation of commercial streets, hotels, residential towers and large retail outlets, the rezoning reengineers this formerly less profitable land into a landscape responsive to a flexible extraction of value (Weber 2002: 531). In its physical manifestation, the plan also delivers a particular image of urban living. This image is manufactured not only through the use of architecture and design, but also through an overhaul of the very "brand" of Coney

Island, which has to be purified of its grittiness and working class pedigree to be marketable to new, more affluent consumers:

> discussions for future developments center around the idea of attracting outside tourists to Coney Island, ignoring the experiences of the thousands of visitors who have continued to come on summer weekends for the past 30 years. Apparently, these aren't the "right" people: namely tourists from outside of New York City with money to spend in the new city of capital and consumption where visions of Times Square dance in the heads of developers and city officials. (Matassa 2006: 40–41)

The revamping of Coney Island's brand is also fostered through specific zoning regulations aimed at favoring a vibrant street activity and a visual sense of "diversity": in an attempt to emulate the honky-tonk of old Coney, the Department of City Planning under Amanda Burden has insisted in more instances on enforcing cosmetic prescriptions to keep street life "vibrant" and to re-create a sense of "picturesque"[39] even in the midst of forced evictions of small local businesses and the burgeoning of ubiquitous chain retail. But the newly produced image of a "reactivated" Coney Island (DCP Plan 2009: np) is also instructive: "it makes assumptions about the spatial practices of the users, their understandings of space, and the symbolism carrying the designer's intentions" (Milgrom 2008: 271). It suggests a set of civic rules (Lefebvre 1991: 56)—strolling, window-gazing, shopping, indoor drinking—while potentially excluding others—lingering on the boardwalk, street vending, and so on. The indoor amusement spaces outlined in the plan may more likely feel like Disney's highly-controlled consumption outlets in the new Times Square than the grungy arcade houses of old Coney. The presence of hotels and residential towers will also take its toll in the surrounding public space, where forms of control, noise ordinances and other regulations may be enforced to protect the comfort of residents. Kipfer (2008: 201) sees the space of urban planners as authoritarian: by assuming an acquiescent passivity of the users, it suppresses responsive forms of engagement, and dissuades creative "spatial practices" from taking place. However, this doesn't guarantee that all users may behave in line with the spatial practices prescribed by this "dominant space."

Matassa (2006) sees Coney Island as "a site of struggle to control the proper meaning of the city"—a struggle between "the city as a space of containment and rational social control, and a space of untamed play and urban difference" (p. 14). Urban planning seeks to create "totalizing" images of the city (Boyer 1996), that are to be consumed voyeuristically and leave no room for a dialectical relationship of mutual exchange between space and its users. Hence, only the unprescribed, appropriative spatial practices of city dwellers are given the power to challenge the visual order or "legibility" (De Certeau [1984] 2002) imposed in the landscape of "dominant spaces": "it is through both conscious and unconscious everyday practice that the city dweller's idea of the city triumphs over that of urban authority" (Matassa 2006: 49). According to this interpretation, the history of Coney Island epitomizes the struggle between the "abstract space" of city planning and the citizens' daily practices of appropriation. Hence, a potential antidote to the prescriptions of "dominant space" lies in its daily appropriation by its users, in their own process of construction of "representational spaces" through their personal, interactive spatial practices. If "processes of producing space (shaped by urban specialists) are potentially hegemonic insofar as they integrate the affective-symbolic sides of everyday life (lived space) into the practical material (perceived) and institutional-ideological (conceived) dimensions of abstract space" (Kipfer 2008: 205), then the cycle of absorption of "representational spaces" (lived space) into "dominant spaces" (conceived space) has to be broken.

This is the way Coney Island's businesses, small amusement operators, nonprofit groups and residents have done all these years. Throughout the many phases of city-led destruction and revival, they have contested and reinvented established meanings of urban space through their daily practices: their businesses have remained opened throughout the darkest days of Coney Island, keeping it alive during the grim decades when the area was agonizing in the midst of soaring gang violence and poverty:

> They were the ones who understood the lessons taught by the likes of Jane Jacobs in the ancient battles to defeat Moses, the idea that city neighborhoods must evolve organically, that they must be tended to and kept to a human scale. Slowly, year by year, piece by piece, it was they who put Coney back together again, made it once again a place with a touch of anarchy but little real danger and a remarkable variety of entertainments (Backer 2010: np).

Likewise, nonprofit organizations such as Coney Island USA have playfully challenged the official discourses of decline with their innumerable parades, sideshows, burlesque, creepshows and freakshows, resurrecting that carnivalesque subculture that had made Coney Island unique in the past.

Together with innumerable Coney Island enthusiasts, residents and tourists, they have subverted the authority of city planning—and while their playful practices may not be inherently political, "it is through them that we resist ordered meanings of the built environment, transforming the city from what it claims to be into what it could be" (Matassa 2006: 49).

Figure 7.8. A rendering of a restored Grashorn Building (built ca. 1889) shows the potential of Coney Island's historic heritage. Rendering courtesy of Save Coney Island.

CONCLUSIONS

The recently approved plan for Coney Island is paradigmatic of a broader framework of commodification of the urban space which was initiated right after New York's fiscal crisis in the early 1970s, and has been strongly boosted by the Bloomberg administration in recent years. Alongside pervasive forms of economic and social restructuring, such process has been carried out by means of a relentless manipulation of the city's built environment through a flexible, piecemeal approach to urban planning. The extensive use of rezoning has become the primary device of production of a new physical and social space, at the same time as it has created new geographies of consumption within the city. By upgrading city land in disadvantaged neighborhoods and making it attractive to larger businesses and wealthier residents, rezoning has performed as a device for the city-led gentrification of low-income districts (Angotti 2009). The much heralded commitment of the City for affordable housing—one of the most dramatic matters the Bloomberg administration had been challenged to confront—has largely proven inadequate. In Darwinian fashion, richer households have moved in over time, while lower income households have been forced out (Newman and Wyly 2006). According to recent surveys (Center for an Urban Future 2009), the city's middle-class is in full flight: over 150,000 middle income residents left New York City in 2006 alone, driven away by the highest rent, food, child care and utilities bills in the United States. As of 2008, the average rent was $2,800, which is 53 percent higher than San Francisco, the second most expensive city in the United States.

Bloomberg's "luxury city"[40] has been expanding unrelentingly out of Manhattan into the outer Boroughs till the third quarter of 2008, when development was stalled because of the recession. The boom in the luxury housing market has been paralleled by the loss of thousands of units of housing affordable to middle- and lower-income New Yorkers: in the third quarter of 2008, only 10.6 percent of housing in the New York City region was affordable to people earning the median area income; in 2009, homeless rates were at record highs (Center for an Urban Future 2009). Between 2006 and 2009, the unemployment rate in New York nearly doubled: in 2009, the city had a local unemployment rate of 10.3 percent—a sixteen-year high—compared with 5.1 percent in 2006 (McGeehan 2009: np). Nearly 62,000 manufacturing jobs have been shed during the mayor's two term. They've been replaced with generally low-paying retail and hospitality jobs, while the city is still massively dependent on Wall Street, which according to the Independent Budget Office generated 21.6 percent of local tax revenue, but accounted for only 4.3 percent of employment in 2009 (Massey 2009).

The ongoing crisis should offer the city a chance to rethink its approach to planning. The reproduction of routinized development practices that changed the face of New York in the times of relentless real estate growth during Bloomberg's first mayoral terms is likely to fail in the newly configured economic framework and in Coney Island's peculiar local context. A sustainable approach to planning should focus on capitalizing on New York City districts' local assets, on nurturing their socioeconomic capital and on strengthening—not disrupting—their local-scale economies. It should encourage the development of housing that is affordable to all income levels, and not just to the upper end of the market. It should be both a participatory and comprehensive approach; the result of a compromise between the demands of local residents and a strategic vision for the socioeconomic well-being of the city as a whole. After the adoption of the Coney Island rezoning plan, on July 30 2009, City Planning Commissioner Amanda Burden stated:

> "Today is a triumphant day for Coney Island and the City. Coney Island's fans in New York City and throughout the world can rest assured that the People's Playground will in fact reclaim its title as the world's most celebrated open, affordable and accessible urban amusement park [. . .] bringing new jobs, retail

services and affordable housing to the Coney Island community" (Burden 2009: np).

To those opposing the rezoning, the City promises again that this plan will provide jobs to locals, in a moment where unemployment in New York City has reached historical highpoints. But the history of the last seventy years of urban development in Coney Island has been the history of a city-led campaign against the only industry that Coney possessed—the amusement area and all related jobs for Coney residents.

NOTES

1. The addition of subway service in 1920 allowed visitors from throughout the City to reach Coney Island for a five cents ticket. It was said that over one million visitors a day visited Coney Island. Many of these were poor immigrants, who at the time made up about 40 percent of the City's population.
2. In 1881, notorious boss John Y. McKane gained control of Coney Island police forces, and with Tammany Hall's tacit permission, indulged the ruffians, pickpockets and prostitutes that operated in the area. Many other impresarios in the early history of Coney Island became known for their visionary ambitions as much as for their ruthless demeanors.
3. The first Steeplechase Park was opened in 1897 by George C. Tilyou, a visionary salesman and entrepreneur. Right after the park was destroyed by fire in 1907, a second Steeplechase Park was opened in time for the 1908 summer season. Tilyou's second Steeplechase Park was rebuilt with steel, glass and concrete.
4. Barry (2003: np): "When plans for a Brooklyn ballpark were being finalized in 2000, Jeff Wilpon—a top New York Mets executive and the man whose minor-league team would play in the new park—mentioned to Mr. Giuliani that the Thunderbolt was an eyesore that looked dangerous. Say no more. Whether by coincidence or design, the Thunderbolt was now squarely in City Hall's sights." The case ended in court. In September 2003, a federal jury in Manhattan ruled that the city had no justification for tearing down the Thunderbolt, and in doing so had trespassed on Mr. Bullard's property. It also determined that one city official, who was integral in the decision to demolish, had acted with "deliberate indifference."
5. Of the twenty-seven acres, fifteen would be occupied by high-rise hotels and indoor shopping and entertainment. Only twelve acres would actually be outdoor amusements of the kind recognizable as traditional seaside entertainment (Save Coney Island 2009a).
6. Angotti (2009: np): "Even though its budget comes fully from the city finances, and its board is entirely under the mayor's control, EDC is set up to work more like a private corporation than a city agency. It exists outside the democratic process, and is unaccountable to the public."

7. In February 2007, City Planning Commissioner Amanda Burden herself told an audience at a breakfast sponsored by local business magazine Crain's Business: "*Amusements are incompatible with immediate adjacent residential* use" (Calder 2007: np).

8. The Department of City planning maintains that through March 2009, the building of 85,089 units of affordable housing has been started through the implementation of the "inclusionary zoning" tool. However, the few units under construction are simply unable to keep pace with the larger number of those lost: a 2005 report conducted by the Furman Center for Real Estate and Urban Policy at New York University found that only between 2002 and 2005, nearly 205,000 housing units affordable to families at 80 percent or below the city's median income level were lost, due to expiring rent stabilizations programs or increasing rents.

9. Local City Councilman Domenic Recchia has been a close childhood friend and a constant ally of developer Joe Sitt since he started buying properties in Coney Island (Bagli, 2009a: np).

10. A few rides are still in storage. One of the stars from the gate was donated to the Smithsonian Air Space Museum. The Rocket was donated to the City.

11. NYCEDC signed a 10-year lease with Zamperla for a $100,000 annual rent plus a reported 10 percent of the gross in the first year of operation. According to Amusing the Zillions (2010a: np): "Interestingly, an Associated Press article about the eviction of the Boardwalk businesses misreported that Zamperla is 'paying the city $1 million plus part of gross receipts.' We got a laugh out of that, but the reporter can be forgiven for thinking the correct $100K figure was so paltry as to be a typo. To put this number in perspective, consider that Boardwalk businesses like Ruby's and Cha Cha's have been paying $100,000 annual rent in recent years."

12. While this Determination of Eligibility does not protect the buildings within the district from demolition, inclusion on the Registers of Historic Places could make grants and tax credits of up to 40 percent available for redevelopment projects that rehabilitate and reuse historic properties in the amusement area. The Determination of Eligibility released on August 12th 2010 states that the amusement district is "nationally significant . . . as the birthplace of the modern American amusement industry." It also claims that the area's surviving historic buildings are "valuable cultural assets worthy of recognition and consideration in preservation planning" (New York State Office of Parks, Recreation and Historic Preservation 2010: 2).

13. The idea of a "Coney Island Historic District"—a two block long corridor along Surf Avenue that would preserve some of the historic structures—was proposed by preservation and advocacy groups including the Municipal Arts Society, the New York Landmarks Conservancy, the Historic Districts Council, Coney Island USA and Save Coney Island. The designation of the area as a "historic district" would have provided tax incentives in order to rehabilitate these historic buildings.

14. Almost ironically, on December 14, 2010, after all properties of Thor Equities had been razed down to rubble to make them ripe for development, the Landmarks Preservation Commission belatedly approved the designation for the Shore Theater, a neo-Renaissance theater built in 1924 and boarded up since the late 1970s, giving it landmark status.

15. The notion that the decisions of the City's Landmarks Preservation Commission are pro-developer and politically influenced by the City/Mayor's office deciding what gets landmarked and when, is common: "Over a decade of whirlwind development, the Landmarks Preservation Commission has repeatedly played dance partner to a potent mix of preservationists, developers and city politicians. It must strike a balance between protecting architecture and accepting economic realities, between a responsibility to history and a knowledge that the city must evolve." And: "The real estate industry controls the agenda in the city," said Tony Avella, a city councilman from Queens. "If they don't want something to happen, it doesn't happen. They pull the strings from behind the scenes, whether in rezoning reform or landmarking. It's just incredible how much influence they have." "The direction comes from the mayor, and the mayor's pro-development," Mr. Avella added" (Pogrebing 2008: np).

16. The Cyclone roller coaster, opened in 1927, was declared a New York City landmark in 1988, and a National Historic Landmark in 1991.

17. Coney Island's Wonder Wheel, opened in 1920, was named an official New York City Landmark in 1989.

18. The Parachute Jump was built for the 1939 New York World's fair in Flushing Meadows and brought to Coney in 1941 as part of the Steeplechase Park. It has been completely restored in 2002–2003.

19. During the 2002–2006 building boom, the number of demolition permits rose from 3,386 in 2002 to a high of 6,480 in 2006. The number fell in 2007 to 5,582 and there have been 2,112 permits issued in 2008, according to data of the Department Of Buildings (Pincus 2008).

20. Broadcasted on September 27, 2010.

21. Yet, the buildings had great potential, as a set of architectural renderings commissioned by the Save Coney Island advocacy groups in June 2010 showed: "These renderings show that the historic buildings of Coney Island still have life in them and still have a future," said Simeon Bankoff, executive director of the Historic Districts Council. "It's now up to the City to say whether that's better than acres of rubble" (Save Coney Island, 2010b). The renderings are available online at: www.saveconeyisland.net/wp-content/uploads/2010/06/Grashorn-Hendersons-flier-6.2.10.pdf

22. In recent years, Sodexo has been sued $80 million for racial discrimination against Black employees, and has been the target of innumerable labor protests against its union-bashing practices. It is also widely referred to as a producer of disgusting food (Maurer 2010).

23. Fortunately, the opening of Zamperla's new "Luna Park" has counterbalanced some of the losses accumulated in such a short time.

24. Source: mail correspondence dated August 1, 2009.

25. Source: mail correspondence dated August 1, 2009.

26. This has indeed a long tradition in a city whose public officials have relied on zoning codes as a key device for land use regulation since the first Zoning Resolution was established in 1916. The 1916 Zoning, as much as the 1811 grid plan, were not meant to guide development, but rather to assess the existing situation of the land market and to accommodate further development (Angotti, 2008: 61).

27. In early 2007, The Municipal Art Society launched the initiative *Imagine Coney*, which included public workshops, a public call for ideas, thorough economic analysis and a charrette with a team of international experts, including amusement industry leaders, to generate a more imaginative and more sustainable vision for development at Coney Island.

28. The Municipal Art Society of New York is a nonprofit organization founded in 1893, whose efforts contributed to establish the New York's Landmarks Preservation Commission and New York's Landmarks Law. The society is currently active in lobbying the city government in support of advocacy planning, historical preservation and sustainable development throughout the metropolitan area.

29. The Prater, in Vienna, has a surface of 50 acres; Tivoli gardens, in Copenhagen is about 20.5 acres; Disneyland is around 80 acres; Magic Kingdom occupies 107 acres, Epcot Center covers 300 acres, Disney-MGM Studios is 154 acres. A new Coney Island with 6 acres for outdoor amusements won't be able to compete with any of the great amusement parks worldwide.

30. The amusement industry is thriving even in times of crisis: because of the role they play as an interlude from the pressures of daily life, parks and attractions tend to fare relatively well during a recession. According to the TEA/ECOM Global Attraction Attendance Report (2009), which analyzes the performance of the top theme parks around the world, urban and regional parks (such as a future, fully functioning Coney Island) have been less impacted by the recession than "destination parks" because of their proximity to their market pools (populated urban cores). According to the same report, in 2008 the number of total visits to the top 20 parks in North America amounted to 121.4 million.

31. City Planning Chief Amanda Burden has warned the Municipal Arts Society against raising any objections: "It is imperative that the rezoning process and timeline not be jeopardized by any reconsideration of our proposed rezoning boundaries or urban design parameters. . . . It is imperative that this rezoning proceed expeditiously, otherwise the Coney Island amusement area that we know and love will cease to exist" (Brown 2008: np).

32. The 421-a tax incentive program was created in 1971 to encourage housing development at a time of shrinking population and falling property values in the City. Under the program, owners are exempt from paying the increase in property taxes that results from the new construction (for example, if the vacant land was valued at $1 million and the new property is worth $10 million after construction, the property owner will not be taxed for the $9 million increase in value for the exemption period, 10 to 25 years). According to a 2003 report by the NYC Independent Budget Office, only 7 percent (4,905) of the 69,000 units subsidized through this program were affordable to low or moderate income families. Affordable housing advocates maintained that the program was a needless and costly taxpayer's subsidy to developers of luxury condominiums. In 2006, the program was marginally reformed; an "exclusion zone" in which developers seeking the tax benefit must provide affordable housing was expanded into parts of all five boroughs; affordable housing was required to be built on the same sites as market-rate units; community residents were given prefer-

ence in the application process for half of all units initially offered for rent or sale; rent stabilization was required for a minimum of 35 years. However, the program still remains very controversial, as 421-a has been used primarily for luxury development at a cost to the city of $408 million in foregone tax revenues in 2006 (Buckley 2011).

33. The program cost the city $408 million in foregone tax revenue in 2006, according to the city's Finance Department, and will cost a projected $930 million in 2011, according to the Independent Budget Office (Buckley 2011).

34. The plan aims at creating or preserving 165,000 affordable housing units by 2013.

35. Data retrieved online on January 12th 2011 from City-Data.com. Available online at: http://www.city-data.com/neighborhood/Coney-Island-Brooklyn-NY.html

36. The bill, proposed in 2009, envisioned a set of new regulations into the rental process for small businesses, giving retailers and small office tenants new rights in dealing with their landlords, and forcing arbitration on new leases when the two sides disagree over a rent. Currently, there is no regulation of rents for commercial property. Once a lease expires, landlords have sole discretion to charge whatever they please, or even to refuse a renewal for no cause. The bill had garnered 30 sponsors in the City Council, more than enough to pass. But it ran into significant resistance from Council Speaker Christine Quinn and Mayor Michael Bloomberg.

37. This has been also the case of the 125th Street Rezoning Plan adopted in Harlem. In March 2008, The Municipal Art Society testified before the City Council's Land Use Subcommittee on Zoning and Franchises that 71 firms that employed about 975 employees on 125th Street were threatened with direct displacement by the rezoning plan (Jones 2008).

38. On July 13, 2009, Hudson Street in the West Village was renamed "Jane Jacobs Way" in her honor.

39. The DCP Plan (2009: np) reads: "New developments on Wonder Wheel Way and Bowery would be required to have amusements occupying half of the total street frontage and the ground floor level of hotels would be required to have active uses such as restaurants, retail and entertainment venues." And again: "parking for new residential buildings will likely be in multi-level [. . .] garages would be required to be wrapped by active uses on all street frontages." (Department of City Planning, 2009) Even the 125th street rezoning plan contains similar "cosmetic" prescriptions: banks and offices are forbidden from having large lobbies on the ground levels so as to keep the street life vibrant; shop owners are prohibited from coating their storefronts with metal grates after they close; and theaters are permitted to build new and extravagant marquee signs, an action not generally permitted citywide with few exceptions, such as Times Square.

40. In January 2003, Michael Bloomberg stated at an economic development summit cosponsored by the Partnership for New York City and NYCEDC: "If New York City is a business, it isn't Wal-Mart. It isn't trying to be the lowest-priced product in the market [...] It's a high-end product, maybe even a luxury product. New York offers tremendous value, but only for those companies able to capitalize on it" (Cardwell 2003: np).

REFERENCES

Amusing the Zillions. 2010a. "Under Construction: Luna Park Coney Island's $1.4M Sodexo-Run Restaurant & More." Retrieved February 5, 2011 (http://amusingthezillion.com/2010/12/02/under-construction-luna-park-coney-islands-1-4m-sodexo-run-restaurant-more/).

Amusing the Zillions. 2010b. "Thor's Coney Island: Tattered Tents, Deathwatch for Historic Buildings." Retrieved June 24, 2010 (http://amusingthezillion.com/2010/04/21/thors-coney-island-tattered-tents-deathwatch-for-historic-buildings/).

Amusing the Zillions. 2010c. "Out With the Old in Coney Island: Only 2 of 11 Boardwalk Businesses Invited Back." Retrieved November 13, 2010 (http://amusingthezillion.com/2010/11/01/out-with-the-old-in-coney-island-only-2-of-11-boardwalk-businesses-invited-back/).

Amusing the Zillions. 2010d. "Meet Sodexo: Luna Park Coney Island's Partner for On-Site Service Solutions." Retrieved February 5, 2011 (http://amusingthezillion.com/2010/11/23/meet-sodexo-luna-park-coney-islands-partner-for-on-site-service-solutions/).

Angotti, Tom. 2008. *New York for Sale: Community Planning Confronts Global Real Estate*. Cambridge, MA: MIT Press.

Angotti, Tom. 2009. "Zoning without Planning?" *Gotham Gazette* May 26, 2009. Retrieved May 28, 2009 (http://www.gothamgazette.com/article/fea/20090526/202/2928).

Backer, Kevin. 2010. "Coney Island's Grand Past and Grim Future—Requiem for a dreamland" *The Village Voice* May 25, 2010. Retrieved June 21, 2010 (www.villagevoice.com/2010-05-25/news/coney-island-s-grand-past-and-grim-future/).

Bagli, Charles. 2009a. "Seeking Revival, City to Buy Land in Coney Island" *The New York Times* November 11. Retrieved November 11, 2009 (www.nytimes.com/2009/11/12/nyregion/12coney.html).

Bagli, Charles. 2009b. "Beyond Sideshows, the City and a Developer Face Off Over Coney Island's Future" *The New York Times* April 10, 2009. Retrieved February 2, 2010 (www.nytimes.com/2009/04/11/nyregion/11coney.html?_r=1).

Barry, Dan. 2003. "About New York; Giuliani Razed Roller Coaster, And the Law" The New York Times October 4, 2003: Retrieved January 4, 2010 (www.nytimes.com/2003/10/04/nyregion/about-new-york-giuliani-razed-roller-coaster-and-the-law.html?scp=1&sq=giuliani%20thunderbolt%20bullard&st=cse).

Bloomberg, Michael 2007. Manhattan Institute. 2007. Bloomberg's keynote speech at the Manhattan Institute's "Thinking Big for New York City" Conference, on November 1st. 2007. (www.rpa-cui.org/newsletter/archive/200711_crd_newsletter.html).

Boyer, Christine 1996. *The City of Collective Memory: Its Historical Imagery and Architectural Entertainments*. Cambridge, MA: MIT Press.

Brenner, Neil. 2004. *New State Spaces: Urban Governance and the Rescaling of Statehood*. Oxford: Oxford University Press.

Brown, Eliot. 2008. "Burden To Municipal Art Society: Don't Mess With City's Coney Plans" *The New York Observer* October 27. Retrieved January 17, 2009 (www.observer.com/2008/real-estate/burden-municipal-art-society-don-t-mess-city-s-coney-plans-0).

Brown, Eliot. 2010. "The New Coney Island? Sitt Sees Fast Food in Place of Current Buildings" *The New York Observer* April 28. Retrieved May 3, 2010 (www.observer.com/2010/real-estate/sitt-demolish-coney-buildings-envisions-fast-food-their-place).

Buckley, Cara. 2011. "City Weighs Extending a Tax-Break Deadline" *The New York Times* February 8. Retrieved February 12, 2011 (www.nytimes.com/2011/02/09/nyregion/09affordable.html).

Burden, Amanda. 2009 From the statement of Commissioner Amanda Burden on the adoption of the Coney Island revitalization plan on July 30, 2009. Retrieved online on June 22 (www.nyc.gov/html/dcp/html/coney_island/index.shtml).

Butler, Chris, 2003. *Law and the Social Production of Space.* Doctor of Philosophy Thesis, Law School, Faculty of Law, Griffith University, Queensland.

Calder, Rich. 2007. "Cyclone swirls around Coney Island builder" *The New York Post* March 26. Retrieved June 22, 2008 (www.nypost.com/p/news/regional/item_uRMWWxL9ZL6xIdBiXNUC2L).

Calder, Rich. 2009. "Coney Island plan might need to seize land" *The Washington Post* March 9. Retrieved February 7, 2011 (www.nypost.com/p/news/regional/item_EBHaDD7TmOoTDEX2prQykO.

Cardwell, Diane. 2003. "Mayor Says New York is Worth the Cost" *The New York Times* January 3. Retrieved January 8, 2003 (www.nytimes.com/2003/01/08/nyregion/mayor-says-new-york-is-worth-the-cost.html).

Caro, Robert A. 1975. *The Power Broker: Robert Moses and the Fall of New York.* New York: Knopf Doubleday Publishing.

Cautela, Giuseppe. 1925. "Coney." *The American Mercury* (New York), edited by H. L. Mencken. Center for an Urban Future, 2008. *Coney Island Visions*. Retrieved November 27, 2008 (www.nycfuture.org/images_pdfs/pdfs/ConeyIslandVisions.pdf).

Center for an Urban Future. 2008. *Attack of the Chains?* Retrieved August 12, 2008 (www.nycfuture.org/images_pdfs/pdfs/Attackofthechains.pdf).

Center for an Urban Future. 2009. *Reviving the City of Aspirations: A Study of the challenges facing New York City's Middle Class*. Retrieved January 17, 2010 (www.nycfuture.org/images_pdfs/pdfs/CityOfAspiration.pdf).

City of New York Department of City Planning. 2007a. *Housing Marketplace.*

City of New York Department of City Planning. 2007b. *PlanNYC 2030.*

City of New York Department of City Planning. 2008. *125th Street Rezoning Plan.*

City of New York Department of City Planning. 2009. *Coney Island Comprehensive Rezoning Plan.*

City of New York Office of the Attorney General. 2010. Retrieved February 6, 2010 (www.ag.ny.gov/media_center/2010/july/july21a_10.html).

Coney Island Development Corporation. 2005. *Coney Island Strategic Plan.*

De Certeau, Michel 2002. *The Practice of Everyday Life*. 2nd edition. Berkeley: University of California Press.

Denson, Charles 2004. *Coney Island: Lost and Found.* Berkley, CA: Ten Speed Press.

Fainstein, Susan. 2005. "The Return of Urban Renewal: Dan Doctoroff's Grand Plans for New York City" *Harvard Design Magazine, Urban Planning Now: What Works, What Doesn't?* 22 (Spring–Summer): 1–5.

Fung, Amanda. 2009. "Coney Island Keeper: Thor Equities' Joe Sitt gives city a ride for its money" *Crain's New York Business* June 28, 2009. Retrieved August 3, 2010 (www.crainsnewyork.com/article/20090628/SMALLBIZ/306289868#).

Goonewardena, Kanishka, Stefan Kipfer, Richard Milgrom and Christian Schmid, eds. 2008. *Space, Difference, Everyday Life: Reading Henri Lefebvre*. London, UK: Routledge.

Goss, Paul. 2010. "Coney Island then and now: A look at the Pyrotechnic Insanitarium 100 years on." *Architecture and Anthropology Curiosity Collaborative* May 16. Retrieved June 12, 2010 (http://architectureanthropology.com/coney-island-then-and-now-a-look-at-the-pyrotechnic-insanitarium-100-years-on).

Gross, Courtney. 2008. "Reshaping the City: Who's Being Heard—and Why?" *Gotham Gazette* August 25, 2008. Retrieved May 21, 2009 (www.gothamgazette.com/article/iotw/20080825/200/2619).

Harvey, David. 1989a. *The Urban Experience*. Baltimore, MD: Johns Hopkins University Press.

Harvey, David. 1989b. "From Managerialism to Entrepreneurialism: The Transformation in Urban Governance in Late Capitalism." *Geografiska Annaler Series B, Human Geography* 71(1):3–17.

Immerso, Michael. 2002. *Coney Island: The People's Playground.* Toronto, Ontario: Rutgers University Press.

Immerso, Michael. 2010. "Coney Island Cornerstones on Surf Avenue face demolition" *The Huffington Post* July 14, 2010. Retrieved July 29, 2010 (www.huffingtonpost.com/michael-immerso/coney-island-cornerstones_b_646400.html).

Jones, David. 2008. "Harlem rezoning critics call for protecting local retailers," The Real Deal, April 1. Retrieved on July 9, 2009 (http://therealdeal.com/newyork/articles/harlem-rezoning-critics-call-for-protecting-local-retailers).

Kasson, F. John. 1978. *Amusing the Million: Coney Island at the Turn of the Century.* New York: American Century, Hill and Wang.

Kipfer, Stefan. 2008. "How Lefebvre urbanized Gramsci: hegemony, everyday life, and difference." Pp. 193–211 in *Space, Difference, Everyday Life: Reading Henri Lefebvre*, edited by Kanishka Goonewardena, Stefan Kipner, Richard Milgrom and Christian Schmid. New York: Routledge.

Koolhaas, Rem [1978] 2001. *Delirious New York: a Retroactive Manifesto for Manhattan*. New York: Monacelli Press.

Lai, Linda. 2008. "Spaces of Experience: the Production of Space." April 10, 2008.

Lefebvre, Henri. 1991. *The Production of Space*. Oxford, UK: Blackwell Publishing.

Lefebvre, Henri. 2003. *The Urban Revolution.* Minneapolis: University of Minnesota Press.

Massey, Daniel. 2009. "Mayor's economy: Grades are in—Bloomberg gets an A for quality of life, a C for budget" *Crain's New York Business* October 11. Retrieved October 12, 2009 (www.crainsnewyork.com/article/20091011/SMALLBIZ/310119987).

Maurer, Daniel. 2010. "Could a 40-Year-Old Coney Institution Be Replaced By a Corporate Cafeteria Giant?" *The New York Magazine* November 29. Retrieved February 6, 2011 (http://newyork.grubstreet.com/2010/11/60-year-old_coney_instituion_t.html).

Matassa, Elizabeth H. 2006. *Whaddya Want? It's Coney Island! Tourism, Play and Memory in the Illegible City*. Master of Arts Thesis, Department of Geography and Anthropology, Louisiana State University.

McGeehan, Patrick. 2009. "Unemployment Hits 10.3% in New York City," *The New York Times* September 17. Retrieved October 11, 2009 (www.nytimes.com/2009/09/18/nyregion/18unemploy.html).

Milgrom, Richard. 2008. "Lucien Kroll: design, difference, everyday life." Pp. 264–82 in *Space, Difference, Everyday Life: Reading Henri Lefebvre*, edited by Kanishka Goonewardena, Stefan Kipner, Richard Milgrom and Christian Schmid. New York: Routledge.

Miller, Michael. 2009. "Whose Coney Island?" *The Brooklyn Rail—Critical Perspectives on Art, Politics and Culture*. Retrieved June 12, 2009 (www.brooklynrail.org/2009/06/local/whose-coney-island)

Municipal Art Society. 2009. *Testimony for the New York City Planning Commission.* Retrieved May 15, 2009 (http://mas.org/images/positions/Coney-Island-City-Council-Testimony-July-09.pdf).

New York State Office of Parks, Recreation and Historic Preservation. 2010. *Determination of Eligibility for Coney Island's historic district.* Retrieved October 21, 2010 (www.saveconeyisland.net/wp-content/uploads/2010/08/determinationofeligibility.081210.pdf).

Newman, Kathe and Elvin Wyly. 2006. "The Right to Stay Put, Revisited: Gentrification and Resistance to Displacement in New York City." *Urban Studies* 43(1):1–35.

Pearson, Erica. 2010. "Summer fun! New Yorkers kick off season at Coney Island's new Luna Park," *NY Daily News* May 30. Retrieved May 39, 2010 (http://articles.nydailynews.com/2010-05-30/local/27065750_1_luna-park-astroland-rides).

Pincus, Adam. 2008. "Demolition permits plunge in November, signal development slowdown" *The Real Deal*, December 1, 2008. Retrieved January 12, 2010 (http://therealdeal.com/newyork/articles/demolition-permits-plunge-in-november-signal-development-slowdown).

Pogrebin, Robin. 2008. "Preservation and Development, Engaged in a Delicate Dance" *The New York Times* December 1, 2008. Retrieved May 21, 2010 (www.nytimes.com/2008/12/02/arts/design/02landmarks.html?ref=nyregion).

Povoledo, Elisabetta. 2010. "Coney Island Getting a $30 Million Italian Makeover" *The New York Times* April 23, 2010. Retrieved April 24, 2010 (www.nytimes.com/2010/04/24/business/global/24coney.html).

Pratt Institute, Center for Community & Environmental Development and Policy Link, 2004. *Increasing Housing Opportunities in New York City: The Case for Inclusionary Zoning.* Retrieved September 22, 2007 (http://prattcenter.net/sites/default/files/users/pdf/Inclusionary%20Zoning%20Full%20Report_0.pdf)

Pratt Center for Community Development, 2006. *Still Subsidizing Luxury Development.* Retrieved May 12, 2007 (http://prattcenter.net/sites/default/files/publications/PrattCenter-421a-Still_subsidizing_luxury_development.pdf).

Rivero, Juan 2004. *Coney Island: Planning Nostalgic Space.* Master of Architecture and Planning Thesis, Columbia University New York. Retrieved May 25, 2007 (http://homepage.mac.com/jjrivero/coney_island/text/introduction.pdf)

Save Coney Island. 2009a. "Save Coney Island on Rezoning Vote: A Sad Day for New York City." Retrieved December 2, 2009 (http://www.saveconeyisland.net/?p=621).

Save Coney Island. 2009b. "As N.Y. Honors Jane Jacobs, Her Son Is 'Appalled' at Coney Island Rezoning Plan." Retrieved December 2, 2009 (www.saveconeyisland.net/?p=435).

Save Coney Island. 2010a. "Save Coney Island Hails New Luna Park, but Warns Coney's History Is in Danger." Retrieved May 27, 2010 (www.saveconeyisland.net/?p=1173).

Save Coney Island. 2010b. "Renderings Show Potential of Endangered Coney Island Buildings." Retrieved June 2, 2010 (www.saveconeyisland.net/?p=1238).

Sargen, Greg. 2005. "The Incredibly Bold, Audaciously Cheesy, Jaw-Droppingly Vegasified, Billion-Dollar Glam-Rock Makeover of Coney Island" *The New York Magazine* September 18, 2005. Retrieved June 12, 2008 (http://nymag.com/nymetro/realestate/features/14498/).

SocioWiki. 2011. "The Presence of the Past: Turning Points in NYC." Retrieved January 12, 2011 (www.macaulay.cuny.edu/seminars/napoli08/index.php/Coney_Island_Context).

Taconic Investments Partners LLC Portfolio. 2011. *Coney Island, North and South Venture.* Retrieved February 13, 2011 (www.taconicinvestments.com/portfolio/coneyisland_nv.html).

TEA/ERA. 2009. "Theme Park Attendance Report 2009." Burbank, CA: Themed Entertainment Association.

Treiman, Daniel. 2009. "How Mayor Bloomberg is killing Coney Island" *The Huffington Post* July 22, 2009. Retrieved July 29, 2009 (www.huffingtonpost.com/daniel-treiman/coney-island-construction_b_242748.html)

Tuccille, Jerome. 1985. *Trump: The Saga of America's Most Powerful Real Estate Baron.* New York: Beard Books.

University Neighborhood Housing Program, 2007. "Shrinking Affordability." New York, NY.

U.S. Census Bureau. 2011. *State and County Quickfacts.* Retrieved January 12, 2011 (http://quickfacts.census.gov/qfd/states/36/36061.html).

Weber, Rachel 2002. "Extracting Value from the City: Neoliberalism and Urban Redevelopment" *Antipode* 34:3.

8

The Gowanus Canal

Local Politics of "Superfunding" Status

Shanna Farrell

As Rachel Carson said, "Water is essential for more than human consumption, irrigation, and transportation. It plays a vital role in terms of the life chain it supports" (Hamilton Lytle 2007: 57). This is absolutely true for the Gowanus Canal, a Brooklyn landmark. What was once an industrial passageway that symbolized prosperity is now an eyesore and a health hazard. The canal represents industrialization, neglect, lack of responsibility, and conversely, hope. As an industrial canal, myriad pollutants have long plagued its waters and vexed the surrounding community. The immense pollution that contaminates the Gowanus Canal violates the Clean Water Act. After years of neglect by the city of New York, a glimmer of hope appeared in the spring of 2009 when the Environmental Protection Agency proposed adding the canal to its National Priorities List, a list of highly polluted sites that are deemed in need of a high priority comprehensive cleanup monitored by the Environmental Protection Agency, which would designate it a Superfund site. However, before community members had a chance to rejoice, Mayor of New York City Michael Bloomberg announced an alternative cleanup plan by the city and promised to take less time to complete than would the Environmental Protection Agency's plan. The city's plan favored development of the neighborhood and would be implemented and ran by the city of New York. The condition of the canal is not only a health issue, but also a political issue, as it tore the social fabric of the community local to the canal.

The Gowanus Canal is almost two miles long, measuring 7,724 feet, and is located in the northwest section of Brooklyn. It runs in a southwest direction, curving at its halfway point. The Gowanus neighborhood surrounds the canal on three sides; the southern end of the canal serves as its fourth side and is where it empties into the New York Harbor. Here, at the mouth of the canal, there is a Lowe's home improvement store. Lowe's shares a parking lot with an industrial landfill of sorts. A tall yellow crane is a permanent fixture among the landscape and is used to pile industrial waste, like metal scraps, into a high mound. If industrial barges need to be used in the canal, they are usually located in this section. Further up the canal on the east side, it is more industrial than residential. There are four inlets that stick out of the east side of the canal. There is a concrete company on this side; from an aerial view their trucks, when parked, resemble toy trucks belonging to a child who has neatly put them away for the night. There is also an iconic sign that reads "Kentile Floors." The sign used to glow in red at night, but since the business is now defunct, the sign's lights have been permanently shut off. To the east of the canal, Gowanus borders the Park Slope and Sunset Park neighborhoods; west of the canal are the neighborhoods of Red Hook and Carroll Gardens. Red Hook was an industrial neighborhood until the 1960s and is mostly residential now. Carroll Gardens is primarily residential. Along the west side of the canal, there are many chain-linked fences intended to keep people away from the water. The area near the head of the canal is also heavily residential and it becomes the Boerum Hill neighborhood just a few blocks north. Five bridges cross the canal, including the Union Street, Carroll Street, Third Street, and Ninth Streets bridges, as well one at Hamilton Avenue. A section of the Brooklyn-Queens Expressway, I-278, is elevated above the canal, as well as two subway stops, the Smith and Ninth Street station and Fourth and Ninth Street station (The City of New York's Community Board Six 2009).

Chemical contaminants sit on the floor of the canal, buried by a layer of naturally occurring soft sediment. The canal's waters are green and often stagnant, save for when raw sewage drains from one of the many pipes connected to sewer lines after a rainstorm.[1] Scrap metal, abandoned cars, steel shopping carts, and miscellaneous trash clutter the banks and the bottom of the canal. Community members that live in Gowanus close to the canal have been subjected to the canal's odor, which is strong enough to waft into the noses of residents and passersby on warm days. People who have lived in the area for a long time can vividly describe the smell has been the inspiration for a local artist, who created color tones that corresponded with the intensity of the canal's stink on any given day. The more pungent the canal's smell was, the deeper and darker the corresponding color was. There are also suspicions of bacteria such as hepatitis, typhoid, and cholera, and residents have lived with the view of the canal's tarnished aesthetic since the 1950s (Prete 1998). While the general health and safety of the canal has been a constant issue and no one disputed that the canal is in dire need of a makeover, there were diverging opinions on how this task should be accomplished and which government entity should assume responsibility for this project. During the controversial time before the canal was granted Superfund status in March of 2010, tensions were high in the surrounding neighborhoods.

For over a hundred years, controversy has swirled around the cleanup of the canal. Brooklyn residents fought a long and arduous battle for the remediation of the canal, a common cause that served as a unifying force for the community. When the EPA expressed their interest in taking responsibility for the canal's remediation, many residents were overjoyed. Marlene Donnelly, a Gowanus resident and environmental activist, said of the Superfund proposal, "When this was announced it brought great hope to our community. We are really surprised about the groundswell of support that everybody has been hearing for the Superfund because we believe that this is our possibility to finally addressing the environmental conditions here in the Gowanus" (Freddy's Roundhouse Brooklyn 2009: np). Just as it seemed that community activists were making progress, evident in the canal's acknowledgement by the EPA, the city stymied their efforts. The city's plan, announced by Mayor Bloomberg, included using funds from the city, polluters, developers, and the federal government to cover the costs of the cleanup. Details of this plan were very vague and not released until several months after the initial announcement. One of the developers interested in developing along the canal, The Toll Brothers, planned to contribute $30 million to the city and the project, and said they would conduct a spot clean, which only intends to remediate certain portions of the water close to where they were planning to build condominiums. A spot cleanup is not comprehensive; it only aims to clean portions of the canal closest to where people live. (This tactic caused a divide among residents and longtime activists.) A number of community members supported the EPA's proposal to add the canal to the NPL. They believed in the merits of this plan, as the EPA had thirty years of experience remediated polluted sites, as well as have legal means of obtaining money to conduct the project from polluters. However, some community members did appreciate the federal involvement and preferred to support the city of New York and Mayor Bloomberg's plan. These residents felt that the city's plan would be quicker and bolster economic development in Gowanus.

Data for this article was obtained through a myriad of research methods. I conducted interviews with Brooklyn residents and activists, as well as government officials. I attended several community meetings about the canal. I analyzed multiple texts, including scholarly essays, current newspaper and magazine articles, transcripts of new radio broadcasts, government documents, community-based blogs that reflected the opinions of local residents, and literature from environmental nonprofit groups and businesses. I viewed documentaries and community based videos made about the canal. I also directly observed the canal and the surrounding neighborhood on a regular basis for approximately eighteen months.

THE GOWANUS CANAL: A BRIEF HISTORY

The Gowanus Canal was originally known as the Gowanes Creek, named after Chief Gowanes of the Native American Canarsee Indian tribe.[2] It was a small inlet and saltwater marsh that both Henry Hudson and Giovanni da Verrazano used as a navigational tool when they were exploring the New York Harbor. Originally owned by the Dutch government, it was sold to New York City for the construction of a tobacco plant in 1636; this was the first real estate deal made by settlers in Brooklyn. In 1645, Adam Bronwer built New York's first tidewater gristmill, located on the canal. Shortly after, a second gristmill was built nearby. When this second mill was built, it was decided that the canal needed to be deepened. It was dredged; this would be the first of many times the canal would be altered to fit human needs. Several Dutch farmers moved to the area, building farmhouses and settling along the waterway. As the population in South Brooklyn increased, the creek became industrialized, signaling the beginning of its identity as a commercial waterway. After the initial dredge, the canal was extended to measure a mile and half and officially renamed the Gowanus Canal (The Gowanus Dredgers Canoe Club 2004). Major David Douglas of the Army Corp of Engineers was hired to design the canal and it was completed in 1869. After the canal was engineered, it became the hub of the commercial shipping industry in New York City. Around this time, Gowanus experienced an industrial, and consequently, an economic boom. Factories that manufactured paint, ink, and soap were built along its banks. Warehouses, tanneries, coal stores, gas refineries, and later stone and coal yards, flour mills, cement works, chemical plants, and sulfur producers[3] were also located along the canal. Due to the jobs that were created by the industrialization of the area, many people began to move in; their arrival incited the formation of the Carroll Gardens, Cobble Hill, and Park Slope neighborhoods (Prete 1998).

With industrialization came an unintended consequence: an incredible amount of pollution. Having no better disposal mechanisms in place, waste from the factories was drained into the canal. Because there was so much chemical waste festering in the water, captains would bring their ships or boats from the New York Harbor to sit in the canal for a few days; the chemicals and pollutants would eat or kill any bacteria or barnacles from the vessel's bottom so the captain would not have to worry about returning to their home ports with potential invasive bacteria or aquatic species back with them (Stanne 2010). Ink manufacturers dumped their waste into the canal, changing its color daily; this earned the canal the popular local nickname "Lavender Lake" (Prete 1998). Sewer connections flushing raw sewage from surrounding neighborhoods also emptied into the canal's water. This raw sewage, combined with industrial by-product and storm water run-off burdened the canal, constantly filling it with sludge. In order to keep the canal in working order and boats from bottoming out, regular dredging became a necessity.

With emerging technology in the 1940s and 1950s the New York City waterfront underwent a major change, "containerization." This process uses large metal containers to transport goods via boat, barge, railroad, and plane. Businesses began to use containers on railroad lines instead of by boat and barge, signaling the beginning of the end of the New York harbor's industrial life (Sharps 2010). Containerization hit Gowanus hard. Though the canal was still a means of transportation for barges carrying fuel oil, sand, gravel, and scrap metal, the canal became an inefficient passageway for many businesses. Factories began to close, and unemployment rose. The declivity of the canal's industrial success caused a substantial loss of jobs. As businesses closed and jobs in the area were lost, industrial buildings were abandoned and people began to move out of Gowanus. Once the canal was no longer seen as viable source of income, it became neglected. For many years, industrial waste was dumped into the water and the canal was never cleaned. Empty lots became filled with rusted cars and shopping carts, tires, and other industrial scraps. A popular past time for local youths was "car surfing," where they tried to keep their balance while jumping from land to floating cars and back (Lucas 2010). Much disposed waste found its way inside the canal and was forgotten about. This caused the canal to become a "derelict dumping place" (Prete 1998). Because it was no longer deemed cost-effective, dredging of the canal stopped in 1975 (Bonanos 2009). The health of the water and the canal had been completely compromised.

Whispers of concern over this issue had begun years earlier, around 1900. Members of the community wanted to clean the canal, but were not armed with the necessary resources and were occluded by local business owners. Instead of a proper cleanup, a large propeller was built in 1901. The propeller was seven feet wide and 6,200 feet long. It was at the head of the canal and meant to flush water out of the canal. The propeller was ultimately a pacification mechanism created to quell the concerns of residents vocalizing their discontent over the health of the water. "South Brooklyn Day" was declared to celebrate the opening of the Flushing Tunnel and fell on June 21, 1911, the first day of its use. A "Miss Gowanus" was crowned, symbolizing a clean future for the canal. Miss Gowanus, a nine-year old girl, floated on a barge through the canal and tossed white flower petals into the water, as onlookers cheered. In 1947, a pumping station was built, also at the head of the canal. It pumped oxygenated water into the canal intended to dilute the noxious odor that emanated from the water, which was particularly strong on a warm day. This method dissipated the smell for a time until 1965, when it stopped working. The propeller wasn't reactivated until 1999 after growing requests from community members (The City of New York's Community Board Six 2009).

A worker from Bayside Fuel and Oil, a company that is still in operation today, said, "The canal is past its prime. This place is a nightmare. It's like bizarro world." While the canal has not been dredged in over thirty years, there were often dead dogs and dead bodies found floating in the water until the 1980s and 1990s. Many residents believe it to be infested with live hepatitis, typhoid, gonorrhea, and cholera (Prete 1998). While many people currently canoe, boat, or even live on houseboats in the canal, longtime residents of Gowanus tell stories about how rainstorms induced diarrhea in their children during the several days that followed, as the chemicals that were stirred from the wet weather had physiological consequences (Appel 2010).

In early December 2009, before the canal was designated a Superfund site, the United States Environmental Protection Agency began a remedial investigation of the canal's water, sediment, and air, something that concerned citizens had been asking for since the 1970s. A remedial investigation is an "in-depth study designed to gather data needed to determine the nature and extent of contamination at a Superfund site" (United States Environmental Protection Agency 2011). The results of this study were released in February 2011. The study confirmed which contaminants were most prevalent in the canal and assessed the risk in two areas, ecological and human health. During the years that the canal was used as a dumping ground for industrial waste, it was polluted most heavily with Polycyclic Aromatic Hydrocarbons (PAHs), Polychlorinated Biphenyls (PCBs), and Volatile Organic Compounds (VOCs). PAHs are byproducts of the incomplete burning of coal, oil, gas, and garbage and are found in coal tar, crude oil, creosote, and roofing tar. PCBs are used as coolants in lubricants in transformers, capacitors, and electric equipment and are not very flammable. VOCs are synthetic compounds and evaporate easily into the air. They are used to manufacture paints, pharmaceuticals, and refrigerants (United States Environmental Protection Agency 2011).

PCBs are a suspected human carcinogen and can compromise the endocrine, reproductive, immune, and nervous systems. PAHs are also suspected to cause cancer in humans. The EPA conducted a human health and ecological risk assessment in 2010 and 2011 and found that "people are at risk from exposure to PCBs if they consume fish or crab caught in the canal" and are at risk from exposure to PAHs if they come into "regular contact with water or sediment from the canal" (United States Environmental Protection Agency 2011). This study confirmed what many residents suspected—that there were toxic chemical contaminants lining the canal. While doing that survey, they spoke with several subsistence fishers, those who live off of the fish that they catch. The majority of the subsistence fishers here are Hispanic and English is usually their second language. They fish in both the Gowanus Canal and off the piers in Red Hook into New York Harbor; these fish and crabs that they catch serve as a cheap meal for their families, even though they are highly contaminated with toxic chemicals that have bioaccumulated in the fish and crab's bodies. The Department of Environmental Protection is tasked with posting signs warning people about fishing advisories and health risks near or along polluted bodies of water, but most of these signs are written in English. Because the information on these signs is written only in English, they do not convey their intended message to the people who stand to benefit the most, or could most be harmed (Tsiamis 2011).

THE NEIGHBORHOOD

There are over 100,000 people living in South Brooklyn, the general region where the Gowanus Canal is located. Residents here are well educated and highly employed. According to the United States Census Bureau, about 82 percent of Gowanus residents have graduated high school, higher than the national average. The neighborhoods next to Gowanus, those of Carroll Gardens, Cobble Hill, and Park Slope, boast a 77 percent, 85 percent, and 83 percent rate of people respectively who have received high school diplomas. Perhaps more striking is the percentage of residents who have received a Bachelor's degree or higher. Fifty percent of Gowanus, 45 percent of Carroll Gardens and Cobble Hill, and 53 percent of Park Slope residents far exceed the national average of 24 percent of those who have been college educated. On average, 68 percent of residents in this area are employed and working (United States Bureau of the Census 2000).

Gowanus was once a working class neighborhood that had a high immigrant population. In the 1950s and 1960s, it mostly had a Hispanic and African-American population. In Red Hook, a nearby industrial neighborhood that was between the southwestern part of the canal and the harbor, it was mostly Irish-American and Italian-American families; in Carroll Gardens, the neighborhood that bordered the northwestern section of the canal, it was mostly Italian-American families. Though Gowanus was mostly Hispanic and African-American, it was lightly infused with Irish-American and Italian-American families. When industry began to decline in the 1950s, people began to leave the area and an influx of artists arrived in the 1960s and 1970s (Lucas 2010). As buildings began to show signs of neglect and abandonment, artists found inspiration and cheap rent in the urban decay. They began to gentrify the neighborhood. With gentrification came respect and caring. People began to care about their community in a new way. The first meeting about the plight of the Gowanus Canal was held in the 1960s in Carroll Gardens by the Italian-American families that had stayed in the area (Hay 2010). Out of this grew pride and people began to try to reverse the negative perception of living in Gowanus. In his fictional book, *The Fortress of Solitude,* about growing up in Gowanus in the 1960s during the beginning of gentrification, author Jonathan Lethem sheds some light on the pride that residents feel: "If someone asks you say you live in *Gowanus*. Don't be ashamed," a mother instructs her son (Lethem 2003: 51).

The neighborhood is very active. Many annual events involve the canal, such as a summer solstice celebration, which features a costumed resident riding a zip line cable across the water (Freddy's Roundhouse Brooklyn 2009). A local gallery, Proteus Gowanus, has rotating exhibits, many of which are centered on the canal itself. During the summer of 2010, they had an exhibit about the changing face of the canal detailed through maps and artifacts. They also offer free lectures and community events, such as a mini-rocket launch in a lot across the street from the gallery. Local restaurants, bars, and music venues near the canal have gotten media attention, their profiles printed on the pages of local magazines. This attention has brought business to Gowanus and fomented exploration of the area by New Yorkers from other boroughs.

This neighborhood is home to many local activists and nonprofit community groups dedicated to environmental causes. Perhaps the most famous grassroots activist in the area is Salvatore Scotto, known to most as Buddy. He attended his very first meeting about the plight of the canal in the mid 1960s when he was a young man. Scotto, an Italian-American born in 1929, dreamed of affordable housing for fellow Italian-Americans that were being forced out of the Carroll Gardens neighborhood, where rent was skyrocketing. Scotto was also embarrassed by the canal in the 1960s and decided to take a stand. Of this experience, he has said, "As an Italian-American, I was embarrassed by the condition of the canal. Where the hell were our people?" He rallied fellow Italian-Americans at the grassroots level to help him fight for his cause (Hay 2010). Scotto formed The Carroll Gardens Association in 1968 and the Gowanus Canal Community Development Corporation, GCCDC, in 1978. He founded the GCCDC to create reasonably priced housing for Italian-Americans, something he had dreamed of doing. "People born and raised in this neighborhood can't afford to live in this neighborhood," Scotto said in 2011. Gentrification caused fewer parishioners for Italian-based churches and fewer customers for Italian-run grocery stores and cafes. More renters moved in and transience became common. This meant that people were less likely to become involved in the area's political affairs. (Hay 2010). Scotto became the self-proclaimed "Mayor of Gowanus" because of his active role in fighting for the revitalization of the canal and his involvement in developing the area. He wanted development that would benefit everyone, something that he calls "social engineering." He was concerned with the availability of affordable housing and jobs in the area. He envisioned "Venice on the Gowanus Canal." He thought that the operation of industrial businesses was an inappropriate use of the canal. As a result of his outspokenness for his highly unique vision for the area, he had a tenuous relationship with local business owners. The owners of Bayside Fuel and Oil, brothers Alfred and Victor Allegretti (though Alfred died in 2001) still use the canal for transport, did not necessarily disagree with Scotto, but have called the canal a "cesspool" and expressed that they had no other place to take their business (Prete 1998).

Though he might have the most experience in working with the canal, many residents began fighting for its health not long after Scotto began his crusade. Newer residents joined forces with lifelong residents and began to take action. Grassroots groups held public meetings, at which the canal was a frequent topic; it was in these forums that residents began to plead with the city to take the initial steps toward cleaning the canal or conducting a study on the human health effects of living nearby.

The health and safety of the water has been a perpetual concern among local residents and has served as the impetus for the creation of several environmental organizations. These organizations have a myriad of missions. Some promote the construction of low-income housing, such as The Gowanus Canal Community Development Corporation, while others, like The Gowanus Dredgers Canoe Club, encourage recreational use of the waterway. There is a bevy of local activists who have created community groups to lobby for the purification of the canal, including Friends and Residents of the Greater Gowanus and Friends of Bond. It is the persistence of community involvement that led to the Environmental Protection Agency proposing that the Gowanus Canal be designated a Superfund site.

WHAT IS SUPERFUNDING?

In 1948, the federal government established the Federal Water Pollution Control Act; it was the first major piece of U.S. legislation enacted to address water pollution. In the late 1960s there was an increasing amount of public awareness due to the rise of the environmental movement that led to growing concerns about water pollution and the limitations of the Federal Water Pollution Control Act. These concerns included pollution in the Chesapeake Bay and the financial consequences wrought by the fishing industry,[4] unsafe bacteria levels in the Hudson River, an usually high amount of fish kills,[5] unsafe chemicals in public drinking water, a record level of mercury in swordfish,[6] and most famously a fire in the Cuyahoga River in Ohio in 1969 caused by a floating oil slick. The fire was responsible for significant damage to two railroad trestles. An investigation determined that "a discharge of highly volatile petroleum derivatives with a sufficiently low flash point was ignited by a chance occurrence," probably from a passing train, and was to blame for the fire (United States Environmental Protection Agency 1977). These events led to an amendment of the Pollution Control Act in 1972, which was the Clean Water Act of 1972. The Clean Water Act of 1972 was amended in 1977 and became what is commonly known today as the Clean Water Act, or the CWA.

The CWA governs flowing waters that discharge into navigable waterways, such as the Gowanus Canal. One of its functions is to call for the elimination of polluted surface waters that impair human sport and recreation. It also seeks to eliminate both point source (a single identifiable source of pollution, like industrial and sewage treatment plants) and non-point source (pollution that comes from several sources, like rainfall or snowmelt that is laced with contaminants and runs-off into a waterway) pollution and the emission of toxic substances. The CWA provides a benchmark against which to measure water quality. Clean water standards were outlined in the CWA and every navigable waterway in the United States was supposed to comply by 1983.

There are several components of the CWA that the Gowanus Canal specifically violates, including Title III and the Water Quality Standards Program. Title III is concerned with technological and water quality-based standards and enforcement of them pertaining to both technology and water quality. Technology-based standards include guidelines for municipal sewage treatment plants and provide New Source Performance Standards for industrial facilities and discharge that calls for treatment plants to have the "best available demonstrated control technology." With only one working treatment plant located in Red Hook, Brooklyn, the canal violates the technology-based standards set by the CWA because this facility does not use the best available technology that would allow the canal to meet the water quality requirements. The Water Quality Standards Program sets hazard-based requirements that determine levels of tolerable pollutants for individual bodies of water. Once the requirements are set, which is Total Maximum Daily Load, a number value that expresses a level of pollution that will not cause human or ecological health risks for a particular contaminant, it cannot be violated. If it is violated, an implementation plan is developed that outlines how the site can meet the standards. (United States Environmental Protection Agency 1977). The Gowanus Canal has never met any of these standards because of the nature and extent of pollutants that are in the water and are buried in the canal bottom. For over thirty years, the Gowanus Canal has violated both Title III and the Water Quality Standards Program, whose compliance is required by the CWA; eight of these years have been under Mayor Bloomberg (Freddy's Roundhouse Brooklyn 2009).

On the heels of the 1977 revision of the CWA, Congress passed the Comprehensive Environmental Response, Compensation, and Liability Act, or CERCLA. It was formally enacted on December 11, 1980. CERCLA provides "broad federal authority to respond directly to releases or threatened releases of hazardous substances that may endanger public health or the environment." The function of CERCLA is twofold. Its first aim is to "establish prohibits and requirements for closed or abandoned waste sites," provide liability of those found responsible for the damage at these sites, and to establish a trust fund to remediate said sites. Its second aim is to elicit response actions. There are two types of response actions that CERLCA implemented, which include short-term and long-term action. Short-term action addresses contamination in sites that require a prompt response and cleanup is immediate. Long-term remedial action is needed when contaminated sites require cleanup to "permanently and significantly reduce the dangers associated with releases or threats of releases of hazardous substances" (United States Environmental Protection Agency 1980). Most of the sites that are Superfunded call for long-term remedial action; these are sites, like the Gowanus Canal, that involved a comprehensive cleanup performed by the Army Corp of Engineers, cost millions of dollars, require a public comment period and multiple community meetings, and take years, if not decades, to complete (United States Environmental Protection Agency 1980).

The long-term response action is perhaps the most important component of CERCLA and many hazardous waste sites fall into this category. It is the response that the EPA recommended for the Gowanus Canal. It also engendered the creation of the National Priorities List, or the NPL. The NPL is a list of sites in the United States that the EPA has recognized to be in the most urgent need of remedial action. When a site is listed on the NPL it is granted "Superfund Status" and designated a Superfund site. Superfund is a colloquial term for the CERCLA. It is a federal enactment to clean abandoned hazardous waste sites. CERCLA was also the impetus for the revision of the National Contingency Plan, or NCP, which outlined the measures that needed to be taken in response to the "releases and threatened releases of hazardous substances, pollutants, or contaminants"[7] (United States Environmental

Protection Agency 1986). In October 1986, CERCLA was amended by the Superfund Amendments and Reauthorization Act, or SARA.

Additionally, the long-term action response is important because it holds polluters financially responsible for covering any costs associated with the cleanup. There is a trust fund that is appropriated for cleanup costs, where an initial $1.6 billion was collected during a five-year period that went to the establishment of these funds. It is common for the remediation costs to exceed $1.6 billion for a single site, which is why the EPA relies heavily on funding from responsible parties. In 1981, the average cost of cleaning a hazardous site was roughly $170 million; the average cost of containing the extracted chemicals per site was $3.6 million. It is estimated that the cost to remediate the Gowanus Canal will be between $300 and $500 million and it will be a twelve-year process (Navarro 2010). As of April 2011, the EPA had sent twenty-one notices of potential liability and information request letters to companies and government entities that may have to contribute the cost of the canal's remediation. Partially responsible parties, or PRPs, that have been informed they must pay include the United States Navy, the City of New York, National Grid, Con Ed, Chemtura Corporation, Rapid American Corporation, Brinks, Beazer East, and Cibro Petroleum Products. Thirteen more companies have been sent information request letters and could potentially become PRPs.[8] It is worth noting that Walter Mugdan, EPA Region 2 Superfund Division Director, at a community meeting in November of 2010, called the contaminated sediment on the bottom of the canal "the most polluted sediment the EPA had seen from any site, ever." This will undoubtedly have financial consequences (The Environmental Protection Agency 2011: 1–6).

THE EPA VS. NEW YORK CITY

In the spring of 2009, The Environmental Protection Agency proposed that the Gowanus Canal be placed on its National Priorities List and labeled a Superfund site. The New York State Department of Environmental Conservation had requested this Superfund designation, as they believed that the state lacked the necessary resources to clean the canal.

When a site is Superfunded, it either receives short-term or long-term remedial action. The Gowanus Canal required long-term action. The process of remediating a site is a lengthy one, and involves a total of nine steps; these steps include Preliminary Assessment/Site Inspection, National Priorities Site Listing Process, Remedial Investigation/Feasibility Study, Record of Decision, Remedial Design/Remedial Action, Construction Completion, Post-Construction Completion, National Priorities List Deletion, and Reuse. Each step has a detailed process. In sum, during the first several steps it is decided what kind of action needs to be taken, how interested the public is, how polluted and with what a site is, and a report of how the site will be cleaned. The last five steps, Remedial Design/Remedial Action through Reuse, the site is actually cleaned, remediated, taken off the NPL, and reused as a viable body of water (The United States Environmental Protection Agency 1986).

Shortly after the EPA made this announcement, Mayor Michael Bloomberg announced on July 1, 2009 that the City of New York had a remediation plan of their own for the canal. This announcement was part of PlaNYC, which is a long-term sustainability plan for New York City. It is meant to prepare the city for an increase in population, boost the economy, fight climate change, and improve the overall quality of life for residents. It has a series of goals that include programs for waterways, solid waste, transportation, public space, food, and housing. PlaNYC was announced in 2007 and aimed to achieve its goals in 2030 (The City of New York 2011). As a part of PlaNYC, the city planned to clean the Gowanus Canal without assistance from the EPA. The city had a timeline for the canal's restoration with a projected completion date of 2013, far sooner than the EPA's schedule. When the original announcement was made by the city, there were no details about how they planned to remediate the canal, except for working with the Army Corp of Engineers and asking potentially responsible parties to contribute financially to the cleanup costs on a voluntary basis (which the city referred to as a "collaborative basis"). They had allocated $150 million of the city's budget to cleaning the canal and would be "fully funded with city capital dollars and [was] indicative of the Bloomberg Administration's commitment to the city's water supply and waterways" (The City of New York 2009). However, the city had partnered with The Toll Brothers, a development corporation. The Toll Brothers were interested in constructing luxury condominiums along the canal. The company struck a deal with the city: if they had exclusive rights to canal front development, they would contribute $30 million to the city for their cleanup effort and during construction, they would conduct a spot cleanup in areas closest to the construction sites for the new real estate. The remainder of the necessary money would come from the federal government, but would be secured only after the city's application for a federal grant was accepted; therefore such funds were not guaranteed (Tsiamis 2009). The city's plan also included the rezoning of twenty-five blocks, so that they would be open for commercial and residential construction. The financial contribution from The Toll Brothers put pressure on Mayor Bloomberg and the city; the company said that they would walk away from the project if the canal was added to the NPL. Whether or not the canal would be added to the NPL became high stakes, as the city felt pressure for their own plan to move forward, as they would lose out financially if the EPA's plan passed.

Details of the city's plan were released on October 1, 2009, several months after Mayor Bloomberg made his announcement. Details about the city's plan were vague for four months after their initial announcement, though they were holding community meetings to rally support. Caswell Holloway, then Special Advisor to Mayor Bloomberg, presented the city's plan to the EPA. (In December 2009, Mayor Bloomberg appointed him Commissioner of the New York State Department of Environmental Conservation). The EPA had several private and public meetings with Holloway and members of his team. Holloway believed that if the canal received Superfund status, it would take an excessive amount of time to clean. The EPA was open to listening and learning about this alternative plan, but remained skeptical. Walter Mugdan, of the EPA, told Holloway during a meeting that the city's plan had "a lot of moving here and this is a complicated project that you are proposing; it's a complicated situation and I'm a little concerned about the complexity of the process" (Spota 2010: np). If the canal became a Superfund site, it would give the EPA veto power over the city's cleanup plan.

Usually, the EPA asks polluters to pay cleanup costs; Holloway didn't think that this was logical for a waterway that is, just under two miles. Instead, he wanted to ask congress to contribute 65 percent of the cleanup costs, which comes out to be between $300 and $400 million ($175 million has already been allocated in New York State's budget to improve water quality, but is not exclusively for New York City). While the EPA relies on polluters to pay for the cleanup, several businesses, such as Key Span, have already been identified as polluters responsible and have committed to making financial contributions to the EPA for the canal's cleanup (Eddings 2009).

SUPERFUND IDEOLOGIES

Often, there is a stigma attached to Superfund status, as it is commonly believed that this designation will elicit a negative perception of the people that live and work in the immediate area. This happened in the 1970s in Niagara Falls with the Love Canal, a site that was contaminated with deadly chemical compounds by Hooker Chemical. A school was built on top of the site and made children sick (Navarro 2009). PCBs, dumped for roughly thirty years by the General Electric Company into the Hudson River from two plants in Hudson Falls and Ft. Edward, New York, caused the Department of Environmental Conservation to create a fishing ban in sections along the Upper Hudson River out of concern for eating contaminated fish

(Mathis 2011). Both of these sites were Superfunded and incited fear over the general health of residents and deferred people from moving to those areas. The concept of a Superfund stigma is pervasive and Gowanus was not immune. Although many people that live near the Gowanus were aware of the general negative perception of the canal, this Superfund designation was viewed as an official warning not only to avoid the waterway, but to circumvent its environs as well. It was feared that consequences of an NPL designation would be manifested in a decline in population, avoidance of the area by tourists, and reluctance to rent or own nearby. Often property values in areas close to Superfund sites decrease for a period of five to ten years, resulting in a downturn of the real estate market (Tsiamis 2009). Many homeowners become frustrated by this reality, which causes them to outwardly oppose a Superfund designation. However, in many cases, the remediation of toxic sites causes property values to actually increase in the long run. They decrease during the years it takes to remediate a site, but once it is restored, property values see a dramatic increase. However, many people feel that Superfunding a site is a good thing. They believe that the risk that contamination poses to humans and the local ecology is serious and that cleaning a site will allow resident's quality of life to improve. As a site is cleaned, people will be more likely to move to the area, even if it takes several years. Once a site is cleaned, then the area can be developed, which would bring in new residents, new apartment buildings, and commercial enterprises, subsequently revitalizing the area.

This speaks to two contrasting Superfund ideologies. In the case of the Gowanus Canal, the more conservative group who favor development (the construction of new residential apartment buildings and commercial spaces) opposed the Superfund designation because they felt it would negatively impact the neighborhood. It did not just have to do with the stigma associated with Superfunding, but also the time they believe a project overseen by the EPA will take. They had been fighting for many years, and felt that the government would impede the progress they had made in years past. The other school, the more liberal and most often involved with environmental groups, believed that the designation would be the best thing that could happen to Gowanus. These people were elated that the government was paying attention to the plight of the canal, signaling the achievement of a goal that had been set long ago. It was seen as progress. They believed that they needed the help of the EPA, as they were the only government entity capable of remedying the canal's ills. A Superfund designation would lead to revitalization of the area, though they acknowledged it would be a slow process. Believing almost the exact opposite of the first group, this school believe that a cleanup, however time consuming, would cause the value of their property to increase, would bring businesses to the area and create jobs, and perhaps most importantly, mean a healthier environment and ecosystem.

THE DEBATE OVER SUPERFUND STATUS

The people of Gowanus, who for so long banded together in their collective mobilization, became divided in April of 2009. The plan proposed by the City of New York, an alternative to the EPA's proposed plan, became one of the biggest controversies that the Superfund program had seen, and proved to be the impetus that divided Brooklyn residents, who for so long had been united in the difficult task of gaining the city's attention for remediation. By October of 2009, after both the EPA and the city had made their announcements, the only universal opinion in the neighborhood was that the canal still needed to be cleaned.

The divide among residents seemed to be a seamless split. Many groups, who revealed themselves to be more conservative, such as Scotto's own organization, the Gowanus Canal Community Development Corporation, sided with the city. Because their primary mission was to provide housing for community members, Italian-American or otherwise, they believed that the city's plan promised to make this possible sooner. Scotto had been fighting this battle for a long time and was tired. This side wanted a clean canal that could be developed with condominiums and commercial enterprises that would bring in tourists and jobs. The city had promised a quick turn-around time with little that would occlude the construction of new Toll Brothers buildings during the cleanup, which was appealing to this group of residents. Those who began to be identified as left leaning, such as environmental groups like Friends and Residents of the Greater Gowanus, or FROGG, and the Carroll Gardens Coalition for Respectful Development, or CG CORD, supported the EPA's recommendation. These residents felt their only viable option was to support the EPA and an NPL designation of the Gowanus Canal. The EPA had thirty years of experience with cleaning highly contaminated sites and a streamlined process for doing so. This camp was also worried about the health effects of the canal's water and about the environment. A healthy environment was more important to them than a thriving local economy, which they believed would happened anyway once the canal's remediation process was complete. While property values may initially decrease, history has shown them to rebound. They were dismissive of any negative connotations associated with the Superfund label, as many say there has *always* been a stigma attached to the canal. Its odor is notorious and has been the source of many negative nicknames given to the canal, like "Lavender Lake." Furthermore, they did not think that the city had a substantial and encouraging record of environmental cleanup, especially with regards to the canal. The city had done a lot of talking about remediating the waterway, but in reality, had done very little. One example of the city's neglect was the functionality of the Flushing Tunnel. The Flushing Tunnel had a long history of ill repair; it would work for stretches and then break for extended periods of time, never to be properly and completely fixed. Most recently, the city had promised that repairs on the tunnel would be completed in 2008. However, Mayor Bloomberg cut the funding that was allocated for these repairs and the tunnel was never fully restored to working order. These community members did not feel that time was an issue, as the canal had been polluted for decades. After all, they had been fighting for this very moment for years. Why stop now?

Residents say that they did not feel unbridled dislike toward neighbors with opposing opinions, or if they did harbor harsh feelings, it wasn't readily apparent (Appel 2010). However, the tension between neighbors was abundantly clear to the EPA. During public community meeting, intense arguments erupted. One EPA staff member said that these arguments resembled "cat fights" (Tsiamis 2011). When pressed about these frequent altercations, residents said that the divide was not more obvious than normal, as "like tends to stick with like" (Appel 2010). Each sides was incredibly opinionated and passionate, and not afraid to vocalize their comments and criticisms. The divisive ideologies splitting community members are both founded in sound reasoning. More conservative groups favored the city's plan because it focused on economics while the more liberal groups reasons were founded in science.

It is not uncommon for people to disagree about an NPL nomination, or the best course of remedial action.[9] However, it was the volume of comments the EPA received during their Public Comment Period, which occurs during the second step of the Superfund process, and the tactics employed by each side that made it so controversial.

Both sides took action. Their tactics included speaking out both at community meetings and to the media, and outreach campaigns to rally support and education fellow community members about each side of the debate. At community meetings, the majority of the seats are filled. Many community members come prepared to take notes, with legal pads and notebooks resting on their laps. Some even bring print hard copies of EPA reports ready to use for reference during presentations. The age of attendees' ranged from young children to older community members, those who have been residents of the area for decades. A common reason for high attendance posited by the EPA is "this is Brooklyn." If there was a slogan or tagline for community engagement, "This is Brooklyn" would be it. At the start of meetings, the EPA has sign-in sheets ready for signatures at tables near the entrance. People patiently stand in line to record their presence in ink on these sheets. They run into neighbors and friendly faces or wave to EPA members they have gotten to know during the lengthy battle for a Superfund listing. During the question and answer periods, the EPA make it clear that they will stay as long as it takes to answer any and all questions, as a line forms in the aisle behind the microphone.

A part of the protocol for granting Superfund status is a minimum of a thirty-day comment period. The comment period for the canal was originally intended to last for sixty days, ending on June 6, 2009. However, it was extended an extra thirty days and ended on July 8, 2009. An example of pragmatic solidarity, it takes the views of affected community members into account. It gives people the chance to have their voices heard in a system that largely ignores their opinions. Education is another component of comment periods. Citizens can ask questions directly to representatives of the EPA and get immediate answers. The information dissemination that occurs here allows for people to make knowledgeable decisions.

What ensued during the public comment period was unprecedented and was reflected at the community meetings. Usually, there are a couple hundred written comments posted to the EPA's website by the general public. Because of the city's proposed alternative plan, the EPA saw a record number of comments, over 14,000. Roughly 80 percent of these comments were in support of adding the canal to the NPL, but there were two voluminous comments from a consultant hired by the city, and the other from the Toll Brothers. The consultant was hired by the city to make a technical argument against the listing, which was explained through their comments. The comment from the Toll Brother reiterated their plan to spot clean the canal and back the city financially. Both of these comments were well crafted and strategic. The EPA is required to respond to every comment, and staff members recall that it took a very long time to complete this task.

Buddy Scotto spoke the most as an individual. He was interviewed by a myriad of media sources including local newspapers, television reporters, and was featured in a short documentary about the Superfund process. In the documentary, Scotto spoke out publically against the EPA's proposal. He did not support the EPA because of funding issues. A popular misconception during this time was that the EPA was broke; Scotto believed that they would have to rely on the financial support of the grassroots groups that have had a history of procuring funds. He said, "Well they're Superfund, I like the way they use that word 'fund;' they don't have any money at all. The only money that's gone into the canal of any consequence that has affected change at all is the money that the grassroots community people [raised]." Bill Appel,

Director of GCCDC, said that the Superfund program, "is not super, and nor do they have any funds. Those affiliated with the GCCDC believed that the EPA would not make any changes and would "slow them down" on their way to revitalizing the canal (Spota 2010). Scotto also commented on this, saying, "Oh great, the federal government can now come in and say 'We'll make this a Superfund site and get it cleaned up.' We want to be damn sure that it does not get cleaned up and that we don't have to wait another twenty or thirty years because we don't think we should have to wait because of all the work we've already done."

The school that supported the EPA also spoke at community meetings, to the media, posted comments to the EPA's website, and used sources like CG Cord's blog as a vehicle to convey their concern over the canal's cleanup plan and educate community members about why they thought Superfunding was a better option. They would post bulletins about upcoming community meetings, write summaries of each meeting, and post new about the canal. To lobby for their cause, FROGG made a video that was posted on YouTube. There are two versions of this video, one running about thirty minutes and the second about ten minutes. In each version, members of FROGG articulate the need for Superfund status, with passion and urgency in their tone. They aimed to clarify the merits of a Superfund listing, remind residents of promises that had been made and broken by the city, like that of repairing the Flushing Tunnel, and encourage people to comment on the EPA's website and sign a petition in support of the Superfund designation. To express her doubt of the city's plan, FROGG member Marlene Donnelly said, "There is no comprehensive alternative—it's a spot cleanup. Toll [Brothers] can't clean what's in the canal . . . Neither can any of the individual development sites deal with the comprehensive conditions of the contaminations that exist in this water. The only process on the table that we have right now is Superfund." Fellow FROGG member, Margaret Maugenest, also spoke of her doubt for the city's plan and said, "Mayor Bloomberg is campaigning right now and I'm seeing ads of him going on roofs and saying 'You know what I see when I look on these roofs? I see opportunity for green.' If he wants to be the 'Green Mayor,' if he wants to see a million trees, why doesn't he want to file a comprehensive clean [for this] canal?" They used science as their platform. Their key point was that the canal lies in a flood zone. If a massive flood were to occur, the canal would overflow, causing its contaminated water to seep into the streets, backyards, and homes of residents. Currently, the canal floods with regularity when heavy rain storms hit Brooklyn, often making bridges impassable. There is footage of Walter Mugdan speaking about this, saying, "In a couple of very wet years during the late 1970s, the water table rose and the contamination rose with it and ended up coming into people's backyards, into their cellars, and things of that sort, the contamination was literally in their backyards and their homes." At the end of both versions, you hear Maugenest exclaim, "What a gift, the EPA! They have experiences with [bioremediation]. They have procedures; they know how to do this. Let's not tie their hands. They need community support, so let's give it to them!" (Freddy's Roundhouse Brooklyn 2009). It was filmed at several locations along the canal.

Aside from speaking out publically, each side ran campaigns to sway undecided community members. A campaign launched by the Pro-City supporters was anonymous flyering. Multiple residents living in Gowanus, near the banks of the canal, were conspicuously slipped flyers under their doors, but only once. It was scarcely mentioned in the media, other than a story written about the division in the community that was published in the Brooklyn Paper briefly discussed these flyers. The article stated that "anonymously written flyers started showing up in area mailboxes claiming that [a Superfund] designation would depress home values and not actually speed the cleanup process of the fetid corpse of water" (Brock and McLaughlin 2009). The purpose of these flyers was to frighten business and property owners about the value of their investments, as well as warn them that the federal government might consider them responsible parties for the canal's pollution and find them liable for payments toward its cleanup. However, this information was unfounded and incorrect, as individual homeowners are never targeted by the EPA or held liable. The source and author of these flyers was never identified, but there is speculation that they came from an umbrella group that was being directed by the Toll Brothers because they were the business entity at the forefront of fighting the Superfund listing. The EPA called these flyers a "scare tactic" (Tsiamis 2011). The GCCDC was dismissive of the flyers, but acknowledged their existence, while other community groups were outwardly unhappy that this had happened.

The people that were Pro-EPA chose to use education and visibility as their primary campaign tactic. FROGG created small "Superfund Me" posters that were distributed and displayed in window fronts throughout the neighborhood. Brandished in the shop windows of many local businesses in Carroll Gardens, Cobble Hill, Boerum Hill, Park Slope, Windsor Terrace, and Red Hook were simply white flyers featuring a blue whale spouting a heart-shaped water formation. Underneath the whale, it read "Superfund Me!" and included the website to sign a petition in support of the NPL listing. The picture was simple, bright, and against a clean white background. It stood in stark contrast to the other event calendars or advertisements hanging next to it. This campaign worked well to represent their support of the EPA. Concerned residents understood that in order to be effective and informative, they have to work at a grass roots level. The flyers were brief and fomented interest, allowing people to take in information quickly. Most importantly, they were prolific and eye-catching. Flyers did not bombard residents with overwhelming statistics or comprehensive legislation; instead, the information given was succinct. This campaign catered to the artistic and politically minded population of Brooklyn.

Local businesses also handed out buttons with the same logo for people to wear. They produced an array of tee shirts, hats, tote bags, mugs, and magnets proudly featuring the "Superfund Me!" logo. They were available to buy online. A few local websites even published photos of people wearing their "Superfund Me!" gear around town. The message advertised on apparel and buttons have allowed for silent, peaceful expression and education.

Below the train station at the Smith and Ninth Street stop was a huge pink paneled poster featuring an extremely large octopus. The poster read "Super Fun Superfund." The panels were attached to a chain link fence that surrounds a Lowe's parking lot and overlooks the canal itself. In the same view, a passerby could see the poster, the water, and all the contaminated debris left to fester on its banks. Tonky Designs, a design firm responsible for the display, has a studio in Gowanus and felt strongly about showing support of the Superfund designation. They hung this design to raise awareness and show their support for the Superfund label.

Aside from these few outspoken groups, there was an incredible response to the debate for Superfund Status among the third party residents. Many concerned residents took to the internet, participating in a debate via blogs; this provided forums where anyone could voice their opinion. Most of them posted updates and links to recent newspaper articles. Not only did they give people a place to speak out, they administered a resource to educate those interested. Others, like members of the Urban Divers Estuary Conservancy and the Dredgers Canoe Club, tried to remain neutral. They believed that the community should work together, as their goals for a clean canal aligned, especially in the face of national attention. They wanted the canal to become an example of restoration and be a legacy for a historic waterway. They urged people to look to their children and give them hope that they will have the chance to interact positively with the canal in the future, to engage with a healthy and clean environment that exists in their backyard.

THE GOWANUS CANAL AS A SUPERFUND SITE

Despite the effort of the city and residents who opposed the Superfunding, on March 8, 2010, the Gowanus Canal was added to the National Priorities

List and designated a Superfund site. It was the first site in New York City to be added since the 1980s when in a site in Queens was listed for its radium contamination. That site was remediated and removed from the NPL in 1995. Judith Enck, the EPA's Region 2 Administrator, said at a community meeting in February 2011 that she hopes that the canal, which was "once an example of urban decay" will become an "an example of urban renewal."

Residents fought hard for the U.S. government, at local, state, and federal levels, to pay attention to the canal's plight. They fought together and they fought alone. They set records. They attended meetings and asked questions. They asked other community members to get involved. They received national attention from the media. Their hard work paid off: action is being taken to remediate the canal. Though many people disagreed about who should take responsibility for the canal's restoration, in the end, their collective plea for help was answered.

Though the parties that supported the EPA and the parties that supported the city might never have congruent Superfund Ideologies, the Environmental Protection Agency's decision to designate the Gowanus Canal a Superfund site reunited members of the community. Meetings are still highly attended and there are a record number of people in the canal's Community Advisory Group, a mandatory provision in the Superfunding process designed to be a forum for community discussion and be a liaison between the government and the general public. Residents realized that they were working toward the same goal and set their differences aside in an effort to effect real change, now that their interpersonal battle was solved for them. Despite the fact that this was an unusual case for the EPA, as more sites begin to be added to the NPL, neighborhoods become gentrified, and people are more interested in the caring for the environment, this level of community involvement may be more common.

While many places throughout the cities and towns in America have been contaminated by industrial pollution and then abandoned, there is no other place quite like the Gowanus Canal. The canal was instrumental in the development of New York City and was once an integral part of the commerce in the New York Harbor. Gowanus' life as an industrial neighborhood was relatively short, lasting about two hundred years, and the time it perceived as an economically successful area was even shorter, less than one hundred years. Brooklyn residents spent over sixty years fighting for the canal to be cleaned, and will have to wait longer than another decade for their dreams of a healthy environment to be realized. However, even though it might take a little bit longer for the canal to be remediated, it will still be cleaned, improving quality of life for those who live nearby. In the end, Gowanus will most likely see another age of ecological health and economic success, no matter how or by whom this will be accomplished.

ACKNOWLEDGMENTS

The author would like to thank Suzanne and Jim Farrell for their support and encouragement. She would also like to thank Alex Alvarez for his time, patience, and insight.

NOTES

1. There are eleven points along the canal where raw sewage is discharged into the water when New York City's sewer system is inundated; these emission points are called Combined Sewage Overflows, or CSOs. It is estimated that about 400 million gallons of untreated sewage is discharged into the waterway each year (Riverkeeper 2011).
2. However, most people that lived in the area in the 1940s and 1950s did not know the canal as the Gowanus Canal, but as Buttermilk Channel.
3. The canal was the first place where chemical fertilizers were manufactured.
4. In 1968, a survey revealed that $3 million was lost by the fishing industry because of pollution.
5. In 1969, over 26 million fish were reportedly killed in Lake Thonotosassa, Florida by discharges into the lake from four nearby food processing plants.
6. In February 1971, The Food and Drug Administration reported that 87 percent of sampled swordfish had a level of mercy deemed unsafe for human consumption.
7. The NCP is what established the NPL.
8. The EPA periodically issues press releases that update the public on the status of partial liability notices and information request letters, which include responses from companies and information about lawsuits and bankruptcy claims.
9. When the Upper Hudson River was Superfunded in 1984, it was not as controversial as when in 2000 and 2001 when the EPA was holding a series of public hearings about whether or not the river should be cleaned by dredging. Community members were either hard-line pro or anti-dredge. When the EPA decided in 2001 that the river would be dredged, it seemed that the issue was resolved. However, when dredging began in 2009, it still angered many local people (Mathis 2011).

REFERENCES

Appel, Bill. 2010. Interview by author, Brooklyn, NY, December 1, 2010.

Bonanos, Christopher. 2009. "A Brief History of Slime." *New York Magazine*, July. Retrieved December 10, 2009 (http://nymag.com/news/intelligencer/topic/57886/).

Brock, Emilia and Mike McLaughlin. 2009. "Superfund Showdown on the Gowanus." *The Brooklyn Paper*, April. Retrieved December 10, 2009 (http://www.brooklynpaper.com/stories/32/17/32_17_mm_superfund.html).

Carroll Gardens Coalition for Respectful Development. 2007. CORD History. Retrieved on December 11, 2009 (http://carrollgardenspetition.blogspot.com).

The City of New York. 2009. "Mayor Bloomberg Announces Start of $150 Million Project to Improve Water Quality in the Gowanus Canal." Retrieved on June 5, 2011. (www.nyc.gov/portal/site/nycgov/menuitem.c0935b9a57bb4ef3daf2f1c701c789a0/index.jsp?pageID=mayor_press_release&catID=1194&doc_name=http%3A%2F%2Fwww.nyc.gov%2Fhtml%2Fom%2Fhtml%2F2009b%2Fpr452-09.html&cc=unused1978&rc=1194&ndi=1).

The City of New York. 2011. "About PlaNYC." Retrieved on June 5, 2011. (www.nyc.gov/html/planyc2030/html/about/about.shtml).

The City of New York Community Board Six. Neighborhoods: Gowanus. Retrieved December 9, 2009 (http://brooklyncb6.org/neighborhoods/?a=detail&content_id=58).

Eddings, Amy. 2009. "Battle Brews Over Gowanus Canal Clean-Up." WNYC, December. Retrieved December 9, 2009 (http://wnyc.org/articles/wnyc-news/2009/dec/09/battle-brews-over-gowanus-canal-clean-up/).

Freddy's Roundhouse Brooklyn. 2009. "The Battle for the Gowanus Canal—Superfund Cleanup vs. the City Plan." Retrieved December 9, 2009 (www.youtube.com/watch?v=YZc96eE_GWg).

Hamilton Lytle, Mark. 2007. *The Gentle Subversive: Rachel Carson, Silent Spring, and the Rise of the Environmental Movement*. New York: Oxford University Press.

Hay, Mark. 2010. "Buddy Scotto, On the Ramparts of Carroll Gardens." *Capital New York*, August. Retrieved June 5, 2011 (www.capitalnewyork.com/category/tags/buddy-scotto).

The Gowanus Dredgers Canoe Club. 2004. Gowanus Canal History. Retrieved December 1, 2009 (www.waterfrontmuseum.org/dredgers/history.html).

Lethem, Jonathan. 2003. *The Fortress of Solitude*. 528:51. New York: Vintage Contemporaries.

Lucas, Peter. 2010. Interview by author, New York. November 4, 2010.

Mathis, David. 2011. Interview by author, Schuylerville, NY, June 12, 2011.

Navarro, Mireya. 2009. "City Proposes New Plan for Gowanus Canal Cleanup." *New York Times*, July. Retrieved December 10, 2009 (http://nytimes.com/2009/07/02/nyregion/02gowanus.html).

Navarro, Mireya. 2010. "Gowanus Canal Labeled Superfund Site, Over City's Objections." *New York Times*, March. Retrieved December 18, 2010 (www.nytimes.com/2010/03/03/nyregion/03gowanus.html).

Prete, Allison. 1998. *Lavender Lake: Brooklyn's Gowanus Canal*. [VHS] Brooklyn, NY: Rough on Rats Productions.

Riverkeeper. 2011. "Gowanus Canal." Retrieved on June 5, 2011. (www.riverkeeper.org/campaigns/stop-polluters/gowanus-canal/)

Sharps, David. 2010. Interview by author, Brooklyn, NY, October 8, 2010.

Spota, Thomas J. 2010. The Gowanus Canal has been designated a Superfund site. Retrieved on January 3, 2011 (www.youtube.com/watch?v=Rc3F_bElDq0).

Stanne, Steven. 2010. Lecture at New York University, New York, NY, September 21, 2010.

Tonky Designs. 2009. Gowanus Canal Super Fun Superfund. Retrieved on December 11, 2009 (http://tonkydesigns.com/blog/?s=superfund+is+superfun).

Tsiamis, Christos. 2009. Interview by author, New York, NY, January 4, 2009.

United States Bureau of the Census. 2000. Fact Sheet for American Community Survey. Washington, DC: U.S. Government Printing Office.

United States Environmental Protection Agency. 1980. CERCLA Overview. Retrieved December 18, 2010 (www.epa.gov/superfund/policy/cercla.htm).

United States Environmental Protection Agency. 1977. Clean Water Act. Retrieved December 18, 2010 (www.epa.gov/oecasgct/lcwa.html).

United States Environmental Protection Agency. 1986. Superfund. Retrieved December 10, 2009 (http://epa.gov/superfund/about.htm).

United States Environmental Protection Agency. 2010. Gowanus Canal. Retrieved December 18, 2010 (www.epa.gov/region02/superfund/npl/gowanus).

United States Environmental Protection Agency. 2010. Gowanus Canal Site Description. New York, NY: EPA Region 2 Superfund Records Center. (Also available at www.epa.gov/Region2/superfund/npl/0206222c.pdf.)

United States Environmental Protection Agency. 2011. EPA Completes Remedial Investigations at Gowanus Canal Site. New York, New York: EPA Region 2 Superfund Records Center.

9

Striving for Sustainability on the Urban Waterfront

The Case of Newtown Creek

Steve Lang

Over the last thirty years, port cities throughout the world have been reimagining and transforming their declining and neglected industrial waterfronts from realms of dereliction into new frontiers of economic opportunity. Increasingly, sustainability has emerged as a dominant discourse and in many of these waterfront planning and redevelopment schemes (Brown 2009; Bunce 2009; Desfor et al. 2011; Miller and de Roo 2004; Pearsall 2010; Raco and Henderson 2006). According to Layard (2001:1), "land use planning and sustainable development seem to be ever more inextricably intertwined. References to the ideas, principles and policies underpinning sustainability are everywhere—from planning policy guidance to good practice guides to inclusions in development." This is particularly true in New York City, where sustainability has become a mantra for waterfront planning strategies. After the launch of its long-term sustainability plan called PlaNYC in 2007, the Bloomberg administration made ideas about sustainability a core component of the city's waterfront revitalization and planning policies. More recently, in 2010, the city updated its 1992 comprehensive waterfront plan in an attempt to create a new "sustainable blueprint for the city's more than 500 miles of shoreline" (Santora 2010:np).

In many of New York City's waterfront neighborhoods slated for remediation and redevelopment, competing visions of what a sustainable waterfront is, how it should be used and what it should become collide with conflicts over how the costs and benefits of environmental remediation and sustainable development should be distributed. Sustainability is not only a top-down affair (Schaller and Novy 2011). There are multiple citizen activist organizations that are working on assorted bottom-up sustainability strategies for the waterways and waterfront. Many are struggling to develop a broader conception of sustainability that is shifting the development debate away from the traditional growth/no growth question to how and where growth should be developed and accommodated. Well aware that green growth does not automatically trickle down, many of these groups and coalitions are struggling to realize a vision of sustainability that promotes environmental quality at the same time that it equalizes the benefits and burdens of growth.

New York City's waterfront sustainability policy, which is still evolving, involves a combination of city planning, national environmental regulations and local citizen activism. This paper explores the consequences and contradictions of this approach to sustainability by focusing on the role that citizen activism plays in struggles to reclaim Newtown Creek, a highly polluted and toxic 3.5 mile industrial waterway in the heart of New York City that flows through an area that has been called an environmental sacrifice zone because of the severity of its multiple health threatening, environmental hazards (Lerner 2010). It will focus on how sustainability is framed and debated paying particular attention to the ways that citizen activists and organizations negotiate and struggle to balance what has been called the three Es of sustainability: the environment, the economy and social equity. In many cases as waterfront planners embrace the concept, the sustainability "balance" heavily favors one E: the economy to the detriment of equity concerns (Pearsall 2010; Kruger and Gibbs 2007; Warner 2002).

In recent years, environmental justice concerns have been incorporated and institutionalized in federal, state and local environmental remediation and sustainability policies. Increasingly, many of these policies tout the need to involve the community in the environmental planning and decision making process (Gandy 2002; Holifield 2004; Sabel, Archon, and Karkkainen 2000). What does this actually mean in practice? This paper will also explore some of the constraints and opportunities associated with these collaborative partnership approaches to sustainability.

METHODS

This case study which explores how community based-environmental groups and coalitions negotiate the three Es of sustainability in their struggles to reclaim the waterways and waterfronts along Newtown Creek is based on ethnographic and historical research. For four years I regularly attended meetings of the Newtown Creek Alliance, the leading advocacy group for the creek as a participant observer. I also attended and observed Community Board meetings and public meetings of the Newtown Creek Monitoring Committee for nine months in 2009, as well as pertinent public events, city council hearings, press conferences, and gallery exhibits that dealt with remediating the creek. Participating in environmental educational walking, bike and boat tours on and around the creek conducted by neighborhood environmental activists was also a valuable source of information.

I analyzed pertinent primary and secondary data sources and documents including newspaper articles, government environmental and planning reports, census data, newsletters, press releases, workshop and conference reports, public meeting records, real estate ads and local blogs that addressed environmental issues on the waterfront. I also analyzed the organizational literature and mission statements of local organizations involved in environmental politics associated with Newtown Creek and the waterfront.

I supplemented the archival and observational data with forty semi-structured interviews based on a snowball sample of key stakeholders involved in sustainability issues on the Newtown Creek waterfront. Using the tools of discourse analysis, I documented and focused on recurrent key themes, storylines, metaphors and rhetoric (Hajer 1995; Philips and Hardy 2002; Quinn 2005;Wood and Kroger 2002). Findings from this particular case study were placed in a larger historical, social, economic and political framework.

THE DISCOURSE OF SUSTAINABILITY

Since it was first popularized by the 1987 Brundtland Commission Report which defined it as "those forms of development that allow people to meet the needs of the present without compromising the ability of future generations to meet their own needs," the word sustainability has been used, misused and fiercely debated" (Weinberg, Pellow and Schnaiberg 2000:3). Although sustainability has become a ubiquitous term in urban environmental discourse, it is elusive and contradictory. Its appeal is easy to understand. The longstanding notion of a fundamental contradiction between economic growth and nature has been superseded by utopian notions of harmony between the two. Nevertheless, despite its promise of win-win scenarios with regard to economic development and environmental balance, the discourse of sustainability stresses goals that are inherently contradictory. It obscures the incompatibility between social, economic and environmental goals: the achievement of one goal precludes the ability to achieve others. Moreover, in many cases, social justice and environmental sustainability are politically incompatible (Campbell 2003; Dobson 2003; Weinberg et al. 2000).

Sustainability is at least as much about politics, injustice and inequality as it is about science or the environment. In an attempt to rectify the "equity deficit" associated with sustainability discourse, Agyeman (2005:26) has developed a

"Just Sustainability Paradigm," which prioritizes justice and equity but does not downplay the environment. Thus, he redefines sustainability as "the need to ensure a better quality of life for all now and into the future in a just and equitable manner whilst living within the limits of supporting ecosystems." When looking at Newtown Creek and its surrounding neighborhoods through the lens of just sustainability the key question becomes sustainable development for whom and for what purposes?

SUSTAINABLE WATERFRONT REDEVELOPMENT AND ENVIRONMENTAL JUSTICE

Throughout its tenure, the Bloomberg administration has aggressively used property-led development schemes and rezoning strategies to transform derelict waterfront spaces into valuable real estate. Recently, the Department of City Planning touted its more than 108 rezonings for creating "a blueprint for sustainable development" that will help to catalyze investment and economic opportunities, "green our city and reclaim our waterfront" (NYCDCP 2011: np).

In New York City, greening the urban growth machine has coincided with a neoliberal urban agenda in which sustainable development and market fundamentalism go hand-in-hand (Hackworth 2007). PlaNYC's sustainability vision for the city's land, air and water has been criticized by many for its overreliance on market—entrepreneurialism to carry out its greening strategy. At the core of PlaNYC, is an implicit faith that "green" economic development will provide the necessary trickle-down effects for overcoming environmental and economic problems facing cities. According to Angotti (2007:np), PlaNYC's "emphasis on sustainability and environment seems to flow from a long-term vision of large-scale real estate growth." This is especially the case with the city's waterfront brownfield development strategies, where sustainability means cleaning up brownfields—sites where previous industrial uses have left behind contamination—and transforming them into attractive sites for real estate investment and capital accumulation (De Pass 2006; Raco and Henderson 2006; While, Jonas and Gibbs 2004).

Such an approach both exacerbates inequalities and downplays potential threats from environmental hazards and pollution. There is a growing body of urban research that shows how sustainable urban planning policy and gentrification are becoming linked (Bunce 2009; Dale and Newman 2009). Much of this research shows the ways in which urban revitalization policies that stress sustainability serve as discursive guises, a form of "rhetorical greenwashing" that promotes and legitimizes gentrification (Angotti 2008; Bunce 2004; Szili and Rofe 2007). In many cases, the discourse of urban sustainability is coupled with a plethora of "re-" words such as "revitalization," "regeneration" and "renaissance." Regeneration is a more neutral, sugar-coated term that obscures the class displacement dimension at the core of the gentrification process (Smith 2002). This ideological reframing is evident in many of the city's long-term waterfront sustainability plans which recast gentrification as a positive and necessary environmental strategy.

Recently the city has begun to stress the importance of supporting economic activity on the working waterfront and called for the protection of significant maritime industrial areas (SMIA). One of these SMIAs is Newtown Creek. With large swaths of the waterfront rezoned for future development and many redevelopment projects stalled because of the recent economic downturn, the city has turned away from relying almost exclusively on real estate development as one of the major engines of growth. According to the NYC Department of City Planning website for its new comprehensive waterfront plan 2020, "By investing in and expanding the working waterfront, we will be creating immediate job opportunities for New Yorkers as well as a source of long-term economic growth for New York City" (NYCDCP 2011:np). It is likely, that if and when the economy recovers, the working waterfront will lose out, once again, to property-led real estate development and gentrification.

In New York City, waterfront redevelopment and environmental justice are inextricably intertwined because many of the city's toxic waterfronts targeted for cleanup and redevelopment are located in low-income and minority communities. The city's waterfront is a tale of two cities. While some areas have become waterfront gold coasts where high-end residential, retail and entertainment venues exist alongside amenities such as esplanades, pubic spaces and parks, other areas have become repositories of waste transfer stations, power plants, sewage treatment plants and a host of locally unwanted land-uses referred to as (LULUs). The waterfront area around Newtown Creek contains both of these extremes.

Environmental justice is concerned with the inequitable distribution of environmental burdens and benefits. The New York State Department of Environmental Conservation (DEC) has an expansive view of environmental justice that includes a focus on the inequitable distribution of noxious facilities as well as the inequitable distribution of environmental benefits amenities, such as parks and open space. It also entails recognition or the need to involve affected communities in environmental decision making and the oversight of environmental problems (Scholsberg 2007). As we shall see, citizen activists and community organizations involved in local sustainability strategies along Newtown Creek have become actively involved in a host of Federal, State and local programs that all place great emphasis on involving the community in environmental remediation processes.

FROM LULUS TO LATTES: THE PERILS OF ENVIRONMENTAL GENTRIFICATION

Newtown Creek and the several communities that it passes through is a microcosm that encapsulates many of the sustainability challenges facing waterfront communities in global cities. Dividing Western Queens from Brooklyn, the 3.5 mile-long waterway is one of the most polluted industrial sites in the United States. The creek which contains hundreds of years of industrial toxins, millions of gallons of oil from one of the largest oil spills in U.S. history and an estimated 2.7 million gallons of raw sewage and polluted storm water from twenty-two combined sewer overflow pipes, moves through some of the most environmentally damaged neighborhoods in New York City before trickling into the East River. The communities along the creek such as Greenpoint and East Williamsburg in Brooklyn and Long Island City and Maspeth in Queens, are home to a disproportionate number of environmental hazards and risks. Within one mile of the Creek there are hundreds of brownfield sites, seventeen State Superfund sites and ninetten waste transfer

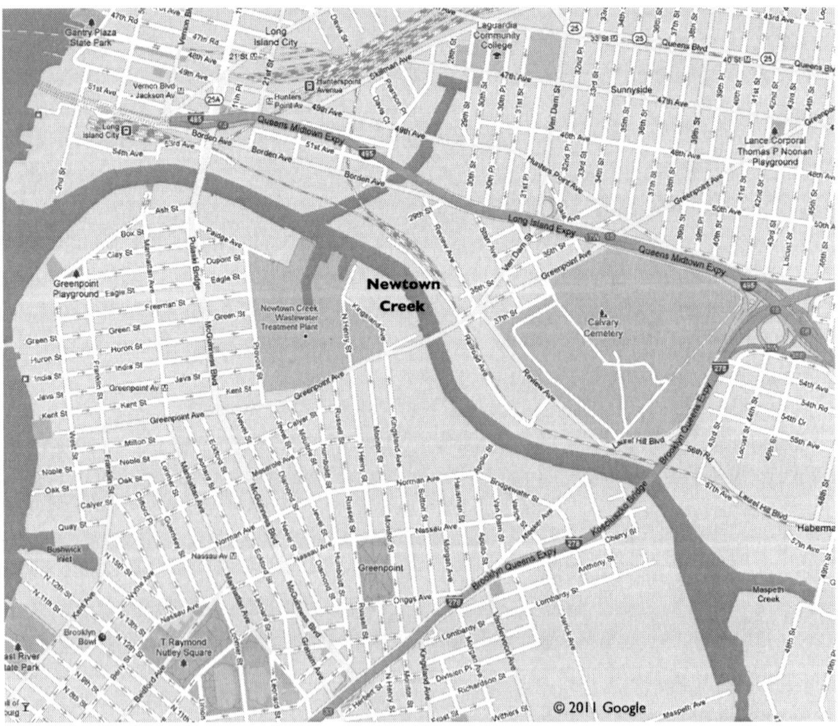

Figure 9.1. Map of Newtown Creek. *Source:* Image courtesy of Google Maps.

stations, which because they rely mainly on tractor trailer use for export, generate a great deal of noise and pollution. There are also several instances of hazardous vapor intrusions into homes and businesses, twelve registered point source air emissions facilities, and the largest sewage treatment facility in New York City (Weiss and Heimbinder 2011).

Historically the shores along the creek were crammed with oil refineries and manufacturing but as deindustrialization set in, the industrial nature of the area shifted and gradually emerged as a vital part of the city's growing waste-based economy. As waste transfer stations began to proliferate, residents were exposed to potentially adverse and environmental health impacts. The land adjacent to Newtown Creek constitutes the largest contiguous industrially zoned area in New York City and has been designated as a SMIA.

The unequal distribution of noxious waste-facilities that serve the entire city is a major environmental justice issue in the city (Angotti 2008; Gandy 2002; Sze 2007). While working class and low-income communities around the creek have dozens of waste-transfer stations that are serviced by hundreds of highly polluting diesel trucks per day, resulting in constant noise and extreme odors, low air quality and high asthma rates, the wealthy borough of Manhattan has none.

Despite the fact that Newtown Creek is considered to be an ecological wasteland, the adjacent waterfront neighborhoods are undergoing gentrification and major demographic changes. During a press conference addressing local efforts to involve the federal government in the remediation of the creek, a local environmental activist from Greenpoint told a reporter that, "The hippest place to live in America is also one of the most toxic places." The first wave of gentrification in the 1980's coincided with the emergence of a waste-based economy that began to reshape the waterfront and has intensified with each successive year, thus blurring the boundaries between and residential uses. At the present time, gentrification is very intensive on the Brooklyn and Long Island City waterfront near the East River mouth of the creek. In 2002, the city broke ground on the Hunter Point South Project, a 5,000 unit, mixed income housing development. The promotional literature for this new sustainable waterfront development stresses its spectacular views but consistently fails to mention that it is located on Newtown Creek. Gentrification is also occurring at a slower but steady pace in the inland section of the creek. This hidden, industrial backyard of the city has been called a "polluted heart of darkness."

According to Marwell (2007:91), "Greenpoint/Williamsburg's decline, rehabilitation and gentrification begins and ends with the growth machine: its abandonment of the neighborhood in the 1950's and its voracious return half a century later." The 2005 rezoning of Greenpoint-Williamsburg has been part of one of the biggest transformations of the city landscape since the rezoning of 1961. Four hundred fifty blocks were rezoned as part of the Bloomberg Administration's long-term vision for the waterfront that includes replacing what it refers to as inappropriate uses such as waste transfer stations and power plants with high-end, high-rise residential housing and parks.

In the early 1990s, much of the Brooklyn waterfront that would eventually be rezoned, became a battleground for environmental justice struggles over noxious and health threatening LULUs such as power plants and waste transfer stations (Angotti 2008; Gandy 2002; Maanaty 2001; Sze 2007). During the 1970's, there was a long history of racial, ethnic and class hostilities and conflicts in the area over municipal services and resources on the deindustrializing waterfront (Ballon and Jackson 2007; DeSena 2005; Susser 1982). In 1992, these differences were set aside as community groups mobilized to fight a city proposal to build an incinerator with potential health risks on the site of the former Brooklyn Navy Yard (Checker 2001; Marwell 2007). While the defeat of the Brooklyn incinerator project has been hailed by many as a major environmental justice victory, the strategic and episodic, single issue oriented environmental coalition that defeated it was short lived.

The benefits of environmental victories are not evenly distributed. During the incinerator battle, activists often claimed that "the Navy Yard is our Love Canal," "everybody breathes the same air," and "toxic clouds don't discriminate." In the aftermath of the incinerator project's defeat, as the Brooklyn waterfront around the Navy Yard become valuable property targeted for redevelopment, the fragile environmental coalitions that mobilized based on a shared interest in defeating a common environmental threat, gave way to zero sum struggles for a piece of the development pie (Marwell 2007). Environmental cleanup was still a priority, but was increasingly subordinated to planning and economic development goals that are intensely in conflict. This is clearly the case with the recent, 2005 rezoning of the waterfront that unleashed struggles and conflicts between different constituencies that are still unfolding.

Leading up to the rezoning, Greenpoint and Williamsburg residents developed their individual community or 197-a plans for the waterfront. According to section 197-a of the New York City Charter, community boards may develop their own land-use plans for a community focusing on social, economic and environmental concerns which can serve as guidelines to be used by city agencies as they embark on a major land use change such as a rezoning. As stated in the Department of City Planning's 197-a Technical Guide:

> At their best, 197-a plans can forge consensus within a community about its future direction, challenge conventional wisdom among decision-makers, and lead to significant shifts in land use policy . . . In a 197-a plan, a community portrays its vision for the future by recommending strategies to address any or

> all of a range of concerns that may include land use, housing, economic development, environmental or social issues (New York City Department of City Planning 1997:7).

Throughout the planning process, environmental concerns and affordable housing loomed large. While there was wide agreement on ridding the waterfront of environmental hazards and health threats associated with the concentration of LULUs and noxious industries, there was disagreement about what to put in their place. While many community groups liked the city's plan for a mix of residential development, esplanades, parks and recreational spaces with increased public access to the waterfront, there was a lot of dissention when it came to building a wall of luxury towers on the waterfront.

To keep the tide of gentrification from tipping the community towards wealth and luxury, the plans called for safeguards and affordable housing provisions to protect residents from being displaced (Angotti 2008). While there was a strong consensus on protecting industry, a division emerged between those who wanted all factories moved off the waterfront and away from residential areas and those who had a vision of mixed-use waterfront with green and environmentally friendly, non-noxious industries. The final rezoning strategy adopted by the city bears little resemblance to the community-based plans. One of the most contentious components of the city's rezoning final plan was its approach to affordable housing that relies heavily on market-based incentives to induce developers to provide affordable housing and waterfront amenities in exchange for the opportunity to make more profits by increasing the height of their buildings. Community groups wanted more affordable housing that was backed by mandatory inclusionary zoning requirements not voluntary incentives.

Overall, when it came to a choice between LULUs and noxious health threatening industries many residents viewed rezoning and redevelopment as a "better evil and a bittersweet victory" for community residents (DeSena 2009:74). Despite some dissatisfaction in both communities, the Bloomberg Administration viewed the rezoning as a major achievement for sustainable waterfront development that should be emulated across the city because of its successful marriage of environmental quality and economic growth. Such win-win rhetoric, so common is sustainable discourse, glossed over the conflicts that took place. By claiming that it acted on behalf of the community, the city was able to use the plan as a legitimating tool for further development (Davila 2004).

The rezoning process encapsulated and helped to crystallize a major dilemma for activists involved in waterfront planning: how to reclaim the waterfront by ridding it of LULUs and noxious industries without encouraging gentrification and displacement (Angotti 2008). In many cases, "environmental gentrification" associated with sustainable development initiatives results in the displacement of incumbent residents. (Angotti 2008; Bullard 2007; Banzhaf and Walsh 2006; Bunce 2009; Dooling 2009; Eckerd 2011; Essoka 2010; Faber 2008; Wolf-Powers 2005). It also threatens to displace small-scale, viable manufacturing industries and businesses that are concentrated on the waterfront (Curran 2007). This dilemma was aptly captured by Elizabeth Yeampierre (2007:np), an environmental justice activist from Brooklyn:

> Our environmental justice successes have turned into gentrification opportunities in our communities. Developers even use our successes in their promotional literature. What our communities are being told is that unless we live next to a waste transfer station or a power plant, we don't deserve to live there and our young people don't deserve to breathe clean air or have open space. So that is the next struggle for the environmental justice movement: to make sure that all of these environmental amenities that we have been fighting for don't end up displacing our people.

In Brooklyn, gentrification was underway before activists became involved in reclaiming the waterfront. In fact, many of these activists were themselves part of the first wave of "pioneer gentrifers who migrated to the area when it was still considered the urban frontier." While environmental activism is in part, both a cause and effect of gentrification on the Brooklyn waterfront, there is a perception on the part of some that revitalizing the waterfront has ushered in gentrification and displacement. During an interview, an environmental justice activist from Greenpoint pointed out that:

> We have been accused of gentrifying the area by cleaning up environmental toxins. An angry long term resident told me that this place would have never been attractive to rich white people if we didn't clean up the environment . . . if you have been removed from your environment you can't reclaim it. We have to make sure that we maintain our presence as we struggle to reclaim our environment.[1]

In short, removing undesirable aspects of a neighborhood and transforming it into an attractive one without causing social, economic and aesthetic disruptions is a major issue faced by all grassroots community revitalization efforts (Zukin 2006).

GREENING NEWTOWN CREEK AND INDUSTRIAL RETENTION

When it came to the three miles of the creek that flowed eastward away from the East River, the Greenpoint 197a plan and the city were both in agreement that the area should be maintained as an industrial zone. The Greenpoint 197-a plan developed by the community specifically addressed environmental conditions and recommended several "greening" strategies for the creek. The following quotations are some of the key recommendations outlined in the plan (Greenpoint 197-a Plan 2002:38–46):

- "Retain Newtown Creek as a Significant Maritime and Industrial Zone" and an industrial sanctuary and at the same time, initiate "high performance standards" for manufactures, enter into good neighbor agreements and reclaim and clean-up the Newtown Creek area"
- "The Newtown Creek itself should be publicly accessible where feasible, even when it adjoins manufacturing uses. The ends of all public right-of-ways should be designated as open space, greened and maintained."
- "encourage clean and environmentally friendly industries"
- "Enforce fair share objectives"
- "Develop Greenpoint as a model sustainable community that demonstrates how solid waste, run off, and transit improvements can be combined to reduce adverse impacts on the environment."
- "Establish and implement a combined sewer overflow abatement plan to maintain a healthy environment for recreational use
- Design and develop the sewage treatment facility to reflect and enhance the existing architectural character of the area, while improving the quality of the environment.
- Dredge the Newtown Creek after the Mobile Oil cleanup to eliminate existing toxic sediments, thus encouraging the return of the natural ecological balance and thereupon promotion of recreational uses such as kayaking in Newtown Creek.

As we shall see, all of these ideas have become core ideas for the Newtown Creek Alliance, the most recent organization that has taken on the task of cleaning up the creek.

INDUSTRIAL AND ENVIRONMENTAL HISTORY OF NEWTOWN CREEK

Newtown Creek's toxic legacy has made it, in the words of a local environmental activist and creek advocate, "a laboratory of urban chemical archeology" (Lerner 2010:248). The area around Newtown Creek was part of an urban-industrial ecological regime that played a major role in the "second industrial revolution" of the nineteenth century (Hurley 1994). In the years following the Civil War, the geography of Newtown Creek was permanently altered by a period of rapid and intense industrial activity which included the storage and refining of oil, chemical production, glue making and fertilizer manufacturing. Along with the industrial pollution that resulted from commercial vessels bringing in raw materials and fuel and carrying out oil, chemicals and metals, the creek became a dumping ground for raw sewage. By 1870 there were more than fifty oil refineries along the banks of the creek and by the turn of the century John D. Rockefeller, founder of Standard Oil, controlled over one hundred distilleries with the result that the environmental conditions of Newtown Creek rapidly deteriorated.

In 1890, a group of Brooklyn citizens, angered by nauseating orders wafting through their community, created the 15th ward smelling committee to monitor the creek's degraded conditions. On a boat trip up the creek, they discovered the source of the nuisances to be the "distilling and boiling of bones, rendering of dead animals, fat, offal and blood, mixing of fertilizer material, escape of sewage, garbage dumping and oil refinery odors and seepage" (Hurley 1994:334).

In the late nineteenth century, capital-intensive industries that polluted the environment were subject to nuisance laws and forced to locate away from the inner city. Such environmental reforms were a mixed environmental blessing because forcing noxious and dirty industries from dense population centers enabled them to win concessions from local governments, which in turn enabled them to mold their surroundings as they wished. Despite widespread citizen protest and calls for political action, the oil corporations' onslaught of the environment remained unabated.

Despite public protest, oil companies were able to use their political clout to exploit the fragmented political authority of the metropolitan region to thwart environmental reform. Prior to being consolidated in 1898, New York City comprised only Manhattan and part of the Bronx. Brooklyn, Queens and Staten Island were independent political entities with their own mayors, legislatures, and health boards. For the most part, these separate governments rarely enforced nuisance laws and thus gave the industries a free ride to pollute with impunity. The oil corporations ability to disregard public indignation and evade regulatory pressures was virtually unchecked until pressures mounted to curb oil pollution at the federal level culminating in the passage of the Federal Oil Pollution Act of 1924. Despite the acknowledgment that land based oil refineries were a major source of oil pollution in urban harbors, lobbyists for the oil corporations persuaded Congress to exempt on-shore facilities from regulations. While the prohibition of discharges at sea brought about significant improvement in harbor waters, poor water quality near the refineries remained unchanged. During World War II, as the creek became one of the busiest ports in the nation, industrial pollution intensified.

While the waters of New York City improved tremendously with the passage of new environmental laws and legislation in the 1970s, Newtown Creek, with its legacy of environmental degradation remained unchanged. In 1978, during a helicopter patrol over Newtown Creek, the Coast Guard detected an oil slick on the surface of the water. A subsequent investigation by the Coast Guard found that the seep was part of a much larger seventeen million gallon oil spill that had saturated the soil underneath nearly fifty-five acres in Greenpoint. The Coast Guard applied temporary measures to collect the oil but very little was done to address what lay beneath the surface until 1990 when the State Department of Environmental Conservation issued a consent order to Exxon to clean up the spill. While Exxon accepted responsibility and agreed to clean up the spill, the State applied very little pressure to the company—there were no timetables, no fines or set outcomes.

In 2002, when the environmental watchdog group Riverkeeper began investigating Newtown Creek, they found the cozy relationship between Exxon and the DEC to be unacceptable. In 2004, they initiated a lawsuit against Exxon Mobil[2] in order to get the company to clean up the oil spill. Since that time, the U.S. Environmental Protection Agency has conducted a study on the oil spill and the New York State Attorney General has reached a major settlement with the company. At the present time, while the creek still remains an "ecological wasteland," a new generation of "smelling committees" and environmental activists are trying to change that.

CITIZEN ACTIVISM AND COMMUNITY BASED ORGANIZATIONS

At the present time there are two key community-based organizations that are following in the footsteps of the late nineteenth century "smelling committees." The Newtown Creek Monitoring Committee (NCMC) is an advisory committee made up of volunteers from the Greenpoint community, several of which have a long history of fighting for environmental quality and protection around the creek that was established in 1996 to oversee the upgrading of what will become the city's largest sewage treatment plant. To comply with the Clean Water Act, the original twenty-five-acre plant, originally built in 1969 was forced to expand to become a fifty-three acre complex. NCMC was formed by the city to help mitigate the impacts that the twenty year process would have on the community. The committee has a community liaison that provides feedback from the community as well as two technical consultants who provide assistance in developing solutions that address negative impacts to the community. In 2008, one of those consultants went to work for the

EPA. The committee was instrumental in establishing a waterfront promenade or nature walk along the plant replete with public art as well as an environmental learning center on the site. Opinion regarding these community benefits varies. Clearly, many people feel that these amenities are a plus for the surrounding community. At the same time there are many local residents who live in the shadow of the plant that feel that a small park, a learning center and a monitoring committee is small compensation given the size of the plant upgrade and its impact on the community.

The Newtown Creek Alliance founded in 2002, represents the interests of community residents and local businesses who are dedicated to restoring community health, water quality, habitat, access and vibrant water dependent commerce along Newtown Creek. The NCA is made up of neighborhood activists with a long involvement in environmental issues as well as recent arrivals to the area. Some of the issues they work on include pressuring government agencies to speed up the Exxon-Mobil Oil spill remediation process, pressing for environmental health studies to assess if there is a link between exposure to environmental toxins and illnesses in the community, working on long-term "green infrastructure" solutions to the creek's massive combined sewer overflow problem and advocating for increasing public access, parks and open space along the creek. The NCA's work with local politicians resulted in a major EPA study of the massive Greenpoint oil spill. They were also actively involved in the struggle to get the creek designated as a Superfund site. Another major achievement for the alliance was receiving a New York State Brownfields Opportunity Area ("BOA") Award that will be used to assess redevelopment opportunities for contaminated sites along the Creek emphasizing environmentally sustainable industrial uses, parks and wetlands creation, and improved environmental infrastructure. The NCA has recently formed a close partnership with HabitatMap, a local not-for-profit environmental health justice organization that leverages local community knowledge "to achieve just and sustainable urban places." In 2002, HabitatMap completed a community-based participatory research study on health concerns of residents living in communities along Newtown Creek. One of the long-term goals of the Alliance is to develop a plan, with the HabitatMAP community-based education program, to address public health issues and risks in neighborhoods along the creek.

The NCA is also involved with protecting industry and fighting against industrial displacement resulting from the creeping gentrification of the area. Although much of the waterfront along the creek is designated as an "industrial business zone," the rate of industrial displacement is steadily increasing as a result of legal and illegal loft conversions by artists and assorted "urban pioneers" who have been migrating to the area, in many cases, as a result of being priced out of other gentrifying areas. Recently, the city's commitment to protect manufacturing in the area has been undermined by new state legislation which allows for the legal conversion of manufacturing lofts into residential spaces. The intense industrial character of the area, does not seem to be a deterrent, and in some cases might be a draw for high income residents interested in industrial chic and the "loft living lifestyle" (Curran 2010; Zukin 1989). During an interview, a Brooklyn community Board 1 member and environmental activist involved in Newtown Creek remediation and affordable housing issues pointed out how "this new migration is blurring the boundaries between manufacturing and residential uses." She went on to say that, "I don't think people are scared off by industrial toxic waste. Give an artist a nice space and a bike and they will move anywhere."

The NCA is not interested in removing LULUs from the waterfront but in reforming them and making them cleaner, greener and more sustainable. They work closely with the Greenpoint Manufacturing and Design Center (GMDC) (which has a member on the board and was a partner for the BOA grant), a local organization devoted to rehabilitating and developing work spaces for light, clean industry around the creek. The Alliance feels strongly that open space, parks and greenways and industry can coexist with each other. They also work on ways to increase use of the waterways for transportation for local industry and municipal services as a way to reduce truck traffic and improve air quality.

The NCA fights environmental battles on many fronts utilizing a variety of strategies and tactics. They organize press conferences and rallies, work with local and state elected officials, and with private and public interest attorneys such as the New York Lawyers for the Public Interests and Riverkeeper, a lawyer driven environmental watchdog group that patrols the waterways and waterfronts in search of environmental polluters. The NCA's relationship with environmental regulatory agencies oscillates between an adversarial and litigious stance and collaborative and partnership approach. They put pressure on polluting companies and keep an eye on environmental regulatory agencies to make sure that they are doing their job of protecting the public and also take advantage of federal, state and local government sponsored environmental remediation and sustainability programs that stress public involvement and provide a role for community groups to participate and weigh in on land use and environmental decision making. The alliance has recently incorporated as a not-for-profit 502c3 and created a board with bylaws. By redefining itself as an incorporated nonprofit organization, the NCA hopes that it will be in a stronger position regarding a multitude of government plans and projects that will fundamentally change the ecology and economy of Newtown Creek over the next decade.

GOVERNMENTAL PLANS AND PROJECTS FOR NEWTOWN CREEK

In 2009, a 10 million dollar Environmental Benefits award, the largest in the state's history was established as a result of a lawsuit between the city's Department of Environmental Protection (DEP) and the State Department of Environmental Conservation (DEC) regarding the failure of the Newtown Creek sewage treatment plant to comply with state regulations. Both the NCA and MCMC were involved in the negotiating process that eventually led to the award. The Environmental Benefits Program was established in 1992, at approximately the same time as the Navy Yard incinerator struggle was taking place, after grassroots environmental activists from Greenpoint/Williamsburg pushed the city and state government to address environmental problems associated with the plant.

The EBP was controversial because it pitted different community groups with different environmental agendas against one another (Sweeny, Shipman and Tassi 1998). During the first application of the EBP in 1992, divisions emerged early over how the program would be administered, how the money would be spent and which particular community within the Community Board 1 area would receive funding. Greenpointers felt that the money should go to programs in Greenpoint since that is where the sewage treatment plant was located. Others to the south in Williamsburg argued that since the entire community was impacted by the plant violations that programs and monies should be distributed equally throughout the entire Community Board 1 area. Also, differences emerged between the priorities of the Greenpoint activists, whose concerns focused on the poorly operated Newtown Creek sewage treatment plant, the oil spill, marine transfer stations and incinerators and those of the Williamsburg activists who focused on health issues such as asthma, lead contamination and cancer. The early negotiations in the program exposed a complex environmental agenda that was crisscrossed by an array of ethnic and ideological schisms (Gandy 2002). Despite conflicts and divisions, the EBP achieved some major environmental accomplishments such as establishing an environmental monitoring project that helped to create maps of environmental health risks in the area. These early accomplishments have formed the building blocks for more recent community based environmental initiatives and policies.

Controversies over how and where environmental benefits and programs should be distributed are alive and well with the recent 2009 EBP process that is still unfolding. Once again, there were debates regarding whether environmental programs and amenities should go to people living in the immediate vicinity of the plant or to people in the wider CB 1 district and even the city at large. There were also questions about who should administer the programs—local grassroots organizations from Greenpoint or more established environmental organizations that focus on the entire city. Since the wastewater treatment plant is just one of fourteen in a citywide sewage system, the EBP raises complex boundary issues about Newtown Creek, which is just one tributary in a vast complex and interdependent estuarine ecosystem. Activists often claim that since the creek is part of a watery commons in what has been called "a city of water," local impacts have regional implications. When it comes to the watery commons "we all live downstream." Should programs to improve water quality be restricted to the creek or the wider system of waterways throughout the city and the region?

The recent EBP has been much more responsive to the needs of residents in the immediate vicinity of the treatment plant than the 1992 program. Some of the projects that have been proposed by community activists include waterfront parks, a boathouse and assorted community restoration and green infrastructure projects will all be close to the plant.

The Brownfield Opportunity Area grant raises similar issues and controversies. What type of development would be good for the community: residential, light green industry or a combination of both? Such conflicts raise complex issues about the meaning of community. While there is consensus regarding environmental ills, this breaks down when the discussion turns to environmental benefits for the community—everyone wants them but they mean different things to different people. Just about everyone wants to turn brownfields into greenfields, but problems emerge because different stakeholders have different green visions.

In the fall of 2010, Newtown Creek was designated a Superfund Site. This followed just a few months after the Gowanus Canal, another nearby Brooklyn industrial waterway received the same designation. Many people in the area regarded the EPA's decision to Superfund the creek as a great victory that will finally bring to bear the funds and resources necessary to clean up the creek. If things go well, the remediation process could take well over a decade. The creation of a Community Advisory Group (CAG), made up a wide assortment of representatives from the affected community is major component of the Superfund cleanup process. The NCA hopes to become one of the leading organizations involved in the CAG process.

In 2010, a settlement was reached by the Attorney General and Exxon Mobil that will provide 19.5 million dollars in community benefit money for the residents of Greenpoint to be used for assorted environmental programs and amenities as well as 5.5 million dollars in other penalties that will help to compensate the state for past and future environmental improvements along the creek. As part of the settlement, the DEC will set up a program, similar to the EBP that will oversee how the funds are distributed and used. Once, again, the NCA hopes to be in a strong position to help negotiate how the monies will be distributed and used.

DISCUSSION

The Bloomberg era of approach to sustainable development of the city's waterways and waterfronts represents an uneasy marriage of professional elite planning with New York style citizen-activism. While the City's comprehensive vision for revitalizing the waterfront, is in large part a blueprint gentrification couched in the language of sustainability and smart growth, there is a great deal of evidence that suggests that strengthening and protecting industrial spaces from being devoured by residential development and gentrification has become a major priority for that vision. What makes this especially curious is the fact that many waterfront activists and grass roots organizations had been calling for such measures for several years, but were unable to make much headway given the steady march of policy backed "neoliberal gentrification."

The various, Federal, State and local government programs and initiatives that provide an avenue for community participation in waterfront sustainability affairs have been a mixed blessing for citizen groups such as the NCA for several reasons. First, there are some drawbacks to collaborations between citizen activism and government policy. While the NCA has strategically used the Environmental Benefits Program to its advantage, relying on permit violations and consent decrees as a source of funding is a tenuous way to ensure long-term continuity of an organization. More importantly, the emphasis on community involvement and enlisting citizens as copartners in environmental remediation processes, while appearing to be a victory for the recognition of community concerns, risk abdication on the part of government. Citizens shouldn't have to become part of environmental advisory groups in order to live in a clean and toxic free environment. As Wilson and Weltman (2000: 49) have argued, citizen activism should act in concert with government action, not in lieu of it; "clean water and air should be a right enjoyed by everyone, not just those 'squeaky wheels' with the time and assistance necessary to take up the battle for a safe environment."

The NCA constantly wrestles with this issue. For example, at a recent pubic meeting in which the DEP announced a new green infrastructure grant program that places great emphasis on involving community groups to help with the city's CSO problems, a member from the Alliance asked a government official if involving citizens was a way to avoid remediation requirements spelled out by a 2004 consent order. Similar concerns are raised with regards to the amenities tied to the Environmental Benefits Program. At a meeting on how the monies from the EBP would be distributed, a member of the Alliance raised the issue of whether the new monies that the community won would be used to build parks that were already promised.

Several critics have pointed out that involving the community in environmental remediation is just veneer that gives off the illusion of transparency (McInroy 1999). In many cases, institutionalized community input sessions and visioning sessions associated with waterfront redevelopment have become ritualistic, "exercises in appeasement" a tool by which city elites have learned to better incorporate dissenting groups and manage potential conflicts more effectively (Bassett, Griffiths and Smith 2002; McCann 2001). Invoking "the community" is a rhetorical strategy that serves as a palliative and tranquillizer that helps to streamline the process of economic redevelopment (Angotti 2008). Given the potential for community resistance to delay or derail a project, community participation helps to legitimate redevelopment projects. This notion was driven home at a 2008 forum on urban revitalization and brownfields entitled "Building the Smart Growth Link between Redevelopment and Sustainable Communities" in which speakers from government agencies constantly stressed that, "bringing the community in to the brownfield planning process can put the seal of approval on a potentially contentious project."

Many environmental justice activists who have been struggling for years to reclaim the waterfront, have a very different view of citizen activism and community involvement. In this regard, it is important to note that the recent version of PlaNYC is the result of a great deal of input and interaction from environmental justice activists whose concerns about the inequitable distribution of risk and burdens on the waterfront were adopted almost wholesale into the city's final plan. This is clearly evident in the decision to use the waterfronts to transport waste and to shift the burdens associated with waste transfer stations from communities such as Greenpoint to neighborhoods in Manhattan. In a similar vein, the city's recent green infrastructure program, that encourages the use of natural "soft" sustainable stormwater management practices as opposed to large-scale "grey," capital intensive technologies, is something that grassroots citizen groups have been advocating for years. In short, the New York City waterfront is a site of successful resistance and struggle and not only of capital accumulation (Schaller and Noy 2011; Rubin 2011).

CONCLUSION

There is a widespread feeling on the part of activists and others in the community that the increased publicity about the creek's environmental ills is less about citizen activism and concerns for environmental justice and more about real estate development. They are aware that the mindset that saw pollution and foul odors as the normal state of affairs for an industrial neighborhood began to change as the neighborhood began to gentrify.

Many activists and residents regard the slow cleanup of Newtown Creek as an environmental justice issue because residents of Greenpoint have inhaled potentially toxic fumes for decades while Exxon Mobil and large oil refinery companies evaded liability. They feel strongly that if the oil spill occurred in a wealthy neighborhood in Manhattan that government agencies would have responded faster to the disaster. According to a fifty-five-year-old Greenpoint resident who has lived near the creek for his entire life:

> The community has known about the oil slick for over fifty years. They pressured the government to do something but nothing was done. The only reason they are doing something now is because there is an economic incentive for cleaning up the mess.

Such anger was reinforced after the city proposed using the mouth of the creek for an Olympic Village. According to a resident who attended several NCA meetings,

> Health concerns only became a public issues after the talk about the Olympics began. They knew about this problem for fifty years and did nothing about it. They only care about cleaning up the creek because the area has become hot real estate. Why did it take so long for the city to get involved? What about the Greenpoint citizens who have lived along the creek for decades but were ignored?

Similar concerns were raised about the city's support for the Superfund designation for the Creek, despite the fact that it lobbied hard against one for the Gowanus Canal out of fear that it would undermine high-end development projects. A forty-six-year-old female public school teacher who has lived five blocks from the creek for twenty years was glad that for the superfund designation but skeptical of the city's support for it. "If this area had potential for real estate development they would have tried to block superfund here too. It's just a bunch of factories. Who cares about the health of thousands or working people?"

Such comments bring us back to the issue of environmental gentrification and how it might influence future sustainability initiatives along the creek. Are community voices and equity concerns influencing waterfront policy or is the city's recent paradigm shift regarding the protection and greening of waterfront manufacturing a result of the recent economic slowdown? Will visions to transform the SMIA around Newtown Creek into a sustainable and green industrial zone melt away if the economy heats up again?

Perhaps more importantly, is the question of whether activists along the creek become victims of their own success. As awareness about the creek grows and more and more people become involved in determining its future, will sustainable visions for the creek change? As community groups like the NCA continue to ratchet up small victories and build more and more parks, esplanades, bike lanes and kayak launches, will new users of the waterfront and waterways feel differently about maintaining the area as a green manufacturing zone? In many cases, parks, open spaces and other waterfront amenities serve as engines of gentrification (Dooling 2009). They are precisely the types of environmental amenities that "creative class gentrifiers" crave as they colonize new urban spaces. As Richard Florida has remarked (2000:8), "The rise of the new economy dramatically transforms the role of the environment and amenities—from a source of raw materials and a sink for waste disposal—to a critical component of the total package required to attract talent and, in doing so, generate economic growth."

When talking about waterfront gentrification it is important to focus on class differences within communities. Not everyone is being hurt by environmental gentrification. In fact some regard it as evidence that their environmental struggles have born fruit. There is a major difference in attitudes between property owners and renters. Many people have benefited from the increased property values that gentrification brings about. Thus, waterfront activists and residents alike view gentrification as a double-edged sword. An artist and member of the NCA who has lived along the creek for twenty years expressed fears during an interview that new development might price him and other longtime residents out of the neighborhood. He also pointed out that the newer middle and upper class residents are pushing along efforts to clean up the waterfront. An ex-City Council member from Queens who was deeply involved in remediating the creek as well as a co-plaintiff on the Exxon lawsuit, spoke about the gentrification of the waterfront around the creek as positive economic strategy for the city. "The Brooklyn-Queens waterfront has the potential to be New York's Gold Coast, with sparkling towers, schools, parks and libraries. Cleaning Newtown Creek is critical to that vision" (Confessore 2007:np). While many activists view increased publicity about the environmental ills of the creek as a way to mobilize support to clean it up, others are deeply concerned that raising environmental awareness about potentially toxic threats will cause their property values to drop.

Gentrification has been a boost for property values while negative publicity about the toxic creek threatens this.

These divergent attitudes about gentrification reflect another tendency in struggles over the three E's of sustainability—the use and abuse of "the community" in local discourse. While the notion of "the community" is constantly bandied about in environmental and policy debates, it is a reified abstraction. The tendency to romanticize and essentialize communities by viewing them as coherent and cohesive bodies obscures divisions and conflicts between different stakeholders (Angotti 2008; Smith 2008). Instead of arguing that "the community" is victimized by particular land-use decisions, it is more accurate to say that some sectors of the so-called community are harmed while others benefit. This is clearly the case with gentrification. For some local residents, a gentrified gold coast is much better than a waterfront sealed off to residents by a wall of potentially noxious industrial sites. For others, a new gold coast is a major threat.

The notion of a conflict and tension free community has much in common with those versions of sustainability discourse that stress win-win scenarios for enduring environmental problems. As Campbell (2003: 446) has argued, the concept of sustainability can "be effective if instead of merely evoking a misty eyed vision of a peaceful ecotopia, it acts as a lightning rod to focus on conflicting economic, environmental and social interests. The more it stirs up conflict and sharpens the debate, the more effective the idea of sustainability will be in the long run." In a similar vein, Weinberg et al. (2000: 188) argue that sustainable community development requires an understanding of the goals of the three E's in an ongoing tension with each other. Striving for sustainability should not be viewed "as a goal, but rather as an ongoing process: Not as a set of irrevocable answers, but as a way of continually asking better questions."

Despite the fact that environmental cleanup and sustainability is a messy affair that involves establishing alliances and partnerships that are fragile and filled with contradictions, activists along the Newtown Creek are negotiating with the three E's and struggling with questions about sustainability. Despite the perils of environmental gentrification and divisions over competing visions for the area, they are struggling to make Newtown Creek and the waterfront a cleaner, greener and more beautiful place for the many not just the few.

NOTES

1. Quotations not otherwise cited are from interview data collected by the author.
2. Mobil merged with Exxon in 1999.

REFERENCES

Agyeman, Julian, Robert D. Bullard and Bob Evans. eds. 2003. *Just Sustainabilities: Development in an Unequal World.* Cambridge, MA: MIT Press.

Agyeman, Julian. 2005. *Sustainable Communities and the Challenge of Environmental Justice.* New York, NY: New York University Press.

Angotti, Tom. 2007. "Daniel Doctoroff's Legacy." *Gotham Gazette*, December. Retrieved December 1, 2010 (www.gothamgazette.com/article/landuse/20071211/12/2373).

Angotti, Tom. 2008. *New York for Sale: Community Planning Confronts Global Real Estate.* Cambridge, MA: MIT Press.

Ballon, Hillary and Kenneth T. Jackson. eds. 2007. *Robert Moses and the Modern City: The Transformation of New York.* London, UK: W.W. Norton Company.

Banzhaf, Spencer H. and Randall P. Walsh. 2006. "Do People Vote With Their Feet? An Empirical Test Of Environmental Gentrification," Discussion Papers: Resources for the Future. Retrieved January 10, 2011 (www.economics.ucr.edu/workshop/papers/RandallWalsh.pdf).

Bassett, Keith, Ron Griffiths and Ian Smith. 2002. "Testing Governance: Partnerships, Planning and Conflict in Waterfront Regeneration." *Urban Studies* 39(10):1757–75.

Benford, Robert. 2005. "The Half-Life of the Environmental Justice Frame: Innovation, Diffusion, and Stagnation." Pp. 37–54 in *Power Justice and the Environment: A Critical Appraisal of the Environmental Justice Movement*, edited by D. N. Pellow and R. J. Brulle. Cambridge, MA: MIT Press.

Brown, Peter H. 2009. *America's Waterfront Revival: Port Authorities and Urban Development.* Philadelphia, PA: University of Pennsylvania Press.

Bullard, Robert D. ed. 2007. *Growing Smarter: Achieving Livable Communities, Environmental Justice, and Regional Equity.* Cambridge, MA: MIT Press.

Bunce, Susannah 2004. "The Emergence of 'Smart Growth' Intensification in Toronto: Environment and Economy in the New Official Plan." *Local Environment* 9(2):177–91.

Bunce, Susannah. 2009. "Developing Sustainability: Sustainability Policy and Gentrification on Toronto's Waterfront." *Local Environment* 14(7):651–67.

Campbell, Scott and Susan S. Fainstein, eds. 2003. *Readings in Planning Theory*, 2nd Edition. London, UK: Blackwell.

Campbell, Scott 2003."Green Cities, Growing Cities, Just Cities? Urban Planning and the Contradictions of Sustainable Development." Pp. 435–58 in *Readings in Planning Theory,* edited by S. Campbell and S. Fainstein. London, UK: Blackwell Publishers.

Checker, Mellisa. 2001. "Like Nixon Coming to China: Finding Common Ground in a Multi-Ethnic Coalition for Environmental Justice." *Anthropological Quarterly* 74(3):135–46.

Confessore, Nicholas. 2007. "New York Moves toward Suit Over a 50-Year Old Oil Spill." *The New York Times,* February 9. Retrieved February 11, 2011 (www.nytimes.com).

Curran, Winifred. 2007. "From the Frying Pan to the Oven: Gentrification and the Experience of Industrial Displacement in Williamsburg, Brooklyn." *Urban Studies* 44(8):1427–40.

Curran, Winifred. 2010. "In Defense of Old Industrial Spaces: Manufacturing, Creativity and Innovation in Williamsburg, Brooklyn." *International Journal of Urban and Regional Research* 34(4):871–85.

Dale, Ann and Lenore L. Newman. 2009. "Sustainability for Some: Green Urban Development and Affordability." *Local Environment* 14(7):669–81.

Davila, Arlene. 2004. *Barrio Dreams: Puerto Ricans, Latinos, and the Neoliberal City*. Berkeley: University of California Press.

De Pass, Michelle. 2006. "Brownfields as a Tool for the Rejuvenation of Land and Community." *Local Environment* 11(50):601–6.

Desfor, Gene, Jennefer Laidley, Quentin Stevens, and Dirk Schubert. 2011. *Transforming Urban Waterfronts: Fixity and Flow*. New York: Routledge.

DeSena, Judith N. 2005. *Protecting One's Turf*. New York: University Press of America.

DeSena, Judith N. 2009. *Gentrification and Inequality In Brooklyn: New Kids on the Bloc*k. Lanham, MD: Lexington Books.

Dooling, Sarah. 2009. "Ecological Gentrification: A Research Agenda Exploring Justice in the City." *International Journal of Urban and Regional Research* 33(3):621–30.

Dobson, Andrew. 2003 *Citizenship and the Environment*. Oxford, UK: Oxford University Press.

Eckard, Adam. 2011 "Cleaning Up Without Clearing Out? A Spatial Assessment of Environmental Gentrification." *Urban Affairs Review* 47(1):31–59.

Essoka, Jonathon. 2010."The Gentrifying Effects of Brownfields Redevelopment." *The Western Journal of Black Studies* 34(3):299–315.

Faber, D. 2008*: Capitalizing on Environmental Injustice*. New York: Rowman and Littlefield Publishers.

Florida, Richard. 2000. "Competing in the Age of Talent:Quality of Place and the New Economy." Final report to the Richard King Mellon Foundation and Sustainable Pittsburgh. Retrieved January 2, 2011 (www.creativeclass.com).

Gandy, Matthew. 2002. *Concrete and Clay: Reworking Nature in New York City*. Cambridge, MA: MIT Press.

Hackworth, Jason. 2007. *The Neoliberal City: Governance, Ideology and Development in American Urbanism*. Ithaca, NY: Cornell University Press.

Hajer, Maarten. 1995. *The Politics of Environmental Discourse*. New York: Oxford University Press.

Holifield, Ryan. 2004. "Neoliberalism and Environmental Justice in the United States Environmental Protection Agency: Translating Policy into Managerial Practice in Hazardous Waste Remediation." *Geoforum* 35(3):285–97.

Hurley, Andrew. 1994. "Creating Ecological Wastelands: Oil Pollution in New York City, 1870–1900." *Journal of Urban History* 20(3):340–64.

Krueger, Ron and David Gibbs. eds. 2007. *The Sustainable Development*. New York: Paradox Guilford Press.

Layard, Antonia. 2001. *Introduction: Sustainable Development: Principles and Practice*, London, UK: Spon Press.

Lerner, Steve. 2010. *Sacrifice Zones: The Front Lines of Toxic Chemical Exposure in the United States*. Boston, MA: MIT Press.

Maantay, Juliana. 2001. "Zoning, Equity and Public Health." *American Journal of Public Health* 19(7):1033–41.

Marwell, Nicole P. 2007. *Bargaining for Brooklyn: Community Organizations in the Entrepreneurial City*. Chicago, IL: The University of Chicago Press.

McCann, E. 2001. "Collaborative Visioning or Urban Planning as Therapy? The Politics of Public-Private Policy Making." *The Professional Geographer* 53(2):207–18.

McInroy, Neil M. 1999. "Urban Regeneration and Public Space: The Story of An Urban Park." *Space and Polity* 4(1):23–40.

Miller, Daniel and Gert De Roo. 2004. *Integrating City Planning and Environmental Improvement: Practical Strategies for Sustainable Urban Development*. Burlington, VT: Ashgate Publishing Co.

Miller, Benjamin. 2000. *Fat of the Land: Garbage in New York The Last Two Hundred Years*. New York: Four Windows, Eight Walls.

New York City Department of City Planning. 2002. *Greenpoint 197-A Plan*. Retrieved Jan 2, 2011 (www.nyc.gov/html/dcp/home.html).

New York City Department of City Planning. 2011. *Vision 2020: New York City Comprehensive Waterfront Plan*." Retrieved April 15, 2011 (www.nyc.gov/html/dcp/home.html).

New York City Department of City Planning. 1997. *197-A Technical Guide*. Retrieved January 4, 2011 (www.nyc.gov/html/dcp/home.html).

Pearsall, Hamil. 2010. "From Brown to Green? Assessing Social Vulnerability to Environmental Gentrification in New York City." *Environment and Planning C: Government and Policy* 28(5):872–86.

Pellow, David and Robert Brulle. eds. 2005. *Power Justice and the Environment: A Critical Appraisal of the Environmental Justice Movement*. Cambridge, MA: MIT Press.

Philips, Nelson and Cynthia Hardy. 2002. *Discourse Analysis: Investigating Processes of Social Construction*. London, UK: Sage Publications.

Quinn, Naomi. 2005. *Finding Culture in Talk: A Collection of Methods*. New York: Palgrave Macmillan.

Raco, Mike and Steven Henderson. 2006. "Sustainable Urban Planning and the Brownfield Development Process In the United Kingdom: Lessons from the Thames Gateway," *Local Environment* 11(5):499–513.

Rubin, Jasper. 2011. "San Francisco's Waterfront in the Age of Neoliberal Urbanism." Pp. 143–65 in *Transforming Urban Waterfronts: Fixity and Flow*, edited by Gene Desfor, Jennefer Laidley, Quentin Stevens and Dirk Schubert. New York: Routledge.

Sabel, Charles, Archon Fund, Bradley Karkkainen. eds. 2000. *Beyond Backyard Environmentalism*. Boston, MA: Beacon Press.

Santora, Marc. 2010. "New York's Next Frontier: The Waterfront." *New York Times*, November 5. Retrieved December 10, 2010 (www.nytimes.com).

Schaller, Susanna and Johannes Novy. 2011. "New York City's Waterfronts as Strategic Sites for Analyzing Neoliberalism and its Contestations." Pp. 167–87 in *Transforming Urban Waterfronts: Fixity and Flow*, edited by Gene Desfor, Jennefer Laidley, Quentin Stevens and Dirk Schubert. New York: Routledge.

Scholsberg, David. 2007. *Defining Environmental Justice: Theories, Movements and Nature*. London, UK: Oxford University Press.

Smith, Neil. 2002. "New Globalism, New Urbanism: Gentrification as Global Urban Strategy." *Antipode* 34(3) 427–50.

Smith, Julia, L. 2008. "A Critical Appreciation of the 'Bottom-Up' Approach to Sustainable Water Management: Embracing Complexity Rather Than Desirability." *Local Environment* 13 (4):353–66.

Susser, Ida. 1982. *Norman Street. Poverty and Politics in an Urban Neighborhood*: London, UK: Oxford University Press.

Sweeney, Jane, Chantal Shipman, and Anthony Tassi. 1998. "Environmental Benefits Program: New York City, U.S.A." Mega Cities Project.

Sze, Julie. 2007. *Noxious New York: the Racial Politics of Urban Health and Environmental Justice*. Cambridge, MA: MIT Press.

Szili, Gertrude and Matthew W. Rofe. 2007. "Greening Port Misery: Marketing The Green Face of Waterfront Redevelopment in Port Adelaide, South Australia." *Urban Policy & Research* 25(3):363–84.

Warner, Kee. 2002. "Linking Local Sustainabiity Initiatives with Environmental Justice." *Local Environment* 7(1):35–47.

Weiss, Rachel and Heimbinder, Michael 2011. *Creek Speak: Voices from Newtown Creek*. Report for the Newtown Creek Alliance. Retrieved January 2, 2011 (www.newtowncreekalliance.org).

Weinberg, Adam. S, David, N. Pellow, and Allan Schnaiberg. 2000. *Urban Recycling and the Search for Sustainable Community Development*. Princeton, NJ: Princeton University Press.

While, Adian, Andrew E. Jonas and David Gibbs. 2004. "The Environment and the Entrepreneurial City: Searching for Urban 'Sustainability Fix' in Manchester and Leeds." *International Journal of Urban and Regional Research* 28(3):549–69.

Wilson, Matt and Weltman Eric. 2000. "Governments Job." Pp. 49–53 in *Beyond Backyard Environmentalism*, edited by Charles Sabel, Archon Fund and Bradley Karkkainen. Boston, MA: Beacon Press.

Wolf-Powers, Laura. 2005. "Upzoning New York City's Mixed Use Neighborhoods: Property Led Economic Development and the Anatomy of a Planning Dilemma," *The Journal of Planning, Education and Research* 24 (4): 379–93.

Wood, Linda A. and Rolf O. Kroger. 2002. *Doing Discourse Analysis: Methods for Studying Talk and Text*. London, UK: Sage.

Yampierre, Elizabeth. 2007. "Comments." *Progressive Planning 171*, Spring. Retrieved February 30, 2011 (www.plannersnetwork.org/publications/2007_spring/yeampierre.html).

Zukin, Sharon. 2006. "Jane Jacobs: The Struggle Continues." *City & Community* 5(3):223–26.

10

Riding the Bus in Brooklyn

Seeing the Spectacle of Everyday Multicultural Life

Jerome Krase

On a sunny morning in June 2007, I took a ride on the B68 bus from its beginning to its end and back again. I had travelled this route hundreds of times over the decades and marveled at the view. This time I took my digital camera to compose this visually enhanced essay that focuses on what can be seen while simply sitting by a window and riding along its approximately four and one-half mile route along Coney Island Avenue, in Brooklyn. A single trip in this vehicle reveals to the viewer, through often dirty windows, an elegant spectacle which passes outside the bus of quotidian multicultural life displayed in what J. B. Jackson terms "vernacular landscapes" that lie "underneath below the symbols of permanent power expressed in the 'Political Landscape'"(1984: 6). For Jackson, and me, what people do in a particular physical territory and how they use objects in them are necessary for a proper understanding of any space (Jackson 1984:118–19).

RIDING THE CONEY ISLAND AVENUE BUS

There are two different ways to use the bus as an observation post in order to explore modes of living with and across difference in neighboring, shopping, and potentially contentious social issues such as multicultural place-sharing, and battles over place identity and belonging. One way is to look out the window and sample the steadily changing streetscapes as you go by. Although the scenes are dominated by diverse storefronts, the pedestrians are also diverse in their physical characteristics and clothing. Another way is to look inside the bus where representatives of varied groups are constantly mixing as different kinds of people get on and off the buses, depending on

Figure 10.1. Inside the B68 bus mid-route on Coney Island Avenue. Photograph by the author.

where you are along the route. In a sense it is a marvelous expression of the acceptance of a multicultural reality for example, as Orthodox Jews, Hindus, Christians, and Muslims, people who might be warring with each other in some other part of the world all getting on the same bus. What makes this possible is that there is something that all groups need; to get from one place to the other. They cooperate with each other in order to get to where it is that they want to go.

The trip was no mere excursion but also a place-based academic exercise as I often give my students similar fieldwork assignments to relate their readings, and my lectures, to the globally connected but still local worlds in which they live. This chapter then is an attempt to demonstrate how to use images in order to better tie the ordinary practices of the people who live, shop, or simply travel along Coney Island Avenue to the often too abstract theories that purport to explain what it is they are doing. For Douglas Harper (1998: 82), this is an example of "visual methods" as I "take photographs in order to study social worlds," as opposed to analyzing images produced by the culture. John Grady, another pioneering visual sociologist, would say that I was "Doing Sociology Visually" by investigating "how the techniques of produc-

Figure 10.2. Outside the B68 bus mid-route. Photograph by the author.

ing and decoding images can be used to empirically investigate social organization, cultural meaning, and psychological processes" (Grady 1996:14).

The images presented in this essay are a small sample chosen from some 550 medium resolution photographs taken by the author from inside an often speeding, bus and they "represent" a small portion of an everyday multicultural panorama. It will be obvious to the reader that a dirty bus window has filtered most of them, and sometimes the vibration of the engine, or the sways of turning and the recoil of breaking, has blurred the image. They are shown here in the way that we most often see social life on buses, and subway cars as well—glanced at, glimpsed, and sometimes purposely unfocused in order to maintain proper social distance.

There is perhaps no better way to appreciate the embodied or inhabited nature of living with cultural difference in what Lyn Lofland (1998) calls "The Public Realm," those spaces accessible to all, than by using public transportation in global cities such as Brooklyn. For Saskia Sassen (2002:162), the global city is also a strategic site where, despite their lack of power, immigrants, people of color, and others emerge as significant subjects (see also Sassen 1999). We might argue that, in essence, multiculturalism is an unintended consequence of globalization. These simple propositions are based on many years of visual sociological research on various versions of what Arjun Appadurai (1996) might call "ethnoscapes," or otherwise visible results of globalization in places as distant as Sidney, Australia and as near as my own home of Brooklyn in New York City.

For most of the twentieth century the borough of Brooklyn, currently with more than two and one-half million residents, has been a virtual Roman Fountain of migration and immigration. During that time, and continuing today, the foreign-born proportion of the total population has averaged about one-third. More strikingly, in the second half of that century, Brooklyn has changed from a community with a 96 percent white non-Hispanic majority to one with a 34.7 percent white non-Hispanic minority. For social scientists, the examination of ethnic and racial diversity usually takes place in number-crunching demographic analysis, but in this essay the question asked, and answered, is: "What do numbers look like on the street?"

The forgoing question is no simple interrogative. History effects what we see on the streets. Shortly after 9/11, the growth, and visibility, of the South Asian population along and near Coney Island Avenue became a major problem for local residents. Mohammed Ravzi, the founder and Director of the Council of Pakistani Organization (which is now the Council of People's

Figure 10.3. Council of Peoples Organization Community Center. Photograph by the author.

Organizations) related that, there was mass confusion as agents of the Federal Bureau of Investigations and Immigration and Naturalization Service descended upon the area to roundup many South-Asians and those who had "Muslim" names similar to names they were looking for. It was about this time that local businesses, owned by immigrants, began to display American flags outside or in their store windows along the route.

The term "multicultural" is often used as an adjective describing ethnic, racial, religious, or other life style diversity. Using such a definition, the United States of America is clearly a multicultural society but diversity in America is hardly uniformly distributed. It is in the large metropolitan areas such as Los Angeles, Chicago, and of course New York, that best fit the bill. Even within large cities diversity tends to be more apparent in some sections than in others. For example, in New York City, Brooklyn as mixed as it is, comes in only second in immigrant diversity to its sister borough of Queens.

Although many think of the idea of multiculturalism as something new, others such as Ronald Takaki (1993), advisedly employed the term in their description of the entire history of the United States. However, it seems more reasonable to argue that America's ethnic diversity paradigm has had three

Figure 10.4. American flag on sidewalk outside the "Taj Mahal" Bangladeshi American grocery. Photograph by the author.

major competing, and conflicting, themes all of which, I have argued in different places, present different visual expressions (Krase 2009). Historically, the themes of "assimilationism," "cultural pluralism," and "multiculturalism" mimic societal responses to the real and imagined threats to the dominant Anglo-conformist culture by immigration and migration. These "-isms" are ideological as well as historical facts. Assimilationism and multiculturalism are at opposite ends of a spectrum of what Michael Walzer calls "Tolerance" and "Toleration." For Walzer (1997) toleration, as a set of institutional and other arrangements, rather than attitudes, of tolerance is crucial for the success of diverse societies. For a situation of toleration, mutual respect is less important than peaceful coexistence. The reality of everyday intergroup life and "minority" relations in America, I believe, falls today somewhere in the middle of the spectrum—in cultural pluralism. While assimilationism abhors difference and multiculturalism idolizes it, cultural pluralism recognizes the positive value of diversity for democratic societies but only in tandem with overarching common values that connect the disparate groups.

The term "cultural pluralism" might be thought of as a precursor of "multiculturalism" and has a long history of usage in intellectual and lay circles. Horace Kallen (1915a, 1915b) was an important critic of the "Melting Pot" (assimilationism) thesis and is credited with coining the term and the idea of cultural pluralism. Another early use of the term was in Randolph Bourne's 1916 essay "Trans-National America." Joseph F. Healey (2006: 50) notes that "Kallen argued that people should not have to surrender their culture and traditions to become full participants in American society . . . and that American society could be a federation of diverse groups, a mosaic of harmonious and interdependent cultures and peoples" (see also Toll 1997).

CONEY ISLAND AVENUE

Ethnic diversity along the Coney Island Avenue corridor in Brooklyn has attracted a great deal of attention during the past few years. As *USA Today* reporter Rick Hampson described his ride on the B68. After noting how the language of store signs and the dress of riders change as the bus moves down the thoroughfare he sees that:

> At Glenwood Road, a Moldavian Jew and a Pakistani Muslim cut hair at adjacent barbershop chairs. At Avenue I, a Muslim grocer boasts that a third of his goods are kosher. At Avenue R, Tayba Islamic Center sits next door to Chabad Jewish Center . . .
>
> Coney Island Avenue isn't the Champs-Élysées. It's noisy, busy, homely: a street of car washes, auto body shops, electronics stores, health clinics and store-

> fronts that traffic in phone cards, discount travel, international money transfers, cellphones, insurance.
>
> There is variety in dining, from Tzar Boris ("Russian Noble Food") to Thai Aroma, El Alamo, Casa Italia (kosher Italian) and HFC, which sells halal fried chicken, pizza and bagels across the same counter.
>
> There's a Walgreens and a Staples and not much else in the way of name-brand retail shopping. The avenue is not even mentioned in the mammoth *AIA Guide to New York City*. 'Architecturally, historically, it really has nothing to point to,' says Brooklyn historian Ron Schweiger, "except for its ethnic diversity."
>
> That, and its tranquility in a crowded, abrasive city where almost anything—a car accident, a slight, a fight—can turn into something bigger—a demonstration, a boycott, a riot. (Hampson 2007:np; see also Voice of America 2004; Wilson 2005)

New York Times reporter, Andy Newman, had a similar experience "On Brooklyn's Avenue of Babel":

> Coney Island Avenue, a five-mile, four-lane strip that runs through or skirts the edges of Midwood, Flatbush and Sheepshead Bay, lacks the global cachet of Broadway or even the local recognition of Flatbush Avenue. To the extent that it is known at all, it is as a fairly ugly thoroughfare lined with auto body shops, car dealers and blocky funeral homes.
>
> Residents of southern Brooklyn and fans of the city's ethnic diversity know it as the place where a Pakistani neighborhood ends abruptly at an Orthodox Jewish neighborhood that eventually melts into a mishmash and emerges on the far side of the Belt Parkway in the Little Odessa of Brighton Beach.
>
> The avenue is all that. But it is much, much more. Not just a cluster of high-concept juxtapositions like the mosque next door to the Jewish day care center or the 99-cent store where the ''Kosher Candy and Snacks'' sign points to a display of Easter bunnies and marshmallow chicks, though the stories behind those places turn out to be interesting enough. Not just ethnic one-liners like the self-proclaimed World's Only Kosher Gym (Newman 2004: np).

Coney Island Avenue has been recognized by the New York City Planning Commission as one the most diverse streets in this very multiethnic city. The thoroughfare can be seen as a product of "globalization" that is often used to describe a combination of factors changing values and norms that are spread across the world. These include new technologies, increased trade, concentration of economic control, reduced welfare state, spatial integration of economic activities, and movement of both capital, and people. The indigenous practices of ordinary people who have been brought together by distant forces and processes are examples of that for which Roland Robertson (1997) coined the term "glocalization." Robertson could have been imagining Coney

Island Avenue when he insisted that homogenizing and universalizing forces of globalization do not obliterate the heterogeneity and particularity of local forces as much as their interaction creates varying degrees of hybrid culture (Osterhammel and Petersson 2005: 7). Like many other places in the New York-New Jersey Metropolitan Area, several sections of Brooklyn are places where people-mixing is simply taken for granted, and therefore virtually unnoticed and unremarkable despite being visible.

According to Kumru Toktamis (2007: 1), "more than half of the population living along Coney Island Avenue was born outside the United States and almost 62 percent of these residents do not speak English at home. Despite the fact the three-quarters of the adults have completed at least a secondary school education, and almost a third have a college degree, more than half of the residents reported that they do not speak English well." In addition to European languages such as Spanish, Italian, Russian, and French that are commonly spoken by more established immigrant groups to the United States other languages identified in her study were: Yiddish, Hebrew, and the Indic languages spoken by Pakistani, Indian, and Bengali people. These South Asians were the fastest growing populations along several parts of the commercial strip. Using boundaries and data from the most recent U.S. Census, Toktamis found that the area is not only very ethnically diverse, it is also better educated, and with less unemployment, than the rest of the borough and the city as a whole.

Coney Island Avenue is a wide, predominately commercial, thoroughfare that traverses four of New York City Brooklyn Community Districts (CDs): CD 12, CD 13, CD 14, and CD 15. All the demographic data which follow are taken from the "Community District Profiles" produced by the New York City Department of City Planning (2005a, b, c, d).

These four CDs contain within their boundaries ten distinct neighborhoods some of which have more or less well-known "ethnic" identities such as "Orthodox Jewish" Borough Park, "South Asian" Kensington, "Russian/ Ukrainian" Brighton Beach, and "Caribbean" Flatbush. In 2000 these CDs had a total population of 629,291 while in the, smaller, census tracts that directly touch the avenue itself the population was only 87,687. The Census data also showed that the commercial strip was a vibrant and active business area and marketplace.

Almost two-thirds of the population along the avenue report that they are "white." This is far higher than the proportion of white residents in Brooklyn (34.7 percent) and NYC (35 percent). As opposed to Brooklyn as a whole, along Coney Island Avenue, African-Americans are a small minority (6.6 percent) of the resident population. The second largest group is Asian (14.1 percent) with Hispanics next (8.5 percent). Toktamis (2007: 3) astutely commented that "whiteness" has several shades—a fact that carries significant cultural and sociological implications." It must be noted for the U.S. Census Bureau "a person having origins in any of the original peoples of Europe, the Middle East, or North Africa" is considered "White" (Toktamis 2007: 3).

Coney Island Avenue acts like a flowing river with tributaries from more distinct ethnic neighborhoods that cause a mixing of populations by degrees along its length. A geographic rule of thumb for the avenue is that, after Church Avenue, from north to south the street names are in alphabetical order. The visible presence of individual groups varies along the route as they come to work, shop, or pass through on the way to somewhere else. Each of the major groups dominates their own specialized shopping district but along the avenue they wax, wane, and occasionally blend. In the process of this multicultural place-sharing one can observe subtle, and not so subtle, competitions and occasional symbolic battles over place identity and belonging.

The B68 Coney Island Avenue bus has one terminus at the northern most end of the route. Here, near the highly gentrified neighborhood of Park Slope, the thoroughfare is named "Prospect Park Southwest" and the streetscape is

Figure 10.5. Pakistani and Buhkari businesses also cater to Bangladeshis and Indians. One also might make out the Orthodox Jewish pedestrian in the right foreground. Photograph by the author.

almost devoid of commerce as it runs along a major urban park and the predominately white middle and upper-middle class residential neighborhood of Windsor Terrace. Further south, at Park Circle where "Coney Island Avenue" officially begins, it is crossed by the Caribbean shopping strip of Church Avenue, followed by South Asian Foster Avenue, and Orthodox Jewish Avenue J. From this point southward the strip becomes more visibly Russian with smatterings of Middle Eastern and Chinese businesses. At the southern-most end of Coney Island Avenue is the ocean side neighborhood of Brighton Beach that in recent years has been named "Little Odessa" reflecting the Ukrainian and Russian speaking population. As to the penchant for ethnic diminutives many refer to the South Asian area on and near Coney Island Avenue as "Little Pakistan," the Orthodox Jewish shopping area on Avenue J as "Little Israel," and the Caribbean shopping strip which links to Coney Island Avenue by several buses as 'Little Haiti" and "Little Kingston (Jamaica)."

We can think geometrically of Coney Island Avenue as a line running north-south that dissects a large square with four quadrants, each having very diverse but distinctive mixings of groups. The northwest quadrant is CD 12 where 185,046 people live. 65.2 percent of the population is white; 14 percent Asian; 13.2 percent Hispanic, 2.9 percent black, 3.4 percent two or more

Figure 10.6. Muslim woman and child walking on Coney Island Avenue between "Little Pakistan" and "Little Israel." Photograph by the author.

races, and 1.1 percent some other races. 41.8 percent is foreign born and 49.2 percent don't speak English well. Yiddish is the language other than English most likely to be spoken at home (27.9 percent), while 17.7 percent speak Spanish or Spanish Creole, 12.4 percent Chinese, and 11.5 percent Russian.

CD 13 is the southwestern quadrant where 55.3 percent of its 168,806 residents are white; 9.5 percent Asian; 16.3 percent Hispanic, 15.7 percent black, and 2.8 percent two or more races. Almost half (47.1 percent) of the population is foreign-born. 60.9 percent of residents don't speak English well and 60 percent of persons older than 5 speak a language other than English at home. Russian is the mostly widely spoken foreign language (28.4 percent) and as

Figure 10.7. Orthodox Jewish man at the B68 bus stop near Avenue J's Orthodox Jewish shopping area. Photograph by the author.

Figure 10.8. South Asian woman walking along Coney Island Avenue near "Little Pakistan." Photograph by the author.

might be expected Russian ancestry is the largest reported, constituting 14.4 percent of the district's population. In 21.1 percent of the households where English is not spoken, Spanish or Spanish Creole is the home language, while 7.2 percent speak Chinese, 4 percent Yiddish, and 3.9 percent speak an Indic language. Although the Russian cohort is growing, the fastest growing population is of Puerto Rican origin and who make up half of the Hispanic population.

District 14, in the northeastern quadrant, is the least populated with only 106,120 people. The largest group is African American (39.2 percent) and the second largest is white (35.7 percent.) Hispanics constitute 13.2 percent, Asians 7.8 percent, and residents reporting two or more races are 3.4 percent of the population. Half of CD 14's population is foreign born (49.8 percent), the largest part of which is Latin American. Mexican immigrants are the fastest growing population whose numbers have increased almost three-fold between 1990 and 2000. The second fastest growing foreign-born group was Pakistani, having more than doubled in the same time. Slightly more than half of those older than five don't speak English well and speak a language other than English at home. Spanish, or Spanish Creole, speakers are the largest (24.3 percent) of this group, with those speaking French or French

Figure 10.9. Nevski Memorial Chapels (Russian) in the southern half of Coney Island Avenue. Photograph by the author.

Figure 10.10. This kosher (and non-kosher) "Super Market" is near the midpoint of the Coney Island Avenue bus route. Photograph by the author.

Figure 10.11. Local public high school students near Church Avenue. Photograph by the author.

Figure 10.12. "Tranfert D'Argent Haiti," Haitian money transfer company near Church Avenue. Photograph by the author.

Creole (23.4 percent) in second place. "Non-Hispanic West Indian" is the largest declared ancestry in the district (21.8 percent) and almost one fifth (18.4 percent) of the non-English speakers are of Russian ancestry. Another 8.4 percent of the population speaks an Indic language, 4.5 percent speak Hebrew, and 4.4 percent speak Yiddish.

District 15 is in the southeastern quadrant. Three-quarters of the 160,319 people living there are white, and Asians are 12.6 percent of the population, 6.4 percent is Hispanic, 3 percent is African American, and 2.2 percent is two or more races. Slightly less than one-half (45.4 percent) of the population is foreign born. More than half (56 percent) of the residents don't speak English well, and an equal proportion of persons older than five speak a language other than English at home. Among those home languages are Russian (42 percent), Chinese (16.7 percent), Arabic (5.3 percent), Italian (5.2 percent), Hebrew (4.8 percent), and Yiddish (3.3 percent). 13.1 percent of the entire population claims Russian ancestry and slightly less (12.9 percent) claims Italian ancestry. The fastest growing language group is Ukrainian with almost and eight-fold increase between the years 1990 and 2000.

Figure 10.13. "Mexico Lindo Y' Q'Rico" Deli and "American and Spanish Record" stores near Albemarle Road in the southern half of Coney Island Avenue. Notice also the Chinese characters at the top of the sign on the left. Photograph by the author.

Figure 10.14. Chinese "Super Sun Lumber" store in the southern part of Coney Island Avenue. Photograph by the author.

Figure 10.15. "Chief, Turkish Mediterranean Food" near Avenue N. Even though the Turkish population is not significant in this area there are several Turkish restaurants that cater to Middle Eastern and Central Asian customers. Photograph by the author.

Figure 10.16. "Russian-American" parcel and courier service near Avenue U. Photograph by the author.

THEORIZING CONEY ISLAND AVENUE

What the residents of Brooklyn, especially those who ride the B68, take for granted has been the subject of study by a wide variety of scholars. In this, final section, we will briefly review of some of those theories about diversity in urban life which can be applied to Coney Island Avenue, and therefore other Brooklyn places and spaces, as examples of a global phenomena. These are theories which also make clear the important contributions of ordinary people in helping to create the multicultural worlds in which they live. Although many today tend to cite Michel de Certeau (1984), or others, my own take on seeing "Everyday Life" comes directly from Erving Goffman (1959). He, and Symbolic Interactionists such as John Lofland (1978), countered the neglect by social scientists of the agency of ordinary people in favor of large scale demographic and survey researches. As I stated in a study of 1970s Brooklyn:

> The micro-social level of life is buried under the weight of macro-social and economic factors responsible for the decline of cities. A more humanistic vision of urban life would show that the ordinary city dweller's experiences and feelings are important *sui generis* . . . What does it mean for a city when the study

of the attitudes and values of its residents is a sociological waste of time? How is a city structured to account for the practical irrelevance of the opinions of its citizens? (Krase 1982: 4).

Many of the newest ethnic flavors Brooklyn are due to changes in American immigration laws since 1965 that increased the diversity of American cities (Portes 1995). Before that time, one would be hard pressed to find more than a handful of South Asians in and around Coney Island Avenue, no less visit the dozens of businesses they operated on the thoroughfare. The street's human variety is also increased by large numbers of Latino undocumented aliens, many of whom are employed in these establishments and take up residence in the least desirable apartments above stores on the street. Some of these new elements in the "Melting Pot" are blending together, but up close others appear more as pieces of a complex mosaic. At the individual street level the symbolic capital of immigrant and ethnic entrepreneurs are reflected in the changing appearance, and therefore the meanings, of commercial streetscapes. For example, each group has their own specialty food purveyors, sometimes on the same block one can find Kosher and Halal food signs not far from where Latinos are ordering pork sandwiches. For Pierre Bourdieu, the production of symbolic capital contributes "to the reproduction of the established order" (1977: 188). Some reproductions such as ethnic store signs and traditional dress are in "plain view" as people follow the course of their everyday lives. Bourdieu's notion of the "habitus" or practices that produce, in this case visible, regularities is also helpful in this regard (1977: 72–95).

Anthony Giddens (1984) describes the deliberate efforts of people thinking and acting, as individuals or collectives, to create or modify the spaces they occupy as "Human Agency," and visual attention to ordinary, yet kaleidoscopic, streetscapes such as those we find in Brooklyn allows us to read conflict, competition, and dominance at a level not usually analyzed. In the heteropolis of Los Angeles, Mike Davis (2001:15) argued that "Hispanic/ Latino" performance can be viewed as practice as well as representation. My simple formula for the process by which agency transforms representation into practice on multicultural Coney Island Avenue is that ethnic groups simply go about their daily business and present themselves to the observer. The observer then re-presents their performances in descriptions that in turn can become representation. The newspaper articles cited in this paper about Coney Island Avenue, as well as this essay, are examples of reportage that, to those who have never visited the strip, are its representations.

Anthony D. King (1996), speaks of cities as "text" to be read and Robert A. Beauregard and Anne Haila note that despite increased spatial complexity modern cites are just as "legible" as their precursors (2000: 23) For Sharon Zukin (1996: 44), visual artifacts make social rules "legible," and "In this enigmatic text immigrant shopping strips sometimes fare better than Madison

Avenue and combative ethnic groups maintain uneasy coexistence in Brooklyn neighborhoods" (1996: 50). Lyn H. Lofland (1985) might add that cities have always been transformed by the entrance of "strangers." The difference today is primarily the rapidity and variety of that change. In the neighborhoods that parallel Coney Island Avenue several catastrophic world events have quickly changed its composition. For example, the fall of the Twin Towers on September 11, 2001 led to the disappearance of thousands of Muslim South Asians, while the Haitian presence increased because of the devastating earthquake in Haiti in January 12, 2010 as friends and relatives sought refuge in Brooklyn.

Spatial semiotics is another tool for deciphering this complexity and is defined by Mark Gottdiener as "the study of culture which links symbols to objects" (1994: 15–16). For a spatial semiotician, multicultural neighborhoods are part of national and global systems, in which "people organize their daily actions according to meaningful aspects of the constructed space" (Gottdiener 1994: 16). The geographer David Harvey, following on the work of Henri Lefebvre (1991), notes, "The appropriation of space examines the way in which space is used and occupied by individuals, classes, or other social groupings. Systematized and institutionalized appropriation may entail the production of territorially bounded forms of social solidarity" (1989: 263-64). Harvey emphasized that: "Different classes construct their sense of territory and community in radically different ways" (1989: 265). This is amply demonstrated though the window of the Coney Island Avenue bus as one passes through consecutive Caribbean, South Asian, Orthodox Jewish, and then Russian shopping areas that represent the different tastes and interests of each community. One of the most obvious of these is the concentration of retail establishments catering to children in the Orthodox Jewish shopping strip. As a group, Orthodox Jews have one of the highest birth rates in the city.

For Manuel Castells (1989, 1996) urban spaces are used, contested, and transformed by different social groups. Territorially defined ethnic groups, for example, call upon their historical roots and collective memory to preserve their identities by symbolically marking local places. For Orthodox Jews, Muslims, and Evangelical Christian Latinos on Coney Island Avenue, this is shown in the strategic locations and varied ritual and temporal uses of synagogues, mosques, and storefront churches along the route.

SUMMARY

According to Howard Becker (2002) as well as Warren and Karner (2005), visual methods are important tools for studying the mundane. Leading visual sociologists Jon Prosser and Donna Schwartz, inform us that: "Taken cumulatively images are signifiers of a culture; taken individually they are artefacts that provide us with very particular information about our existence. Images provide researchers with a different order of data, and, more importantly, an alternative to the way we have perceived data in the past" (1998: 29). I hope therefore in this chapter that I have demonstrated how my own, sometimes blurry, images can help to connect the ordinary practices of the people who live, shop, or travel along Coney Island Avenue to the demographic data that claim to describe them as well as the theories of globalization and multiculturalism that claim to explain how they create their moving panorama of everyday multicultural life.

ACKNOWLEDGMENTS

The author would like to thank the people who ride the Coney Island Avenue bus and who live, work, and shop along the route.

REFERENCES

Appadurai, Arjun. 1996. *Modernity at Large: Cultural Dimensions of Globalization.* Minneapolis: University of Minnesota Press.

Beauregard, Robert A. and Anne Haila. 2000. "The Unavoidable Continuities of the City." Pp. 22–36 in *Globalizing Cities: A New Spatial Order?*, edited by P. Marcuse and R. Van Kempen. Oxford, UK: Blackwell.

Becker, Howard S. 1995. "Visual Sociology, Documentary Photography, and Photojournalism: It's (Almost) All a Matter of Context." *Visual Sociology* (10)1–2: 5–14.

Bourdieu, Pierre. 1977. *Outline of a Theory of Practice.* New York: Cambridge University Press.

Bourne, Randolph. 1916. "Trans-National America." *Atlantic Monthly*, July, pp. 86–97.

Castells, Manuel. 1989. *The Informational City.* Oxford, UK: Blackwell.

Castells, Manuel. 1996. "Conclusion: the Reconstruction of Social Meaning in the Space of Flows." Pp. 494–98 in *The City Reader* edited by R. T. LeGates and F. Stout. London, UK: Routledge.

de Certeau, Michel. 1984. *The Practice of Everyday Life*, translated by S. Rendall. Berkeley: University of California Press.

Davis, Mike. 2001. *Magical Urbanism: Latinos Reinvent the U.S. City.* New York: Verso.

Giddens, Anthony. 1984. *The Constitution of Society: Outline of the Theory of Structuration.* Cambridge, UK: Polity.

Goffman, Erving. 1959. *The Presentation of Self in Everyday Life.* Garden City, NY: Doubleday.

Gottdiener, Mark. 1994. *The New Urban Sociology.* New York: McGraw-Hill.

Grady, John. 1996. "The Scope of Visual Sociology." *Visual Sociology* 11(2):10 24.

Harvey, David. 1989. *The Urban Experience*. Baltimore, MD: John Hopkins University Press.

Hampson, Rick. 2007. "Brooklyn Street Proves Yes, We All Can Get Along." *USATODAY*, August 15. Retrieved May 1, 2011 (www.usatoday.com/news/nation/2007-08-14-coney-island_N.htm).

Healey, Joseph F. 2006. *Race, Ethnicity, Gender, and Class: The Sociology of Group Conflict and Change*, 4th ed. Thousand Oaks, CA: Sage/Pine Forge.

Jackson, John B. 1964. *Discovering the Vernacular Landscape*. New Haven, CT: Yale University Press.

Kallen, Horace M. 1915a. "Democracy versus the Melting Pot." *The Nation*, February 18, pp. 190–94.

Kallen, Horace M. 1915b. "Democracy versus the Melting Pot." *The Nation*, February 25, Pp. 217–22.

King, Anthony D. 1996. *Re-Presenting the City: Ethnicity, Capital and Culture in the Twenty-First Century Metropolis*. London, UK: Macmillan.

Krase, Jerome. 1982. *Self and Community in the City*. Lanham, MD: University Press of America.

Krase, Jerome. 1993. "Traces of Home." *Places: A Quarterly Journal of Environmental Design* 8(4):45–55.

Krase, Jerome. 1997. "Polish and Italian Vernacular Landscapes in Brooklyn." *Polish American Studies* 59(1):9–31.

Krase, Jerome. 2002. "Navigating Ethnic Vernacular Landscapes Then and Now." *Journal of Architecture and Planning Research* 19(4):274–281.

Krase, Jerome. 2003. "Italian American Urban Landscapes: Images of Social and Cultural Capital." *Italian Americana* 22(1):17–44.

Krase, Jerome. 2004. "Visualizing Ethnic Landscapes." Pp. 1–24 in *Race and Ethnicity in New York City*, edited by J. Krase and R. Hutchison. London, UK: Elsevier Press.

Krase, Jerome. 2009. "A Visual Approach to Multiculturalism." Pp. 1–38 in *Beyond Multiculturalism*, edited by G. Prato. Aldershot, UK: Ashgate Publishing Ltd.

Lefebvre, Henri. 1991. *The Production of Space*. Oxford: Blackwell.

Lofland, John. 1978. "The Qualitative Strategy Approach to Interaction in Everyday Life." Pp. 5–15 in *Interaction in Everyday Life: Social Strategies,* edited by J. Lofland. Beverly Hills, CA: Sage.

Lofland, Lyn H. 1985. *A World of Strangers: Order and Action in Urban Public Spaces*. Prospect Heights, IL: Waveland Press.

Lofland, Lyn H. 1998. *The Public Realm: Exploring the City's Quintessential Social Territory*. New York: Aldine de Gruyter.

Newman, Andy. 2004. "On Brooklyn's Avenue of Babel, Cultures Entwine." *The New York Times*, March 26. Retrieved June 18, 2011 (www.nytimes.com/2004/03/26/nyregion/on-brooklyn-s-avenue-of-babel-cultures-entwine.htmlp).

New York City Department of City Planning. 2005a. "Community District Profile: Brooklyn Community District 12," New York, NY: New York City Department of City Planning.

New York City Department of City Planning. 2005b. "Community District Profile: Brooklyn Community District 13," New York, NY: New York City Department of City Planning.

New York City Department of City Planning. 2005c. "Community District Profile: Brooklyn Community District 14," New York, NY: New York City Department of City Planning.

New York City Department of City Planning. 2005d. "Community District Profile: Brooklyn Community District 15," New York, NY: New York City Department of City Planning.

Osterhammel, Jurgen and Neils. P. Petersson. 2005. *Globalization: A Short History*, translated by Dona Geyer. Princeton, NJ: Princeton University Press.

Portes, Alejandro. ed. 1995. *The Economic Sociology of Immigration: Essays on Network, Ethnicity, and Entrepreneurship*. New York: Russell Sage Foundation.

Prosser, Jon and Dona Schwartz. 1998. "Photographs within the Sociological Research Process," Pp. 115–29 in *Image-based Research: A Sourcebook for Qualitative Researchers*, edited by J. Prosser. London, UK: Falmer Press.

Robertson, Roland. 1997. "Comments on the 'Global Triad' and 'Glocalization" in *Globalization and Indigenous Culture*, Institute for Japanese Culture and Classics, Kokugakuin University. Retrieved October 10, 2007 (www2.kokugakuin.ac.jp/ijcc/wp/global/index.html)

Sassen, Saskia. 1999. *Globalization and Its Discontents Essays on the New Mobility of People and Money*. New York: The New Press.

Sassen, Saskia. 2002. "From Globalization and Its Discontents," Pp. 161–70 in *The Blackwell City Reader,* edited by G. Bridge and S. Watson. Oxford, UK: Blackwell.

Takaki, Ronald. 1993. *A Different Mirror: A History of Multicultural America*. Boston. MA: Little, Brown and Company.

Toktamis, Kumru. 2007. "The People of Coney Island Avenue: A Demographic Portrait of Diversity." Unpublished paper. Center for the Study of Brooklyn, Brooklyn College CUNY, February.

Toll, William. 1997. "Horace M. Kallen: Pluralism and American Jewish Identity." *American Jewish History* 85(1):57–74.

Van Kempen, Ronald and Peter Marcuse. eds. 1997. "The Changing Spatial Order in Cities." *American Behavioral Scientist* 41(3).

Vergara, Camilo J. 1995. *The New American Ghetto*. New Brunswick, NJ: Rutgers University Press.

Voice of America. 2010. "Board the Magic Bus' for Tour of Coney Island—A Multicultural, Multiethnic Community." Retrieved January 11, 2010 (www1.voanews.com/english/news/a-13-2004-11-23-voa38.html).

Walzer, Michael. 1997. *On Tolerance*. New Haven, CT: Yale University Press.

Warren, Carol A. B. and Karner, Tracy X. 2005. *Discovering Qualitative Methods: Field Research, Interviews and Analysis.* Los Angeles: Roxbury Publishing Company.

Wilson, Claire. 2005. "Cortelyou Road, Brooklyn: A Commercial Strip Gaining in Charm," *The New York Times,* June 5. Retrieved June 16, 2011 (http://query.nytimes.com/gst/fullpage.html?res=9E0CEEDD1738F936A35755C0A9639C8B63).

Zukin, Sharon. 1996. "Space and Symbols in an Age of Decline." Pp. 43–59 in *Re-Presenting the City: Ethnicity, Capital and Culture in the Twenty-First Century Metropolis,* edited by A. D. King. London, UK: Macmillan.

11

Brooklyn and Belleville

On the Visual Spatial Semiotics of Ethnic Identity in Two Immigrant Neighborhoods

Timothy Shortell

Globalization has increased the flow of capital, goods, ideas, and people from place to place in the contemporary world. Cities on every continent have been facing all manner of challenges as a result of these flows. On the streets of global cities, the flow of people and their cultures can be easily seen in the mosaic of "cultural strangers" who move around and through urban neighborhoods during the course of everyday life on the streets, in the shops, and in the public spaces that make up the vernacular landscape. How different groups live together in urban communities, sometimes peacefully and sometimes less so, needs to be investigated if the impact of globalization on urban space is to be fully understood.

Although urban communities in global cities appear at first glance quite different—with different groups of native-born majorities, minorities, and immigrants, as well as different built environments and different rhythms of urban life—there are structural similarities that can be revealed by spatial semiotic analysis. People change the meaning of urban public places by changing the way these spaces look, through their activities and by their presence (Krase and Shortell 2011). Comparative analysis of global cities is urgently needed to fully explain the "on the ground" effects of globalization.

In this chapter, I pose the question, "what do immigrant communities in global cities look like?" The answer to this question concerns the lived nature of globalization; the circulation of people (and their cultural practices) changes the way urban neighborhoods look, and as a result, alters the way that urban dwellers—both immigrants and the ethnic majority—experience the city. Analysis of how members of different cultural groups interact within an overall pattern of micro-segregation must bring together insights from literatures on mobility, micro-level theories of culture, semiotics, and urban public space in the analysis of empirical data from vernacular landscapes. I argue in this research that visual data is necessary to understand how urban vernacular neighborhoods are changing as majority and immigrant cultures meet.

This research is based on data collection from a series of journeys through immigrant communities in Brooklyn and Paris. Though Brooklyn and Paris don't look alike at first glance, travelling through immigrant neighborhoods offers an opportunity to see urban communities in a new way. A sociological gaze reveals a structural similarity of immigrant urban spaces based on the way that signs of collective identity get socially embedded through the course of quotidian mobility and other modifications of the appearance of these neighborhoods. The cultural practices of immigrants produce signs of collective identity which mark their spaces as multiethnic, and this representation of their "otherness" is understood by both the ethnic majority and ethnic minorities.

The journeys in Brooklyn follow Coney Island Avenue from Prospect Park to Brighton Beach Avenue. Among the distinct neighborhoods along this four mile commercial street are Caribbean, Hispanic, South Asian, Orthodox Jewish, Russian, and Chinese. In Paris, I followed a winding path of immigrant areas from Belleville, the traditional neighborhood of migrants to Paris and now mainly East Asian, along commercial streets in the 10th arrondissement, passing through North African and South Asian neighborhoods, and ending in La Goutte d'Or, home to many West Africans. I collected data using a photographic survey method and ethnographic observation of social life in an effort to describe the local streetscapes of these two places, but also to generalize about the nature of immigrant neighborhoods in global cities.

MIGRATION, MOBILITY, AND VISIBILITY IN URBAN SPACES

Investigating the urban vernacular landscape is part of an attempt to explain how collective identity gets embedded in the social space of particular places. Borer (2006:181) points out that "the urban culturalist perspective prompts the researcher to begin with a place and ask an open and inductive question: 'what happens or happened here?'" This is a method for documenting empirical instances of culture rather than culture in the abstract. Such an "on the ground" approach is necessary to apply sociological reasoning to "glocal" culture; one has to find the places where hybrid culture is practiced and to describe "what happens or happened" there. I argue here that "glocal" culture is produced in immigrant neighborhoods in global cities in part by the patterns of quotidian mobility in public places in these neighborhoods.

Scholars of mobility have theorized the multitude of ways that people move in and through places, and how these patterns of movement are structured by power in the form of class, racial/ethnic, and gender differences. Urry (2007) notes four main aspects of mobility: (i) objects (people, products, technologies) moving or capable of movement; (ii) the crowd, or movement that is actually or potentially disordered and a challenge to social control; (iii) social mobility, or movement "up or down" in a class hierarchy; and, (iv) migration. My concern here is with two levels of mobility in urban spaces: migration and the quotidian circulations of people that fill the resulting immigrant spaces. I see crowds as part of the normal dynamism of urban public space. As Simmel (1950) noted, this dynamism is the essence of urban life. Migration brings together "cultural strangers" and urban space is marked by their competition and cooperation, their ambivalence and their occasional hostility, in all manner of everyday social practices as people inhabit and "take possession" of their neighborhood by moving around and through it. This mobility is tied to the rhythms of everyday life: working, commuting, shopping, socializing, walking.

One of the most important ways that urban dwellers perform identity is by using public space. For Certeau (1985), the urban dweller appropriates social space by walking through it. For the time that we are in it, he explains, the space is ours to use. Demerath and Levinger (2003: 218) agree, observing of American cities, "Had urban designers not overlooked the social benefits of pedestrian activity, and had they designed communities more around walking and less around driving and parking, we might not have so many social scientists in the United States concerned with 'problems' such as a lack of community, moral disintegration, and social isolation." Using public space binds us to the community. We realize social structure and enact social relations by interacting with others in the course of moving around and through the vernacular landscape. Through these interactions, we form interpretations of ourselves and others; Demerath and Levinger (2003: 231–34) call this "collaborative creativity." Urban dwellers understand that "being seen" is a form of power in public space; Lofland (1998) has enumerated some of the types of interaction by which this occurs.

The meaning of urban public space depends, in part, on who is present and how urban dwellers act within it. People, and their identity performances, become meaningful objects in the social space of urban public places. In this way, mobility shapes public space by partially determining the groups of people who share the social spaces of urban neighborhoods and the details of their spatial practices—which groups are advantaged, for example, or which practices are normative.

As global population flows bring together "cultural strangers" in urban public spaces, the mixture of signs of collective identity is partly what ascribes a place as an "immigrant neighborhood." In addition to signs of majority ethnic culture, there are markers of "glocal" culture easily visible; the greater the concentration of these signs, the stronger the identification of the space as belonging to particular minority groups. The specific meaning of individual signs—such as the message denoted by foreign language lettering or the specific geographic location of a traditional costume—often doesn't matter as much as the signification of "otherness," especially in immigrant neighborhoods. Sometimes, as Pan (2009) has demonstrated, language is a signifier of class status.

As groups practice their culture in local social spaces, through their quotidian mobility and performances of identity, they embed signs of their collective identity in those places. This is sometimes done intentionally, but most often is simply the by-product of people using and inhabiting urban space. These signs become meaningful to members of both the in- and out-groups—though not necessarily communicating the same thing to members of the majority and minorities. The simultaneous practice of different cultures in particular places creates tension. Sometimes this tension is what we might call ordinary, that generated when strangers share urban space. On occasion, this tension can become conflict.

In global cities, conflicts about public space can occur between ethnic groups or between immigrants and the majority. The current nativist backlash in the United States and Europe is an example of such conflict. In this sense, urban public space becomes a public sphere where struggles regarding the inclusivity of the polity take place. The presence of people in urban public space becomes a claim to belonging, to a voice in the deliberations on the public good, and to a share of public resources. Ethnic relations often become a competition for visibility in public space.

The majority sometimes tries to render unwanted groups—ethnic minorities, the poor, "rebellious youth," etc.—invisible in order to shore up its own power. More and more, as urban public space is subordinated to private economic interests, the intersection of ethnicity and class becomes a powerful exclusionary incentive; Atkinson (2003:1834) observes, "The rights conferred by citizenship are increasingly predicated on being a consumer—consumers of private and government services." Being seen as the "wrong kind" of consumer can bring to bear the mechanisms of social control with regard to access to and use of public space, and by extension, participation in the public sphere (White and Sutton 1995; see also Smith 1996 on the "revanchist city").

When the public sphere directly acknowledges the debate about who is to be included in "our nation" (or "our city"), a number of signs of collective identity embedded in public space that were previously easily seen but routinely unnoticed suddenly become "visible"—often accompanied by expressions of concern about how “they” are “taking over” the spaces in which these signs of identity are observed. The current strain of anti-Islam in American and European public discourse is one potent example of this process. In both New York and Paris, a visibility conflict involving Muslims (who have long been in these cities, in these urban spaces) is currently unfolding.

SPATIAL SEMIOTICS OF THE VERNACULAR LANDSCAPE

In sociology, discussion of the nature and importance of the visual in understanding urban environments owes much to the work of Simmel (1924:360), who notes that: “Modern social life increases in ever growing degree the role of mere visual impression which always characterizes the preponderant part of all sense relationships between man and man [*sic*], and must place social attitudes and feelings upon an entirely changed basis.” Combining Simmel and other seminal urban theorists, such as Lefebvre (1991), Lofland (1973, 1998), and Jackson (1984), Krase (1997, 2002, 2004) has argued that ordinary people change the meaning of social spaces by changing how the spaces look. This is often done intentionally, but can also be accomplished by simply inhabiting the location.

Harvey (1989a, 2006) recognizes that those who have the power to command and produce space are therefore able to reproduce and enhance their own power. This power is manifest in the ability to create distance between the in-group and outsiders and to define the legitimate uses of social space so as to bring mechanisms of social control to bear on how particular spaces are used (White and Sutton 1995; Atkinson 2003; Raco 2003). Through appropriation and domination, the powerful differentiate public space. Though disadvantaged in conflicts with elites, ordinary urban dwellers express their agency in the ways they challenge and sometimes subvert the official uses of social space.

From a spatial semiotic perspective, social meanings are embedded in the physical and social landscapes that structure urban neighborhoods. Gottdiener (1994:16) refers to “settlement space” as that “built by people who have followed some meaningful plan for the purposes of containing economic, political, and cultural activities. Within it people organize their daily actions according to meaningful aspects of the constructed space.” In this regard, it is important to note that perceptions and valuations of residential or commercial neighborhood spaces, for example, may be significantly different for insiders and for outsiders. Urban dwellers and their identity performances become objects for interpretation by others with whom they share the settlement space.

The markers of collective identity must be understood from a semiotic perspective. The meaning of these signs is constructed in the analytical space between the producer of the signs and the viewer of them. Summarizing Jakobson's analysis of the communicative act, Hawkes (2003: 65–66) explains:

> All communication consists of a message initiated by an addresser, whose destination is an addressee. But the process is not as simple as that. The message requires a contact between addresser and addressee, which may be oral, visual, electronic or whatever. It must be formulated in terms of a code: speech, numbers, writing, sound-formations etc. And the message must refer to a context understood by both addresser and addressee, which enables the message to "make sense" . . . "Meaning" then, according to Jakobson's account, is not a stable, predetermined entity which passes, untrammelled, from sender to receiver.

Though sensibility, or perhaps just consensus, may cease to exist if there is no common context, interpretability does not. That is, the producer and viewer of a sign of identity may form different readings of its meaning; the meaning of the sign, in effect, can change in transmission. In social space, there is often some kind of competition to control the meaning of signs of identity.

The context of the signs of collective identity under consideration here is the urban vernacular landscape. Signs have meanings that relate to the patterns and places of urban life. These give the sense to the "visual impressions" that Simmel, and later Lofland (1973, 1998) and Krase (1997, 2002, 2004) so thoughtfully observed. The vernacular landscape includes both the built and social environments—that is, urban settlement spaces. Social activities in public spaces give as much meaning to the vernacular landscape as its physical properties, though we are often unreflective of the significance of people in public space because the presence of strangers in urban settings is so common. Urban dwellers are generally adept at reading public spaces, even if they don't always realize when they are doing it.

The code for messages of ethnic identification is multimodal, including both verbal and visual signs. There are codes for appearance, for example, and nominal codes. There are visual codes that relate colors to identity and codes for alphabets as physical signs of geography. Distinctive cultural practices are also a code; perhaps the most common of these relate to food and dress.

Jakobson (1960, 1972) identified three functions of signs that can help us interpret the visual representations of identity in urban neighborhoods: the expressive, the conative, and the phatic. Jakobson was theorizing about the structure of language, but the functionality he describes may be applied to visual markers also. In doing so, I am extending Jakobson's semiotics in a manner that may be useful for urban sociologists. The starting point is Jakobson's, but the application is mine.

Expressive signs give the subject a voice; they are an important component of social agency. According to Jakobson, these signs are oriented toward the addresser; they reveal his or her emotive state. In the context of urban neighborhoods, people create expressive signs in the course of their everyday practices when they enact rituals of identity. Among the most visible of these practices is the use of flags, national colors, or place names to proclaim origins.

In Jakobson's view, conative signs attempt to influence others' behavior. In language, the use of vocative case or imperative mood signals the conative function. Conative signs highlight the relationship between the addresser and addressee, and place an obligation on the latter. Markers of exclusion are one important type of conative sign in the urban vernacular landscape. Graffiti can be said, in some instances, to be of this type. So too can the uses of native alphabets. To the extent that social space is contested, conative signs are more common; they call attention to group boundaries, marking the space between the in-group and out-groups.

Jakobson describes phatic signs as those that are oriented toward contact (Hawes 2003). In language, this includes, among other things, phrases which facilitate continued communication rather than are strictly denotative. For example, "How are you?" is often used not as an inquiry into the health of the other as much as an invitation to have a conversation. Other examples include questions like "You know what I mean?" which function as tests of the connection between addresser and addressee—that is, are you still paying attention to me? Applied to visual codes, phatic signs are those that serve as an inducement to social interaction. They work not through denotation primarily, but by confirming the connection between individuals, and between people and places. They signal shared culture and confer insider status even among strangers.

In the end, visual signs that facilitate social relations, like these linguistic customs, might be the most common signifier in the urban vernacular. Phatic signs are artifacts of ordinary social interaction. They imply that a social space belongs to a particular group, that its cultural practices are acceptable there. Through phatic signs, "cultural strangers" can assert their agency in the multiethnic social spaces of the host country.

The main distinction between expressive and phatic signs is that production of the latter is not primarily about advertising identity. Goffman (1959: 2, emphasis in the original) makes a similar distinction in contrasting two kinds of sign activity, "the expression that he [*sic*] *gives*, and the expression he *gives off*." The former is intentional communication, often with verbal behavior, and the latter involves the interpretations observers make of a wide range of attributes and behaviors performed in public. People generally impute motives when interpreting expressive signs, but phatic signs are material manifestations of in-group normative practices in local spaces. Outsiders can read them as indicators of collective identity, even if that was not the motive of those whose practices enacted the signs. As Demerath and Levinger (2003: 229) note, "By reading others we read meaning into the world. We see the world as meaningful partly by observing symbols of identity." Urban dwellers of vernacular landscapes are generally literate with regard to signs of collective identity, but attribution errors are common. We tend to see other groups' identity performances as directed toward us even when they are not.

METHOD AND DATA

Sociologists generally use three different kinds of images in research. Some researchers have research subjects produce images. Other researchers use found or preexisting images as data. In the present research, I employ the third kind, researcher produced images (Warren and Karner 2005; Pauwels 2008). I use a visual method called the photographic survey, developed in collaboration with Krase (Krase and Shortell 2007, 2008, 2009; Shortell and Krase 2009, 2010a, 2010b, 2010c) to collect data for this project. The photographic survey is a technique for taking photographs of urban neighborhoods in order to record visual information at a particular place and time. The photographs are taken as the researcher walks through the neighborhood in a systematic manner, street by street, photographing public spaces on both sides of the street, without regard to particular content. In fact, with a bit of practice, a researcher can take photos in this manner without even looking through the camera's viewfinder. Whatever is visible in public space at the time of the survey may be recorded.

The photographic survey records both the physical and social streetscapes. It is important for the data collection not to be determined by the researcher's attention—that is, the researcher must not photograph *only* that which seems, at that moment, to be of interest. Often the signs of collective identities are subtle and can be recognized in a photograph only after studying it closely. The photographic survey is designed to collect images in which the social content might not be immediately noticed. It is also important that the data collection not be distorted by the act of photographing the spaces. The photographic survey emphasizes more distant content rather than foreground; this is because the inhabitants of neighborhood spaces may regard being photographed as invasive (Prosser and Schwartz 1998) and also because the recognition of the act of data recording can change the nature of human behavior. The aim is to avoid taking photographs in which individuals are recognizable.

(This can be assured, if necessary, by digital processing before the images are coded.) A blurry shot might not be regarded as a "good photo" but it is often an effective source of data.

Some of the images gathered in this way have little interesting or sociologically important content, but many record aspects of the physical and social space that may be analyzed as visual semiotics. Multiple trips are required to adequately cover a particular neighborhood. Because social life in urban neighborhoods is dynamic, varying by time of day, day of week, and week of year, as well as year to year, multiple trips to photograph a neighborhood results in data with greater validity. It becomes possible to see patterns when the set of images extends beyond the boundaries of particular urban cycles. For example, it is possible to see variation in the use of public space (people walking on the sidewalks, people in the park, etc.) by season only if one has photographs from different times of the year. The end result of data collection using the photographic survey is thousands of photographs. Digital photography is a necessity for this technique, which might otherwise be prohibitively expensive.

Photographs from Coney Island Avenue were taken by Krase in 2003 and 2010 traveling in the Coney Island Avenue (B68) bus from Park Circle to Brighton Beach Avenue and by the author in 2010 and 2011 on the same bus route, and on walks in 2009, 2010, and 2011 from Church Avenue to Brighton Beach Avenue. Photographs from Paris were taken by the author in 2007, 2009, and 2010 while walking from Belleville through the 10th arrondissement to La Goutte d'Or. I began on Rue de Belleville from Rue Julien Lacroix, up and down Boulevard de la Villette/Boulevard de Belleville, down Rue du Faubourg du Temple to Place de la République, along Place Johann Strauss and right onto Rue du Faubourg Saint-Denis to Boulevard de Magenta, continuing along Magenta to Rue La Fayette, turning right, and then left onto Rue du Faubourg Saint-Denis, then left on Boulevard de la Chapelle to Boulevard Barbès, and right on Barbès ending at Rue Ordener.

Field observations were taken by the author in Brooklyn in 2009, 2010, and 2011, and in Paris in 2010. Field sketch notes were taken in a small notebook during walking and bus trips along the two journeys and written into field notes on a computer soon after, the usual method of observational data collection (Babbie 2001; Berg 2007).

CONEY ISLAND AVENUE AS MULTICULTURAL BROOKLYN

As Krase (chapter 10 of this volume) has shown, signs of collective identity are embedded in both the built and social environments all along Coney

Figure 11.1. "Norteña Express," a Mexican car and messenger service on Coney Island Avenue. An example of an expressive sign using a flag icon and national colors to signify ethnic identity. Photograph by the author, 2010.

Island Avenue, the backbone of Brooklyn. Commercial signage, national colors, and flags are among the ubiquitous expressive signs of immigrant identity on the Avenue. Moreover, phatic signs such as styles of dress and appearance, as well as the concentration of certain types of businesses, such as communication, currency, and travel services, are commonplace and mark the space as belonging to immigrant groups.

Figure 11.1 shows a Mexican car and messenger service whose awning displays Mexico's national colors: red, white, and green. This is a common motif; there are numerous similar businesses on the Avenue. Along with national colors, such businesses often include flag icons and place names as indicators of place of origin. Some similar signs, such as the ubiquitous Italian pizza place, have become so generalized that they may not always indicate the ownership or clientele.

A common phatic sign is shown in figure 11.2. Businesses such as "Travel Home Services" provide services that are in demand in immigrant neighborhoods, as a result of people wanting to maintain connections with kin and the home community. Along the Avenue, there are dozens of businesses like this, including communications, money transfer, legal services, package services, and so forth. In our online photo archive of immigrant neighborhoods in global cities, we have literally hundreds of photographs of these businesses

Figure 11.2. "Travel Home Services" on Coney Island Avenue. An example of a phatic sign of immigrant identity. Note, also, the Statue of Liberty icon. Photograph by the author, 2010.

Figure 11.3. Orthodox Jewish women on Coney Island Avenue. An example of style of dress as a common phatic sign of ethnic identity. Photograph by the author, 2010.

(Krase and Shortell 2011). Incidentally, figure 11.4 also shows a storefront of this kind.

Figure 11.3 shows another ubiquitous sign of collective identity, styles of dress. Most of the people one can see moving about on the Avenue are wearing typical Western fashions. In some cases, costume is determined by the norms of ethnic or religious minorities, as is the case of these women, whose appearance is consistent with the rules of the Orthodox Jewish community in the area. The concentration of people dressed similarly is one of the primary means by which this stretch of urban space is ascribed as belonging to a particular group.

There are two significant conative signs communicating ethnic identity that are easy to see but generally unnoticed. The first is graffiti—what might be considered the quintessential territory-marking conative sign; as a sign of urban disorder, it certainly commands a great deal of attention from those who attempt to control urban public space (White and Sutton 1995; Atkinson 2003; Raco 2003). Perhaps more significant in its influence on quotidian mobility, though, is the concentration of monolingual foreign language signage, particularly in non-Roman alphabets. This tends to influence the users of the space by virtue of the inscrutability of information about the purposes of the businesses and other buildings to members of out-groups. As urban dwellers understand, if you can't read the signs, you probably don't belong there.

Figure 11.4. Monolingual foreign language signage with non-Roman alphabet on Coney Island Avenue. An example of a conative sign of immigrant identity. Photograph by the author, 2010.

Figure 11.4 shows a typical example of this kind of conative sign. The signage on most of the façades on this block contains Arabic script, alone or with some English. The concentration of these "geosemiotics," especially on the informal signage in shop windows, ascribes the place as an immigrant space (Scollon and Scollon 2003). Up the Avenue, the concentration of signage in Hebrew (especially the monolingual texts) effects the same kind of conative sign.

Much of the quotidian mobility along Coney Island Avenue is commercial. Urban sociologists have long understood the importance of commercial interactions in urban life, particularly with regard to lifestyles and their relation to collective identity (see, for example, Stone 1954; Zukin 2004; Zukin and Maguire 2004). Both workers (as well as owners) and consumers are in motion in these interactions. But these places—what Oldenburg (1999) calls "third places," different from work and home—are also sites of social interaction.

Figure 11.5 shows one instance of this combination of place and interaction. The two women pictured are socializing as they walk to the "Mini Market" to shop. The majority of interactions observed along the Avenue are like this one; because most of the businesses here are oriented to local consumers (rather than tourists or business-to-business), there is a great deal of pedestrian activity during the day. The concentration of people functions as a

Figure 11.5. "Mini Market" fruit and flower shop on Coney Island Avenue. An example of how shopping is an important site for social interaction. Photograph by the author, 2010.

Figure 11.6. Bus stop at Coney Island Avenue and Kings Highway. Walking and public transportation are primary means of mobility for many in the neighborhood. Photograph by the author, 2010.

sign of collective identity, as people read strangers as indicators of to whom the neighborhood belongs.

Another important site along the length of Coney Island Avenue where urban dwellers do identity work is the bus stop. Like much of Brooklyn, despite the many pedestrians, the Avenue is dominated by car traffic. But, particularly for young people and many immigrants, public transportation is a primary means of mobility. This makes the subway stop at Brighton Beach Avenue and the B68 bus stops all along Coney Island Avenue hubs of activity. Figure 11.6 shows several people waiting for the bus at Kings Highway, another important commercial street in this part of Brooklyn. Sites like this, as with the bus itself, are places of significant multicultural mixing.

"AROUND THE WORLD" IN PARIS

Immigration has been a contentious issue in France, particularly since labor migration was officially ended in 1973. (Because of the continuing influence of the republican ideals of the revolution, France continues to receive refugees, though the denial rate for asylum cases has spiked since 1973.) Unlike the United States, mass migration to France occurred after the modern national identity was formed; resistance to the idea of a multiethnic society has been so strong that only recently did public discussions admit to recognize "visible minorities" and "diversity" (Hargreaves 2007). Nonetheless, France has been the most important European host of population inflows since the beginning of the twentieth century. Until the 1960s, most of the migration to France was from other European nations and was mainly a combination of economic pushes and pulls. Since the end of the French colonial period, however, the inflow has been primarily non-European. As Hargreaves (2007: 22) notes,

> Maghrebis, who were the first non-Europeans to make their presence felt on a significant scale, have since 1982 represented around 30 per cent of the total immigrant population, making them by far the largest non-European minority in France. During the last thirty years rapid rates of growth have been recorded among other Africans (up from 2.4 per cent of the immigrant population in 1975 to 9.1 per cent in 1999) and Asians (up from 3.6 to 12.7 per cent during the same period.

Until quite recently, these migrants were mostly men; in the latest census, the gender ratio is approaching 1:1, signaling, in part, a policy of allowing families to reunite. These numbers, of course, only include official migration. The number of "personnes sans-papiers" (undocumented persons) is significant.

The *Lonely Planet* guidebook for Paris (Fallon and Hart 2006) describes a two-and-a-half hour walk of Paris' immigrant neighborhoods, showing the diversity of people living in the "City of Light." The walk begins in Belleville, the traditional immigrant neighborhood in Paris. The initial wave of non-Europeans who came to France were attracted by the cheap housing stock. Originally home to Maghrébin Jews and then Muslims, the neighborhood more recently became the "new Chinatown" in the city.

The streetscape is currently dominated by signs of East Asian immigration, as shown in figure 11.7. Along Rue de Belleville, most of the businesses have Chinese on the signage and in the windows. Most of the workers in the shops—mostly restaurants, cafes, and food shops, but including also clothing stores and other usual urban services—appear to be East Asian. Many of the people on the street are East Asian, but there are Maghrébins, South Asians, Africans and majority Parisien/nes (or other white Europeans) also.

The neighborhood is pan-Asian, even if the Chinese signage is by far the most common. Figure 11.8 shows the scene north of Boulevard de Belleville, which turns into Boulevard de la Villette, where one can see shops advertising to Vietnamese, Thais, and Koreans as well as Chinese. The tree-lined street attracts a lot of pedestrians and bikers; among the young people I observed in the neighborhood, the proportion of majority Parisien/nes was higher than for the older adults.

Figure 11.7. Mostly Chinese businesses on Rue de Belleville. An example of a street scene, with its concentration of phatic signs, that ascribes the neighborhood as a "Chinatown." Photograph by the author, 2007.

Figure 11.8. On Boulevard de la Villette, a Vietnamese/Thai restaurant. One of many businesses demonstrating that this is a pan-Asian neighborhood. Note the Asian pedestrian with shopping bags in the lower left. Photograph by the author, 2007.

As in Brooklyn, the public transit hubs were especially crowded, attracting a diverse group of people. Commuting is an important form of quotidian mobility and one of the primary places where "cultural strangers" are forced to interact—as Lofland (1998) points out, the norms of public transportation required a subtle but sustained form of interaction. As with the Coney Island Avenue bus (Krase, chapter 10 of this volume), people have to cooperate to get where they want to go. Figure 11.9 shows the crowd around, and coming in and out of, the Belleville Metro stop.

Boulevard de Belleville hosts a market twice a week that might be the most diverse public event in the city. The vendors and the shoppers include both immigrants and majority Parisien/nes. Phatic signs of collective identity were omnipresent in the goods for sale and the appearance of the vendors and shoppers, as seen in figure 11.10. On a visit to the market in 2009, among the shoppers included persons who appeared to be majority French, East Asian, Maghrébin, and West African. The majority Parisien/nes and Asians were exclusively in Western attire. Many of the Maghrébin and West Africans were also, but some were wearing dress from their home cultures. On either side of the market near the Metro stop were a few "unofficial" vendors who spread their goods on blankets; these consisted of mainly cheap leather goods and used clothing. The vendors were exclusively Maghrébin or Turkish, including

Figure 11.9. The Belleville Metro stop. Public transportation is one of the important settings for multicultural interaction in the neighborhood. There are Asian, African, and majority French visible in the image. Photograph by the author, 2007.

Figure 11.10. The public market on Boulevard de Belleville. The vendors and the crowd here are as diverse as any public space in Paris. In the image are visible Asian, North African, African, and majority French buyers and sellers. Photograph by the author, 2007.

a few wearing traditional dress. They attracted very little attention from shoppers as far as I could see.

On the western side of Boulevard de Belleville, along Rue du Faubourg du Temple, heading toward Place de la République, the streetscape changes from mostly Chinese to mostly Muslim. As the Paris guidebook says, we're now in a North African (Maghrébin) and Turkish area. One of the most common phatic signs of ethnic identity in this area is the commercial signage of the halal food shops. Figure 11.11 shows a halal butchery on Rue du Faubourg du Temple, one of several on the nearby blocks. Customers for these places include both Maghrébin and majority French.

Northwest of Place de la République, Boulevard de Magenta runs diagonally toward La Goutte d'Or, cutting across the top of the 10th arrondissement. The lower part of the Boulevard, between République and Gare du Nord and Gare de l'Est, is filled with beauty shops, food stores, and restaurants advertising to Paris' black population, with signage noting "Afro Coiffure" and "Specialite Afro-Caraibe." Figure 11.12 shows a typical salon, whose awning includes icons for the North African and West African francophone nations. (There is also English on the sign, "Beauty Center.") The window includes photographs of dark-skinned models with African hair

Figure 11.11. "Boucherie Musulmane," a halal butchery on Rue du Faubourg du Temple, opens in time for the morning commuters. An example of how food is an important phatic sign of ethnic identity. Photograph by the author, 2010.

Figure 11.12. "Le Marché Beauty Center" on Boulevard de Magenta. The awning includes icons for the North African and West African francophone nations. Note the use of English on the signage. Photograph by the author, 2010.

styles. Many of these beauty shops, such as the "Fair & White" chain, include English on the signage and window displays.

Along Magenta past the train stations, there is a concentration of discount clothing and shoe shops, including many wedding boutiques. Many of the sales staff observed in these shops are of African origin, though the goods are all typical Western fashions. Many of the people observed on the busy sidewalks are also dark skinned, and typically wearing Western fashions. Occasionally one sees a few men or women in traditional West African dress or Maghrébin women in religious attire. Toward Boulevard de Rouchechouart/Boulevard de la Chapelle, more Maghrébin men and women can be seen. At the intersection, a busy transit hub, with a Metro stop and bus stops on every corner, young Maghrébin men hawk "American cigarettes" on the street.

The area along Rues du Faubourg Saint-Denis and Saint-Martin is filled with phatic signs of South Asian immigrant identity. The shops include food stores and cafes, as well as the usual immigrant services such as travel services and money transfer. The restaurants packed into Passage Brady, a popular destination for inexpensive "Indian" cuisine, constitute both phatic and expressive signs. (The population in the area is mostly Sri Lankan.) The alley is packed with workers from the neighborhood around lunchtime, but the area also attracts a lot of tourists from the area, which is filled with discount hotels.

In January 2010, the town hall for the 10th arrondissement, a magnificent building on Rue du Faubourg Saint-Martin and Rue de Château d'Eau, displayed a banner expressing solidarity with students of undocumented parents, as shown in figure 11.13. The banner is an expressive sign of the immigrant identity of the neighborhood. In April of that year, a protest march in support of "personnes sans-papiers" moved along nearby Boulevard de la Chapelle, shown in figure 11.14. Collective action such as this is another powerful expressive sign of immigrant identity.

Along Rue du Faubourg Saint-Denis north of Rue La Fayette, the majority of shops are also South Asian. These include food shops and restaurants, clothing shops whose window displays feature discount saris, boutiques selling cultural products, and at least one salon. Figure 11.15 shows the window of one of the clothing stores. These window displays are a common phatic sign of ethnic identity. Many of the shops have posters advertising events of interest to the South Asian community here. These are significant phatic signs which ascribe the neighborhood as immigrant space. Most of the people observed on the street are South Asian. A common sight is of families, with men, women, and children together, shopping. Another typical vista is the crowds, mostly younger South Asians, at the bus stops. Around the side entrance to Gare du Nord, the rush of commuters includes mostly majority Parisien/nes.

Figure 11.13. Banner declaring the 10th arrondissement's solidarity with students of undocumented parents. The banner hangs on the 10th arrondissement's town hall. Photograph by the author, 2010.

Figure 11.14. March for undocumented persons along Boulevard de la Chapelle. An example of collective action as an expressive sign. Photograph by the author, 2010.

Figure 11.15. Discount saris on display in a window on Rue du Faubourg Saint-Denis. Clothing stores constitute an effective phatic signs of ethnic identity. Photograph by the author, 2010.

Figure 11.16. Storefront mosque in La Goutte d'Or. The building bears only a small sign announcing itself, but there are often worshippers in the vicinity. Photograph by the author, 2010.

In contrast to the mixed gender streetscape of Faubourg St-Denis, the street life in La Goutte d'Or is starkly gender segregated. Nearer Boulevard de la Chapelle the neighborhood is mostly Maghrébin; nearer Rue Myrha, it is mostly West African. In both places, one can observe small groups of men socializing on many corners. In trips in 2009 and 2010, only one group of women was observed in this manner. There are many women on the streets here, but they appeared more often in motion: shopping or otherwise moving from place to place, often with children. Interestingly, there were quite a few Maghrébin women—but no men—dressed in traditional attire, begging on the street. The only place where there was a great deal of interaction between men and women in the neighborhood, including migrants and majority Parisien/nes, was at the market on Rue Dejean, famous for its West African fish-sellers.

There are three storefront mosques in the neighborhood. Figure 11.16 shows Mosquee al Fath on Rue Poissonniers. Despite the fact that most of the migrants in the neighborhood come from Islamic nations, these mosques are all far less prominent than the historic church, Saint-Bernard de la Chapelle, in the area. There are often worshippers, in traditional costume, near the mosque. Prayer rugs can sometimes been seen in front of the building. Next door is a shop selling West African foods.

ETHNIC IDENTITY IN THE VERNACULAR LANDSCAPE OF GLOBAL CITIES

Although Brooklyn and Paris do not look alike, there are important similarities in the spatial semiotics of immigrant neighborhoods in both places. Phatic signs of ethnic identity define the public space, creating a powerful frame by which urban dwellers—residents and visitors, ethnic majority and ethnic minorities—interpret the neighborhood as immigrant space. As Harvey (1989b:66) notes, the ubiquity of signs in so many different languages (and sign systems more generally) leads urban dwellers to construct "one knowable world from the infinity of possible worlds" opened up by this multitude of inscrutable signs.

Because food and dress are such important aspects of the practice of culture, the presence of these places and activities fill the urban streetscape with phatic signs. In Brooklyn and Paris, these signifiers are often different—different foods on sale or different styles of dress—but the semiotic function is the same. Along Coney Island Avenue, to give one example, one can see many instances of food shops and restaurants selling halal or kosher products. In the immigrant neighborhoods of Paris, one can see the same thing.

Most of the people one sees on the streets and in the shops along Coney Island Avenue or on the commercial streets from Belleville to La Goutte d'Or, as I've described, are likely to be wearing Western dress—a sign of acculturation or, perhaps, the hegemony of majority culture in Brooklyn and Paris. But in both places, there are significant numbers wearing the attire that is traditional of their home culture. Sometimes this is also a phatic sign of religious identity, as in the case of Orthodox Jews or Muslims. But the urban spaces I've investigated are also filled with people wearing the traditional styles of West Indian, Maghrébin, Turkish, South Asian, and East Asian local cultures.

Appearance functions as a phatic sign beyond styles of dress. Physical appearance, and especially skin tone, communicates collective identity. Race is a significant social factor in both Brooklyn and Paris. The American and French majority views on race are different, but in both cities "color" is a signifier of minority status, and places where people with darker complexions are present get ascribed as minority or immigrant spaces. As Mason (chapter 2 in this volume) has shown, Brooklyn remains strongly segregated by race (most especially in terms of Black/Not Black). In Paris, skin color and immigrant status are strongly associated in the common perceptions of the majority (Begag 2007; Thomas 2007).

Another ubiquitous phatic sign concerns businesses providing services of use to people with connections to faraway places. Communication services, and particularly vendors of low-cost phone cards and hourly internet access are obviously useful for immigrants. To illustrate the semiotic similarity, figures 11.17 and 11.18 show windows of such businesses in Brooklyn and Paris, respectively. In both places these shops are on blocks full of immigrant services. Travel shops in both neighborhoods tend to advertise, on signage and with window displays, special deals to particular places; this is another reliable indicator of the groups one is likely to encounter in the area. Currency transfer shops are useful in the same sense. In both Brooklyn and Paris, the familiar brown "Western Union" sign with gold block letters is a reliable indicator of immigrant space. Newspaper (and other media) vendors often function in the same way.

Flags, national symbols, and national colors are the most common expressive signs of collective identity in urban public space. Often the immediate context of these signs, particularly on commercial signage, is to attract customers. In a narrow sense, these signs could be called "commercial phatic" signs because they are intended to influence, but outside of "ethnic theme parks" (see Krase

Figure 11.17. The posters on the fascia of this Western Union office along Coney Island Avenue advertise phone cards with cheap foreign rates. Businesses providing travel, currency, and package services are common in immigrant neighborhoods. Photograph by the author, 2010.

Figure 11.18. The window display of the film developer in Belleville is full of posters advertising cheap calling card rates to East Asia. Commercial logic—businesses seek customers—reveals important information about who is likely to be found in particular urban spaces, which can be confirmed by observation of the pedestrian traffic. Photograph by the author, 2007.

1997) most of the potential customers are locals, and these businesses constitute an important signifier of "home," and in this sense are expressive. One can see flags in residential windows performing this same function. As Borer (2006) notes, people form emotional attachments to places as a result of certain kinds of interactions, reflective of "lifestyle" or various forms of quotidian mobility; one important kind of attachment is pride, which gets attached to the expressive signs of places where significant forms of in-group interactions occur, such as corner stores, restaurants, and cafés or bars.

Collective action is an important, if rarer, expressive sign. The use of public space for social movement activity often involves spectacular mobility, such as protests, parades, marches, or riots. The basis of collective action might be primary or secondary affiliations, but the action itself constitutes a sign of collective identity that in urban environments is usually connected with minority status. Sometimes the collective action is specifically about immigration issues, as the march shown in figure 11.14, and other times it is about events in the home nation, such as the solidarity with Egypt actions that occurred in many cities in early February 2011.

There are two conative signs of collective identity that play a significant role in the interpretation of public space in immigrant neighborhoods. The first is the effect of foreign language (from the perspective of the majority, but also to other language groups) alphabets on commercial signage and other forms of "geosemiotics" (Scollon and Scollon 2003). We do not need to be able to parse these messages to understand them as signifiers of "otherness." The density of such signs can, in the aggregate, constitute a conative sign by making the place feel welcoming (to those who can read the messages) or alienating (to those who cannot).

The second important conative sign occurs when the make-up of the crowd in a public space is such that the space "belongs to" the temporary "majority." As Lofland (1998) pointed out, this is not strictly a matter of numbers. This effect depends in large measure on how people are acting and interacting in the space. Small groups, acting aggressively—transforming the space from public to their own private space—can exert a powerful influence over others. This is a conative sign of collective identity, when the group shares a visible feature.

In both Brooklyn and Paris, young people in particular ethnic groups are often accused of this kind of behavior, and a social problem of "urban disorder" is constructed out of the conative reading of their presence in public spaces. As Demerath and Levinger (2003) noted, the quotidian mobility of young people is sometimes transgressive, and this can constitute a conative sign for others, especially the not-so-young.

Much of the attention to the connection between identity and place focuses on the built environment, and particularly to the ways in which the built environment enhances or inhibits forms of social interaction. This is important sociological analysis. But the data that I've collected in Brooklyn and Paris suggests that the social environment is every bit as significant as the built environment in terms of understanding this connection. The ways that ordinary urban dwellers, both majority and minorities, use public space—various forms of quotidian mobility—fills the vernacular landscape with signs that are interpreted by the "cultural strangers" that cohabit immigrant neighborhoods in global cities.

These ordinary practices create opportunities of visibility. In global cities, they give immigrants and ethnic minorities the opportunity to "take possession" of urban spaces and thereby to make a claim on the public sphere. At the same time, they sometimes become the context of nativist backlash, as is the case in the political present in the United States and Europe. In both ways, as agency and as backlash, as forms of cooperation and conflict, the signs of collective identity that flow from quotidian mobility in vernacular spaces represent "glocal" culture, the "on the street" meaning of globalization.

ACKNOWLEDGMENTS

The author would like to thank Jerry Krase, Judy DeSena, and Greg Smithsimon for helpful feedback on earlier drafts. The research was made possible, in part, by the PSC-CUNY Award program and a generous grant from Leonard and Claire Tow Faculty Travel program at Brooklyn College CUNY.

REFERENCES

Atkinson, Rowland. 2003. "Domestication by Cappuccino or a Revenge on Urban Space? Control and Empowerment in the Management of Public Spaces." *Urban Studies* 40(9):1829–843.

Babbie, Earl. 2001. *The Practice of Social Research, Ninth Edition*. Belmont, CA: Wadsworth.

Begag, Azouz. 2007. *Ethnicity & Equality: France in the Balance*, translated by Alec G. Hargreaves. Lincoln: University of Nebraska Press.

Berg, Bruce. 2007. *Qualitative Research Methods for the Social Sciences, Sixth Edition*. Boston, MA: Allyn and Bacon.

Borer, Michael Ian. 2006. "The Location of Culture: The Urban Culturalist Perspective." *City & Community* 5(2):173–97.

de Certeau, Michel. 1985. *The Practice of Everyday Life*. Translated by S. Rendall. Berkeley: University of California Press.

Demerath, Loren, and David Levinger. 2003. "The Social Qualities of Being On Foot: A Theoretical Analysis of Pedestrian Activity, Community, and Culture." *City & Community* 2(3):217–37.

Fallon, Steve and Annabel Hart. 2006. *Paris City Guide*. Melbourne, Australia: Lonely Planet Publications.

Goffman, Erving. 1959. *The Presentation of Self in Everyday Life*. New York: Anchor Books.

Gottdiener, Mark. 1994. *The New Urban Sociology*. New York: McGraw-Hill.

Grady, John. 1996. "The Scope of Visual Sociology." *Visual Sociology* 11(2):10–24.

Hargreaves, Alec C. 2007. *Multi-ethnic France: Immigration, Politics, Culture and Society, Second Edition*. New York: Routledge.

Harper, Douglas. 1998. "An Argument for Visual Sociology." Pp. 24–41 in *Image-based Research: A Sourcebook for Qualitative Researchers*, edited by Jon Prosser. London: Routledge.

Harvey, David. 2006. *Paris, Capital of Modernity*. New York: Routledge.

Harvey, David. 1989a. *The Urban Experience*. Baltimore, MD: Johns Hopkins University Press

Harvey, David. 1989b. *The Conditions of Postmodernity: An Enquiry into the Origins of Cultural Change*. Cambridge, MA: Blackwell.

Hawkes, Terence. 2003. *Structuralism and Semiotics*. London, UK: Routledge.

International Visual Sociology Association. 2008. "About the IVSA." Retrieved October 3, 2008 (www.visualsociology.org/about.html).

Jackson, John B. 1984. *Discovering the Vernacular Landscape*. New Haven, CT: Yale University Press.

Jakobson, Roman. 1972. "Verbal Communication." Pp. 39–44 in *Communication*, edited by *Scientific American*. San Francisco, CA: Freeman.

Jacobson, Roman. 1960. "Closing Statement: Linguistics and Poetics." Pp. 350–77 in *Style In Language*, edited by T. A. Sebeok. Cambridge, MA: MIT Press.

Krase, Jerome. 2011. "Riding the Bus in Brooklyn: The Spectacle of Quotidian Multicultural Life." Pp. 237–58 in *The World in Brooklyn: Gentrification, Immigration, and Ethnic Politics in a Global City*, edited by Judith N. DeSena and Timothy Shortell. Lanham, MD: Lexington Books.

Krase, Jerome. 2004. "Visualizing Ethnic Landscapes." Pp. 1–24 in *Race and Ethnicity in New York City*, edited by J. Krase and R. Hutchinson. London, UK: Elsevier/JAI Press.

Krase, Jerome. 2002. "Navigating Ethnic Vernacular Landscapes Then and Now," *Journal of Architecture and Planning Research* 19(4):274–81.

Krase, Jerome. 1997. "The Spatial Semiotics of Little Italies and Italian Americans." Pp. 98–127 in *Industry, Technology, Labor and the Italian American Communities*, edited by Mario Aste, et al., Staten Island, NY: American Italian Historical Association.

Krase, Jerome, and Timothy Shortell. 2011. "On the Spatial Semiotics of Vernacular Landscapes in Global Cities." *Visual Communication* 10(3):371–404.

Krase, Jerome, and Timothy Shortell. 2011. "Brooklyn Soc Photo Gallery." Retrieved February 14, 2011 (www.brooklynsoc.org/blog/gallery3).

Krase, Jerome, and Timothy Shortell. 2009. "Visualizing Glocalization: Semiotics of Ethnic and Class Differences in Global Cities." Paper presented at the annual meeting of the Eastern Sociological Society, Baltimore, MD.

Krase, Jerome, and Timothy Shortell. 2008. "Visualizing Glocalization: Changing Images of Ethnic Vernacular Neighborhoods in Global Cities." Paper presented at the First ISA Forum of Sociology. Barcelona, Spain.

Krase, Jerome, and Timothy Shortell. 2007. "Imagining Chinatowns and Little Italies: a Visual Approach to Ethnic Spectacles." Paper presented at Le Beau Dans La Ville: Colloque International. Tours, France.

Lefevbre, Henri. 1991. *The Production of Space*, translated by Donald Nicholson-Smith. Malden, MA: Blackwell.

Lofland, Lyn. 1973. *A World of Strangers*. New York: Basic Books.

Lofland, Lyn. 1998. *The Public Realm*. New York: Aldine.

Mason, Lorna. 2011. "Mapping a Changing Brooklyn, Mapping a Changing a World: Gentrification, Immigration and Outmigration in Brooklyn 2000-2008." Pp. 7–50 in *The World in Brooklyn: Gentrification, Immigration, and Ethnic Politics in a Global City*, edited by Judith N. DeSena and Timothy Shortell. Lanham, MD: Lexington Books.

Oldenburg, Ray. 1999. *The Great Good Place: Cafés, Coffee Shops, Bookstores, Bars, Hair Salons and Other Hangouts at the Heart of a Community*. New York: Marlowe and Company.

Pan, Lin. 2009. "Dissecting Multilingual Beijing: the Space and Scale of Vernacular Globalization." *Visual Communication* 9(1):67–90.

Pauwels, Luc. 2008. "An Integrated Model for Conceptualising Visual Competence in Scientific Research and Communication." *Visual Studies* 23(2):147–61.

Prosser, Jon, and Dona Schwartz. 1998. "Photographs within the Sociological Research Process." Pp. 115–30 in *Image-based Research: A Sourcebook for Qualitative Researchers*, edited by J. Prosser. London, UK: Routledge.

Raco, Mike. 2003. "Remaking Place and Securitising Space: Urban Regeneration and the Strategies, Tactics and Practices of Policing in the UK." *Urban Studies* 40(9):1869–887.

Scollon, Ron, and Suzie Scollon. 2003. *Discourse in Place: Language in the Material World.* London: Routledge.

Shortell, Timothy, and Jerome Krase. 2009. "Spatial Semiotics of Difference in Urban Vernacular Neighborhoods." Paper presented at the 9th European Sociological Association Conference, Lisbon, Portugal.

Shortell, Timothy, and Jerome Krase. 2010a. "Place, Space, Identity: A Spatial Semiotics of the Urban Vernacular in Global Cities." Paper presented at annual meeting of the European Sociological Association Culture Research Network, Milan, Italy.

Shortell, Timothy, and Jerome Krase. 2010b. "On the Visual Semiotics of Collective Identity in Urban Vernacular Spaces." Paper presented at the annual meeting of the International Sociological Association. Gothenburg, Sweden.

Shortell, Timothy, and Jerome Krase. 2010c. "Seeing Islam in Global Cities: A Spatial Semiotic Analysis." Paper presented at the annual meeting of the Society for the Scientific Study of Religion. Baltimore, MD.

Simmel, Georg. [1908] 1924. "Sociology of the Senses: Visual Interaction." Pp. 356–61 in *Introduction to the Science of Sociology*, edited by R. E. Park and E. W. Burgess. Chicago: University of Chicago Press.

Simmel, Georg. [1903] 1950. "The Metropolis and Mental Life." Pp. 409–24 in The Sociology of Georg Simmel, translated and edited by Kurt H. Wolff. New York: Free Press.

Smith, Neil. 1996. *The New Urban Frontier: Gentrification and the Revanchist City.* London: Routledge.

Stone, G. 1954. "City Shoppers and Urban Identification: Observations on the Social Psychological of City Life." *American Journal of Sociology* 60(1):36–45.

Strauss, Anselm, and Juliet Corbin. 1998. *Basics of Qualitative Research: Techniques and Procedures for Developing Grounded Theory.* Thousand Oaks, CA: Sage.

Thomas, Dominic. 2007. *Black France: Colonialism, Immigration, and Transnationalism.* Bloomington: Indiana University Press.

Urry, John. 2007. *Mobilities.* Cambridge, UK: Polity Press.

Warren, Carol A. B., and Tracy X. Karner. 2005. *Discovering Qualitative Methods: Field Research, Interviews and Analysis.* Los Angeles, CA: Roxbury Publishing.

White, Rob, and Adam Sutton. 1995. "Crime Prevention, Urban Space and Social Exclusion." *Journal of Sociology* 31(1):82–99.

Zukin, Sharon. 1995. *The Cultures of Cities.* Cambridge, MA: Blackwell.

Zukin, Sharon. 2004. *Point of Purchase: How Shopping Changed American Culture.* New York: Routledge.

Zukin, Sharon, and Jennifer Smith Maguire. 2004. "Consumers and Consumption." *Annual Review of Sociology* 30:173–97.

12

Constructing an Oppositional Community

Sunset Park and the Politics of Organizing Across Difference

Mark Treskon

In a late 2010 segment on the MSNBC show *Morning Joe*, NBC anchor Brian Williams argued (rather sardonically) that the biggest media story of the year had been the *New York Times* "discovery of Brooklyn" with its "open air markets, like trading posts in the early Chippewa tribe, where you can make beads at home and then trade them for someone to come over and start a small fire in your apartment that you share with nine others. Artisanal cheeses. For sale, on the streets of an entire American borough. It's been fascinating to watch the paper venture over the bridge" (Fischer 2010: np) As the *Times* and other media have picked up stories and trends out of Brooklyn in recent years, the borough has come to be framed in a couple of different ways: either, as per Williams' rant, as a repository of do-it-yourself 'hipster' types gentrifying ever-widening swaths of land, or as a site where tourists can consume the products of ethnic and immigrant communities increasingly valorized in contemporary tourist guides and economic development policies. While these two frames are wholly inadequate as descriptors of the various social and economic processes taking place within a borough of over two-and-a-half million people, this chapter argues they nonetheless influence how Brooklyn residents understand their changing neighborhoods.

This chapter illustrates how cultural frames influence political action. I trace a 'rezoning' debate in the Sunset Park neighborhood in Southwestern Brooklyn. In recent decades, Sunset Park has seen both growing Latino and Chinese populations and a smaller influx of young white professionals. Concerns from community residents about new housing construction, displacement of low-income populations, and population change, coupled with the City government's desire to update its land use planning and channel population growth in particular ways, resulted in the undertaking of a neighborhood rezoning process in 2007. As initial organizational and planning efforts from neighborhood groups gave way to the officially-sanctioned City-led planning process, tensions between politically active local residents and representatives of City government grew: residents described the City's process as designed explicitly to push out existing lower-income, minority, and immigrant populations and replace them with wealthier—and whiter—new residents.

The gentrification of many parts of New York City—and Brooklyn—has been under intense scrutiny by academics and the popular press in recent decades (Lees, Slater, and Wyly 2008). In Brooklyn, authors have covered the process from a number of angles and within a number of communities: from the increasing aesthetic attraction of 'brownstone' living in South Brooklyn (Osman 2011), to the often fraught relationships between long-term working-class, minority, or immigrant residents and newcomers in areas such as Clinton Hill (Freeman 2006) or Greenpoint (DeSena 2009). However, there are two reasons why the 'traditional' understandings of gentrification defined by (often white) professionals displacing lower-income and minority populations are inadequate in Sunset Park. First, there has been an increasing demographic 'split' between two portions of the neighborhood largely separated by Green-Wood Cemetery. While the northern portion has seen an influx of white residents, population growth in the larger portion of the neighborhood south of the cemetery being rezoned starting in 2007 has largely been through increases in the Hispanic and Asian populations. Second, as debates about rezoning developed they came to pivot around incommensurable understandings of the way displacement actually worked. While the City argued that housing production needed to be encouraged to satisfy growing demand, opponents of 'upzoning' argued that new construction was aimed at wealthy newcomers instead of existing residents and would actually speed up the gentrification process through inducing demand in the neighborhood. This chapter argues that while concerns about gentrification and 'induced demand' have merit, they became the dominant oppositional frames because they were the most effective way that activists had for creating themselves as an active political 'subject.' Using a mix of media accounts, document analysis, and three years of participant observation research, I argue that both popular media accounts of Sunset Park *and* the rezoning process itself treated residents as passive objects, albeit in different ways, and the relationships between these two dominant sources structured the development of neighborhood opposition to the rezoning process. While in the short term opposition managed to join some of the 'multiple publics' (Hum 2002) in the neighborhood together in constructive public debate, the particular frames used to achieve the eventual coalition of rezoning opponents, coupled with the City's unwillingness to engage with a wider range of potential concerns, limited those involved from dealing with the most pressing challenges facing the community.

FRAMING A COMMUNITY

Although any measure of the extent to which a neighborhood is 'known' by the general populous is crude, some neighborhoods, through dint of history, media, the arts, or politics are better-known than others. In New York, neighborhoods such as Harlem and Greenwich Village in Manhattan have been joined (to an extent) in the national consciousness in recent years by Park Slope and Williamsburg in Brooklyn as illustrating particular *types* of places: from African-American culture and a certain type of intellectual bohemianism in the former two neighborhoods to yuppie (to use a rather out-dated term) and hipster (to use a rather underspecified term) culture in the latter two. Not all neighborhoods have this sort of cultural renown, and Sunset Park, in Brooklyn, is one such example. For instance, the 1996 movie *Sunset Park* featured Rhea Perlman of *Cheers* fame as a high school basketball coach attempting to overcome cultural differences between herself and the African-American youth she coached. Here, 'Sunset Park' was little more than a catchy title for a generic 'inner-city black' neighborhood: in reality Sunset Park did not have a high school until 2009, and its African-American population makes up significantly less than 5 percent of the community's overall population (3.3 percent as of 2009 American Community Survey estimates).

Other fictional accounts have taken more pains to treat Sunset Park as an actual place. The novelist Paul Auster's 2010 book, *Sunset Park*, describes it as:

> Home to more than a hundred thousand people, including Mexicans, Dominicans, Poles, Chinese, Jordanians, Vietnamese, American whites, American blacks, and a settlement of Christians from Gujarat, India. Warehouses, factories, abandoned waterfront facilities, a view of the Statue of liberty, the shut-down Army Terminal where ten thousand people once worked, a basilica named Our Lady of Perpetual Help, biker bars, check-cashing places, Hispanic restaurants, the third-largest Chinatown in New York, and the four hundred and seventy-eight acres of Green-Wood Cemetery, where six hundred thousand bodies are buried, including those of Boss Tweed, Lola Montez, Currier and Ives, Henry Ward Beecher, F.A.O Schwarz, Lorenzo Da Ponte, Horace Greeley, Louis Comfort Tiffany, Samuel F. B. Morse, Albert Anastasia, Joey Gallo, and Frank Morgan—the wizard in *The Wizard of Oz* (Auster 2010: 80).

Auster's interest lies, however, not with the 'facts' of the neighborhood as such, but with a few characters—creative class types, really—squatting in an abandoned building on the edge of the cemetery. Throughout the novel, Sunset Park as a place, when it comes up at all, is treated as something alien and depressed. One character states: "There is something dead about the place, he finds, the mournful emptiness of poverty and immigrant struggle, an area without banks or bookstores, only check-cashing operations and a decrepit public library" (132). These are the thoughts of a character in a novel to be sure, but in interviews Auster described the neighborhood similarly. To one interviewer he noted that Sunset Park was not "a desperate place" but "mournful" (Neary 2010). To another, that it: "is a real neighborhood, as you know—it is a sort of downtrodden place. It is not a beautiful part of Brooklyn. There are a lot of poor, struggling people. The architecture's fairly ugly; it has a whole industrial zone near the water. There are a lot of things that make it unattractive. And it seemed to me that this was the kind of neighborhood where young people, such as the characters in my book, would be able to find a spot" (Pierce 2010:np). Finally, although he had used an actual building for the model of his squatter house, he expressed some delight in interviews when he discovered it had been demolished. While this expressly was because it highlighted the ephemeral relationship of his characters to the neighborhood (Pierce 2010), it also fit within the narrative of the 'mournful' or struggling place slowly coming apart.

While neither the movie nor the book *Sunset Park* were made with verisimilitude their foremost goals, in recent years Sunset Park *has* become increasingly visible in local media accounts; not for its basketball players or its decrepit housing stock, but for the food its ethnic and immigrant communities produce. While this chapter does not focus on the reasons for this newfound interest, others have argued that in recent decades ethnic and minority cultural practices have been increasingly valorized and integrated into 'mainstream' conceptions of local economies (Hoffman 2003: 295). A recent piece by Susan Fainstein and John Powers, while noting that New York City policy has not worked to encourage tourism to ethnic neighborhoods, argues that: "increased tourism can play a role by changing urban imagery, causing places formerly regarded as scary to seem interesting or edgy and daring instead" (Fainstein and Powers 2005: 2).[1] Critics of these changes have argued that this revalorization has increasingly led to direct government encouragement of tourism (and consumption more generally) and indirect encouragement of gentrification (Hoffman 2003; Shaw, Bagwell and Karmowska 2004; Fox Gotham 2005; Brown-Saracino 2009). Making a neighborhood 'open' for business makes it 'open' to newcomers and the changes they may bring.

The lack of City interest in promoting ethnic tourism has in a sense been taken up by those outside of official government, in particular the mix of newspaper and magazine columnists, bloggers, and others focused on food.

Part of the interest in Sunset Park in particular stems from the location of multiple ethnic communities in close proximity to each other—broadly speaking the Hispanic community and its 'main street' of Fifth Avenue and the Chinatown centered on Eighth Avenue. A 2010 *New York Times* 'Local Stop' article on the neighborhood, recommended that the visitor "feast on some of the most authentic Mexican food in New York" (Dunham 2010:np), the *Village Voice* restaurant critic has written that the Sunset Park Chinatown is his favorite of the five in the city: not as tourist-filled as Manhattan and not as crowded as Flushing, but more developed than Elmhurst or Homecrest (Sietsema 2008), and a number of websites and magazines have listed the restaurant Ba Xuyên as making the best Vietnamese banh mi sandwiches in the city. *New York Magazine*, listing the restaurant as a 'Critics' Pick, even has an online slideshow of the restaurant (*New York Magazine* 2011).

But the draw—and something that the *Voice* critic points to—is not simply the food alone but in the environment within which it is presented. Residents here are not explicitly catering to outsiders, and that helps the neighborhood retain a sort of charm *for* outsiders. A 2010 story on Sunset Park from the *More Intelligent Life* culture magazine published by *The Economist* posited that:

> Sunset Park, however, is something of a relic. This is not a fashionable place to live, or even to visit. In a city where streets host relentless reincarnations, Sunset Park's stasis, its imperviousness to gentrification, is the source of its charm. An archetypal immigrant community, this area is seemingly immune to the changes that have swept through much of the borough, despite its proximity to Park Slope, its grandly transformed posh neighbour (Rodriguez 2010: np).

This article and its viewpoint, while celebrating the neighborhood in a way that Auster did not, nonetheless essentializes it. Tourists and visitors are supposed to seek out neighborhoods where they can be ignored (but served) by residents: once a place is too welcoming to outsiders, it no longer is 'authentic,' and loses its cachet.

In a 2010 interview, Sharon Zukin, who had recently released *Naked City: The Death and Life of Authentic Urban Places*, was asked what she thought was an 'authentic' neighborhood. She answered:

> An authentic neighbourhood is Sunset Park in Brooklyn, home to New York's third Chinatown on Eighth Avenue, a bustling community of Latino stores on Fifth Avenue, and an ethnically mixed group of homeowners and renters between them. I've heard a lot of worries recently, though, about whether Sunset Park can keep its authenticity as an ordinary neighbourhood instead of turning into a "destination" (Gierasimczuk 2010: np).

Zukin's 2010 book deals expressly with the problems that ensue once economic development gets linked to cultural practices and notions of 'authenticity.' However, while the concept of authenticity has been used extensively to describe a number of expressed practices by realtors, developers,[2] tourists, and others, it remains a slippery analytic concept. If authenticity itself is an object of desire, then one is always fighting a losing battle to protect it. And if Sunset Park is such an authentic community, then how is an increasing interest in the neighborhood from outsiders diminishing that authenticity 'on the ground'? Further, how do residents of an 'authentic' community under attack from inauthenticity respond?

Obviously, cultural framings of 'Sunset Park' are open to interpretation, whether or not one thinks that there exists some sort of Platonic ideal of a banh mi sandwich. Defining Sunset Park—or any spatial entity as a 'community'—is problematic: as Craig Calhoun has argued, 'community' can refer to both a physical setting *and* a "morally valued way of life" (1980: 107). Nonetheless, as outsiders have constructed some sort of coherent 'thing' referred to as Sunset Park, so too have area residents. Part of this stems from a simple political reality: the imposition of a Community Board system in 1977 has delimited a geographic area broadly bounded by 15th Street to the north, New York Harbor to the West, and Eighth Avenue and Green-Wood Cemetery to the east as Community District 7. Broadly speaking, there are three population concentrations within the district. To the north of Green-Wood Cemetery there is Windsor Terrace and an area increasingly referred to by realtors and growing numbers of white residents as Greenwood Heights. Along the west and central portion of the neighborhood, Hispanics are concentrated closer to the waterfront with the Chinese population located further up the hill and over the Eighth Avenue boundary with Community Board 12 to the east.

While Sunset Park has long had large Hispanic and Chinese communities, with a Puerto Rican population dating back to the 1950s and a Chinese population dating back to the 1970s (Winnick 1990), these broad outlines mask significant change in recent years. According to Census American Community Survey data, while the overall population of the Community District increased by nearly 20,000 between 2005 and 2009, the overall Hispanic or Latino population has remained relatively constant, the white population has more-or-less kept up with the overall district population growth, and African American and Asian populations increased at rates greater than that for the district (see table 12.1).[3] But decomposing the Hispanic and Latino population shows another significant change: while the Puerto Rican population has dropped, the Mexican population has grown, part of broad trends within the city over the past two decades (see Lobo, Flores and Salvo 2002: 720).

Table 12.1. Sunset Park Population Change, 2005–2009

Year:	*2005*	*2009*	*% Change*
Total	139,547	158,333	13.5%
Total Hispanic or Latino	61,678	63,370	2.7%
Mexican	14,663	22,259	51.8%
Puerto Rican	24,617	20,322	–17.4%
Cuban	466	867	86.1%
Other Hispanic / Latino	21,932	19,922	–9.2%
White Alone	36,041	40,097	11.3%
African-American Alone	3,008	5,273	75.3%
Asian Alone	35,874	48,266	34.5%

Source: U.S. Census American Community Survey PUMS Data

Changes are also noticeable when looking at home lending data. While much of Sunset Park is a renter community, many of its side streets are lined with row-houses and sold as single-family homes (often with a renter unit). Home purchase loans made by year in the neighborhood show the rapid change in borrower characteristics since the market collapse starting in 2007. In short, while loans overall have decreased from their peaks, these declines have been especially notable among Hispanics: while in 2006 about 20 percent of home purchase loans in Sunset Park south of 24th Street were made to Hispanics, in 2009 Hispanics received only *six* loans (2.3 percent of the total) in the area. Conversely, Asian home buyers have received an increasing share of loans in the area: from 46 percent in 2006 to 79 percent in 2009 (see table 12.2).

Combined, tables 12.1 and 12.2 reflect how demographic change is shaping neighborhood characteristics. While broadly speaking Sunset Park remains a

Table 12.2. Sunset Park Home Purchase Lending, 2000–2009

	Race/Ethnicity					
	# Asian	*# Black*	*# Hispanic*	*# White*	*# No Info*	*Totals*
2000	158	11	88	74	21	361
2001	190	9	81	69	19	374
2002	145	9	69	76	24	326
2003	190	17	72	79	16	388
2004	177	11	79	83	46	400
2005	196	13	118	104	32	469
2006	185	15	83	78	40	407
2007	280	16	65	93	26	480
2008	246	4	20	50	19	341
2009	204	2	6	32	14	259

Home purchase loans for 1–4 family, owner-occupied housing. Loans made in Sunset Park south of 24th Street and extending east to Ft. Hamilton Parkway. Source: Home Mortgage Disclosure Act (HMDA) data.

largely Hispanic and Asian community, the composition of that community is not in stasis. Homebuyers are increasingly coming from the Asian community, with the growing Mexican population going into renter housing.

PLANNING FOR CHANGE

Social change within Sunset Park has not taken place in an institutional vacuum. Released in 2007 after a series of meetings with community organizations and 'town halls,' New York City's *PlaNYC 2030* was an attempt to provide long-term guiding principles, couched in the notion of 'sustainability,' to New York City policymakers in the fields of land, water, transportation, energy, air, and climate. Within the context of 'land,' the plan's focus on housing is of special note. The report predicts that the population of New York will increase by nearly one million residents by 2030 (from a current population of just over 8 million), and those residents will need 265,000 housing units (Angotti 2007). The plan attempts to grapple with a number of constraints in confronting this influx of population, from the limited number of vacant parcels ready to be developed, the growing cost of land, and increasing shares of household income going to housing costs. For instance, more than half of the city's renter households are paying more than 30 percent of their incomes on rent, a figure that generally designates a 'cost-burdened' household (City of New York 2007: 18). These are all related. Because there are fewer spaces for development within the city, land costs go up, new construction gets more expensive, and affordability plummets.

PlaNYC 2030 serves not just as a broad outline for future City initiatives, but also contains what Tom Angotti has referred to as an implicit policy recommendation. In a critique of the plan, Angotti quoted a *Planning* magazine article by Chris Williamson: "If a city plans for a projection, is it also implicitly recommending growth policies for future councils?" (Agnotti 2007). Simply put, if the City projects it will grow by a million residents, a large portion of its effort must go towards fitting those residents in somewhere. Further, as part of the cost of property comes from its potential for revenue-generation, neighborhoods and properties targeted for intensified land use become more valuable. While the plan notes the various difficulties in attaining these goals, it nonetheless assumes a 'growth machine' logic of continuing economic intensification and population growth (Molotch 1976; Logan and Molotch 1987). It is only within this context that *PlaNYC* then attempts to channel that growth into politically palatable (and broadly-defined) recommendations.

These broad recommendations have filtered down in a number of ways to concrete policy practice, illustrated by the City's recent rezoning efforts.

A 2009 Department of City Planning's (DCP) webpage touted the completion of 100 neighborhood rezonings (totaling 8,400 blocks). Letters from Commissioner Amanda Burden and Mayor Michael Bloomberg pointed to innovative ideas and community-responsive plans. Burden's letter stated, in part: "First off, we start by listening to communities, spending time with them, and walking neighborhoods, to understand what makes them special, what challenges they face, and what opportunities exist. Then, as planners, we develop detailed neighborhood plans." The letter also notes the City's Zoning Handbook, and efforts to make the overall process and zoning tools more easily accessible to the general public.

In practice, public involvement has been highly constrained. In designated growth areas of the city such as Hudson Yards in Manhattan or Atlantic Yards or Williamsburg-Greenpoint waterfront in Brooklyn, the Planning Department has pushed for significant intensification of land uses and population growth, while in 'contextual' rezonings, it has generally 'upzoned' wide commercial avenues with good transit access to encourage the development of bulkier (but shorter) buildings than had been allowed for under the older zoning regime, while it has 'downzoned' residential side streets to discourage the demolition of contextual housing stock. The goal of this strategy is to protect the character of the side streets of a neighborhood while providing for some of the housing units called for in *PlanNYC* along transit-accessible corridors.

Although aimed at encouraging additional housing and based on the basic economic rationale that more supply leads to lower prices, the actual ramifications of this zoning strategy have been controversial for a number of reasons. Setting aside massive building projects such as Atlantic Yards, the City's general efforts to upzone avenues and downzone sidestreets have implications for lower-income residents. In neighborhoods targeted for this sort of contextual rezoning, buildings large enough to fall under rent stabilization protections (those with six units or more) are considerably more likely to be located on the avenues than sidestreets. Given the paucity of vacant parcels (as pointed out by *PlaNYC*), this means that lower-income residents are living on increasingly-valuable land. While the City is encouraging new development to build supply and to indirectly increase affordable housing, this new development may directly be replacing already-existing *actual* affordable housing. An October 2009 New York University study bears out this tension, showing that since 2002, while the city had financed preserving or creating 94,000 units (72,000 for low-income residents), approximately 200,000 units affordable to low-income residents had been lost (Fernandez 2009). Critics have charged that this process simply encourages gentrification, whether directly through demolition of existing affordable housing or indirectly through pushing out working-class social and economic infrastructures (everything from stores to social service centers) in favor of middle- or upper-class ones (see Marwell 2007; Angotti 2008). In other words, construction induces demand.

As rezoning is, at best, indirectly able to encourage affordable housing, the City has also used a few other tools to encourage affordability. The first is inclusionary zoning. This program lets a developer build a bigger building if a project includes a certain number of affordable units. Under current regulations (and in contrast to mandatory programs in a number of other cities), the New York City program is voluntary (Pratt 2007: 19). As such, while developers have occasionally taken advantage of the bonus in large-scale residential towers, the economic incentive for smaller-scale buildings remains small enough that as of 2010 no mid-size building within an 'inclusionary zoning' district had taken advantage of the program.[4] Additionally, 'affordability' is defined as a household making 80 percent or less of the area median income of the metropolitan area—and not of the neighborhood or even the city as a whole. This means that 'affordability' as the program defines it is only 'affordable' to those with relatively high-incomes. In the context of a lower-income community, this means that residents of newly-constructed 'affordable' units are likely to have significantly higher incomes than other area residents *and* to come from elsewhere in the City. The second tool, used more rarely than inclusionary zoning, is the creation of special districts designed to protect existing affordable housing stock (Pratt 2007: 27).

IMPOSING UPON A NEIGHBORHOOD

New construction in Sunset Park has increasingly been debated in recent years. Part of this stems from the borough- and city-wide construction boom of the 2000s and its effects on the built and social fabric of various neighborhoods. While Sunset Park has not been immune from these changes, other neighborhoods have seen significantly wider-scale building and demolition. When looking at permits issued for new buildings by the City between 2003 and 2010, one can see that the density of new construction in the northern Brooklyn neighborhoods such as Greenpoint, Williamsburg, and Bushwick has been significantly higher than elsewhere (see figure 12.1). If we focus in on Community District 7, which includes Sunset Park, we see that while permits have been issued across the area, the greatest concentrations have been in its northern and southeastern extremities bordering Park Slope and Borough Park, respectively.

Although central Sunset Park has seen relatively fewer new developments than other parts of Brooklyn, by the middle of the 2000s there was a notice-

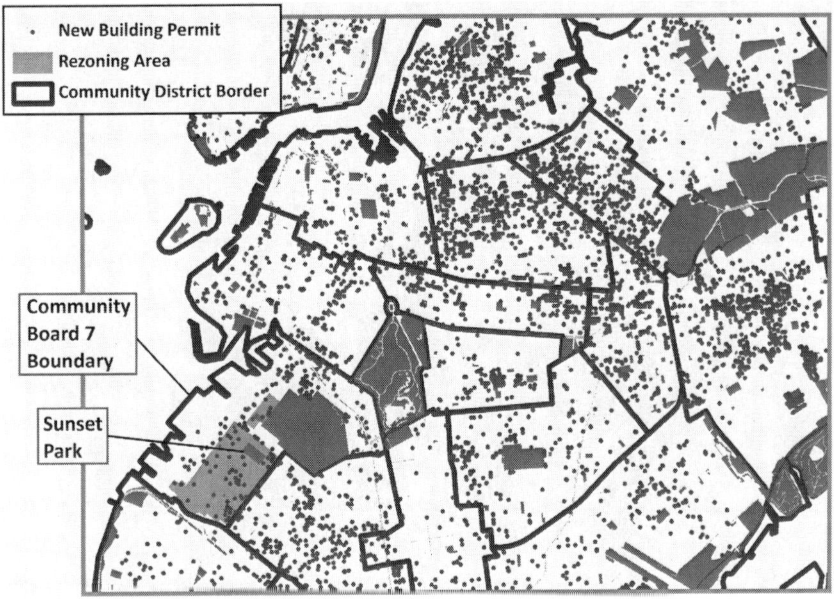

Figure 12.1. Building Permits Issued, February 2003 through December 2010 (Initial permits for new buildings). ***Source:*** **New York City Department of Buildings, Permit Monthly Statistical Reports, 2000–2003.**

able uptick in new construction along both residential side streets and wider avenues (see figure 12.2). These two types of developments reflected two types of imposition on the neighborhood. Demolishing an older row house for somewhat-larger new construction could be seen as an attack on the neighborhood's physical patrimony. But demolishing a relatively larger building on an Avenue had clearer social ramifications: since many of Sunset Park's affordable rental units were located on its avenues, demolishing an existing building for new construction was a sign that existing residents were being physically displaced. While both the northern portion of the Community District to 24th Street and the Bay Ridge neighborhood south of the Gowanus Expressway had been rezoned in 2005, central Sunset Park remained under the city's 1961 zoning code. The miles of Fourth Avenue north of Sunset Park had been largely rezoned and were already seeing the construction of numerous large projects that would supposedly transform the street into what Brooklyn Borough President Marty Markowitz had (rather aspirationally) called the 'Park Avenue' of Brooklyn. Whether Markowitz was referring to the aesthetics of Park Avenue or the income bracket of its inhabitants, these new buildings stood in the eyes of many Sunset Park residents as signs of impending 'luxury' construction and concomitant displacement of lower-income populations (see Moses 2005). Elsewhere in the neighborhood,

Figure 12.2. Sunset Park New Development. Photograph by the author.

especially on Seventh and Eighth Avenues, several new six- to ten- story buildings advertising availability in Chinese; further east in Borough Park new apartments built for the growing Hasidic community were also replacing smaller-scale, older buildings. In a sense, Sunset Park was surrounded by growing development on all sides.

Throwing these changes into relief, in January 2007 plans were filed for a ten story building that, taking advantage of the 1961 code's size bonus for buildings with community uses, would have included a twenty-nine foot high first floor daycare center. This project, located on 42nd Street just off of Fourth Avenue was downhill from Sunset Park but between the park views and New York Harbor. Although the proposed building was potentially legal within the 1961 rezoning, a group of local residents organized a new group known as the Sunset Park Alliance of Neighbors (SPAN) to fight the proposal. Although there was some talk that the issue could become contentious, a March 2007 agreement between local politicians, the developers, and SPAN worked out a compromise limiting the building height to sixty feet (Brownstoner.com March 12, 2007). Further, local politicians, notably Councilwoman Sara González, requested that the Department of City Planning (DCP) look at rezoning the neighborhood to be more in line with contemporary planning practices. DCP agreed and began work on their study of the area as a prelude to a formal rezoning proposal. González also contacted the Pratt Center for Community Development, an organization that links professional resources to address community planning and policy issues, to undertake its own study of the needs of Sunset Park. This rezoning study area was to include much of the southern portion of CB7: south of 24th Street, down to the boundary with Bay Ridge around 63rd Street (following a railroad line), and between Third and Eighth Avenues.

BUILDING A COALITION

In addition to the City and Pratt, a number of groups, some already-existing, some newly formed, began to organize responses to the rezoning. During the summer of 2007, members of two local community organizations organized the Affordable Housing Working Group (AHWG) to explore the potential ramifications and opportunities that the rezoning held for the neighborhood. Originally convened as a part of SPAN, the Working Group aimed to explore the technical details of the relationship between zoning and affordable housing. Although nominally open to the public, participants largely came from SPAN or worked with neighborhood community organizations. Members, already plugged into professional networks, were largely white—something the head of one organization (who did not participate in subsequent meetings) noted as a significant problem. In subsequent meetings, Working Group participants would convene a number of subcommittees to study technical aspects of rezoning.[5]

SPAN was also active, planning and hosting a summit in a local school on Sunday, September 23, attended by between 150 and 200 people. It was heavily represented by younger participants and non-profit workers in the neighborhood, and included an organized group of about twenty from La Union, a local immigrant-advocacy organization. Notably absent, however, was any presence from the Chinese community, a fact that would be brought up during the summit and also during subsequent meetings.

The summit started with a presentation from the Center for Urban Pedagogy (CUP), a nonprofit organization focused on urban planning public education, on the issues around rezoning and housing. While noting possible tools such as inclusionary zoning and special districts, the presentation argued that in general zoning was *bad* for keeping existing housing affordable. Afterwards, the head of the Fifth Avenue Committee, another local nonprofit, stressed the importance of community involvement. Citing the projected population growth in the city, and the fact that twenty-five communities in the city were undergoing rezoning, she argued that intensive community involvement in areas such as Greenpoint-Williamsburg and Clinton was crucial for procuring positive neighborhood outcomes. After these presentations participants broke out into nine smaller groups (five in English, four in Spanish) to discuss topics[6] and came up with ideas and general recommendations. People then reconvened to present their findings and recommendations, and SPAN members promised to look through and attempt to consolidate recommendations.

Summit participants expressed a number of concerns about changes to Sunset Park. One participant expressed concern about the intersection of population change, gentrification and the City's involvement forcefully: "they want to eliminate the poor. It's all about money and power." Others expressed more detailed worries, such as new members of co-op buildings pushing for amenities and improvements that longer-term residents could not afford, the loss of manufacturing jobs, and the displacement of low-income residents. While much of this concern was expressed in terms of worries about 'gentrification' from Park Slope to the north, issues about overcrowding and the financial backing for new development touched on the practices of immigrant communities. During one breakout session, when the issue of overcrowding and unsafe living conditions came up, a SPAN organizer noted that these concerns could be used to attack the cultural practices, notably the existence of extended families, of immigrant groups.[7] At another point, while one participant asked about the extent that new development was coming from Chinese developers (incidentally, the same person quoted about 'money and power' above), this concern was not taken up by others in the breakout session.

During the summit, participants overall expressed a measure of pragmatism: a few noted that development would happen no matter what Summit participants wanted, so the goal was to make it 'respect' and take account of the community. As such, final recommendations offered a mix of specific and general recommendations to address concerns expressed during the summit, a range of which included calls for a special anti-displacement and anti-demolition district, more supportive units, green building, view corridor protections and 'contextual' development, *true* affordability measured according to the income of existing residents instead of metropolitan area-wide designations, and strong inclusionary zoning provisions.

In the weeks after the summit SPAN and AHWG members attempted to reach out with members of the Chinese Community, meeting with the Chinese Staff and Workers' Association (CSWA). This was seen as especially important given an organization, the Eighth Avenue Improvement Association (EAIA), had organized a pro-growth petition, arguing that ten thousand Chinese would settle in the neighborhood within the next ten years and that new construction was needed (Hum 2010: 11). In subsequent months, SPAN and the CSWA would form a close alliance that at least in part served to reject the idea that Chinese immigrants were responsible for out-of-context development.

BOUNDING AGENCY

Parallel to the efforts by SPAN, Councilwoman González organized a series of meetings run by the Pratt Center. The Pratt program consisted of three meetings which loosely corresponded to the single SPAN summit: the first meeting, titled "Zoning and Land-Use 101," was designed to discuss the context and issues of the rezoning, while the later two meetings were workshops and speak-outs designed to collect input from residents. Attendance at the Pratt sessions was somewhat smaller than the SPAN and included a relatively larger share of older residents, fewer Latino participants, and more from the Chinese community—including a number from the Chinese Staff and Workers' Association.

Although nominally organized in a similar manner, the environment at the Pratt sessions was notably more contentious. There are a number of reasons that could explain the different responses: First, while SPAN summit organizers were made up of community residents, Pratt meeting organizers were brought in from 'outside' the community. Especially given that as of late 2007 the City had not been actively involved in *any* of deliberations around Sunset Park, Pratt's link to Sara González and the Community Board meant it was closest thing to a voice of the 'official' city view. Pratt had been involved in the controversial Williamsburg-Greenpoint rezoning, for instance, and in meetings some SPAN members had expressed concerns that their work had not truly taken account of community concerns. Finally, this 'outsider' dynamic was also highlighted by the ways the two sets of meetings closed: while SPAN summit participants were encouraged to work to formulate positions and attend subsequent meetings, Pratt meeting participants would have their concerns compiled by Pratt researchers who in turn would produce a recommendation report (which was released in December 2007).

The second difference between the SPAN and Pratt sessions, and one exacerbated by the first difference, was the focus on what rezoning could *not* do. While presentations during the SPAN summit had also noted the limits of rezoning to address affordable housing, the Pratt presentations treated the relationship as a fundamental conflict: contextual development versus affordable housing. Pushing for a decrease in development would limit the amount of new development that could take pressure off existing housing stock. As the head of Pratt put it, "if you wanted more affordable housing, you wouldn't start a rezoning campaign." Further, Pratt representatives noted the relatively precarious position of local activists: if residents pushed too hard for things such as mandatory inclusionary zoning or if the City noticed widespread dissention within the community, it would likely set the rezoning aside entirely and not address *any* local concerns. Some participants were incensed at this dynamic: one member of the Chinese Staff and Workers' Association asked the Pratt head if he was "telling people in the community to go screw themselves?"

The third difference was at least in part because SPAN had in a sense beaten Pratt to the punch: since a number of community groups and residents had already been discussing the minutiae of rezoning, they had already built up a store of knowledge to push Pratt organizers on particular issues. For instance, one community group member involved with the Affordable Housing Working Group asked the Pratt representative about 'special districts' less for his own benefit (as he had participated in discussions on the subject in other meetings) than for that of meeting attendees. At another point, an audience member asked the Pratt representative to define 'affordable' in regards to the inclusionary zoning program, pointing out its problematic definition in the context of a largely lower-income neighborhood such as Sunset Park.

Together, these elements represented a growing activism of differences between community concerns and the City's plans—all before the Department of City Planning even released its proposal. While during the speakout one local resident and business owner argued that downzoning increased crowding and gentrification pressures on existing housing stock, a more broadly expressed concern was with the implications of new development. As one SPAN member put it: "gentrification is what's going on with this new development. Immigrants aren't buying condos; babies aren't buying condos." Whether or not rezoning was undertaken, the neighborhood would develop according to the needs and desires of new residents, not existing ones.

BUILDING AN OPPOSITIONAL FRAME

Notable in these debates was that the official process had not even started yet: as the head of Community Board 7 stated during one of the Pratt sessions: "This is preseason. We're going to have regular season once ULURP starts." 'ULURP' stands for the 'Uniform Land Use Review Procedure' used by the City to structure the official rezoning process. It requires public reviews and a particular chain of decision-making to be used in any rezoning. Rezonings and ULURP experiences elsewhere in the city had provided both organizers and participants working with SPAN and Pratt with some guidelines for what the city would do. Given Sunset Park's relative distance from Manhattan, a massive rezoning along the lines of Williamsburg-Greenpoint was not in the cards; neither would be the rezoning of industrial to residential uses. More likely would a plan that upzoned the avenues—Fourth and Eighth in particular (the December 2007 Pratt report also noted that Seventh Avenue could be upzoned)—and downzoned the sidestreets to encourage some new construction and units along traffic and transit corridors while protecting smaller-scale residential districts. Less certain would be whether the city would implement other protective measures to retain affordable housing or the view from the park.

Nonetheless, when the City's proposal was released in January 2008, it caught many residents by surprise. While it downzoned residential sidestreets and upzoned Fourth and Seventh Avenues, it determined Eighth Avenue to be outside of the proposal area because of its location on the border between Community Board 7 and Community Board 12. This meant that the avenue facing some of the most intense development, and a focus of many discussions, would remain for the time being under the older rezoning regime. A letter sent to Councilwoman González, the Community Board Chair, and the City Planning representative from members of SPAN, the CSWA, the Asian American Legal Defense and Education Fund, two local pastors, and Queens College Professor Tarry Hum expressed strong concern about this exclusion and the sense "that 8th Avenue has been 'conceded' to the developers."

As the city's zoning review process developed, the constellation of organizations involved would change significantly. Recommendations by the Affordable Housing Working Group to limit the upzoning of Fourth Avenue may have influenced the City's decision to propose a slightly lower designation than the one used to the north in Park Slope (personal communication), but the group largely disappeared once members determined that neither the zoning proposal nor politically realistic alternatives would do much one way or the other to address issues of displacement or affordability. A small group of homeowners, more focused on protecting the physical fabric of Sunset Park's sidestreets than seeing zoning as a tool to protect affordability left SPAN to form the Sunset Park Alliance for Re-Zoning. SPAN formally joined with the Chinese Staff and Workers' Association to form the Coalition to Protect Sunset Park, and this new group took on the most visible and oppositional stance to the rezoning process as it went forward during 2008 and 2009. Activists still encouraged residents to attend meetings and to speak out, but as one flyer (in English and Spanish) put it, less to put forth recommendations for improvement than to make sure opposition was on the record:

"[o]therwise the government can say that no one objected to their plan and that the neighborhood wanted it."

Flyers handed out before rezoning hearings encouraged audience members to express particular talking points: that 'affordable' housing as defined by the city was out-of-reach to area residents, that avenue upzoning would accelerate the loss of affordable housing, and that side street downzonings were insufficient to stem demolition. A Coalition to Protect Sunset Park memo argued that the exclusion of Eighth Avenue "was done to try to split the Latino and Asian communities so that we couldn't organize together as easily," and that the rezoning proposal "continues a pattern of discriminatory rezoning aimed at displacing low-income communities of color and small businesses." While the claims themselves could be somewhat at odds with one another—both the rezoning of Fourth and Seventh Avenues and the *lack* of rezoning of Eighth Avenue were cited as evidence that the City was pushing existing residents out—they pointed to a developing frame put forth by local activists: low-income communities of color were being intentionally kicked out by City policy in general and through zoning in particular. For instance, one flyer stated that previous rezonings had "down-zoned and protected the predominantly wealthy white communities of Park Slope and Bay Ridge, while promoting high-rise development on Fourth Avenue, where predominantly low-income Latino residents reside."

This frame not only split Sunset Park residents from City government, but also split residents within the community as well. In part, this stemmed from the arbitrary lines of community district boundaries. First, the northern portion of Community Board 7 included the relatively wealthier and increasingly 'gentrified' neighborhoods of Windsor Terrace and Greenwood Heights.[8] Second, it did *not* include residents living on the eastern side of Eighth Avenue. Further, given that many community board members—including its chair—were white and resided in the northern parts of the Community District, they were increasingly attacked as not truly representing the community. Towards the end of a rezoning speak-out meeting, a resident and SPAN member shouted "Randy doesn't live here!" in order to lump the board chair with the 'outsiders' both because of his formal role as community board chair and rezoning facilitator and because of his residence *outside* of Sunset Park proper. This split worked both ways, however: in another speakout the chair noted that a number of Chinese residents denouncing the rezoning did not actually live in the community, either, as their addresses put them on the far side of Eighth Avenue and outside of the district, at least as it was officially demarcated.

As it became increasingly clear that the rezoning would go through, opponents resorted to other tactics. In August 2009, a group made up of area residents, five churches, and the Chinese Staff and Workers' Association filed a lawsuit against the city arguing that it had failed to conduct a full socioeconomic review through an environmental impact assessment (Fung 2009). A press release argued "that the rezoning plan will encourage more luxury development and large chain stores, resulting in widespread residential and commercial displacement and gentrification among Sunset Park's low-income Asian and Latino Communities." It argued that the plan would upzone "Fourth, Fifth, Sixth, Seventh, and Eighth Avenues to allow for larger residential buildings" and quoted an organizer with the Chinese Staff and Workers' Association repeating the argument that the plan would encourage more luxury housing: "We know this will happen because we have seen this displacement happen in other low-income and immigrant neighborhoods" (Legal Services NYC 2009: np).

INSIDERS, OUTSIDERS, AND THE FRAMING OF CHANGE

Tarry Hum, in her study of the Sunset Park rezoning process, argues that while Community Board 7 did not provide an inclusive public space for participants, both the Chinese Staff and Workers' Association and SPAN did: presenting "a more viable venue for making policy claims and articulating alternative development visions to sustain immigrant neighborhoods" (Hum 2010: 13). While I agree that the City-led planning process only nominally took account of community concerns, her take on the transition of community concern from an influx of "Immigrant Asian capital" and its role in changing the neighborhood's built form (Hum 2010: 7) to one focused on the displacement and affordability issues facing lower-income residents ends up trading one problematic frame for another. While it is true that the City has shown very little interest in protecting existing residents from displacement, replacing the 'bogeyman' of foreign capital with that of government-led gentrification has let those involved in the rezoning process off the hook, in a sense. Instead of dealing with and responding to a multifaceted set of social, economic, and demographic change, proponents and critics increasingly saw the issues involved in oppositional, binary, terms.

Of course, the impact of the political process itself should not be understated. By refusing to make changes to the inclusionary zoning program (either to make it mandatory or to define 'affordability' in terms of local populations) and by refusing to make use of 'special district' provision aimed to stem unnecessary demolition or displacement, the Bloomberg administration has significantly curtailed any relevance that zoning could have for the creation or retention of affordable housing. Similarly, while nominally the rezoning process involves community input, any actual evidence for the *effect* of this input is difficult to discern. Comparing the March 2008 initial City proposal, the April 2009 formal proposal, and the final map approved in September 2009 shows that the Department of City Planning made *no* changes to its initial map once the formal process was initiated (despite a request from the Community Board to zone Fourth Avenue at the lower 'R6A' rather than the proposed and final 'R7A' designation). While, as noted above, the R7A designation itself may actually represent a compromise, any pertinent discussions took place before the formal public process was initiated. Finally, while numerous people pointed out throughout the process that rezoning tools were nearly useless in encouraging or retaining affordable housing, it is also true that rezoning remains just about the *only* means by which community members can meet to discuss—or to argue about—widespread changes to the neighborhood. In other words, while addressing affordability through rezoning is a bit like hammering a square peg through a round hole, no 'square hole' presently exists. Given the current planning regime in New York, community members are forced to choose between spectacular or incremental displacement: the Atlantic Yards development reflects one pole, while Sunset Park may reflect the other.

The changing dynamics of debate over the rezoning process shows us that the 'public' is not a constant feature of political life, but is a process (Sennett 2009:18) constantly being produced and shaped. In Sunset Park, a number of potential cleavages could have broken out as diverse populations living within an arbitrarily drawn political district were forced to confront a host of issues. Initial efforts such as the SPAN summit, free of constraints subsequently set by City government, started to build something approaching a 'public' which, as Nancy Fraser has argued, "better than that of a community, can accommodate internal differences, antagonism, and debates" (Fraser 1990: 80n29). As it became increasingly clear that rezoning Sunset Park would do little to address significant problems facing the neighborhood, opponents increasingly framed the debate in us-versus-them terms that reflected a perception that it was being carved up for the sake of outsiders without regard to already-existing residents. But by building an oppositional voice so focused on contrasting itself to outsiders, gentrifiers, and City government, important challenges to the future of Sunset Park and Brooklyn at large remain. After all, while in Paul Auster's novel the squatter's home was taken over by the City after the owner had missed tax payments, in reality the property was sold to developers who, as of June 2011, had plans for a five-story, eighteen unit apartment building approved by the City's Department of Buildings.

The Sunset Park rezoning did not take place in a vacuum. While a few commentators have argued that Sunset Park is at least partially "immune" to larger forces shaping present-day Brooklyn, the reality is that Sunset Park—and the rest of Brooklyn—is, and has always been, constantly changing. What makes Brooklyn so fascinating is not just its diversity, but the flux of that diversity. This obviously makes undertaking political projects a tricky proposition for would-be activists: organizing across diversity is a daunting challenge. This becomes even more difficult, however, when media accounts and tourist guides celebrate this diversity only to the extent that it can be consumed, and when political processes acknowledge that diversity only as a formality.

NOTES

1. It should be noted that Fainstein and Powers discuss the potential that encouraging local tourism could lead to commercial and residential displacement of existing communities.
2. To take one example, a 2009 slideshow on the Congress for the New Urbanism website was entitled: "Developing Authentic Places: The Hipster Effect." Accessed online March 1, 2011 (www.cnu.org/node/3011).
3. Note that the 'planned' growth predicted for Sunset Park between 2010 and 2030 in the PlaNYC 2030 report shows the population of Sunset Park south of Green-Wood Cemetery and west of Fifth Avenue to be only between 1,000 and 2,499, with the area west of Fifth Avenue predicted to grow between 2,500 and 4,999 (City of New York 2007: 19).
4. Activist quotations come from data collected for the study.
5. Groups studied the 421a tax-break system, special districts, affordable housing preservation, inclusionary zoning, general development trends, and issues facing undocumented and very-low-income residents.
6. The six given topics were: manufacturing and small business, new development, affordable housing, architecture and historical character, overcrowding and unsafe conditions, and displacement; participants could add other topics as well.
7. According to American Community Survey 2005–2009 data, 31 percent of Asian households and 19 percent of Hispanic households versus 7 percent of white (not Hispanic) households were living in 'crowded' conditions (more than 1.0 people per room); in five census tracts, more than 40 percent of Asian households were 'crowded.' The measure of 1.0 people per room is a problematic metric by any means, but these numbers point to the ways in which housing conditions vary.
8. Although 2000 Census data are somewhat out of date, median household income in this northern section was $41,840, while that to the south was $29,032.

REFERENCES

Angotti, Tom. 2007. "Plan NYC 2030." *Gotham Gazette*. February.
Angotti, Tom. 2008. *New York for Sale: Community Planning Confronts Global Real Estate.* Cambridge, MA: MIT Press.

Auster, Paul. 2010. *Sunset Park.* New York: Henry Holt and Co.
Brown-Saracino, Japonica. 2009. *A Neighborhood That Never Changes: Gentrification, Social Preservation, and the Search for Authenticity.* Chicago: University of Chicago Press.
Brownstoner.com. 2007. "420 42nd Street Building Gets Cut in Half." March 12. Accessed March 1, 2011 (www.brownstoner.com/brownstoner/archives/2007/03/420_42nd_street_2.php).
Burden, Amanda. 2011. "Letter from the Commissioner." Neighborhoods Count: Celebrating DCP Rezonings. Accessed August 17, 2011 (www.nyc.gov/html/dcp/html/rezonings/index.shtml).
Calhoun, Craig. 1980. "Community: toward a variable conceptualization for comparative research." *Social History* 5(1):105–29.
City of New York. 2007. *PlaNYC: A Greener, Greater New York.* Accessed March 1, 2011 (www.nyc.gov/html/planyc2030/html/downloads/the-plan.shtml).
DeSena, Judith. 2009. *Gentrification and Inequality in Brooklyn: the New Kids on the Block.* Lanham, MD: Lexington Books.
Dunham, Jillian. 2010. "Local Stop: Sunset Park. Vistas, Tacos and Bowling." *The New York Times.* March 18.
Fainstein, Susan and John C. Powers. 2005. "Tourism and New York's Ethnic Diversity: An Underutilized Resource?" Accessed March 1, 2011 (www.gsd.harvard.edu/people/faculty/fainstein/text/Diversity%20tourism%20edited%20version.pdf).
Fernandez, Manny. 2009. "As New York Adds Housing for Poor, Market Subtracts It." *The New York Times.* October 14. Accessed February 8, 2012 (http://www.nytimes.com/2009/10/15/nyregion/15housing.html).
Fischer, Max. 2010. "Brian Williams Mocks NYT Over-Coverage of Brooklyn." *The Atlantic Wire.* December 29. Accessed August 17, 2011 (www.theatlanticwire.com/entertainment/2010/12/brian-williams-mocks-nyt-over-coverage-of-brooklyn/18116/).
Fox Gotham, Kevin. 2005. "Tourism Gentrification: The Case of New Orleans' Vieux Carre (French Quarter)." *Urban Studies* 42(7):1099–121.
Fraser, Nancy. 1990. "Rethinking the Public Sphere: A Contribution to the Critique of Actually Existing Democracy." *Social Text* 25/26:56–80.
Freeman, Lance. 2006. *There Goes the' Hood: Views of Gentrification from the Ground Up.* Philadelphia: Temple University Press.
Fung, Amanda. 2009. "Sunset Park Fears High-rises Will Spring from New Zoning." *Crain's New York Business.* November 23.
Gierasimczuk, Tom. 2010. "Where is Authentic New York?" *Up Magazine.* May 17. Accessed March 1, 2011 (www.upmagazine.com/blog/where-authentic-new-york).
Hoffman, Lily M. 2003. "The Marketing of Diversity in the Inner City: Tourism and Regulation in Harlem." *International Journal of Urban and Regional Research* 27(2):286–299.
Hum, Tarry. 2002. "Asian and Latino Immigration and the Revitalization of Sunset Park, Brooklyn." Pp. 27–44 in *Contemporary Asian American Communities: Inter-*

sections and Divergences, edited by Linda Trinh Vo and Rick Bonus. Philadelphia: Temple University Press.

Hum, Tarry. 2010. "Planning in Neighborhoods with Multiple Publics: Opportunities and Challenges for Community-Based Nonprofit Organizations." *Journal of Planning Education and Research* 29(4):461–477.

Lees, Loretta, Tom Slater, and Elvin Wyly. 2008. *Gentrification.* New York: Routledge.

Legal Services NYC. 2009. "Immigrant Groups File Lawsuit to Stop Sunset Park Rezoning in Brooklyn." Press Release. August 20. Accessed February 8, 2012 (http://www.legalservicesnyc.org/index.php?option=content&task=view&id=363).

Lobo, Arun Peter, Ronald J. O. Flores and Joseph J. Salvo. 2002. "The Impact of Hispanic Growth on the Racial/Ethnic Composition of New York City Neighborhoods." *Urban Affairs Review* 37(5):703–727.

Logan, John and Harvey Molotch. 1987. *Urban Fortunes: The Political Economy of Place.* Berkeley: University of California Press.

Marwell, Nicole. 2007. *Bargaining for Brooklyn: Community Organizations in the Entrepreneurial City*. Chicago: University of Chicago Press.

Molotch, Harvey 1976. "The City as a Growth Machine." *American Journal of Sociology* 82(2):309–330.

Moses, Paul. 2005. "Poor Excuse: rezoning Plan for Brooklyn's Fourth Avenue Forces Lower-income Neighbors Out." *Village Voice*. July 5.

Neary, Lynn. 2010. "Paul Auster Tackles Homelessness And Broken Hearts." *All Things Considered.* National Public Radio. Accessed March 1, 2011 (www.npr.org/templates/story/story.php?storyId=131196031).

New York Magazine. 2011. "Ba Xuyên profile." Accessed August 17, 2011 (http://nymag.com/listings/restaurant/ba-xuyen/).

Osman, Suleiman. 2011. *The Invention of Brownstone Brooklyn: Gentrification and the Search for Authenticity in Postwar New York.* Oxford, UK: Oxford University Press.

Pierce, Leonard. 2010. Interview with Paul Auster. *The A.V. Club.* November 9. Accessed March 1, 2011 (www.avclub.com/articles/paul-auster,47376/).

Pratt Center for Community Development. 2007. *Sunset Park Voices in the Rezoning Process.* Prepared by the Pratt Center for Community Development. December 17. Accessed March 1, 2011 (http://prattcenter.net/sunset-park-rezoning).

Rodriguez, James. 2010. "Sunset Park Standstill." *The Blog. MoreIntelligentLife.com.* Accessed March 1, 2011 (http://moreintelligentlife.com/blog/james-rodriguez/sunset-park-standstill).

Sennett, Richard. 2009. "Quant: The Public Realm." Accessed March 1, 2011 (www.richardsennett.com/site/SENN/Templates/General2.aspx?pageid=16).

Shaw, Stephen, Susan Bagwell and Joanna Karmowska. 2004. "Ethnoscapes as Spectacle: Reimaging Multicultural Districts as New Destinations for Leisure and Tourism Consumption." *Urban Studies* 41(10):1983–2000.

Sietsema, Robert. 2008. "Footloose Food Tours Through Brooklyn and the Bronx." *The Village Voice*. May 13.

Winnick, Louis. 1990. *New People in Old Neighborhoods: The Role of New Immigrants in Rejuvenating New York's Communities*. New York: Russell Sage Foundation.

Zukin, Sharon. 2010. *Naked City: The Death and Life of Authentic Urban Places.* Oxford, UK: Oxford University Press.

13

An Ethnography of Local Politics in a Brooklyn Caribbean Community

Evrick Brown

Discussions of urban public life include the properties, norms and codes regarding the interactional dynamics among the throng of strangers (Goffman 1963; Gardner 1980; Lofland 1998; Duneier 1999; Jenks and Neves 2000; Demerath and Levinger 2003), which sometimes leads to racial tension and hostility (Durr 2009). Other studies investigate a phenomenological, emotional and collaborative link that individuals experience with the physical environment (Bendiner-Viani 2005; Pink 2008). Such behaviors on sidewalks and other areas of heavy pedestrian traffic, more often associated with interim or between places, provide an opportunity not only for social research but neighborhood activism specifically in the form of political campaigns. In community politics, social space is often used by those campaigning for public office who need to establish and increase their base of power due to a lack of resources that are often at the command of an incumbent. Often this involves spending more time out on the field and exposing oneself to the greater fluctuations of the crowd but, on an ethnic community, there is an understanding through common identification that those who are present are not entirely strangers, thus this defines them as entrants in the parochial realm, partially defined as a space occupied by those who share some form of kin-like traits, in this case, in the form of common regional ancestry. It is the interactional dynamics of this type of social space which, in part, lead to a recent surge of Afro-Caribbean[1] activism in Brooklyn, New York. Further instigators of this cause are linked to an historical precedent of ethnic based machine politics in which political leaders garner voter support through circulating their political districts. More recently, the formation of the community boards as administratively carved semi-sovereign ethnic niches empowered residents with social and political control over their neighborhoods.

MOBILITY METHOD IN COMMUNITY ETHNOGRAPHY

A key component of ethnography which involves a successful immersion of the researcher who shares the experiences of those studied is its ability for adjustment through self-reflexivity (Fox 2004; Hsiung 2008). The researcher is enabled to apply changes to their mode of inquiry possibly shifting from interviews to the ranges of participant-observation and back. Here, certain properties of a community based in Brooklyn, New York, have been learned by the implementation of a mobility method of data gathering which partially involves the canvassing and "purposeful drifting" within a neighborhood (Jenks and Neves 2000). The utility of this method has been shown in past studies of urban neighborhoods which focused on how the larger forces, mostly economic in nature, preceded the development of dense and diverse communities of residentially unstable renters with a lapse of tight communal bonds. Unfortunately, such studies did not provide equivocal discussion of permeating the field (Burgess [1925] 1967; Zorbaugh 1937; Cressey 1932) with exceptions (Whyte [1943] 1981; Jonassen 1949).[2]

In his Boston neighborhood study, Whyte (1943) engaged in several attempts to "gain entry" into an Italian neighborhood, his first two attempts were unsuccessful. Initially, he used a "formal survey" questioning residents of slum conditions which lead to limited results and distrust. Afterwards, he tried through an informal gathering at a local "Royal Hotel," which resulted in near physical harm when he approached two women and one male at a table in a bar. His final and successful effort was through an informal walking tour of the area when he observed young men and women congregating in groups at a local settlement house where he made his first successful contact with an informant who would help launch his study and establish a friendship that would last several decades, "Doc." Through Whyte's "footwork" or circulation of the community he discovered the semiformal nature of the settlement house where norms permitted the "invasion" of an outside researcher, in this case an Irish-American, into an Italian community. The initial and continuing process leading to this eventual understanding could be grasped when a researcher does an informal walking survey of the community.

The engagement and outcomes of the mechanisms and techniques of this process have been documented in various studies that emphasized the necessity of comprehending the social and cultural context of the research site (Gans 1962, 1999; Anderson 1990, 1999; Fong 1994; Sanjek 1998; Venkatesh 2002; Kusenbach 2003; Scott 2004; Britton 2008).

NAVIGATING THE COMMUNITY CULTURE

Community residents are active authors of their subcultures. Such an apparent truism enabled Gans, through his study of the West End Community in Boston Massachusetts, to specify a definition of community that initially had, at its core, the peer group with limited involvement in their local government. Consequently, elements of their definition of community changed to involve patterns of interaction external to their daily routine. For a West Ender during the late 1950s, community was synonymous with activism. Residents who were involved in saving the West End Community from destruction could be identified as engaging in communal activity. Years later Fong (1994), through his study Monterey Park California, came across a somewhat different variation of community. Although he does not define community, its definition was implicit through the actions of residents, there were times when the informal groups or associations became "formalized" and participated in politics through either pro-growth or antigrowth coalitions. Fong documents this through the "kaffe klatch," an informal antigrowth/conservative group made up of residents and business interests. Krase defined the community via a theatrical construct in which residents form ecologically based organizations to solidify their area identity. This enables groups to seek the approval and aid of city and state public officials who later co-opt and undermine such organizations (Krase and La Cerra 1991).

For a period of time Elijah Anderson was involved with a local organization working for the improvement of public school education which eventually yielded a potent understanding of the social-psychological interplay of street-level interaction (Anderson 1990: x). The results of his ethnographic work yielded informative accounts and explicit descriptions of neighborhoods in Philadelphia while explaining the norms which guided fragile and strained interactions of pedestrians (Anderson 1990, 1999). During his study of the Taylor houses in Chicago, many residents initially saw Venkatesh (2002) as one of the intrusive state agents which made his foray into the field problematic. As a compromise, he volunteered information by voicing his angst concerning a lack of viable income and employment. Residents were eventually able to reestablish his role from state agent to academic "hustler." Given the nature of poverty for residents in public housing, the role of a "hustler" as one who seeks economic survival, possibly through enterprising informal means, was contextually pertinent to residents eventually permitting his access to data. Scott employed this understanding of researcher repertoire as he studied the relationship of gang members prior to and after incarceration in Chicago. His purposeful "ethnographic immersion" involved a revelation of past deviant activity to informants as a streetwise academic hustler which increased his level of access and confidentiality with respondents (Scott 2004: 114).

Kusenbach engaged in a similar strategy pinpointing the activity of what she called the "go-along" in which the fieldworker accompanies individual informants in their "natural" settings while they engage in their daily routines. This facilitates the researcher's access to data by observing personal biographies; thereby, uncovering ways individuals apply depth and meaning to their daily round in their lived social experience and not by the interviews or, as she refers, the "static encounters" which forces recall.

In summary, research which highlights the sociocultural aspects of communal life reveal properties that distinguish certain semiotics of space under the guise of realms (Lofland 1998). The latter are defined as space with social meaning and significance that varies according to usage. Space which is characterized by a continuous presence of strangers or "other" is noted as the public realm. In such an environment, particularly an urban one, individuals have a categorical, and thus limited, repertoire of knowledge to base assessment of one another which is often limited to manner of dress, body language, and other mainly non-verbal cues. Despite the variations in presentation, what is often common and understood in this realm, is the notion of "civil inattention" as a protocol of social rules that govern interaction based on an informal consensus of recognized social distance or personal space (Goffman 1963). These rules are often adhered to and respected with few folkway violations. Most often; however, individuals seek and create their own private space or, in the case of groups, parochial realms which represent carved social niches. Often such social spaces are defined as situational and temporary as a group that claims a niche does so for a specific event or culturally specific ceremony as when a family decides to occupy a portion of a public park for a picnic. In this manner, communities, particularly ethnic communities, can represent forms of relatively non-situational and stable parochial realms. The claim for turf is understood to be taken by those who share semi-primary kin-like bonds. Thus, community and neighborhood members may not only claim a similar ancestry but engage in historically significant shared cultural practices such as a carnival or parade. If such is the case then their common identities can reinforce aspects of the parochial realm through territory or turf (Jacobs 1961). This adds another dimension to the discussion of access for the researcher who must permeate boundaries, possibly hardened by the territorial claims, which includes an understanding and approval drawn from a cognitive repertoire of a researcher's role from the residents' perspective.

The similarities between the ethnographic practice explained thus far and the actions of political activists are to be clarified. Rather than gaining access to interviews and informants, candidates seek votes through potential constituents who assess the viability of these political contenders. Thus, circulating the community proved necessary not only methodologically for access to and gathering data but in understanding how residents, politically active and otherwise, negotiate identity within a portion of Brooklyn they designate as their own.

HISTORICAL AND POLITICAL IMPLICATIONS OF A MOBILITY METHOD IN BROOKLYN

Place-based identity construction is not without precedent and has its roots in the ethnic political machine of communities in the past that was largely displayed in an amalgam of behaviors couched in a historical practice of canvassing (Chisholm 1970; Caro 1975; Krase and LaCerra 1991). Caro, in covering the life of road baron, Robert Moses discusses how Al Smith, an Irish-American power broker and eventual governor of New York utilized the Irish ethnic machine as leverage towards a successful gubernatorial race eventually helping Moses acquire an influential position revolutionizing New York City roadways and the public authority structure. Krase and LaCerra (1991) noted how machine politics in Brooklyn was utilized to facilitate and maintain the political power of State Assemblyman Stanley Steingut, through his Madison Club, despite the racial and ethnic changes in the neighborhood. What they note as leading to the eventual downfall of the latter was, in part, their complacency, and the political efficacy of the insurgents through canvassing.

Along with the sudden changes in Brooklyn's racial landscape through the discovery of a "Harlem Community" there, insurgent or "reform" democratic political clubs and associations formed to challenge the establishment.[3] One such organization dubbed the Unity Club was founded with the aid of such insurgents as Thomas R. Jones and Shirley Chisholm (Chisholm 1970). The club's tactic to challenge the county organization was through the personal microinteractional form of canvassing to people within the neighborhoods. This form of electoral organizing involves a candidate physically presenting themselves to the community away from the safety of a political club's office or an indoor forum. The candidate makes themselves vulnerable to verbal and sometimes physical attacks, although the latter are presumably rare. It is also seen as a way of building the confidence of a constituency in one's ability and is one of the most effective tactics a candidate from an insurgent club can do when campaigning against the choice of an entire county organization. However, this mobility campaigning was even effective against a well known national activist at the time, James Farmer, an African American of the Congress of Racial Equality who had participated in the nationally known

Civil Rights movement and was coming to challenge a congressional seat. Running as a Liberal Republican, Farmer had the backing of actors, scholars, as well as other nationally known entertainers. Meanwhile, Chisholm continued to run under her Unity Team Chisholm, maintained her *Unbought and Unbossed* slogan and proceeded with her grassroots organizing tactics which suggests a strong and potent knowledge of the community. For example, when news reporters asked for the two candidates' opinions of a school board race both candidates supported the decentralization and greater community control; however, Chisholm was more specific and detailed in her response than her challenger. Such displays often indicate increased knowledge, interest and attention into community affairs which residents can relate and note. These tactics helped to secure Chisholm a victory and a "walloping" defeat of Farmer by a margin of more than two to one (13,777 votes for Farmer and 34,885 for Chisholm) (Chisholm 1970: 77).

During the three decades between Shirley Chisholm's insurgent congressional campaign and the study for this chapter, there was the formal adaptation of the community boards and a significant growth of the Caribbean population in the south and central portion of Brooklyn including an area designated as Community District 17, the area of focus. The interim has been described as the black Caribbeans' early "political" representation in the form of voluntary organizations in an effort to sustain their cultural existence in the midst of inimical prescribed racial pressure. As the immigrant population grew, the organizations' role expanded to include access to jobs and housing for those who required it and eventually assumed a greater stance in asserting their presence as a potentially viable political group (Basch 1987). Kasinitz (1992) chronicles the next step of representation with the growth of ethnicity entrepreneurs. He defined these entrepreneurs as those who did not hold public office but had influence in the political structure as representatives of their fellow immigrants.[4] Thus, for a time, they served as informal liaisons between the community and local representatives. As the immigrant population grew; however, ethnicity entrepreneurs became solely inadequate to accommodate the needs of the group (Sengupta 1996). The demands for social and economic amenities required more formal political representation eventually leading to Caribbean office holders and their ever present insurgents who desire to topple them.

EAST FLATBUSH AND THE MOBILITY METHOD

The central portion of Brooklyn, defined as District 17 by the New York City Planning Department, was the research site for this study. District 17 has a western boundary that zigzags along Bedford, Nostrand and Glenmont Avenues and East 32nd Street. The northern boundary includes the avenues of Clarkson, Utica and East New York bounded by the L.I.R.R. (Long Island Railroad) tracks to the south. Within the administrative boundaries that define this district that sits in the south-central portion of Brooklyn are a collection of four neighborhoods Flatbush, East Flatbush, Rugby and Remsen Village. Although residents simply refer to the area as East Flatbush it is unofficially recognized as a physical extension of the various islands of the Caribbean.

During the weekdays, most heavily during the spring and summer months, one can find residents strolling the sidewalks loosely holding their groceries or purchased items at their sides seemingly without the need to rush while scanning other pedestrians for a familiar face or listening for a familiar sound—often an accent. Many find time to loiter and chat with friends or associates that they may not have seen for many years since they immigrated or the day before, there is not much need for an excuse to strike up a conversation in such a familiar environment. On weekends one might find additional visual and vocal presentations:

> At the busy intersection of Church and Utica Avenue a mobile flatbed is stationed as a makeshift platform layered with three foot high stereo speakers overlaid with signs featuring a local religious institution. In front of this display is a preacher gesticulating wildly while verbally admonishing the crowd to convert to Christianity as he yells out scriptures from the bible, this is followed by a return to the blaring music that attracts the attention of some pedestrians who begin to jive or "get caught up in the spirit" to the gospel music donning a heavy calypso base, while an attendee sells various CDs, books and other paraphernalia. Meanwhile, the hustle and throng of pedestrians continue as the presentation coalesces with the collection of various tonalities from car horns of "dollar cars" or vans and music blaring from other vehicles.[5]

Within the confines of this vibrant district includes those who engage in an assortment of political activism ranging from marginal to influential activist citizen and political insurgent to incumbent, one of the main forums in which all of these groups mingle is through the local planning board meetings.

The community boards' purpose is to provide a forum for civic engagement and as information conduits to the neighborhood residents. Their perhaps unintended consequence is the sanction of governmental endorsed freedom and appearance of self-reliance that supplants a localized belief in community and self-efficacy. Although the fifty board members are legal residents appointed by either the Brooklyn Borough President (25) or City Council Members whose district falls within the Board boundaries, the remaining twenty-five are divided among those council members, participation at monthly board meetings is extended to all present. Consequently, any person can attend board meetings and participate. The monthly general meetings are officially guided by Roberts Rules of Order which are arbitrarily followed often with little rebuke. Thus, board meetings are often conducted according to the discretion of members with little active oversight by the Borough President (Goodman, 1974). This arrangement strengthens the belief of autonomy that all board members and many community activists have. In District 17, the continued vibrancy of the Afro-Caribbean population has been shown, in part, by political representatives who are openly either first or second generation Afro-Caribbean at the city, state and federal levels along with a Caribbean population of 51.5 percent in comparison to a non-Caribbean population of 48.5 according to the 2000 U.S. Census.

The data reported below was based on ethnographic research conducted between the beginning of 1999 to the fall of 2002 when I began my initial "entry" into the field by attending the general planning board and several committee meetings from the beginning of 1999 to the summer of 2002. Such meetings are open to the public which allows for unobtrusiveness and understanding of the social protocol and practices of board and committee members. After attending meetings for several months, the local Community Board president was interviewed for public endorsement and interviews were obtained with community board members. Through this medium, I imagined that I would be able to interview and gain access to the politicians and other community activists in the area. While this enabled interviews and referrals to other members of the school and community board, I discovered that such recommendations were not the preferred method for acquiring respondents. There was always the mien of paranoia and mistrust among those in and seeking positions of political power. Possibly because of the tenuous nature of these positions, none are safe from removal in any elected and politically motivated position. Thus, being too aggressive could have been seen as divisive and interpreted as trying to gain a foothold through searching for any exposed friction for a political gain. Moreover, the depths of the tenuous relations between African Americans, Caribbeans and within the latter group themselves was initially unknown.

My first interview with a politically active member of the community was seemingly a success. I was greeted rather warmly and held a forty-five minute interview—when I spoke to this person on the phone I was told that I had fifteen minutes and gladly accepted whatever time I could have.[6] I was then invited to the opening of their political campaign office, at the time I was desperate for information and did not have the savvy to question the person's motive. In the meantime, I was given a list of names of other contacts and people who would be willing participants in my study. I was overjoyed as my list of potential respondents was growing. I quickly discovered that gaining this list was not advantageous. It appeared that the activist whom I interviewed and referred me was testing a relationship they had with others. Since I carried this person's name as a reference, hopefully as a gaining-entry tool, I was also representing that person, which meant it was assumed that the information that I gained through the interview, despite going over the consent letter and assuring respondents of confidentiality, would be repeated. Thus, the referred interviews were extremely guarded and somewhat confrontational—I assumed if they did not want to be interviewed that they would simply deny the opportunity and say "no." However, not denying an interview belies another measure and characteristic of community politics in Board 17. If the interview was denied then the message would be that the relationship between the activist who referred me and the potential interviewee was closed. In doing so, could mean a possible end of a weak tie which could represent future support or flow of information—another guarded resource. Thus, it was beneficial for me to "tread lightly" and become a fixture in the community to gain trust—a common practice, and to not ask too many questions. Since one of the main properties and functions of the meetings is for individuals to present their grievances and concerns, I thought that would be a superb opportunity to gain interviews through those intermittent guests of the community. Such people would be less likely to withhold feelings and opinions of their neighborhood and representatives. In such cases I was able to accomplish on the spot interviews while the feelings and opinions were still pristine and thus I could get reactions. Although in quite a few of such cases I did schedule interviews, the potential respondents were willing to be interviewed but not willing to sign a consent form. Despite my efforts to quell any fears they had for attaching their name to anything, technically I was unable to gain information as formal interviews; however, the respondents were willing to talk and often expressed their feelings. In such cases I neither recorded nor wrote anything in front of them, I took notes when I went home. I found that although my continued presence facilitated the opportunity to gain further interviews, the mien of suspicion was difficult to permeate for reasons that will become clearer. It became apparent throughout the research that the mobilization of alternative research methods was necessary as it proved an effective means for gaining critical insight into the community.

INFORMAL STRUCTURES

A key technique of acquiring data in this East Flatbush Community as a component of an ethnographic process took place through such informal

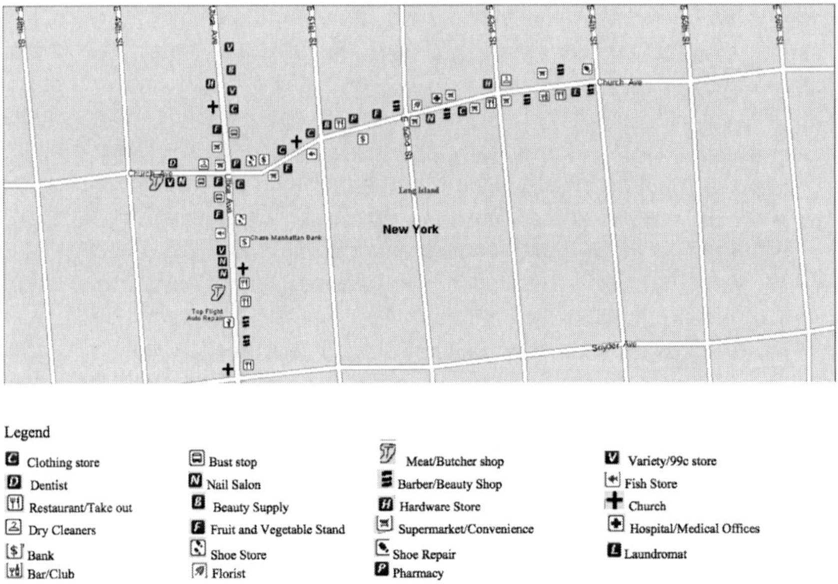

Figure 13.1. Detailed section of pedestrian activity. *Source:* Compiled by the author.

means as undirected walks throughout the district where I learned of meetings and events as I came across "community activists" engaging in their own purposeful strolls. Although my walks were initially undirected, I soon recognized that particular pedestrian venues were advantageous.

Commercial strips such as Church, Utica and Avenue D during the spring to summer months are locations where one can find relatively heavy foot traffic and access to information (figure 13.1). For example, the following was acquired while taking a casual, unplanned walk on Church Avenue:

> I decided to take a walk today and by a wild chance came across "L." She told me of a magazine entitled "Everybody's" which had on Major Owens and Una Clarke on the cover has been around since 1974. I went to the location and purchased three copies from a man in the window of an apartment. From the outside I could tell that the first floor was actually an office but there was no sign outside indicating that it was a magazine. The man inside, "B," told me that they have no sign because if they did then they might subject themselves to robbery but that they mostly function on subscriptions. By doing this they desire to remain hidden and functioning on their own terms which can be perceived as anti-community. They present themselves but they are not "out there" where passersby can see them and discover their presence.[7]

Such ostensibly undirected walks within a community lead to purposeful ends. I gained the advantage of not only being seen but information concerning a neighborhood based periodical and a political debate between two candidates. The informal nature of conventionally formal structures became more evident and widespread as multiple homes and residential dwellings have signs displayed of commercial interests such as "Copy/Fax Services" or "Accounting/Tax Services." There is often the uncontested appropriation of public space displayed through the cooking of jerk chicken or roasting of corn on the cob on makeshift grills by independent entrepreneurs (figure 13.2).[8] This enables a "pausability" or the interruption of foot traffic as hungry or curious passersby examine the food meanwhile engaging in idle conversation with other pedestrians or even the chef; thereby, increasing the possibility of experiencing shared meaning if not simply through the ambience and conversation (Demerath and Levinger 2003).

The billowing smoke from the grill, conversations in accented dialects accompanied, during the summer, with stalks of sugarcane are characteristics of sidewalk use that provides room for fortifying the notion that space has been infused with meaning and identity geared to those of Caribbean ancestry such as the Coconut Man (figure 13.3). One has to engage in a stroll or circulate the community to find such services and general interaction that is advantageous. Ethnic communities such as this one in Brooklyn embolden residents to delineate and construct an informal environment that is comfortable to their needs with little oversight from outsiders. It is often understood that the

Figure 13.2. Two men share an appropriated space on Church Avenue in front of a makeshift grill. Photograph by the author.

Figure 13.3. "Coconut Man" street vendor. Photograph by the author.

environments they create, as immigrants, often reflect the ones they left behind with perhaps some variation leading to a cultural amalgam often referred as ethnogenesis. Thus, in this Caribbean community in Brooklyn this casual disposition is taken for granted and utilized in community politics. Further characteristics of the community acquired through ethnographic means reveal greater political implications for candidates running for office.

THE BIKEMAN EXPERIENCE

It is argued that in parochial realms, social spaces infused with a collective meaning, there is a familiarity among those who see each other regularly in passing leading to "fleeting relationships" among strangers which can include a nod or a casual glance indicating familiarity (Lofland 1998). Various visual or otherwise perceptible cues surrounding customary practices can be used to label and categorize strangers with appropriate titles. As illustrated in the following case when for a period of two months I rode my bicycle regularly around the community more so in the evening to night hours while there was less automobile traffic on a main commercial strip and on side streets stopping regularly at a few all night convenience stores and fruit markets known as the "identity pegs" of Church Avenue in the East 50s. One particular evening with sparse pedestrian traffic I decided to walk directly to one of the convenience stores instead of going for an evening bike ride and one of the workers at a local fruit market, a West Indian gentleman, had greeted me with a yell of "Bikeman!" from across the street. He had apparently seen me from my previous rides and provided a semi-generic label of acquaintance. This title not only provides familiarity but can be taken as an open invitation to engage in a more lengthy conversation at another time which can lead to a lengthy quasi-primary relationship. At a later date, when he was asked about the label the following answer was given:

> "I see you all the time ridin' 'round on your bike sometimes you come here to shop so me recognize you even though ya' walk this time. It was late and I saw someone walking down the street, I like to know and see if I recognize somebody because it is so dangerous out at night and you don't know who's who. So me recognize you and call you like I know you."[9]

Note, because of the dangerous and precarious nature of urban life which is often magnified by, but not limited to, night life familiarity with the surroundings is often sought. In this case, a recognizable face is found and categorized if not only for safety but to maintain control over the environment through the power of labeling. Whether one is categorized as a "Beanie Man"[10] or "Yardie" from Jamaica, a "Trini" from Trinidad, "Rude Boy" or generalized under "Big Man," the latter indicating physical size or social status, there are categories based upon social assessments. For political candidates seeking a vote from residents, circulation is not only an expectation but a necessity:

> "I know on the Islands, ya' can't meet with them [politicians], ya' never see them on the street like I see them here. That's important we have to see who we voting for. If we don't how can we vote for them when J.S. [District Leader] sees us he talks to us. He can expect a vote from us because we see him out here with us."[11]

Here "being seen" is in contrast with the character of politicians and elected officials in the home countries who are perceived as socially removed from the electorate. This is particularly helpful for candidates who are running for political office and find a constituency with a common island ancestry although, because of the pan-Caribbean identity in Brooklyn, it is not limited to them. Such forms of circulation by canvassing can be taken to an extreme.

PROFILING

A candidate, particularly an insurgent, often hopes to display a certain status through some material item or through the typical barrage of campaign flyers embossed with a pictorial collage showing the local hopeful standing next to a slew of the politically established—of a different district or office. If this is not possible, an alternative approach can be taken:

> On chilly Friday evening in September an event called "Candidate's Night" was held in the basement auditorium of a local church that often doubles as a gym. The forum's purpose is to allow members of the community to meet candidates that were running for various local offices. There were about fifty people present in the audience and six candidates on stage. The event started around 7:30 when each candidate running for elective office was announced. For the next two hours, each candidate gave a speech, debated each other and answered general questions concerning job growth and education. With the exception of two, all were insurgents and all but one of the Candidates were African-American with the rest Caribbean. Before the forum finished one of the insurgent candidates abruptly left the stage as if stirred by a sudden emergency. A few minutes later a crowd of people begin to flow outside to be greeted by a shiny silver gray late model Mercedes-Benz idling a few feet away near an intersection, cross wise in the middle of the street, in full profile and highly visible to all those leaving the forum at its only entrance with the insurgent candidate in the driver's seat.[12]

By capturing the attention of those leaving with such a display of a luxury item, the insurgent was attempting to convey success and suggest that occupying a local political office was the next natural phase since he already commanded a high status as "Big Man." This act is amplified, of course, by the commandeering of a portion of the roadway, albeit for a time, in an atypical and illegal way to imply that when such a status surpasses legal barriers how can one not consider the candidate worthy. Unfortunately, such measures are not always received as well as canvassing on foot. While in a car, experience with the public is limited; interaction with other community residents, potential votes is grossly delineated to horn blowing and boisterous commands blaring out of mobile megaphones. Pausability, or interrupting the flow of traffic by immediately stopping to engage in conversation, is impossible without a serious outcome. This limits the possibility of the collaborative creativity linking shared meaning and experience concomitant with the ease of pace within the pedestrian environment. Consequently, although the particular candidate above may earn a cursory term of "Big Man" it is without substance as being briefly admired from afar reminding residents of the politicians back home unapproachable and unwilling to interact with residents on their own terms sharing a physical locale and absorbing a communal ambience. The potential for success of political campaigns by incumbents or insurgents is magnified once they are able to acquire greater resources in the form of personnel who can circulate the community and be a continual presence on their behalf. Their presence affords the opportunity of residents to implement the characteristics mentioned above through the informal labeling of supporting a "Trini," "Yardie" or "Bajan" or "Beanie Man" candidate, someone who potential voters in the district can relate. When an insurgent mixes resources with an understanding of the social relations of a community their campaign can become problematic for the incumbent. Such was the case in the contested political race for the 11th congressional district in Brooklyn between African American incumbent Major Owens and Jamaican born Una Clarke who was a member of the New York City Council representing a portion of East Flatbush Brooklyn.

MAJOR OWENS AND UNA CLARKE CAMPAIGN

Major Owens, a librarian from the south, became acquainted with the community through the New York City Community Development Agency and later entered politics in 1974 eventually earning a position in the State Senate then a run for a federal seat in the newly reapportioned 12th Congressional District in 1982 after a brutal political campaign against rival African American state Senator Vander Beatty. Eventually Owens became a seasoned Federal Representative for central Brooklyn.

Jamaican born Una Clarke migrated to the United States in the 1950s where she obtained a bachelor's degree in Business Management and eventually earned a Master's degree in Early Childhood Education which she used to operate day care centers in Brooklyn. When a city council district with a sizable Afro-Caribbean population became available during the early 1990s, Clarke ran with the support of Major Owens and acquired the political seat. During her tenure in office, what the ethnic and local newspapers often focused on was her stance on legalizing the notorious Caribbean-based "dollar" vans which were faster and more available than public transportation.[13] In effect, her functioning resembled that of the "old style" bosses who performed favors for immigrants who were not familiar with the city's structure or process for obtaining social services. Clarke's office was often teeming with West Indian immigrants seeking aid.

It is still debatable but believed that due to term limits, Una Clarke decided to run against Major Owens in the 11th Congressional District. Partially because of Clarke's discussion and aggressive talk of Afro-Caribbean rights and the failure of the current leadership, the Kings County Democratic Organization representing the ensconced and seasoned politicians under the predominantly African American Coalition for Community Empowerment dispatched a team headed by then Assemblyman Al Vann to persuade Clarke not to run citing the need to retain the eighteen years of experience and seniority Major Owens acquired. The Coalition for Community Empowerment also feared if Clarke remained steadfast she would cleave divisions among blacks along ethnic lines. At the meeting, Clarke brought an entourage of her own much to the dismay of the Empowerment group, they wanted a "friendly" chat in which to dissuade her—the presence of "others" altered that possibility. By the time the meeting took place, Clarke and her supporters had already established a Clarke 2000 committee and had their first fund raising event most assuredly committing her to the Congressional race.

As the political campaigns gained momentum, local publications *Carib News* and *Caribbean Life* carried articles featuring the campaign of both candidates. Both publications saw themselves as the voice of the Caribbean community. Despite claims, a common thread between residents and planning board members was their lack of acquiring news through the Caribbean based or major publications in the area. Residents noted that they "rarely" or "vaguely" read the *Carib News* or *Caribbean Life*, more so the *Caribbean Life* because it is a free publication with a more extensive circulation. Copies of the *Caribbean Life* can be found in various locations ranging from the frequented fast food Chinese-American stores to the modest convenience stores. One doesn't even have to be a patron to quickly grab a copy of the *Caribbean Life* placed at a pile by the entrance to the shops. However most residents preferred to receive and share information through less formal means:

> I call my brother at home and of course I have friends who reads those papers anything that comes up they call me and say J— did you know that such and such happened my friends also keep me up to date, but I don't read the *CaribNews*. [14]

If, on those rare occasions, they acquired any news from home through more formal means, it was either through the papers from the respective islands which can be found at the newsstands located at busy intersections such as Church and Utica or Utica and Eastern Parkway, the location of the annual Caribbean Carnival. Such locations may have copies of the less circulated *Carib News*. Clarke was aware of the partial futility of such formal means and it was her adaptation of the "village" or small town trait that bolstered her campaign. She would often meet her constituents and Caribbean immigrants from other districts with an openness and warm attitude resembling kin, something seen as atypical for a public servant/diplomat but customary when greeting a neighbor at home.

Such behavior often stirs fond memories of their home countries and emboldens residents in this east Flatbush community when they experience it which is not surprising considering what it evokes:

> I remember . . . an elderly person maybe 80 years sitting on a sidewalk with maybe 200 dollars on a stack of each paper and not a police officer in sight and that money is safe there. You would never see a police officer with a nightstick and there is that interaction where people respected the police because they were like their brother, you were a family you were a relative not that you had to know the individual but from top down you had to respect the citizen and the citizen had to respect you that was an ongoing relationship an unwritten contractual relationship.[15]

In this case, Afro-Caribbean residents apparently accepted Clarke's interpretive representation of what is Caribbean, a humble well-spoken servant that often escorted official guests from Caricom, the Economic and Political Union of countries in the Caribbean, in her city council district making sure that she was visibly seen with the overseas officials to reinforce her alliance with constituents who may have interests, nostalgic or otherwise, with their home countries; thereby, reinforcing their identity and imputing their cultural footprint in the East Flatbush neighborhood. Thus it appeared that Clarke had an advantage as her support base was growing with residents within Major Owens' Congressional District.

As the summer of 2000 approached, Major Owens' campaign (Friends of Major Owens) rented an office on Eastern Parkway and Utica Avenue. Meanwhile the Clarke 2000 team was functioning one mile west at Montgomery and Nostrand. During the course of this political contest, members of the Clarke campaign, whose office was opened more than twelve hours a day, were heavily attending the multiple block parties and public forums by making rounds to block association meetings which were often held outside in resident's driveways if Una Clarke was unable to attend. Meanwhile, the Owens contingent piled leaflets on unmanned tables and hired a full time staff consisting of workers from New Jersey who maintained the formal business hours of 9 a.m. to 5 p.m. with very little circulation throughout the community. For this incumbent, much of the canvassing was left to the neighborhood-based established political clubs in which members and District Leaders, those who head the neighborhood-based clubs, would familiarize residents with local political campaigns and public officials, in essence, the political clubs are to bridge the gap between the community and local politics. However, what often happens with established political clubs that are ensconced in formalized political machines is their communal complacency and change in focus. For example, Krase and LaCerra

(1991) reported that in the beginning Madison Club members in Brooklyn often involved direct contact with constituents. Club operatives often knew their voters and were engaged in their day to day activities. However, this changed as the interest of local clubs in the community diminished to a focus on campaign contributions and generating ties with municipal unions. These political outposts to the community often become relics of a mobilized past as in the case of one political club during the Clarke-Owens campaign. Around the corner of this club's office, residents did not know who their District Leader was nor were they familiar with the title of District Leader or its formal name, State Committee Person. They were neither familiar with the concept of a political club nor were they in contact with any of its members. As Krase and LaCerra (1991) noted, such unfamiliarity with the populous marked the end of the Madison club and perhaps marked the waning influence of a political incumbent. Sensing the pernicious route of his campaign, Owens hired entrenched, communal savvy "old timers" from his heavily contested election in 1982. The Owens campaign office remained open and active after typical business hours for the remainder of the race, a stark contrast to its previous operation. The veterans of the Owens campaign engaged in the "old-fashioned" canvassing done by the political bosses of long ago. Due to attrition, many of the Owens supporters of the past were no longer present and there was a need to garner new support with the primary just weeks away. "Contracts" were made between the altered "Friends of Major Owens" committee and entrenched urban political operatives in the areas fortified by Clarke 2000. The agreement involved nocturnal flyer "lit drops" to private homes days before the primary of a smiling Una Clarke standing next to a grinning Mayor Rudolph Giuliani days before the primary in September of 2000. Residents who were not familiar with the campaign were aware of the racial tensions garnered between Giuliani and the black community at-large in New York City due to two racially charged incidents of that time which became problematic for the Clarke 2000 campaign contributing to her defeat.[16]

In essence, the tactic of canvassing, highlighting pedestrian activity, contributed to the African American incumbent's victory and almost a loss. Residents developed a shared sense of identity with insurgent Una Clarke facilitated by their shared Afro-Caribbean identity. Canvassing, as being a pedestrian act, enables collaborative work as residents and candidates express sentiments that highlights shared awareness and meanings. It was the canvassing that enabled the incumbent to understand and develop shared meanings with those in the community. This highlights the importance of an uncertainty reduction as residents are able to develop a social connection with those whom they perceive as socially removed from them.

DISCUSSION AND CONCLUSION

The "sensory sociality" which involves and an understanding of how people construct their urban environments by overlaying structure and agency with an emphasis on the embodied phenomenological experience is obtained, in part, through the process of walking as part of a collaborative experience (Pink 2008). This ethnographic practice has been engaged by urban sociologists since the days of Robert E. Park and others (Hughes 1984) under the name of Participant Observation (Becker 1958). It is worthwhile and interesting to note that Howard Becker, in the beginning of his instructional essay, indicated that the researcher as participant observer: "gathers data by participating in the daily life of the group or organization he studies . . . he is studying to see what situations they ordinarily meet and how they behave in them" (Becker 1958: 652). The reflexive work appears as a natural outgrowth of the process in which the researcher must "learn how the group members define him" (Becker 1958: 655). His concern, not dissimilar to the more recent studies, was for researchers to understand their implied role from informants and how it may jeopardize validity and access. A logical outgrowth of this understanding, particularly for urban-based community research, is for the researcher to comprehend how residents perceive their neighborhoods. This not only involves walking, but an array of mobile activity in the presence of and in collaboration with others in an effort to understand, through embodied experience, the multiple meanings of a community.

Political candidates have to address this as well; for all intents and purposes they play a similar role with ethnographers in permeating "the field" to "access" votes to give the appearance of being trustworthy through canvassing. A more successful effort involves engaging in the lived-experience of potential constituents through an embodied phenomenological collaboration of place-based identity through sharing stories or remembrances of home in terms of island identity and various visual and verbal importations and interpretations in the United States. Historically, and even in the present, incumbents often attempt this through political clubs which are mostly informal community-based groups whose main purpose is to mobilize a loyal constituency to fulfill this role. This diluted form of canvas by proxy becomes less ineffective once an aggressive insurgent desires to run and circulate the community. Once this happens and residents begin to make an island affiliation with the candidate, a labeling process can begin where the latter is known as "Trini," "Yardie" or addressed on first name bases in either case an informal kin-like relationship is begun and residents will perceive less of a barrier between them and the political hopeful. In East Flatbush, the casual is preferred to the formal as most residents favor approaching an elected official who is willing to attend their block association meeting, block party and does not mind strolling the main commercial strips to engage in on-the-spot impromptu conversation, a normative practice with consequences for those who violate them.

The evaluative characteristic which makes political candidates vulnerable to public assessment is similar to the research process that ethnographers experience. Canvassing and permeating the field are strikingly similar with a major exception. As a legal prerequisite, political candidates must reside in the community they wish to represent and are assumed to have a certain familiarity with the normative, hence, cultural components that are the web of a community's structure which allegedly gives them an "insiderness" to their permeating component in contrast to a researcher who may live outside of the community. However, this does not exempt either from being mobile, preferably through foot-traffic, and actively practicing and sharing in the daily events of residents. As Pink (2008) observed, "by attending to the sensoriality and materiality of other people's ways of being in the world . . . we can . . . [attune] our bodies, rhythms, tastes, ways of seeing and more to theirs . . . and thus feel that we are similarly emplaced" (2008: 193). This can only be possible if the candidate becomes an ethnographer and rediscovers their own community.

NOTES

1. There are hundreds of islands in the Caribbean. For the purposes of this research I will primarily be referring to those whose ancestry can be traced to the African continent. I use the terms Afro-Caribbean and Caribbean interchangeably to refer to black immigrant groups or those who identify themselves as such. In New York City this group has primarily settled in the East Flatbush, Flatbush and Crown Heights sections of Brooklyn and is largely comprised of Jamaicans, those from Trinidad and Tobago, Haiti, Guyana and the smaller islands of the Caribbean economic community (CARICOM) such as St. Kitts and Nevis. Unless explicitly noted in the text, I will refer to English-speaking and non-English speaking West Indian groups as a whole.

2. Although he did not document his entry into the field Jonassen's article emphasized the cultural factors in the spatial trends of a Norwegian Settlement in the metropolitan area of New York City. He noted that, in contrast to a strictly "biotic" or economic based trend of social forces which include rising real estate values due to business development that Norwegians settled in areas of the city which reflected their cultural roots. Thus, since Norway is a bucolic fishing and boating culture, Norwegians who migrated here during the late nineteenth and early twentieth century often sought areas that were characterized by greenery and close access to the sea or waterway. Rather than emphasizing the push factors of economic growth and residential development Jonassen suggests that there was a pull factor of residential preference in which the residents moved to areas that were strongly influenced by

their cultural roots. Thus, through field research he was able to find evidence suggesting the resilience of community.

3. On July 16, 1961, a 16-year-old black male named James Powell was shot and killed by a police lieutenant Thomas Gilligan. Four days of rioting ensued as the police, NAACP, Core and local ministers tried to cease the violence.

4. Krase and LaCerra call Kasinitz's ethnicity entrepreneurs old style machine politicians or "power brokers." The latter took advantage of the immigrants' fear of government and the bureaucratic process in order to provide patronage services for whatever personal gains (economic or political) they could acquire.

5. Field Notes, July 2001.

6. In all of the interviews that I scheduled over the phone I was told by the respondent that my time would be limited to fifteen minutes or less only to have them extend to an hour or more. I learned not to challenge the lack of time availability only to accept it in an attempt to later pry as much information I could gain once the interview started. Once I asked questions and urged for extra information most if not all of the respondents were willing to divulge. My point was to have them play the role as teacher and I as student which most of them could not resist.

7. Field Notes, August 29, 2000.

8. Many grills are located in front of restaurants where the food is sold. However, "independent contractors" are prevalent and pay proprietors rent for sidewalk use in front of their establishments.

9. Field Notes, September 15, 2002.

10. Reggae singer from Jamaica.

11. Interview, July 23, 2000.

12. Field Notes, September 20, 2001.

13. The "dollar cars" or jitney vehicles are a continuous presence in this East Flatbush community as an informal alternative means to the mass transit system. Often the drivers conveniently ignore the rules of the road and receive encouragement from potential passengers who "create" their own "bus" stops by either standing at any corner or off the sidewalk between two parked cars.

14. Interview, April 14, 2000.

15. Interview, July 15, 2000.

16. The Amadou Diallo and Patrick Dorismond cases were well known. Amadou Diallo was an African immigrant who was shot forty times by a special tactical unit of white police officers while Patrick Dorismond was a Haitian immigrant shot and killed as a result of struggle with an undercover New York City police officer posing as a drug addict.

REFERENCES

Anderson, Elijah. 1990. *Streetwise*. Chicago: University of Chicago Press.

Anderson, Elijah. 1999. *Code Of The Street*. New York: W.W. Norton.

Anderson, Ralph E. and Irl Carter. 1984. *Human Behavior In The Social Environment: A Social Systems Approach*. 3rd ed. New York: Aldine de Gruyter.

Basch, Linda. 1987. "The Vincentians and Grenadians: The Role of Voluntary Associations In Immigrant Adaptation To New York City." Pp. 159–93 in *New Immigrants in New York*, edited by Nancy Foner. New York: Columbia University Press.

Becker, Howard. 1958. "Problems Of Inference And Proof In Participant Observation." *American Sociological Review* 59(1): 652–60.

Bendiner-Viani, G. 2005. "Walking Emotion And Dwelling." *Space And Culture* 8(4):459–71.

Britton, Marcus. 2008. "My Regular Spot: Race and Territory In Urban Public Space." *Journal Of Contemporary Ethnography* 37(4):442–68.

Burgess, Ernest. [1925] 1967. "Can Neighborhood Work Have A Scientific Basis." Pp. 142–55. in *The City: Suggestions for Investigation of Human Behavior in the Urban Environment*, edited by Robert E. Park and Ernest W. Burgess. Chicago: University of Chicago Press.

Cannato, Vincent J. 2001. *The Ungovernable City*. New York: Basic Books.

Caro, Robert. 1975. *The Power Broker*. New York: Vintage Books.

Cressey, Paul G. 1932. *The Gold Coast and The Slum*. Chicago: University of Chicago Press.

Chisholm, Shirley. 1970. *Unbought and Unbossed*. Boston: Houghton Mifflin.

Churchill Jr., Christian J. 2005. "Ethnography As Translation." *Qualitative Sociology* 28(1):3–24.

Demerath, Loren, and David Levinger. 2003. "Social Qualities Of Being On Foot: A Theoretical Analysis of Pedestrian Activity, Community And Culture." *City & Community* 2(3):217–37.

Duneier, Mitchell. 1999. *Sidewalk*. New York: Farrar, Straus and Giroux.

Durr, Marlese. 2009. "A Small Town Life." *Ethnography* 10(2-3):387–403.

Fong, Timothy P. 1994. *Suburban Chinatown: The Remaking of Monterey Park*. Philadelphia: Temple University Press.

Fox, Renee C. 2004. "Observations And Reflections Of A Perpetual Fieldworker." *Annals of the American Academy of Political and Social Science* 595(1): 309–26.

Gans, Herbert. 1962. *Urban Villagers*. New York: Free Press.

Gans, Herbert. 1999. "Participant Observation In The Era Of 'Ethnography.'" *Journal of Contemporary Ethnography* 28(5):540–48.

Gardner, Carol Brooks. 1980. "Passing By: Street Remarks, Address Rights And The Urban Female." *Sociological Inquiry* 50(3):328–56.

Gieryn, Thomas. 2000. "A Place For Space In Sociology." *Annual Review Of Sociology* 26(1): 463–96.

Glaser, Barney G. and Anslem Strauss. 1967. *The Discovery Of Grounded Theory*. New York: Adline De Gruyter.

Goffman, Erving. 1963. *Behavior in Public Places*. New York: Free Press.

Goodman, Roy M. 1974. *Community Boards*. New York: NY State Charter Revision.

Harrington, Brooke. 2003. "The Social Psychology of Access in Ethnographic Research." *Journal of Contemporary Ethnography* 32(5):592–625.

Hsiung, Ping-Chun. 2008. "Teaching Reflexivity In Qualitative Interviewing." *Teaching Sociology* 36(3):211–22.

Hughes, Everett C. 1984. *The Sociological Eye*. New Brunswick, NJ: Transaction Books.
Jackall, Robert. 1997. *Wild Cowboys: Urban Marauders And The Forces Of Order*. Cambridge, MA: Harvard University Press.
Jacobs, Jane. 1961. *The Death and Life of Great American Cities*. New York: Vintage Books.
Jenks, Chris, and Tiago Neves. 2000. "A Walk On The Wild Side: Urban Ethnography Meets The Flaneur." *Cultural Values* 4(1):1–17.
Jonassen, Christen. 1949. "Cultural Variables In The Ecology Of An Ethnic Group." *American Sociological Review* 14(1):32–41.
Kalmijn, Matthijs. 1996. "The Socioeconomic Assimilation of Caribbean American Blacks." *Social Forces* 74(3):911–30.
Kasinitz, Phillip. 1992. *Caribbean New York*. Ithaca, NY: Cornell University Press.
Katz, Jack. 1997. "Ethnography's Warrants." *Sociological Methods & Research* 25(4):391–423.
Kleinman, Sherryl, Martha Copp, and Karla Henderson. 1997. "Qualitatively Different: Teaching Fieldwork To Graduate Students." *Journal of Contemporary Ethnography* 25(4):469–99.
Krase, Jerome and LaCerra, Charles. 1991. *Ethnicity and Machine Politics*. Lanham, MD: University Press of America.
Kusenbach, Margarethe. 2003. "Street Phenomenology: The Go-along As Ethnographic Research Tool." *Ethnography* 4(3):455–85.
Levitt, Peggy. 1998. "Social Remittances: Migration Driven Local-Level Forms of Cultural Diffusion." *International Migration Review* 32(4): 926–48.
Lofland, Lyn. 1998. *The Public Realm*. New York: Aldine de Gruyter.
Logan, John and Harvey Molotch. 1987. *Urban Fortunes: Political Economy Of Place*. Berkeley: University of California Press.
Malinowsky, Bronislaw. 1967. A *Diary In A Strict Sense Of The Term*. New York: Harcourt Brace.
Marwell, Nicole P. 2007. *Bargaining For Brooklyn: Community Organizations In The Entrepreneurial City*. Chicago: University of Chicago Press.
May, Tim, Beth Perry, Patrick Le Galès, Saskia Sassen, and Mike Savage 2005. "The Future of Urban Socioloogy." *Sociology* 9(2):343–70.
Mollenkopf, John H. 1992. *A Phoenix In The Ashes*. Princeton, NJ: Princeton University Press.
Model, Suzzane. 1991. "Caribbean Immigrants." *International Migration Review* 25(2):248–76.
Model, Suzzane. 1993. "Ethnic Niche And The Structure Of Opportunity Immigrants And Minorities In NYC." Pp 161–93 in *The Underclass Debate: Views From History*, edited by Michael B. Katz. Princeton, NJ: Princeton University Press.
Patillo, Mary. 2003. "Negotiating Blackness, For Richer Or For Poorer." *Ethnography* 4(2):61–93.
Pink, Sarah. 2008. "An Urban Tour: The Sensory Sociality Of Ethnographic Place-Making." *Ethnography* 9(2):175–96.
Rieder, Jonathan. 1985. *Canarsie: The Jews and Italians of Brooklyn against Liberalism*. Cambridge, MA: Harvard University Press.

Sanjek, Roger. 1998. *The Future Of Us All: Race and Neighborhood Politics in New York City*. Ithaca, NY: Cornell University Press.

Sengupta, Somini. 1996. "Neighborhood Report: Brooklyn Up Close: A Snapshot Of Influence Of Caribbean." *New York Times,* August 18, sect. 13, p. 8.

Slack, Sara. 1968. "Children Are First." *New York Amsterdam News,* September 28, p. 27.

Scott, Greg. 2004. "It's A Sucker's Outfit: How Urban Gangs Enable And Impede The Reintegration Of Ex-convicts." *Ethnography* 5(1):107–40.

Toennies, Ferdinand. 1957. *Community and Society*, edited by Charles P. Loomis. East Lansing: Michigan State University.

Venkatesh, Sudhir. 2002. "Doing The Hustle: Constructing The Ethnographer In The American Ghetto." *Ethnography* 3(1):91–111.

Vickerman, Milton. 1999. *Crosscurrents: Caribbean Immigrants And Race*. New York: Oxford University Press.

Whyte, William F. [1943] 1981. *Street Corner Society*. Chicago: University of Chicago Press.

Wirth, Louis. 1938. "Urbanism As a Way Of Life." *American Journal Of Sociology* 44(1):1–24.

Wolfinger, Nicholas H. 1995. "Passing Moments: Some Social Dynamics Of Pedestrian Interaction." *Journal Of Contemporary Ethnography* 24(3):323–40.

Zorbaugh, Harvey. 1937. *The Gold Coast And The Slum*. Chicago: University of Chicago Press.

14

The Dual Roles of Brighton Beach

A Local and Global Community

Phyllis Conn

In southwestern Brooklyn along the shore between Manhattan Beach and Coney Island lies a small community that is part ethnic enclave and part seaside resort. Brighton Beach has been home to entertainments of all kinds, including horse racing, vaudeville, sports competitions, and dance halls, in addition to the primary attraction of the Atlantic Ocean beach. As Little Odessa, it has also been home to the most concentrated Russian-speaking community in the United States and a vibrant Jewish émigré community, and it has been home to members of an organized crime family. At times events and trends in Brighton Beach have reflected changes specific to New York City; in other respects, it has truly been an international community, reflecting and affected by events thousands of miles away. Brighton's development from the mid-nineteenth century onward echoes in many ways the dual roles played by Brooklyn: a unique urban area with its own distinct patterns, and a global community that resonates with world events.

A RESORT COMMUNITY GROWS

Brighton Beach was founded as a seaside resort just after the Civil War. Named after the resort in England, the area offered many of the new leisure attractions available to the growing populations of Manhattan and Brooklyn in the second half of the nineteenth century, including swimming, horse racing, and other outdoor activities. Henry Cruse Murphy, one of the area's early developers, was also the founder and owner of the *Brooklyn Daily Eagle*, which ran regular advertisements for the area's attractions, and the owner of the Brooklyn, Flatbush, and Coney Island Railway, which provided transportation to Brighton from Manhattan and northern Brooklyn neighborhoods.

In the early years, thoroughbred horse racing and pari-mutuel betting at the Brighton Beach Racetrack drew the largest crowds and the most money from visitors and investors. However, the racetrack faced a severe downturn in its fortunes when the New York State legislature passed the Hart-Agnew law in 1908 that essentially outlawed racetrack betting as part of a national antigambling movement. Brighton's racetrack owners tried adapting to the new legislation (reducing the amount of the purse, for example, or offering automobile racing instead), but the betting population was far less interested in that type of entertainment ("Brighton's Test a Success" 1908). Within a few years after passage of the Hart-Agnew law, the era of horse racing in Brighton came to an end. When the racetrack hosted games in 1914 to benefit widows and orphans of New York City police officers killed in the line of duty, visitors to the games were reminiscing about "how much 'like old times' was the appearance of the Brighton race track, with the exception of horses and jockeys" ("Police Games Bring $61,000" 1914).

By the 1910s, Brighton largely appealed to two groups: summer visitors interested in the beach, hotels, swimming pools, and theaters, and middle-class families interested in the area's new year-round housing. Real estate investors had already begun developing beachfront properties before the racetrack closed. The Brighton Beach Bath and Racquet Club, founded in 1907, claimed to be world's largest beach resort. Club members who wanted to visit the beach passed through the Bath Club's ticket booth and gained access to bath houses where they could change into swimming attire (beachgoers were not allowed to dress or undress on the beach itself). The Bath Club also offered swimming pools, steam rooms, game rooms, team sports, and a band shell that in later years featured performers like Milton Berle, Lionel Hampton, and Tallulah Bankhead.

As the population of Brooklyn grew and transit lines were established, cultural institutions and entertainment venues continued to spread beyond Brooklyn's central business district, following the population into south Brooklyn neighborhoods. The New Brighton Theatre, founded in 1909, featured performers like Al Jolson, who was discovered performing at Brighton; Fred and Adele Astaire; and Will Rogers and his horse. The Brighton Theatre and similar venues in the area were part of the Subway Circuit, where major stars and successful Broadway shows performed in local theaters throughout New York City. At times the Brighton theaters competed with each other. The New Brighton Theatre at Ocean Parkway competed with Brighton Beach Hall, which was owned by interests of the Brooklyn Rapid Transit Company (BRT). At times, the owners of the BRT refused to stop the train at Ocean

Parkway to make it more difficult for riders to get to the New Brighton Theatre. When trains reached the station for the BRT's Brighton Beach Hall, BRT employees told riders to exit the train for the best vaudeville at Brighton ("The Drama to Brighton" 1930).

At the same time, Brighton Beach experienced the surge in residential development that was occurring throughout Brooklyn, with housing built for middle-class families seeking to move from overcrowded areas in Manhattan. Brighton saw consistent residential development through the 1910s, 1920s, and 1930s, with new residents attracted by the ease of transportation to Flatbush and Manhattan, ocean views, and the offerings of the Boardwalk. The Brighton subway line, extended with full service to Manhattan in August 1920, cost only five cents under Contract No. 4 between the BRT and the New York Public Service Commission. The availability of inexpensive rapid transit encouraged middle-class families to take advantage of rapid transit to Manhattan while living in neighborhoods like Brighton and Harlem ("Coney Island Now Five-Cent Ride" 1920; "New Subway Link Opens" 1920).

The developer Brighton-by-the-Sea Inc. built bungalows along the old racetrack and the oceanfront and through the area. Called the Riegelmann bungalow colonies after Edward Riegelmann, Brooklyn borough president from 1918–1924, these homes were built on small lots, often about forty feet by forty feet, along pedestrian lanes and on local streets. Riegelmann promoted the interests of Brighton, Coney Island, and the waterfront area in many ways, perhaps most notably through his efforts to renovate and extend the Boardwalk along the waterfront up to Manhattan Beach.

Through the 1920s the question of ownership of the Boardwalk, responsibility for repairs, and general questions of beach access periodically rose to the level of legal challenges. The developer Joseph Day had claimed for years that his businesses controlled the main beachfront and tried to prevent unauthorized, namely unpaid, access to the beach. In 1921, Samuel Gumpert, manager of the Brighton bungalows and the Parkway Baths, built a fence there to prevent guests of the Brighton Beach Hotel from entering the area he claimed belonged to the Baths. Reigelmann claimed that the city owned the entire Boardwalk and arranged to have the fence torn down. However, the Brooklyn Supreme Court determined that summer that that part of the Boardwalk had been built and maintained by the Brighton-by-the-Sea Company, then the owner of the baths, and could not be a public thoroughfare, granting the company the right to maintain a fence there ("City Loses Beach Fight" 1921; "City Razes Fence" 1921).

With the exception of the Riegelmann bungalows (some of which remain in Brighton in the twenty-first century), single-family housing began disappearing in the 1930s. Developers instead began construction of multifamily buildings in response to Brighton's rapidly increasing real estate values. New apartment buildings in art deco style were built along Brightwater Court and nearby streets (New York City Department of City Planning 2010b). Within short order, some of these buildings became home to large numbers of retired garment workers, especially Russian and Ukrainian Jewish immigrants who had arrived in New York during the immense immigration wave before and after World War I, generally referred to as the first wave of Russian and East European immigrants.

Brighton remained a resort and leisure area as well as a residential neighborhood through the 1920s. The Brighton Beach Baths, bought by the developer Joseph P. Day from the Brighton Development Company in 1922, and other clubs and bathhouses brought up to a million visitors a day to the beach during the summer months. The clubs and hotels hosted competitive athletic events that also drew visitors. Swimming competitions were especially popular, with results published regularly in *The New York Times* and other newspapers. The Brighton Beach Theatre began offering dramatic performances in summer 1930 with a Moss Hart-George S. Kaufman play, "Once in a Lifetime" ("The Drama to Brighton" 1930).

ECONOMIC DECLINE, 1930s–1970s

Brighton began a slow decline in the 1930s, initially due to its own popularity as a summer resort and then due to the availability of alternative summer destinations in the New York area and elsewhere. This change was visible as early as 1933, as *The New York Times* commented on the reasons for the decline of Coney Island and nearby beaches and resort areas like Brighton. First, day visitors suffering from the effects of the Depression found ways to spend less money at the beach: they brought their own food and drinks, they wore beach attire under kimonos or bathrobes so they did not need to pay to change in the bath houses, or they changed quickly under the Boardwalk or elsewhere. Second, new amusements offered similar entertainment either closer to home or on a larger scale: star performances could be seen at local movie theaters, and movies also offered full-blown reenactments of historical scenes that had previously been offered at the Brighton theaters on a smaller scale. Third, most of the amusements and attractions at Brighton and Coney Island had either been discredited (like the tallest man or the wild man) or had been outstripped by what had become everyday technology (like elevators in skyscrapers in midtown buildings, or riding in automobiles or small airplanes, supplanting the thrill of the Ferris wheel and the roller coaster) (Harlow 1933).

Brooklyn Rapid Transit, which had owned and operated the Brighton Beach Hotel, a few Brighton theaters and other businesses as well as transportation lines, was deeply affected by inflation after World War I and then by the Depression. The company was still bound to Contract No. 4, limiting the cost of a subway ride to five cents; even with continually increasing ridership, the company's income was far outpaced by expenses for repairs, maintenance, fuel, and other items. After twenty years of financial difficulties, BRT finally collapsed and the City of New York acquired BRT's assets in 1940 under Mayor Fiorello La Guardia. Throughout the 1930s, similar difficulties were affecting other private businesses that had profited from their access to and maintenance of the beach as a result of reduced numbers of visitors and reduced spending by those who did visit the area.

In 1938, responsibility for all of New York City's beaches and boardwalks was transferred from the borough presidents to the New York City Parks Department under Robert Moses. That summer, Moses proposed buying eighteen acres of Brighton Beach along six city blocks of the beachfront. The proposed purchase price, which was approved by the City Planning Commission and the Board of Estimate and finalized in 1941, was $75,000, although the land was valued at $750,000. The purchase also included 173 acres of land under water along the Brooklyn shore. Both parcels were previously owned by the real estate developer Joseph P. Day ("Brighton Baths in 99-Year Lease" 1955; "City Plans to Add 18 Acres" 1938).

Within a few years, Moses had the Boardwalk extended from Coney Island through the Brighton area and new white sand brought for the beaches to replace the brown sand that had become a signature of the waterfront ("Coney Island to Get White Beach Sand" 1941). In the 1950s, Moses sought to extend the Boardwalk to the Manhattan Beach esplanade, which would have made the Boardwalk stretch across almost the entire Brooklyn seashore. Manhattan Beach residents opposed the plan, wanting to preserve their quiet residential community. The Board of Estimate agreed with local residents and the Brooklyn borough president, John Cashmore, and Moses did not add the esplanade to the Parks Department holdings.

Through the Depression, the war, and the postwar years, Brighton and Coney Island experienced a gradual but consistent loss of summer visitors to places like the newly constructed Jones Beach (built by Moses and opened to the public in 1929) and, after World War II, to newly opened amusement parks like Disneyland (opened in 1955) and other new theme parks. The advent of air conditioning in public places and private homes reduced the need for New Yorkers to turn to the beaches for relief during hot summer days and nights.

As Brighton's role as a summer resort diminished, the year-round population also changed as a result of wider trends, beginning with the effects of the

Depression and continuing after World War II. Extended immigrant families facing unemployment moved in together to save money on housing and food, creating greatly overcrowded pockets of poverty throughout Brighton. After World War II, echoing the general economic decline in Brooklyn with the out-migration of the middle-class to the suburbs, year-round residents in Brighton Beach were increasingly poor, elderly, and disadvantaged. A large number of those who remained in the area were elderly Jewish émigrés from Russia and Ukraine who had arrived in New York as young people, especially those who had worked in the garment district in the 1910s and 1920s (Orleck 2001:123).

In the years just before and after World War II, Brighton increasingly become home to East European Jews escaping persecution and those who had survived the war. This second wave of Russian and East European immigrants first had to gain admittance to the United States under the severely limited quotas established by the 1924 Immigration Act. After they arrived, these second-wave immigrants turned to aid agencies like the New York Association for New Americans (NYANA, founded in 1949) and the Hebrew Immigrant Aid Society (HIAS, an international organization founded in 1881). Leaders at both organizations believed that it would be easier for Jewish refugees to move to neighborhoods with large, settled Jewish populations like Brighton Beach. They believed that long-term residents would help the new arrivals find employment and adjust to the new culture, and that the new arrivals would feel more at home in a community with shared traditions, culture, and languages. This hope for an easy transition in Brighton was met with the reality of tension between first-wave and second-wave immigrants. In part the tensions were due to competition for low-cost housing and jobs. At first, some among the first-wave also questioned the extent of the Holocaust and Jewish suffering in Europe described by the second wave before widespread publication of photographs and stories from the concentration camps confirmed their stories. Later, some first-wave immigrants asked second-wave immigrants how they survived when so many others died (Abramovitch and Galvin 2002: 97).

Refugees arriving in Brighton Beach after World War II included large numbers of Ukrainians from the Black Sea area who were especially attracted to living on the waterfront. Along the way, the area became known as Little Odessa. With the arrival of large numbers of immigrants lacking English-language skills, many street names in Brighton were changed to numbers (for example, Brighton 1st Street, Brighton 2nd Street, and so on) (Brooklyn Public Library n.d.). Postwar refugees included the parents of singer-songwriter Neil Diamond, who, like many refugees at the time, opened their own business (Diamond's dry goods store). Neil Simon later used his family's experiences in the neighborhood to write *Brighton Beach Memoirs*.

In 1964, the Amalgamated Clothing Workers of America opened the Warbasse apartment houses on the west side of Brighton Beach. Named after Dr. James Peter Warbasse, a former physician and surgeon who became active in the cooperativist movement in the 1910s, the Warbasse houses attracted still more retired immigrant garment workers to Brighton Beach, most of whom were from Eastern and Southern Europe. According to Annelise Orleck (2001:124), by the late 1960s, Brighton Beach had the nation's second-largest concentration of senior citizens, outranked only by Miami Beach.

As middle-class residents left the area, Robert Moses saw Brighton Beach and nearby Coney Island as appropriate places to build some of the new low-income housing projects of the postwar period, particularly housing under New York's Mitchell-Lama program, established in 1955, directed toward middle-income and moderate-income residents. To build new housing, some of the older buildings had to be demolished. Single-family homes were converted to single-room-occupancy (SRO) dwellings for welfare families, the elderly, and other disadvantaged populations. This trend especially affected the streets north of Brighton Beach Avenue (Brooklyn Public Library n.d.; "For A Brighter Brighton Beach" 1992). The Brighton Theatre at Ocean Parkway and Brighton Beach Avenue was demolished in early 1955 to make way for new apartment houses. That year, Joseph P. Day, Inc. leased the Brighton Beach Baths property and twenty-one acres on Brighton Beach Avenue, Coney Island Avenue, and the public beach and Boardwalk, to the Oxford Manor Corporation for ninety-nine years, with an aggregate rental reported as more than $20,000,000. This lease was reported to be the largest deal in the Day corporation's history to that time (Bennett 1955).

Alexander Muss, the real estate investor who headed Oxford Manor and himself the son of a first-wave Russian immigrant, built an apartment community called Seacoast Towers A and B on six acres of the site next to the Baths (Fowler, "Brighton Beach Gets Mid-City Air" 1962a; Fowler, "Tall Apartment Houses Rise" 1962b). Muss was able to complete two large towers with a total of 591 apartments before New York City's 1961 rezoning changes went into effect (Oser 1989). Muss continued to operate the Brighton Beach Baths, later renamed the Brighton Beach Bath and Racquet Club, and held the lease for the remaining land as he planned more development.

Plans to build more housing for persons of low and moderate incomes encountered delays that lasted years, such as the plan to build public housing from Brighton Second to Brighton Fourth Streets in the late 1960s and 1970s (Fried, "City is Accused," 1975b). Among the reasons for long delays with this project, Oceanfront Gardens, were disagreements about which groups the project should serve (with most Brighton residents advocating housing for the elderly and others involved in public housing advocating for moderate income families); disagreements about the size and purpose of a proposed community center within the building; and problems in designing the project to meet requirements from the Mitchell-Lama program and federal housing subsidy programs (Fried 1972; Fowler 1974). The city's fiscal crisis of the 1970s delayed, downsized, or derailed housing projects throughout the five boroughs including a project in Brighton, the Scheuer House, a housing development for the elderly proposed for Brighton Seventh Street and the Boardwalk (Fried 1975a).

Those housing developments that were completed like Seacoast Towers, Mitchell-Lama housing, and other new tall rental apartment buildings kept the population density high in the area. However, Brighton Beach suffered from problems that were affecting similar New York neighborhoods in the late 1960s and 1970s. Connected to the city's spiraling financial crisis, Brighton's general financial decline began by affecting area businesses. There were empty storefronts on Brighton Beach Avenue for the first time. Crime began to increase as Oceanside Avenue became known as regular place for picking up prostitutes (New York City Department of City Planning 2010b). Landlords began to avoid regular maintenance of their buildings. Abandoned buildings were burned down. Decrepit SROs north of Brighton Beach Avenue became home to drug dealers and prostitutes. Drugs became a consistent problem, as did youth gangs and vandalism. Arson attributed to teenagers destroyed a wooden pavilion and 1500 square feet of the boardwalk in July 1974 ("Suspicious Fire" 1974). Pat Singer, then the Co-Director of the Brighton Neighborhood Association, remembered the 1970s: "We weren't exactly a Bedford-Stuyvesant, but it was definitely a pocket of poverty here" (Rangel 1986). Housing problems continued through the 1980s and early 1990s: one SRO had 243 pending violations in March 1992 (Tabor 1992c). Those who remained in the area through this time experienced substantial increases in reported unemployment rates.

SOVIET POLICY TOWARD JEWISH EMIGRATION

Russian and East European immigration to Brighton Beach through the twentieth century reflected Soviet immigration policy and the effects of the culture's anti-Semitism. Jewish Ukrainians suffered in particular from the effects of Josef Stalin's collectivization and grain requisitioning policies, including the death of five million Ukrainians during the famine of 1933. Another two million Ukrainians, mostly Jews, died during World War II in daily battles or in large-scale massacres like the one at Babii Yar where

70,000 Jews were executed. After the Soviet Union broke off diplomatic relations with Israel in 1953, only a few hundred Soviet Jews were allowed to emigrate each year. Denial of an exit visa was frequently followed by loss of employment and sometimes loss of citizenship. As unemployed workers, these "refuseniks" (otkazniki) then faced further persecution under Soviet laws against "parasitism" enacted in the late 1950s and 1960s.

As the numbers of those seeking to emigrate grew, Soviet authorities became concerned about the loss of highly educated and trained professionals, assuming that Jews in the Russian, Ukrainian, and Baltic republics were mostly urban and well-educated. Their assumption was based on historical anti-Semitic perceptions that Jews were over-represented in professional and intellectual circles and tended to live in cities to practice their professions. Soviet authorities were also concerned that allowing large numbers of well-educated Jews to emigrate might encourage other well-educated professionals to emigrate.

In 1972 the Soviet government enacted a "diploma tax" that required emigrants to repay the state for their public schooling—between $5,000 and $25,000, depending on the emigrant's level of education. At the same time, the U.S. and Soviet governments were negotiating improved trade terms as part of détente. Some American politicians worked to link détente to human rights concessions, including a repeal of the diploma tax. Leonid Brezhnev was inclined to repeal the tax and permit larger-scale emigration in order to gain the benefits of détente, but there was opposition within the Politburo.

According to recently released records from Soviet archives, the Committee for State Security (KGB) conducted a study to determine whether in fact Jews seeking exit visas were urban and well-educated. The study concluded that, contrary to popular opinion, only 13 percent of Soviet Jews emigrating at that point had college educations, and most were from Georgia and the Baltic Republics, not from the Russian Republic or Ukraine (the former Jewish Pale of Settlement). The study helped Brezhnev convince other members of the Politburo to reach a compromise in spring 1973: the diploma tax would remain in effect, but it would not be enforced (Beckerman 2010; Krasikov 2007).

Larger numbers of Soviet Jews requested exit visas through the 1970s. As détente fell into place, most received permission to emigrate (Krasikov 2007). In the early 1970s, Israel was still the only state that Soviet Jews could emigrate to, and family reunification was still the only acceptable reason for emigration (Orleck 1999). The numbers of Soviet Jewish émigrés continued to hold strong through the 1970s and 1980s. American politicians had clearly linked Soviet-American trade to human rights, including the right to emigrate, most notably in the 1975 Jackson-Vanik Amendment to the Trade Act of 1974 (Cornell University Law School Legal Information Institute 2010). In addition, Soviet authorities at times saw exit visas as an opportunity to rid the nation of dissidents or others considered undesirable.

The ultimate destination for many of these émigrés was the United States, which represented freedom from the persecution and shortages of the Soviet Union and freedom from the constant ethnic tensions and violence of the Middle East. By 1975, the possibility of immigrating to the United States began drawing more well-educated Soviet Jews who were from Russian and Ukrainian cities—the same groups who had been suspected of seeking immigration earlier. In 1976, despite strongly expressed concerns among Israeli officials that Israel would lose educated professionals to the United States, HIAS and most American Jewish aid societies were helping Soviet Jews navigate the road from the Soviet Union through Vienna, then Rome, then on to the United States.

The number of Jewish and Ukrainian applicants for exit visas swelled through the 1980s in response to the anti-Semitism of the Russian right-wing party Pamyat' and still further after the explosion at the nuclear plant in Chernobyl, Ukraine in 1986. This immigration was so large that, according to Ines Miyares (1998), Soviet refugees between 1975 and 1994 became the third-largest refugee group entering the United States since World War II (after Southeast Asian refugees and Cuban refugees). By 1990, the Soviet Union was ranked the fifth most common country of origin for New York City immigrants (New York City Department of City Planning 2004). The destination of many of those third-wave immigrants was Brighton Beach.

ETHNIC ENCLAVE, 1971–1991

Third-wave émigrés headed toward Brighton Beach for several reasons. First, several not-for-profit aid organizations that helped in resettlement (such as NYANA) were concentrated in New York City, and it was easier for the organizations and the refugees to find housing and employment in local neighborhoods. Second, refugees and aid organizations expected New York and especially Brighton Beach to provide greater employment opportunities for Soviet émigrés, given both the size of the city and the existence of established communities of large Russian and Jewish populations. Third, some refugees had friends or relatives among those already living in Brighton Beach from whom they hoped to receive assistance and companionship. Fourth, Soviet émigrés after 1975 were increasingly likely to come from large cities in the Soviet Union and sought similar urban environments in the United States, especially with easily accessible public transportation as available in Brighton Beach (Chiswick 1993). Fifth, due to the economic decline in Brighton Beach through the 1970s, the area offered available housing and high vacancy rates, resulting in lower housing costs for new arrivals. Sixth, in the late 1970s and 1980s Soviet émigrés included a significant population of older men and women. Since Brighton Beach had already become home to a large elderly population formerly from the Soviet Union, the city had already established social services that the new older émigrés were expected to need. According to Orleck (2001), by the late 1990s about one-third of Soviet émigrés in New York City were elderly; according to U.S. Census data (U.S. Census Bureau 2000 American Community Survey), by the late 1990s the average age in much of the Brighton Beach area was over fifty.

The U.S. government anticipated social problems in the integration of other large refugee populations at this time, creating the Office of Refugee Resettlement in the Refugee Act of 1980 to help newly arrived refugees learn the English language and become economically independent as quickly as possible (Office of Refugee Resettlement n.d.). Most of those active in refugee assistance expected that Soviet émigrés would not need much federal assistance, believing that Jewish aid societies and previous Russian and Ukrainian émigrés would help the new arrivals (Chiswick 1993). However, the relationship between the new arrivals and the previous group of immigrants quickly became tense in areas like Brighton Beach. The tensions were part of a common trend among immigrant groups, where new arrivals and previous immigrants of the same ethnicity or religion assume that they will share values, traditions, and cultures, but in fact find that their experiences in the home country and in the new country differ significantly, leading to unexpected and often serious tensions. With the new Soviet émigrés in Brighton Beach, the main issue was the question of Jewish identity.

Jewish immigrants who had arrived in Brighton Beach as refugees from the Holocaust or as World War II survivors expected that the new arrivals would be actively involved in Jewish communal life at synagogues, Jewish community centers, Jewish day schools, and similar places (Chiswick 1993). Most of the third-wave arrivals had received assistance from Jewish aid organizations based on their religious identity. The older group tended to see it as their duty to teach the new arrivals how to "be Jewish," recognizing that the new émigrés' practice of religion had been repressed in the Soviet Union.

However, new émigrés resented the implication that they were not Jewish enough, since they had been persecuted for Jewishness while living in the Soviet Union. They saw the older group's actions as another form of harassment for their particular type of Jewish identity, which was sometimes dominated by nationality (for example, Russian or Ukrainian), sometimes by religion (Jewish), and sometimes by class based on former occupation or socioeconomic status in the Soviet Union. Among the third wave émigrés, older men and women particularly resented the fact that while they had been in the Soviet Union suffering from famine, Stalin-era purges, employment and education quotas, discrimination, shortages, and fallout from the Chernobyl power plant, the World War II-era immigrants had been living peacefully in the United States (Orleck 2002).

In many respects, the experience of Soviet émigrés from 1970 to 2000 was similar to other immigrant and refugee groups. Many experienced downward occupational mobility. Looking at statistics for all Soviet émigrés, about two-thirds had been employed in professional fields in the Soviet Union, but only one-third found similar jobs in the United States (Chiswick 1993). Nearly all émigrés had been at least partially employed in the Soviet Union, but on arrival in the United States, perhaps 20 percent became unemployed or retired. Those most likely to be employed in New York's thriving economy in the 1980s and 1990s, especially in jobs similar to those they held in the Soviet Union, were immigrants who adapted to their new home most easily, which were usually the younger immigrants, those with greater English-language fluency and those in the best health. Those who were older, who lacked college degrees, who had poor health (for example, as a result of the Chernobyl disaster), or who lacked relatives in the United States tended to experience downward occupational mobility or face unemployment, similar to the patterns for other immigrant groups in New York City. In addition, gender and class played significant roles: male émigrés tended to find employment more easily than females, and professionals and urban émigrés tended to find more employment opportunities than less-educated and more rural émigrés. Older professional women generally faced difficult employment prospects. Many older third-wave professional women had been pediatricians in the Soviet Union, and their training tended to be perceived as substandard by U.S. medical professionals (Orleck 2001:120–21).

Immigrants from Byelorussia, Moldova, and the Baltic republics tended to have stronger English language skills. Stronger English language skills generally corresponded with a higher level of education earned in the Soviet Union. Those who were older at the time of their immigration tended to have weaker English language skills. According to Chiswick (1993), the positive effect of previous education on English-language skills was smaller among Soviet émigrés than among other refugee groups, and the negative effect of age was larger. Enclaves with a strong ethnic density like Brighton Beach tend to attract and create populations that are less fluent in English, further delaying the development of English-language skills.

With the arrival of third-wave immigrants in Brighton Beach, the area began a slow revitalization, mirroring efforts to revitalize other Brooklyn neighborhoods in the 1970s, including the downtown business district. In Brighton Beach, in part this gradual rebirth was the result of the new population arriving to the area, and in part it represented the work of organizations like the Brighton Neighborhood Association, created in 1977, working to force landlords to tend to repairs, fighting crime and drugs in the area, seeking a greater police presence, and promoting economic development. Real estate values began to increase; the streets were filled with families with children alongside elderly second-wave immigrants. Brighton Beach Avenue, under what were now called the B and Q trains, saw ownership of its nightclubs, restaurants, and markets transitioning to third-wave immigrants. The gradual shift toward a younger population can clearly be seen in the decline of the Brighton Beach Baths. In 1971, the Baths had 13,000 members; by 1987, there were only 3,270. Between 1986 and 1987, 587 "regulars" died or left the area. The older population was leaving for warmer climates, especially Florida, or moving to nursing homes, or passing away (Freedman 1987). After several years of proposals and protests, the State Supreme Court finally granted the developer Alexander Muss and Sons the right to tear down the Baths to build a new housing complex in 1994.

Supermarkets and groceries served as community centers, highlighting the distinctions between the Soviet Union and its consumer shortages and the abundance of consumer goods in the U.S. Most members of the third wave who became active in politics supported the Republican Party, especially with the election of Ronald Reagan in 1982. This group saw Reagan as the embodiment of opposition to communism and the Soviet Union, and eventually saw him as the primary force behind the collapse of the Soviet Union and end of the Cold War. Dr. Oleg Gutnick, a politically active physician from Kazakhstan, said, "Back in the USSR, when I heard how the Soviet government was denouncing Ronald Reagan, I knew there was something special about him. I was a Reaganite before I was even American" (*Gotham Gazette* 2001: np).

THE FOURTH WAVE

The breakup of the Soviet Union in 1991 and changes in federal immigration law beginning in 1990 dramatically affected Soviet immigration patterns. The 1990 Immigration Act maintained priorities for immigration based on family reunification and refugee and asylum status, but also made it easier to gain entry based on employment and diversity visas. For most former Soviet émigrés, family reunification and refugee status were the basis for their immigration applications. While third-wave immigrants had far outnumbered the second wave, the number of fourth-wave immigrants (after 1991) was larger still. By 2000, the former Soviet Union was ranked fourth among the sources of immigration in New York City, up from fifth in 1990. Over 80 percent of all refugees in New York City in the 1990s were from the former Soviet Union. The increased number of post-Soviet era refugees helped to push the percentage of refugees among all immigrants in New York City up to 14 percent in the 1990s from 5 percent in the 1980s (New York City Department of City Planning 2004). Post-Soviet refugees generally received assistance from organizations that had helped previous generations, including HIAS, which received matching grants from the federal government (Miyares 1998).

It was critical for post-Soviet immigrants to qualify for refugee status under the 1980 Refugee Act both for entry into the United States and for assistance after they arrived. Refugees, in contrast to immigrants, qualified for cash and noncash assistance from the federal government, as well as assistance with training and housing from aid organizations. Refugees sometimes also qualified for incentive capital for opening businesses. This was especially helpful to well-educated post-Soviet refugees who were competing with other first-generation immigrants who had arrived in New York under the new federal immigration laws.

Some of the trends from the third wave carried over to the fourth wave. Ukrainian immigration to New York City remained strong. Ukraine was the only European country of origin that was in the top five source countries for immigrants in each borough in 2000. Russian immigrants continued to flock to Brooklyn, home of almost two-thirds of Russian-born immigrants in New York (New York City Department of City Planning 2004). Russian immigration to Brooklyn from 1990 to 1994 was approximately seven times as large as the 1980s Russian immigration (Miyares 1998). Russia ranked seventh among the countries of origin of foreign-born residents of Brooklyn. Russian-born immigrants were found in large numbers in Gravesend-Homecrest, Sheepshead Bay-Brighton Beach, and Bay Ridge-Bensonhurst. The Russian "corridor" from Brighton Beach north to Gravesend held the largest concentration of Russians in the United States by 2001 (*Gotham Gazette* 2001; Miyares 1998). Brighton Beach maintained its immigrant-oriented character, with over 50 percent foreign-born in 2000 (New York City Department of City Planning 2004). For Ukrainian-born immigrants, almost eight tenths were living in Brooklyn, with the largest numbers in the Sheepshead Bay-Brighton Beach area. Ukraine ranked fifth among countries of origin of Brooklyn's foreign-born.

As the third wave grew through the 1970s and 1980s, a subculture of Russian criminal activity emerged in Brighton Beach. Referred to as the Russian Mafia, at first it seemed that these groups were loosely organized and engaged in activities similar to those of other criminal gangs in the neighborhood (drugs and small weapons sales, gambling, and prostitution) as well as fraud involving Medicare payments, counterfeit credit cards, and gasoline taxes (Iverem 1987; Raab 1994). They were attracted to Brighton Beach because of its proximity to international airports, especially John F. Kennedy International; because they hoped to blend in with other Russian émigrés; and because Brighton still possessed a stock of vacant apartment buildings where the gangs could meet (Orleck 2001:131).

The Russian Mafia in Brighton Beach grew still more through the 1990s after the breakup of the Soviet Union brought ever-increasing numbers of former Soviets to New York. By the early 1990s, the gangs became more violent, more closely tied to criminal activity in the Soviet Union and other countries, and more tightly organized. Without the travel restrictions that had been imposed by Soviet authorities, the new Russian Mafia was able to travel easily between Brooklyn, Berlin, Amsterdam, and other major émigré centers, as well as Moscow and similar cities in Russia (Kinzer 1994). In Brighton Beach, their crimes expanded into money laundering, large-scale narcotics trafficking, and extortion. By early 1994, the U.S. Justice Department placed the Russian Mafia on the highest investigative priority and the FBI created an office exclusively dedicated to Russian criminals in New York (Raab 1994).

Fourth-wave post-Soviet immigrants reflected some demographic changes from previous groups. In the 1990s and 2000s, new immigrants tended to identify less often with the Jewish religion, and sometimes in fact were not Jewish but Christian or not identified with any religion. Often their main motive for immigration was economic rather than to escape persecution, although most managed to qualify for immigration under refugee status. Previous Jewish immigrants sometimes referred to this group as the "sausage immigration" in derisive terms (Idov 2009). Fourth-wave Russian immigrants tend to come to the United States with a strong educational background (New York City Department of City Planning 2004). An estimated thirty percent of Russian-born immigrants held a graduate or professional degree in 2009, compared to ten percent for the U.S. population as a whole (United States Census American Community Survey 2007–2009). In contrast to the third wave, female refugees who arrive with high levels of education and professional and technical backgrounds generally expect that they will find ways to use their training in the United States. The fourth wave is also more likely to be well-traveled than earlier immigrants.

Fourth-wave immigrants tend to support the Democratic Party rather than the Republican Party like the third wave. As expressed by a Moscow-born immigrant, Inna Stavitsky, who became property manager for the Jewish

Association for Services for the Aged (JASA), "People understand the Democratic line is much closer to the needs of immigrants" (*Gotham Gazette* 2001). Compared to earlier generations, more post-Soviets had some English-language training before entering the U.S., which may have accelerated their acculturalization and improved their employment opportunities, although Russians and especially Ukrainians were more likely than most other immigrant populations in New York City to consider themselves not proficient in English (Miyares 1998; New York City Department of City Planning 2004).

Alec Brook-Krasny in many ways exemplies the fourth wave. He was born in Moscow, where he graduated with a degree in economics and engineering from Moscow Technological Institute. An early member of the fourth wave, he immigrated to the United States in 1989, where he continued his education at Columbia University Graduate School of Business while living in Brighton Beach. Within a few years, he became a local business owner, earning accolades from the New York City Council and owners of similar businesses. He ran for political office as a Democrat at the local and state level, becoming the first elected U.S. official born in the former Soviet Union. He was a founding director of The Council of Jewish Émigré Community Organizations (COJECO), which coordinates over three dozen local Russian émigré organizations (Assemblymember Alec Brook-Krasny n.d.; Belenkaya and Monahan 2006).

Brook-Krasny's election to the State Assembly in 2006 reflected some of the contemporary tensions in Brighton Beach and surrounding neighborhoods. His main opponent in the Democratic primary, Ari Kagan, is also an émigré from the former Soviet Union. In the leadup to the primary, there were rumors first that Kagan had been a member of the Communist Party, and second that he had served in or been linked to the KGB (Belenkaya and Monahan 2006). Kagan acknowledged that he had been a Party member, but said that he had never had any ties to the KGB. Kagan charged Brook-Krasny with becoming too much part of the local Democratic establishment, drawing figurative parallels to establishment candidates in the former Soviet Union. When the primary votes were counted, Kagan appeared to have carried the day in Brighton Beach (where recent voter registration drives have brought thousands of Russian voters to the polls), but Brook-Krasny won the primary through support from Irish, Italian, and African-American voters in the Assembly district beyond Brighton (Saltonstall 2006).

Brook-Krasny, like many successful fourth-wave immigrants, may well find that his future lies outside Brighton Beach. In many ways Brighton's recent history resembles the stories of Little Italy and the Lower East Side as newer generations find that their economic, social, and cultural needs are not met in the neighborhoods of previous generations. This may be especially true for Brighton Beach, since the second and third waves built an émigré community that reflects a nation that no longer exists. Post-Soviet émigrés are far more likely to see Brighton Beach as a place to live for a short time on first arrival, if at all, before moving to Staten Island, New Jersey, Westchester, or other surrounding areas. Since their identities are often less Russian and Jewish than cosmopolitan, they find less need to live in a neighborhood that has identified itself based on language, nationality and religion. Those who move away come back to Brighton Beach for events like bar and bat mitzvahs, weddings, and holy day celebrations, as well as occasional shopping for authentic foods. As one recent Russian émigré put it, Brighton Beach is "like a museum" (Tavernise 2003).

That perspective belies significant demographic and economic changes underway in Brighton Beach. Some of the area's businesses that had fallen into decline after World War II have been rejuvenated. The Oceana Theater was transformed into the home of a restaurant and caterer on the ground floor and a performing arts center that features Russian performers on the second floor (Brooklyn Community Boards 2010). Brighton Beach Avenue remains the main commercial strip in the area, and its clubs and restaurants have been featured in prominent local reviews. The housing stock in the area has maintained high occupancy rates in large part due to the continued attraction of immigrants to the area. The City's Department of City Planning estimated in 2000 that perhaps 70 percent of recent occupancy in the Brighton Beach area was attributed to immigrant households (New York City Department of City Planning 2004). Indeed, of all local businesses, the housing stock has seen perhaps the most significant change with the construction of the Oceana-Muss condominiums on the former site of the Brighton Baths.

The Oceana-Muss condominiums, like numerous housing developments before, took years to bring to fruition. The site had been part of the package leased from the Day Corporation in 1955 by Alexander Muss. Alexander's son, Stephen Muss, bought the site in 1980, and began the process of acquiring city approval for a development plan in 1989. Although Stephen Muss received city approval in 1993, building was never begun due in large part to the recession that year. A few years later, Joshua Muss, Stephen's cousin, took over the project and reworked its size and cost, resubmitting it for City approval. The Muss Development Company broke ground for the Oceana in summer 1999 (Oser 1999). Between 1989 and 1999, some Brighton residents supported the proposed project, particularly local business owners who saw it as a potential draw for more customers. Others protested that the project would overload the local sewage system, remove desperately needed parking spaces in a congested area, change the nature of the neighborhood, or place nearby homes in shadows due to the proposed height of the project's buildings

(Tabor 1992a; Tabor 1992b). The Oceana opened in stages as buildings were completed, quickly selling its apartments and penthouses.

The residents at the Oceana represent the new multiethnicity of Brighton Beach. Although many are first- or second-generation Russian, Ukrainian, and/or Jewish, typical of Brighton's past, others have arrived from other former Soviet republics or other nations. Just after the Oceana opened, new buyers were mostly from the Brighton area, reflecting the long wait in the neighborhood for the complex to open. However, by 2001, residents' countries of origin already included Italy, the Dominican Republic, Hong Kong, and China (Oser 2001).

Multiethnicity at the Oceana reflects trends in Brighton Beach overall. The area now includes families that identify themselves as Afro-American, Mexican, South American, Korean, Chinese, Arabic, Turkish, and Puerto Rican (New York City Department of City Planning n.d.). Out of 73,993 residents five years old or older identified in zip code 11235 in Sheepshead Bay-Brighton Beach in 2000, significant minorities spoke Spanish or Spanish Creole (6,148) or Chinese (4,159). In contrast to trends from earlier times, only one-third of that population reported speaking Russian, and just under 2,000 residents reported that they spoke Yiddish (New York City Department of City Planning 2004).

As of 2011, visitors to Brighton Beach could see Jewish temples and Islamic mosques on the same street (New York City Department of City Planning 2010b). A Spanish Evangelical Pentecostal Church was located on Neptune Avenue near Coney Island Avenue; a Metro PCS telephone store on Brighton Beach Avenue displayed window signs in Russian, English, and Spanish; and newsstands on Brighton Beach Avenue carried the traditional Russian and Jewish newspapers as well as publications like El Diario, Diario de Mexico, El Vocer del Puerto Rico, and Impact de New York. On Brighton 11th Street near Oceanview Avenue, a series of small shops included a deli, a clothing store, and a cell phone store that catered to English speakers; a Georgian bread store offering the traditional Georgian khachapuri; and a car service named after the Virgin of Guadalupe (La Morenita).

Brighton's multiethnicity can easily be seen in local cuisine. In 2005, the Kashkar Café on Brighton Beach Avenue served Chinese specialties prepared by Muslim Uighurs, while Bulgarian cheeses were available at M & I International Foods and Korean market owners sold traditional Korean snacks as well as fruits and vegetables (McEvers 2005). In 2011, a walk up Coney Island Avenue from Brighton Beach Avenue brought a visitor past Tacos El Ray, the No Pork Halal Kitchen, and a Chinese restaurant advertising that it was strictly Halal. Customers at the Starbucks store on Brighton Beach Avenue (in the long-established center of the Brighton business district) spoke in

English, Russian, and various bilingual blends. Still, the Brighton Bazaar on Brighton Beach Avenue played Russian radio on the loudspeaker and carried products that were primarily Russian and kosher.

Many of Brighton Beach's main challenges in 2011 are common among older neighborhoods. The infrastructure was originally designed for small streets, one-family homes, and bungalows and has become overwhelmed by the dense population that has settled there. The local Community Board has lobbied for changes in zoning ordinances to prevent developers from tearing down smaller homes to build more apartment buildings, hoping to avoid more pressure on the schools, the streets, the sewage system, and other local services. One of the biggest problems continues to be parking in the neighborhood, both for residents and for customers of local restaurants and businesses; this problem has only worsened with the rejuvenation of some businesses (New York City Department of City Planning 2010b).

Yet for all this recent growth, the area generally remains poor. In 2000, the median household income in 1999 dollars was under $45,000, in part because of the number of SROs still found in Brighton. There is a significant homeless population, especially near and under the Boardwalk. Despite the fact that the area under the Boardwalk has been largely fenced in, homeless men and women continue to seek shelter there. The fires that sometimes occur under the wooden Boardwalk may be caused by someone cooking or lighting a fire for warmth (New York City Department of City Planning 2010). The continued presence of poverty and homelessness in the area is due in part to its large elderly population and in part a reflection of recent increases in the number of those living below the poverty line in New York City overall.

CONCLUSION

With the fourth wave of post-Soviet immigrants and recent changes in Brighton Beach, the neighborhood continues to echo both global trends and developments found throughout Brooklyn. From a global perspective, Brighton Beach continues to reflect events in the former Soviet Union with recent immigrants often remaining closely connected to families and businesses in their former homes. This transition to transmigration is occurring in immigrant neighborhoods throughout Brooklyn and indeed in urban areas worldwide.

Brighton Beach also reflects local trends. Gentrification (as seen in new condominium developments) and the entry of more immigrants from Mexico follow trends in Brooklyn as well as citywide trends. Brighton's transition from an isolated ethnic enclave to a more diverse community mirrors changes in Little Colombia in Queens and the Lower East Side in Manhattan, as previously ethnic communities become multiethnic neighborhoods. In addition, recent and planned development of Brighton's waterfront properties can be seen as part of renewed interest in waterfront development in other Brooklyn neighborhoods like Coney Island, Greenpoint, and Williamsburg.

Growing out of large-scale immigration and development of local resources, the history of Brighton Beach illustrates themes repeated in many other Brooklyn communities: a clear identity linked to a group of immigrants; small businesses run in an urban environment; the importance of the waterfront; dependence on public transportation; periods of decline and periods of revitalization; the continued presence of cultural institutions that reflect the identity of the neighborhood; and the role of real estate developers in helping to determine the future of the area. In some ways, the periods of decline in the past helped to preserve the historical identity of Brighton Beach, leaving the small businesses, bungalows, and street names intact. As real estate development continues in the twenty-first century, Brighton Beach will undoubtedly continue to lose much of its particular identity as a Russian Jewish neighborhood as national business chains replace small businesses, as high-rise apartment buildings replace bungalows, and as a multiethnic middle class moves into the area. In that way, too, Brighton Beach represents the greater story of Brooklyn.

ACKNOWLEDGMENTS

This article was written with the support of the St. John's University Writing Initiative under the leadership of Dr. Anne Geller and Dr. Maura Flannery.

REFERENCES

Abramovitch, Ilana, and Seán Galvin, eds. 2002. *Jews of Brooklyn*. Hanover, NH: University Press of New England for Brandeis University Press.

"Apartment Project to be Scaled Down." 1989. *The New York Times*, January 19, p. B2. Retrieved January 2, 2011 (http://proquest.umi.com).

"Assemblymember Alec Brook-Krasny: Biography." 2011. Retrieved February 11, 2011 (http://assembly.state.ny.us/mem/?ad=046&sh=bio).

Barron, James. 1990. "Luxury Brooklyn High-Rise Fails to Win Planning Votes." *The New York Times*, January 23, p. B3. Retrieved January 4, 2011 (http://proquest.umi.com).

Beckerman, Gal. 2010. *When They Come for Us, We'll be Gone: The Epic Struggle to Save Soviet Jewry*. Boston, MA: Houghton Mifflin Harcourt.

Belenkaya, Veronika, and Rachel Monahan. 2006. "Russian Pols Slinging Mud." *Daily News*, September 14. Retrieved March 5, 2011 (http://proquest.umi.com).

Bender, Marilyn. 1972. "Many U.S. Jews are Torn Over Trading with Soviet." *The New York Times*, October 16. Retrieved January 4, (http://proquest.umi.com).

Bennett, Charles G. 1955. "Our Changing City: Flatbush-Coney Island: Once-Dowdy Section is Acquiring Polish and Population." *The New York Times*, July 25. Retrieved February 12, 2011 (http://proquest.umi.com).

"Brighton's Baths in 99-Year Lease: Corporation Headed by Muss to Operate Brooklyn Area Developed by Jos. P. Day." 1955. *The New York Times*, July 13. Retrieved February 13, 2011 (http://proquest.umi.com).

"Brighton Beach Growing: Fifteen Apartments Completed Or Under Construction." 1928. *The New York Times*, December 9, p. W16. Retrieved February 15, 2011 (http://proquest.umi.com).

"Brighton Beach History." 2011. Brooklyn Public Library: Our Brooklyn. Retrieved January 25, 2011 (www.brooklynpubliclibrary.org/ourbrooklyn/brightonbeach/).

"Brighton Beach Neighborhood Association: Social Services. New York." 2010. Retrieved January 29, 2011 (www.brightonbeach.com/About_Us.html).

"Brighton's Test a Success: Racing Begins a New and Promising Growth Under Changed Conditions." 1908. *The New York Times*, July 13, p. 11. Retrieved February 20, 2011 (http://proquest.umi.com).

Brooklyn Community Boards, Brooklyn. *Community District Needs: Fiscal Year 2011*. DCP #10-05 Winter 2010 Vol. New York: New York City Department of City Planning, 2010. Accessed online January 29, 2011.

Chiswick, Barry R. 1993. "Soviet Jews in the United States: An Analysis of their Linguistic and Economic Adjustment." *International Migration Review* 27:260–85.

"City Leads World in Beach Resorts: New Yorkers have a Score of Splendid Pleasure Grounds to Choose from. Sunburn for Everybody. Long, Tedious Journeys from Town for a Summer Outing no Longer Necessary." 1912. *The New York Times*, July 28, p. X5. Retrieved February 16, 2011 (http://proquest.umi.com).

"City Loses Beach Fight: Court Enjoins Riegelmann from Interfering with Boardwalk Fence." 1921. *The New York Times*, June 19, p. 16. Retrieved February 16, 2011 (http://proquest.umi.com).

"City Plans to Add 18 Acres to Coney; Purchase of Brighton Beach Tract and Extension of Boardwalk Proposed by Moses." 1938. *The New York Times*, August 5, p. 19. Retrieved January 25, 2011 (http://proquest.umi.com).

"City Razes Fence in Bathhouse Row: Contends that Barrier at Brighton Beach is on Municipal Property." 1921. *The New York Times*, April 5, p. 7. Retrieved January 25, 2011 (http://proquest.umi.com).

"Coney Island Now Five-Cent Ride." 1920. *The New York Times*, May 2, p. 12. Retrieved January 27, 2011 (http://proquest.umi.com).

"Coney Island to Get White Beach Sand: Whole Front to be Covered—Boardwalk Will be Extended." 1941. *The New York Times*, February 21, p. 21. Retrieved February 13, 2011 (http://proquest.umi.com).

Cooper, Ann. 1989. "U.S. Foresees Rush in Soviet Emigres." *The New York Times*, July 13, p. A1. Retrieved February 12, 2011 (http://proquest.umi.com).

Cornell University Law School Legal Information Institute. 2010. United States Code: Title 19, Subchapter IV—Trade Relations with Countries Not Receiving Nondiscriminatory Treatment, As of 2010. Ithaca, NY: Cornell University Law School Legal Information Institute. Retrieved February 26, 2011 (www.law.cornell.edu/uscode/html/uscode19/usc_sup_01_19_10_12_20_IV.html).

"The Drama to Brighton: After Twenty Years the Acrobats make Way for the "Legitimate" Theatre." 1930. *The New York Times*, June 1, p. X3. Retrieved February 13, 2011 (http://proquest.umi.com).

Finder, Alan. 1986. "Brighton Beach is Proposed Site of New Project." *The New York Times*, June 25, p. B3. Retrieved February 12, 2011 (http://proquest.umi.com).

"For a Brighter Brighton Beach." 1992. *The New York Times*, July 6, p. A12. Retrieved February 13, 2011 (http://proquest.umi.com).

Fowler, Glenn. 1962a. "Brighton Beach Gets Mid-City Air." *The New York Times*, September 2. Retrieved February 11, 2011 (http://proquest.umi.com).

Fowler, Glenn. 1962b. "Tall Apartment Houses Rise on Seashore at Brighton." *The New York Times*, March 24, p. 36. Retrieved February 24, 2011 (http://proquest.umi.com).

Fowler, Glenn. 1974. "Mitchell-Lama Supporters Cool to Aid Tied to Poor Outsiders." *The New York Times*, January 31, p. 37. Retrieved February 24, 2011 (http://proquest.umi.com).

Freedman, Samuel G. 1987. "A Gradual Fade to Memories at the Baths." *The New York Times*, July 25, p. 33. Retrieved February 22, 2011 (http://proquest.umi.com).

Fried, Joseph P. 1972. "Feud Stymies Housing Start in Brighton: A Feud Stymies Brighton Housing." *The New York Times*, January 9, p. A1. Retrieved March 1, 2011 (http://proquest.umi.com).

Fried, Joseph P. 1975a. "9 Housing Projects in Doubt." *The New York Times*, November 9, 1975, p. NJ12. Retrieved February 15, 2011 (http://proquest.umi.com).

Fried, Joseph P. 1975b. "City is Accused of Stalling on Housing." *The New York Times*, August 31, p. 71. Retrieved March 1, 2011 (http://proquest.umi.com).

Gwertzman, Bernard. 1973. "Soviet is Said to Stop Jamming of Voice of America." *The New York Times*, September 13, p. 16. Retrieved February 28, 2011 (http://proquest.umi.com).

Harlow, Alvin F. 1933. "The Coney of the Thrills Tones Down." *The New York Times*, August 13, p. SM6. Retrieved January 20, 2011 (http://proquest.umi.com).

"History Of Amalgamated Warbasse Houses." 2008. Amagalmated Warbasse Houses, Inc. Retrieved February 27, 2011 (http://amalgamatedwarbassehouses.com/history.htm).

Idov, Michael. 2009. "The Everything Guide to Brighton Beach." *New York Magazine*, April 12. Retrieved January 25, 2011 (http://nymag.com/guides/everything/brighton-beach/).

Iverem, Esther. 1987. "Russian Immigrant Dies Gangland-Style in Car in Brooklyn." *The New York Times*, November 19, p. B9. Retrieved February 16, 2011 (http://proquest.umi.com).

Kinzer, Stephen. 1994. "The Long Shadow of the Russian Mob." *The New York Times*, December 11, p. E1. Retrieved February 20, 2011 (http://proquest.umi.com).

Krasikov, Sana. 2007. "Declassified KGB Study Illuminates Early Years of Soviet Jewish Emigration." *Forward*, December 14. Retrieved March 3, 2011 (www.forward.com/articles/12254/).

"Leasing Coney Island Lands." 1882. *The New York Times*, October 8, p. 14. Retrieved January 20, 2011 (http://proquest.umi.com).

Lewine, Edward. 1999. "From Brighton Beach to America; the Wave of Immigrants Began 25 Years Ago. Soon Russian Filled the Streets. Now, the Tide is Ebbing." *The New York Times*, March 14. Retrieved February 28, 2011 (http://proquest.umi.com).

McEvers, Kelly. 2005. "Close-Up on Brighton Beach." *The Village Voice*, May 3, p. 1. Retrieved February 11, 2011 (www.villagevoice.com/2005-05-03/nyc-life/close-up-on-brighton-beach/).

Miyares, Ines M. 1998. "Little Odessa—Brighton Beach, Brooklyn: An Examination of the Former Soviet Refugee Economy in New York City." *Urban Geography* 19: 518–30.

Navarro, Mireya. 1989. "Aging Baths in Brighton Face Demise." *The New York Times*, November 29, p. B1. Retrieved February 11, 2011 (http://proquest.umi.com).

"New Subway Link Opens: Service Started through Queens and Montague Street Tubes." 1920. *The New York Times*, August 1, p. 12. Retrieved February 9, 2011 (http://proquest.umi.com).

New York City Department of City Planning. 2004. *The Newest New Yorkers 2000: Briefing Booklet: Immigrant New York in the New Millennium*. New York: New York City Department of City Planning. Retrieved January 30, 2011 (www.nyc.gov/html/dcp/pdf/census/nny_briefing_booklet.pdf).

New York City Department of City Planning. 2009. *Brighton Beach Zoning Text Amendment (Withdrawn)*. New York: New York City Department of City Planning. Retrieved January 29, 2011 (www.nyc.gov/html/dcp/html/brighton_beach/index.shtml).

New York City Department of City Planning. 2010a. *Community District Needs, Borough of Brooklyn; Fiscal Year 2011*. New York: New York City Department of City Planning.

New York City Department of City Planning. 2010b. *Brooklyn Community District 13 Community District Profile*. New York: New York City Department of City Planning. Retrieved February 1, 2011 (www.nyc.gov/html/dcp/pdf/lucds/bk13profile.pdf).

Orleck, Annelise. 1999. *The Soviet Jewish Americans*. Westport, CT: Greenwood Press.

Orleck, Annelise. 2001. "Soviet Jews: The City's Newest Immigrants Transform New York Jewish Life." Pp. 111–40 in *New Immigrants in New York*, edited by N. Foner. New York: Columbia University Press.

Orleck, Annelise. 2002. "Waves upon the Sand: Jewish Immigrant Life in Brighton Beach." Pp. 83–106 in *Jews of Brooklyn*, edited by I. Abramovitch and S. Galvin. Hanover, MA: Brandeis University Press.

Oser, Alan S. 1989. "A Revised Proposal for the Baths Site." *The New York Times*, November 19, p. R9. Retrieved February 5, 2011 (http://proquest.umi.com).

Oser, Alan S. 1999. "A Developer Reshapes a Brighton Beach Project." *The New York Times*, September 5, p. RE9. Retrieved January 26, 2011 (http://proquest.umi.com).
Oser, Alan S. 2001. "On Brighton Beach, a Tide of Immigrants." *The New York Times*, December 23, p. RE1. Retrieved January 31, 2001 (http://proquest.umi.com).
"Police Games Bring $61,000 for Heroes." 1914. *The New York Times*, June 27, p. 3. Retrieved February 15, 2011 (http://proquest.umi.com).
Raab, Selwyn. 1994. "Influx of Russian Gangsters Troubles F.B.I. in Brooklyn." *The New York Times*, August 23. Retrieved March 1, 2001 (http://proquest.umi.com).
Rangel, Jesus. 1986. "In Brighton Beach, Another Time of Change." *The New York Times*, July 23, p. B1. Retrieved February 10, 2011 (http://proquest.umi.com).
Saltonstall, David. 2006. "Russian Rise: Primary Wins Prove Ethnic Groups Gaining Clout." *Daily News*, September 24. Retrieved March 5, 2011 (www.nydailynews.com/archives/news/2006/09/24/2006-09-24_russian_rise_primary_wins_pr.html).
Schwartz, David. 2001. "Mitchell-Lama." *Gotham Gazette*, April 9. Retrieved February 27, 2011 (www.gothamgazette.com/iotw/mitchell-lama/).
"Searchlight on Campaign 2001: New York City District 47." 2001. *Gotham Gazette*, August 29. Retrieved January 29, 2011 (www.gothamgazette.com/searchlight2001/dist47.html).
Shabad, Theodore. 1972. "47 Soviet Jews Petition Podgorny on Exit Taxes." *The New York Times*, September 4, p. 3. Retrieved February 5, 2011 (http://proquest.umi.com).
Shabad, Theodore. 1973. "105 Jews, Refused Exit Visas by Soviet, Appeal to Congress." *The New York Times*, April 13, p. 5. Retrieved February 5, 2011 (http://proquest.umi.com).
Simon, Neil. 1995. *Brighton Beach Memoirs*. New York, NY: Plume.
Smith, Hedrick. 1972. "Soviet Jews' Monthly Departure Rate Reported at 2,500 Despite Slackening." *The New York Times*, August 22, p. 3. Retrieved February 11, 2011 (http://proquest.umi.com).
"Suspicious Fire Destroys Part of Boardwalk Pavilion." 1974. *The New York Times*, July 28, p. 40. Retrieved February 18, 2011 (http://proquest.umi.com).
Tabor, Mary. 1992a. "Brighton-by-the-Sea Housing Proposal Endures a Stormy Hearing." *The New York Times*, June 11, p. B1. Retrieved February 5, 2011 (http://proquest.umi.com).
Tabor, Mary. 1992b. "Dismal Section of Brighton Beach Resists Revival Efforts." *The New York Times*, March 16, p. B3. Retrieved February 28, 2011 (http://proquest.umi.com).
Tabor, Mary. 1992c. "Plan Revised for Brighton by Developer." *The New York Times*, July 20, p. B3. Retrieved February 5, 2011 (http://proquest.umi.com).
Tabor, Mary. 1992d. "Residential Complex for Brighton Beach in Progress, again." *The New York Times*, April 10, p. B2. Retrieved February 11, 2011 (http://proquest.umi.com).

Tabor, Mary. 1992e. "Two Sides Clash Over Project for Brighton Beach." *The New York Times*, May 7, p. B3. May 7 1992. Retrieved February 27, 2011 (http://proquest.umi.com).

Tavernise, Sabrina. 2003. "Too Young, a Russian Enclave is Too Much the Old Country." *The New York Times*, October 8, p. B8. Retrieved February 19, 2011 (http://proquest.umi.com).

Thompson, William C. 2004. *Affordable No More: New York City's Looming Crisis in Mitchell-Lama and Limited Dividend Housing.* New York, NY: New York City Office of the Comptroller.

United States Census Bureau. 2010. "United States—Selected Population Profile in the United States (Russia)." 2007–2009 American Community Survey 3-Year Estimates. Retrieved February 2, 2011 (http://factfinder.census.gov/servlet/IPTable?_bm=y&-geo_id=01000US&-qr_name=ACS_2009_3YR_G00_S0201&-qr_name=ACS_2009_3YR_G00_S0201PR&-qr_name=ACS_2009_3YR_G00_S0201T&-qr_name=ACS_2009_3YR_G00_S0201TPR&-TABLE_NAMEX=&-ci_type=B&-ds_name=ACS_2009_3YR_G00_&-reg=ACS_2009_3YR_G00_S0201:919;ACS_2009_3YR_G00_S0201PR:919;ACS_2009_3YR_G00_S0201T:919;ACS_2009_3YR_G00_S0201TPR:919&-_lang=en&-format=)

United States Department of Health and Human Services Office of Refugee Resettlement. n.d. *The Refugee Act of 1980: 8 U.S.Code 1521.* Washington, DC: Office of Refugee Resettlement. Retrieved March 3, 2011 (www.acf.hhs.gov/programs/orr/policy/refact1.htm).

Vinkurov, Andrey, Dina Birman, and Edison Trickett. 2000. "Psychological and Acculturation Correlates of Work Status among Soviet Jewish Refugees in the United States." *International Migration Review* 34.2: 538–59.

Williams, Lena. 1997. "Brighton Beach Memories, Sold!" *The New York Times*, November 9, p. CY10. Nov 9 1997. Retrieved February 25, 2011 (http://proquest.umi.com).

"World Jewish Aides Meet on Soviet Tax. Special to the New York Times." 1972. *The New York Times,* September 5, p. 5. Retrieved February 24, 2011 (http://proquest.umi.com).

15

Hood Politics

Charter Schools, Race and Gentrification in Fort Greene

Noel S. Anderson

Much of current research on charter schools centers on the impact of race and parent choice (Saporito and Lareau 1999; Stambach and Becker 2006; Tomlinson 1997; Wells, Slayton, and Scott 2002); parents and access to social capital (Goldring and Phillips 2008; Horvat, Weininger and Lareau 2003); and achievement measures (Berends, Goldring, Stein and Cravens 2010; Deluca and Hinshaw 2006; May 2006; Scott and Villavicencio 2009). Yet research is limited on the role of charter schools in the gentrification process in under-resourced urban settings. Traditional public schools are impacted by gentrification as new waves of more affluent parents reintegrate urban neighborhoods and encounter poor performing schools. In the recent past, it was common for gentrifying parents to seek public or private schools outside of the community (DeSena 2009; Freeman 2006). However, gentrifying families are increasingly seeking charter schools as alternative learning environments, the majority of which are being housed in traditional public school buildings in New York City (Smith 2010).

This chapter is taken from a larger case study examining gentrification and school change in Fort Greene. It is based on an analysis of Public School (P.S.) 67, a school that houses one of the more popular charter schools in Brooklyn. P.S. 67 is situated between the Walt Whitman and Ingersoll Public Houses and serves as a zone school for predominately African American children residing in the public housing projects.[1] Historically, P.S. 67 is the site of the first school erected for colored students in Brooklyn established in the mid-1800s. A popular charter school, the Community Roots Charter School (CRCS), was recently founded in 2006 and resides within the P.S. 67 building. Despite that 90 percent of the students in P.S. 67 being black, the Community Roots has a racially diverse student body, with just under 40 percent of the student body being white, the majority of whom reside outside of the housing projects. The difference in racial composition of students attending two separate schools in one building is glaring, creating a DuBoisian dual identity of sorts for P.S. 67. These two schools have very distinct identities, missions, curriculum and differing student populations. Black students, the majority of whom are poor, with 97 percent qualifying for free lunch, isolated to the housing projects, disproportionately attend the traditional public school, P.S. 67. However, located on one floor in the P.S. 67 building is a relatively new, highly sought after charter school, Community Roots Charter School, with just under half its population being white, middle class students from mostly the gentrified community of Fort Greene and other neighboring communities. In the Community Roots Charter School, just 30 percent of the student body qualifies for free lunch, clearly a low-poverty population. Yet the two schools, one black and largely poor, and one surprisingly more white and more resourced, coexist in an historical building in the middle of one of the largest and poorest housing projects in Brooklyn.

In the context of gentrification, some may argue that the establishment of CRCS benefits a previously highly segregated school community by increasing educational options and reintegrating more white and middle class residents into public schools. However, given the limited number of quality public schools in the Fort Greene community and with the increased competition for a small, yet growing number of charter schools, questions emerge about who truly benefits from these educational changes in a gentrified neighborhood. In fact, the demand for charter schools as an alternative to failing traditional public schools has advanced the process of gentrification in previously under-resourced communities, and exacerbated social class divisions.

SCHOOL COMMUNITIES AS POLITICAL SYSTEMS

Bacharach and Mundell (1993) assert that school communities are natural sites of political activity. Many macropolitical studies of school community change look at the role of external interest groups, groups not subject to formal administrative control, applying political pressure attempting to influence the internal operations of schools or a district (Lutz and Mertz 1992; Wirt and Kirst 1997). In these macropolitical studies, interest groups (i.e., parents or community groups) push schools and/or school districts (i.e., school boards, administrators and teachers) to implement some type of desired change (i.e., curriculum, shared decision making). Much of this research centers on a presumed external-internal conflict as the site of examination.

However, Bacharach and Mundell's (1993) framework for analyzing school politics and change allows us to examine the belief systems and logic of action underpinning decision-making as well as behavior in schools. It is through the examination of underlying belief systems and assumptions of decisions the researcher gains better insight into the political dynamics taking place in a school building (Bacharach and Mundell 1993). In the case of P.S. 67 and the CRCS, it allows several questions to be raised in the study: given that two schools share one building, is there a shared or a distinct educational mission and governance structure for the student populations each school serves? Are the teaching and learning, and curricula approaches of each school shared or distinct from each other?

Bacharach and Mundell's (1993) framework is further strengthened by Critical Race Theory (CRT) advanced by educators Ladson-Billings and Tate (1995). CRT is a way of interrogating or uncovering the ways in which race, racism and race-based assumptions and predilections underlie seemingly neutral decision-making practices, educational policies and school protocols from ostensibly objective institutions (e.g., public schools) in society. Therefore it attempts to serve as a lens to examine social phenomena to illuminate the way race "hides in plain sight" (Ladson-Billings and Tate 1995). CRT enables us to look closely at, for instance, how two schools in one school building that are surrounded by a predominately black population of students from the housing projects could have an observable mismatch in populations they are serving, specifically along racial and class lines.

Utilizing these lenses, and through document analysis and selected interviews with parents who have children in both CRCS and P.S. 67, we gain some insight into the politics of gentrification, race and school change in one neighborhood in Brooklyn. We argue that analyzing the change that is taking place at P.S. 67 can increase our understanding of how, in fact, charter schools reinforce the process of gentrification in a neighborhood and compound social class divisions among residents.

THE CHARTER SCHOOL MOVEMENT

Emerging from the politically charged educational choice movement of the 1980s, charter school legislation, now passed in over thirty-eight states, allows individual schools greater autonomy from state education regulations and local district guidelines. Charter school laws generally provide more flexibility in how schools are staffed (e.g., allowing them to hire nonunion, uncertified teachers and nonunionized classified staff), curriculum and education innovations and release from requirements of state laws and court orders governing the use of public funds, including procurement laws (Wells et al. 2002).

In many state and national policy making circles, charter school reform is viewed with an antigovernment sentiment that has become increasingly popular among neoliberals across the country. However, as Wells, Slayton and Scott (2002) state "the charter school movement cannot be simply characterized as a 'neoliberal' reform" (p. 345). Although the movement embraces and furthers many of the central tenets of neoliberal ideology, namely the view that the private market is sufficient to manage and oversee public services, advocates and founders of charter schools represent very different political and philosophical perspectives—from neoconservative members of the religious right to more leftist and progressive educators who seek autonomy from a state-run system to provide viable educational alternatives to students who have not succeeded in the traditional educational system (Wells et al. 2002).

Over the last forty years, advocates for school choice have ranged from civil rights leaders, Black nationalists/Afrocentrists, progressive or free school educators and conservative free-market economists. The types of school choice policies include alternative schools, magnet schools, charter schools, voluntary transfer and open enrollment plans, and tuition voucher programs. These groups have shaped charter school reform from state to state, have run the political spectrum and have garnered bipartisan support from lawmakers. Yet charter school reform under the same state law and guidelines can look dramatically different in different school districts and local school communities.

These broad and divergent historical and ideological roots, coupled with the different political contexts in each state, have led to wide variations in the scope and content of each state's charter school law. In New York State, for instance, the Charter Schools Act of 1998 authorized the establishment of charter schools. The first year of operation for charter schools in New York City was 1999–2000, and twelve schools were operating by 2000–2001. By the 2005–2006 school year, thirty-six more charter schools had opened. By 2009, seventy-eight charter schools were operating, with another twenty-six scheduled to begin in 2010. Brooklyn is one of the boroughs with the fastest growing number of charters in the city, with several more slated to start in Fort Greene/Clinton Hill in 2010 (Smith 2010).

Based on 2010–2011 data in New York City, over 40,000 students attended charter schools in 2010–2011. Over 58 percent are African/Black American, 31 percent are Latino, and 10 percent are classified as "other." The bulk of charter schools are elementary schools, with many of them co-located in a traditional school building. Currently 62 percent of charter schools are located in school buildings, while the remaining 38 percent are in private buildings (Department of Education 2011).

However, across the board, the data highlight that students who attend charters do not fare any better or worse on tests than students who attend traditional public schools (Smith 2010). In fact, other than a different learning environment and school culture, there is no distinguishable difference between the academic performances of students across settings. Furthermore, other than charter schools serving specific religious communities, they are disproportionately created in poor and working-class communities, not in the wealthy, better resourced communities, where traditional public schools tend to already perform well. Despite the questionable nature of the educational outcomes, charter schools are growing in demand and becoming the model of urban school choice, in Fort Greene and other parts of New York City.

GENTRIFICATION OF FORT GREENE

Fort Greene evolved as a neighborhood due to the establishment of the Brooklyn Navy Yard. Developed in 1801, the Navy Yard shaped housing patterns, businesses and services in the area to serve primarily shipyard workers. For much of the early 1800s, Fort Greene was made up of squatter camps, many of which lined Myrtle Avenue. Walt Whitman, a Brooklyn native, once labeled a section of the Myrtle Avenue squatter camps, “Little Dublin,” given the sizeable Irish squatters residing there.

According to Freeman, during the middle decades of the nineteenth century, Fort Greene grew rapidly.

> A case could be made that gentrification began to occur in the middle decades of the 19th century as more of the new housing was upscale in nature and targeted those solidly in the middle class. Toward the end of the 19th century, the section of Fort Greene that has come to be known as Clinton Hill became even more upscale, attracting robber barons of the day, such as Charles Pratt (benefactor of Pratt Institute), who was a partner at Standard Oil, and coffee merchant John Arbuckle (2006).

Fort Greene’s close proximity to downtown Brooklyn and lower Manhattan made it an attractive location for settlement by robber barons and their stately mansions and a century later for gentrifiers seeking to rehabilitate homes and brownstones with classical architecture. By the late 1960s and early 1970s, however, the Fort Greene neighborhood became a ghetto. Fort Greene Park, the centerpiece of the neighborhood, became a dangerous place, frequented by drug addicts and prostitutes. Despite falling to disrepair, the neighborhood soon became a hub for gentrifying activity, with ebbs and flows over the next three decades. *The New York Times* referred to “Brownstoneurbia” to describe the rehabilitation of the brownstones in the Fort Greene area by young professionals (Freeman 2006). Yet by the late 1990s, there were sections of the neighborhood that were not gentrified, but well on their way. According to Freeman, The Home Mortgage Disclosure Act data suggest that during the

1990s there was a resurgence of gentrification as evidenced by the increasing flow of mortgage capital into Fort Greene (2006: 46). Incomes did not change much in Fort Greene, but the nature of the real estate market and availability of mortgage capital changed the neighborhood's trajectory.

BLACKS IN FORT GREENE

There was always a sizable black population in Fort Greene since its development. In 1860, approximately half of Brooklyn's black population lived in the Fort Greene area and Colored School # 1 was built in 1847 in Fort Greene to accommodate the children of black Navy Yard workers. Further, many notable black abolitionists lived in Fort Greene, organizing to eliminate slavery in New York and eventually in the southern states (Scheiner 1965).

By the middle of the twentieth century, the black community grew. Great migrations from southern states to northern cities such as New York increased the black populations in Brooklyn. Black migrants settled mostly along the axis of Fulton Street and Atlantic Avenue stretching from the downtown and Fort Greene areas through Bedford Stuyvesant and into Brownsville and East New York.

Unfortunately, blacks arriving were increasingly isolated to declining and increasingly under-resourced neighborhoods, due to housing discrimination. With the arrival of blacks, services and resources were withdrawn, and white flight to the newly established inner-ring suburbs like Levittown, Long Island, and black in-migration coupled with the other symptoms of neighborhood decline, including red-lining, housing deterioration, and rising crime, accelerated the downward spiral of Fort Greene. In fact, blacks were relegated to poor, segregated public schools through a combination of housing segregation and deliberate racist policies administered by the Board of Education (Rogers 1968). Fort Greene declined during the middle twentieth century, due to divestment and racial hyper-segregation. For instance, the sprawling Fort Greene public housing projects, the Walt Whitman and Robert V. Ingersoll Houses, established in 1944, had also become overwhelmingly minority, home to one of the largest black populations in the world.

According to Freeman (2006), the largest groups of gentrifiers in Fort Greene are educated and middle-class blacks. Interestingly, Census data suggest that white flight from large cities may have bottomed out in the 1990s. For instance, Brooklyn has seen its proportion of whites grow to 36.1 percent in 2006 from 35.9 percent in 2000, the first increase in white share in about a century (Dougherty 2008).

However, despite the "reverse migration" of whites back into urban areas from suburban communities, according to Census tract data for Fort Greene, less than 10 percent of the population is white, with the majority of this white population clustered around Fort Greene Park, just blocks from the Walt Whitman and Ingersoll Housing Projects. Fort Greene remains a predominately black neighborhood, despite gentrification and a white presence.

SCHOOLING IN THE HOUSING PROJECTS

In NYC, public housing developments accommodate an estimated 130,000 students, or about one out of every nine students in City's public schools (Schwartz, McCabe, Ellen and Chellman 2010). Yet, about a quarter of all NYCHA elementary school students attend 4 percent of the City's elementary schools, or thirty-three schools. Half of the elementary school-aged students in public housing attend just 10 percent of the City's elementary schools, or 83 schools. This concentration of populations is mirrored at the high school level as well (Schwartz et al. 2010).

A growing body of research suggests that neighborhoods are an important determinant of how students perform in school. In neighborhoods with concentrated poverty, high unemployment and few neighborhood institutions, students are likely to perform worse than their peers in neighborhoods with more advantages. Schools with high concentrations of students in public housing have fewer white students and more poor students than most schools throughout the city. Further they tend to perform lower on tests than non-NYCHA students, only 38 percent and 41 percent passed their reading and math exams, respectively, compared to 50 percent and 52 percent for non-NYCHA. NYCHA students living in high-poverty neighborhoods score lower on standardized tests than NYCHA students living in lower poverty neighborhoods. Teachers in the average school attended by NYCHA students have slightly less education and experience than their peers in the average school attended by non-NYCHA students (Schwartz et al. 2010).

Completed in 1944, Walt Whitman Houses and the Robert V. Ingersoll Houses in Fort Greene Brooklyn consist collectively of thirty-five buildings, ranging from six to thirteen stories tall with over 3,000 apartments housing over 8,000 people. These two complexes represent one of the largest housing projects in the United States. In the 1970s, the Whitman and Ingersoll houses were a hotbed of criminal activity and violence, which escalated during the 1980s crack cocaine epidemic. The majority of the children residing in these projects attend just three elementary schools in the zoned area, mirroring the reality of hypersegregation. All three of the elementary schools under perform on state and city exams in English Language Arts (ELA) and mathematics.

Since the gentrification boom in Fort Greene, there have been major private residential developments, many of them skyscrapers, engulfing the housing project. Further, since 2003, major needed renovations have taken place in the Walt Whitman and Ingersoll Houses, leaving many apartments observably vacant. Estimates are that 60 percent of the apartments are vacant, leading to much speculation that many poor and working class residents are being forced to leave the Whitman/Ingersoll Houses to make room for middle class occupants.

In New York City, housing development has outstripped school construction, leading to overcrowding of schools. In neighborhoods where new housing construction is leading to surging population, the demand for elementary and middle school seats are growing, and schools are performing near or above capacity. However, it appears that the growth in residential development in Fort Greene has not precipitated higher demand for quantity of schools seats. It has, inadvertently, pushed for demand for quality schools, particularly among gentrifying parents. For instance, City Councilwoman Letitia James, who represents the Fort Greene community, was approached in recent years by predominately white parents asking her to redirect their local tax money toward schools in a nearby neighborhood. The parents stated they wanted their kids in schools with a more diverse racial mix, according to Ms. James, rather than the majority black schools in her district. The parents felt "tax dollars should follow the children and not the school." But Councilwoman James denied the request (Dougherty 2008).

TWO UNRECONCILED STRIVINGS IN ONE SCHOOL BUILDING

The Charles Dorsey Elementary School (P.S. 67) is a kindergarten through fifth grade school that sits directly in the middle of the Ingersoll Houses. It is a large sprawling brick building, mirroring the design of most public schools in New York that were built in the first half the twentieth century. Yet P.S. 67 is unique in that it is also the historic site of Colored School #1, the first school for black children in Brooklyn established in 1847, twenty years after the abolition of slavery in New York. After the closing of the African Free Schools, which were developed by the New York Manumission Society to educate the children of slaves and freemen, the Colored Schools evolved under the newly established public school system. Colored School #1 in Fort Greene was the largest school educating the children of Navy Yard workers (Scheiner 1965). Charles A. Dorsey, an African American educator, served as principal from 1863 to 1897. Over time, in an attempt to comply with the passing of the federal Civil Rights Act of 1873, the New York City Board of Education moved to abolish "colored schools." Subsequently, the Board of Education simply changed the name from "colored" to "ward" schools, simply keeping already segregated schools in tact. Colored school #1 became designated P.S. 67 in 1887, taking on the name of its longest serving principal, Charles Dorsey, many decades later.

Currently P.S. 67 serves as the primary school for children living in the Ingersoll and Whitman public houses. P.S. 67 has a predominately black student population, with 97 percent of students qualifying for free lunch. The school utilizes the standard city curriculum, but has been chronically under-resourced and low performing for decades, with the majority of its students falling below New York City averages on academic measures, namely city-wide reading and math exams. A recent report card on P.S. 67 highlighted that the school received a "D" for student performance on the English Language Arts (ELA) and Math exams, an improvement from an "F" in previous years. The grading system for schools is a relatively new initiative from the Department of Education, and is rife with controversy due to the questionable methodology for measuring school improvement and success. Many view it simply as a public relations ploy, with no real merit. And P.S. 67 has made strides in improving, with incremental changes in student achievement over the years. However, students' academic performance still falls well below the state and city average for K–5 students.

P.S. 67 is an example of a hypersegregated public school in New York City, a school with an overrepresentation of one racial group. This hypersegregation is exacerbated in schools serving the children residing in housing projects. Children residing in projects are disproportionately attending poor performing and overcrowded schools in districts across the city. In community school district 13 (CSD 13), which encompasses Fort Greene, the population is expected to increase by 7.2 percent between 2000 and 2010. Yet, interestingly as of 2008, the public schools in Fort Greene/Clinton Hill were under capacity, functioning at approximately 75 percent capacity, with space for nearly 7,000 more students (Thompson 2008). Currently P.S. 67 is at 65 percent capacity, with approximately 280 students enrolled with room for a total of 425 students.

What accounts for the underutilization of P.S. 67? A number of factors may be at hand. The relatively high vacancy rate in the Walt Whitman and Robert Ingersoll housing projects as of recent, due to increasing renovations of apartments and the displacement of families may be a cause. A number of families have been relocated to other public housing complexes in the borough, perhaps reducing the potential enrollment rolls for P.S. 67.

Moreover, the saturation of private housing development in the area has outstripped demand. The population has increased slightly in Fort Greene, yet it has not kept pace with the large-scale development that has occurred.

For instance, Forte, a large condominium building bordering Whitman and Ingersoll houses was only at 30 percent capacity in 2009, over a year after it was completed. As with much of the NYC, residents tend to rent housing units as opposed to buying. Further, the economic recession triggered in late 2007 has caused banks to reduce mortgage lending, thus curtailing home buying in much of the city.

Subsequently P.S. 67 is underperforming and underutilized, serving disproportionately poor children from poor housing projects. Its condition is exacerbated by the chronic underfunding of schools that has been the ongoing legacy of New York City, as well as the overdevelopment occurring in the vicinity. The low enrollment of students and poor performance raises questions about P.S. 67, about its longevity as a traditional public school.

COMMUNITY ROOTS CHARTER SCHOOL: FILLING THE VOID

While P.S. 67 struggles to serve more students and help them pass city and state tests, Community Roots Charter School is thriving. Chartered in 2006, Community Roots now occupies space in P.S. 67, and boasts a progressive, interdisciplinary and engaging curriculum for elementary students. Each classroom has two teachers who instruct a group of 25 elementary students, a small class size compared to the thirty-plus students in traditional public school classrooms like P.S. 67. The school is small but growing, serving approximately 250 students K to fifth grade, the majority of whom live in District 13, which comprises the Fort Greene/Clinton Hill neighborhood. Under New York State charter law, charter schools can draw on the wider district for recruitment of students, and not just the zone school area. Given this reality, unlike traditional P.S. 67, which can only admit students from the zone area, CRCS has been able to cast a wide admissions net, capturing the racial and class diversity of the Fort Greene community. In fact, due to its success in such a short time, its charter was recently renewed for another five years, allowing the school to now expand to an eighth grade.

The impetus for creating the school, according to Emily, one of the first parents in the school, was "there was not a decent elementary school in the area, one that we parents found suitable, academically, to send our kids." Emily, a white female from Ohio, moved to Fort Greene in late 1996, at the height of a postrecession gentrification boom in the area. Unmarried at the time, she was unconcerned with schools and their performance. "I didn't really give schools a second thought, at first. But when reality set in, I had to now pay attention."

When Emily gave birth to her son she eventually placed him in a cooperative nursery school that was started by parents in the area. "We started the cooperative nursery on the first floor of a parent's brownstone because there were also not any quality nurseries in the area. The ones that were good were private and cost too much."

Emily navigated alternative schooling environments in Fort Greene from the time her son was born. So when Community Roots started, she was one of the first parents admitted (her son is now in the fifth grade at CRCS). Inquiring as to whether the traditional P.S. 67 was a viable option, Emily retorts, "The irony is that we are zoned for that school. CRCS shares the same building with P.S. 67, and the students do things together like community service days and other events. But CRCS has a different philosophy and approach. A strange fact of life in this school." For Emily, there are clear distinctions between CRCS and P.S. 67. She lauded the "different philosophy and approach" of CRCS without specifically commenting on the poor performance of P.S. 67. Clearly P.S. 67 was not a viable choice for her son, although it shares the same building with CRCS.

The demand for Community Roots has grown. In the beginning, the school started as a kindergarten, with a small number of families applying to the school from the neighborhood. Overtime the reputation has led to more families inquiring and applying for a limited number of seats. "It used to be two to three open houses per season. Because of the demand for seats, currently, there are about two to three open houses per month for parents to tour and learn about CRCS," according to David, a parent with a third grader in the school. David is African American, and grew up in Bedford Stuyvesant. He moved to neighboring Fort Greene in the early 1990s, primarily to be a part of the burgeoning filmmaking scene in the area. A filmmaker himself, he wanted to be in proximity to other filmmakers, like Spike Lee, who set up his production company, 40 Acres and a Mule Filmworks on Dekalb Avenue, just a block from David's brownstone.

As Freeman (2006) highlights, many of the gentrifiers in Fort Greene/ Clinton Hill are black, having moved from neighboring communities to take advantage of the limited housing stock in the area. David is just such a person. "I like what this neighborhood has become. When I got here it was still not safe to walk the streets at night . . . now my kid goes to one of the better schools in the area. I don't feel guilty about this change. It was needed."

Parent involvement is high at CRCS, with parents like David participating on the "community council," which is an iteration of a traditional parent-teacher association (PTA). This council, and its various subcommittees, ranges from coordinating the chaperoning of school trips, to overseeing the community garden to helping to raise additional funds through auctions and other activities. David believes it is his right as a resident to demand the best for his child, and to "push public schools" to respond to "our needs."

The "our" for David, after much discussion, refers to parents who "understand their rights and demand better schools," namely the parents who have children in CRCS. When confronted with the notion that parents in public housing may be demanding similar things from P.S. 67, David laments "it's a resource game too. Parents with financial resources, networks can create a bigger stir . . . not that the parents in the projects don't deserve good schools, but it's an uphill climb without money and networks."

Recently, CRCS received an "F" from the Department of Education (DOE) for its slow improvement on citywide test scores for students, a lower grade than what P.S. 67 received, creating an outcry from vocal CRCS parents that the grading system is unfair. Subsequently the blogsphere exploded with criticism of the grading system and the Department of Education, generating e-mail from parents attesting to the quality teaching and learning at CRCS. Interestingly, the failing grade has not slowed applications to the school. The oversaturation of applicants from the district for seats in CRCS has led to implementation of a lottery system. As with most popular charters in New York City, the lottery system has become a fact of life. Every year come spring, thousands of families cram into gymnasiums and auditoriums to hopefully hear their child's name called for a coveted seat in a desirable charter school. Although no exact numbers could be garnered for this study, it is estimated that hundreds of families apply each April for under fifty seats at CRCS. Many families are wait-listed, hoping that a student will drop out or a parent will suddenly move away, leaving the seat vacant.

"PARALLEL PLAY": DISTINCT AND CONFLICTING IDENTITIES IN A PROJECT SCHOOL

Although CRCS and P.S. 67 share space and at points in the year, students collectively engage in community service events like mural painting, community gardening or fifth graders serving as "ambassadors" in the schools, both schools have a clear and distinct identity from each other. They coexist in the building but do not overlap, explicitly, in the areas of curriculum and teaching. Initially when the New York Charter Law was established, it required newly formed charter schools to be sites of innovation that would share knowledge and instructional ideas with traditional public schools in the district. For the most part, this has not happened with the CRCS and P.S. 67. The two schools have a seemingly parallel existence, where students, parents and staff engage daily in, what child psychologists refer to as, "parallel play." Parallel play is when children play in close proximity to each other but do not engage each other nor influence each other's behavior. Other than targeted events both schools have their own culture, values and daily rituals that do not mesh, and students do not interact much. Given the racial and class make up of the two schools, with an increasingly white and low-poverty student body in CRCS drawn from the wider district 13, and a disproportionately black and high poverty student population pulled from the housing projects and placed in P.S. 67, this makes for a surreal contrast. This disparity is exacerbated by this skewed recruitment and admissions procedures for each school. P.S. 67 as a zoned school, which means it must take every student who lives within the immediate vicinity (or zone of the school). And as a traditional public school, it must accept all kids, regardless of their background. However, under charter law, CRCS can and does recruit from the wider district 13, which encompasses the housing projects and gentrified areas nearby. Given its larger catchment area, the result has been an increased number of applicants from the gentrified areas of Fort Greene, many of them racially mixed but solidly middle class, overwhelming the number of applications for the admissions lottery. Further, CRCS can cap admissions after a certain point, and if there is turnover in a grade (students leaving the school), they are not required to fill that seat with another student, automatically.

Hence, the colocation of P.S. 67 and CRCS is not without conflict. Divergent interests between the schools have led to tension over shared "common space" in the building (i.e. lunchroom, gymnasiums, classrooms, etc). A number of parents from the housing projects and longstanding black community residents argue that CRCS "is taking over the building, promoting small class sizes, and two teachers per class, while P.S. 67 is struggling to find suitable space." For instance, Jumilah, a resident of Ingersoll houses and mother of a daughter who attended P.S. 67 asserts, "that school [CRCS] believes that it's God's gift. It was put there for the white parents in the neighborhood to put their kids someplace. They are trying to take over the building." Jumilah views CRCS as an encroachment on P.S. 67 and sought of an "island of privilege" for white parents in the gentrified area of Fort Greene. Even though the school has a lottery, the overrepresentation of white parents seeking to get their kids in the school fuels the suspicion.

Further, resentment is also growing that CRCS, like many charters, is favored by the Department of Education, and P.S. 67 is seen as the prodigal son when it comes to budget allocations. Research on New York City charters has also highlighted that charters in school buildings tend to receive more funds than ones with their own buildings (Smith 2010). This has fueled speculation by parents of children in P.S. 67 that resources are not being allocated equitably to all in the building, with CRCS benefitting from a larger slice of the budget and resources.[2] Given its growing white student population, CRCS, like all charter schools, has its own board of directors and raises additional funds from private sources to supplement its budget. This arrangement, by design, leads to a disparity in funds between the traditional school and the charter school.

Recently, the Department of Education allowed CRCS to expand to a K–8 model, growing each grade each year to the middle school level. As part of the process, public hearings were held so that the community can hear the details of the plan and make suggestions on how to proceed. At the first hearing, protests erupted. Many community members voiced resentment that CRCS could grow as a "white" school in the "first black school for Brooklyn" (alluding to P.S. 67 as Colored School #1). Fliers were handed out to passers-by depicting the expansion as a "take over" of the school, and teachers and students from P.S. 67 (and P.S. 367) took to the street chanting that they were "being displaced by charter schools." Black elected officials, who initially supported CRCS, publicly reversed their stance and supported the predominately black protesters. In a matter of a few days, the CRCS and P.S. 67 conflict became less about the struggles of colocation and more about racial divisions. Subsequently, the protests did not terminate the expansion plan, but slowed the time line down. So CRCS will continue to grow into a K–8 model, just not as rapidly as was first planned.

CONCLUSION

The dual existence of P.S. 67 and the Community Roots Charter School raises questions about which population's needs are being targeted and subsequently served by the creation of a charter school. For the parents of CRCS, the school fulfills a need for a quality neighborhood elementary school, one that provides an innovative curricula and lower student to teacher ratio. Given the racially diverse make up of the school, with just under half the students in CRCS being white and higher income, and given the popularity and demand from families in the neighborhood, it appears CRCS is attempting to serve the needs of the growing population of residents in the surrounding neighborhoods, not the students in the housing projects.

The subsequent resistance by primarily black residents to the expansion of CRCS was highlighted in the media as a race conflict, a knee jerk response to festering racial divisions in the Brooklyn neighborhood. But this issue cannot be simply reduced to an issue of race and gentrification. It truly illustrates the dynamics of the social class divide under gentrification. Many of the residents who send their kids to CRCS are like David, black and middle class or mixed race families, looking for a suitable school for their kids. The class divide between P.S. 67 with over 90 percent of the students qualifying for free lunch, and CRCS with only 30 percent receiving free lunch, in one school building is a glaring reality of how race is accentuated but class undergirds the tension around gentrification and school change in the building. When David, the CRCS parent, refers to schools needing to respond to "our needs," he is speaking primarily of gentrifying families in the school, those aligned by class and ideological interests. In fact, the shared class interests among white and black gentrifiers to find a suitable public elementary school fueled the creation of CRCS, and similar charter schools in previously under resourced communities. It is a cheaper alternative to private schools, given the rising private school costs in Brooklyn (the average tuition at a private school was approximately $30,000 per year and approximately $15,000 for a parochial school).

Parents seeking better housing in gentrified areas are also seeking better schools in the same community. As a result, charter schools, as an engine of urban school reform, will continue to fuel gentrification and lure families to once under resourced neighborhoods, creating an oasis of educational choice in a sea of poor and failing schools.

NOTES

1. There is a third school in the building, P.S. 367, which serves students with learning disabilities, and it resembles the population in P.S. 67, a mostly black and poor demographic.
2. This claim could not be substantiated since we did not have access to the Community Roots' budget.

REFERENCES

Bacharach, Samuel B. and Bryan L. Mundell. 1993. "Organizational Politics in Schools: Micro, Macro, and Logics of Action." *Educational Administration Quarterly* 29(4):432–52.

Berends, Mark, Ellen Goldring, Marc Stein and Xiu Cravens. 2010. "Instructional Conditions in Charter Schools and Students' Mathematics Achievement Gains." *American Journal of Education* 116(3):303–36.

De Luca, Barbara and Steven Hinshaw. 2006. "Comparing Academic Achievement in Charter Schools and Public Schools: The Role of Money." *Journal of Educational Research and Policy Studies* 6(1):67–90.

DeSena, Judith N. 2009. *Gentrification and Inequality in Brooklyn: The New Kids on the Block*. Lanham, MD: Lexington Books.

Dougherty, Conor. 2008. "The End of White Flight." *The Wall Street Journal*, July 19, p. A1.

Freeman, Lance. 2006. *There Goes the Hood: Views of Gentrification from the Ground Up*. Philadelphia, PA: Temple University Press.

Goldring, Ellen B. and Kristie J. R. Phillips. 2008. "Parent Preferences and Parent Choices: The Public-Private Decision about School Choice." *Journal of Education Policy* 23(3):209–30.

Horvat, Erin McNamara, Elliot B. Weininger and Annette Lareau. 2003. "From Social Ties to Social Capital: Class Differences in the Relations between Schools and Parent Networks." *American Educational Research Journal* 40(2):319–51.

Ladson-Billings, Gloria and William F. Tate IV. 1995. "Toward a Critical Race Theory of Education." *Teachers College Record* 97(1):54–64.

Lutz, Frank W. and Carol Mertz. 1992. *The Politics of School/Community Relations*. New York: Teachers College Press.

May, Judy Jackson. 2006. "The Charter School Allure: Can Traditional Schools Measure Up?" *Education and Urban Society* 39(19)19–45.

Rogers, David. 1968. *110 Livingson Street: Politics and Bureaucracy in the New York City School System*. New York: Random House.

Saporito, Salvatore and Annette Lareau. 1999. "School Selection as a Process: The Multiple Dimensions of Race in Framing Educational Choice." *Social Problems* 46(3):418–39.

Scheiner, Seth M. 1965. *Negro Mecca: A History of the Negro in New York City, 1865–1920*. New York: New York University Press.

Schwartz, Amy Ellen, Brian J. McCabe, Ingrid Gould Ellen and Collin C. Chellman. 2010. "Public Schools, Public Housing: The Education of Children Living in Public Housing." *Urban Affairs Review* 20(10):2–22.

Scott, Janelle and Adriana Villavicencio. 2009. "School Context and Charter School Achievement: A Framework for Understanding the Performance 'Black Box'." *Peabody Journal of Education* 84(2):227–43.

Smith, Yolanda. 2010. "Comparing the Level of Public Support: Charter Schools versus Traditional Public Schools" *Fiscal Brief*. New York: New York City Independent Budget Office.

Stambach, Amy and Natalie Crow Becker. 2006. "Finding the Old in the New: On Race and Class in the Charter School Debates." *Race, Ethnicity and Education* 9(2):159–82.

Thompson, William C. 2008. "Growing Pains: Reforming Department of Education Capital Planning to Keep Pace with New York City's Residential Construction." *Policy Report*. New York: Office of the New York City Comptroller and Office of Policy Management.

Tomlinson, Sally. 1997. "Diversity, Choice and Ethnicity: The Effects of Educational Markets on Ethnic Minorities." *Oxford Review of Education* 23(1):63–76.

Wells, Amy Stuart, Julie Slayton and Janelle Scott. 2002. "Defining Democracy in the Neoliberal Age: Charter School Reform and Educational Consumption." *American Educational Research Journal* 39(2):337–61.

Wirt, Frederick M. and Michael W. Kirst. 1997. *The Political Dynamic of American Education*. Berkeley, CA: McCutchan Publishing.

16

Revising Canarsie

Racial Transition and Neighborhood Stability in Brooklyn

Jennifer Candipan, Roberta Cordeau, Mark Peterson, Nicole Riordan, Bengisu Peker, Danielle Shallow and Gregory Smithsimon

In the early morning hours of July 17, 1991, a homemade firebomb crashed through the window of Fillmore Real Estate agency on Flatlands Avenue in the Brooklyn neighborhood of Canarsie. This bombing was the second of three bias-related attacks on the real estate agency which had been court ordered to show homes to black and Hispanic buyers in the mostly white neighborhood. On August 11 of the same year, police arrested twenty-year-old Brian Fining, a lifelong resident of Canarsie's Avenue M, an all-white block where no homes had been sold in twenty eight years. Although he acted alone in all three attacks, Fining's explosive anger over minorities moving into the neighborhood was a familiar sentiment among many of Canarsie's longtime white residents (Kurtz 1991).

From the 1970s through the 1990s, the neighborhood of Canarsie in South Brooklyn underwent a dramatic period of racial tension and transition, triggered by the in-migration of black residents to what had formerly been a predominantly Italian and Jewish community.[1] In his book *Canarsie: The Jews and Italians of Brooklyn Against Liberalism,* Jonathan Rieder chronicled the angry, sometimes violent response of white residents against new black residents (Rieder 1985). Whites were convinced that the safety, status, and physical quality of the neighborhood would precipitously decline if blacks moved in, and their resistance metastasized into a generalized dismissal of integrationism, liberal politics, the Democratic Party, and even rule of law. We conducted an ethnographic revisit to compare whites' expectations to how the neighborhood actually changed—and remained the same—as black residents became the majority.

According to U.S. Census figures, by 2000, Canarsie's black population had grown to 60 percent from less than 20 percent a decade earlier. This drastic racial transformation, however, is more complex than these numbers suggest, because not only were native-born African Americans moving into Canarsie, but significant numbers of Caribbean people (also called West Indians) were as well.[2] In fact, according to Butterfield (2004:288), by the year 2000, West Indian immigrants and their children comprised 54 percent of New York City's black population. This transformation from Italian and Jewish white residents to Afro-Caribbean blacks exemplifies what Chicago School sociologist Ernest Burgess called "succession." The racial transition that accompanied this otherwise classic case of succession dramatically redefined the meaning of the change in the minds of white residents.

White Canarsians viewed their world as under attack from outsiders who were aided by a liberal government (Rieder 1985). They reacted angrily and sometimes violently to new black residents. Whites were convinced that the arrival of blacks would destroy their middle-class enclave and render it unrecognizable. More than twenty five years after Rieder's study, our ethnographic revisit found that, while whites are still convinced that "things have changed," the story of Canarsie is remarkable for how similar black Canarsie is to white Canarsie and how expectations of dramatic change and deterioration were incorrect.

Black newcomers, according to a woman who moved to the neighborhood in 1997, simply "wanted a suburb. Living in Canarsie made you feel like you didn't have to leave Brooklyn . . . You could sit on your porch" (Fahim 2009:np). Black migrants to Canarsie shared the same goal as the Jews and Italians who had preceded and fought to exclude them: to live a middle-class life in a part of the city that offered elements of a suburban environment.

Black Canarsie residents were able to achieve that goal to a much greater degree than their white predecessors had ever imagined. That said, two forces have reconfigured the neighborhood. First, neoliberal economic policies that have reshaped the city since the period when Canarsie was all white have changed the structural context in which a "middle-class" existence is possible. Second, while contemporary racial inequality does not preclude the establishment of a black middle-class community such as Canarsie, it continues to impose particular costs on black Americans, regardless of class. During the period of our study, this additional burden was most evident in the foreclosure crisis facing Canarsie.

METHODS

The research team conducted twenty ethnographic observations in a range of settings in Canarsie, including meetings, community centers, and businesses. Researchers used several convenience samples focused on residents and business owners. The research team conducted forty formal interviews of respondents age eighteen to eighty. Interview subjects were evenly split between men and women. Interviewees included two Asian and one Hispanic respondent, the rest were nearly evenly split between blacks and whites, The ethnographic work of the team mirrored the techniques of a rapid ethnographic assessment project, or REAP (Low, Taplin, and Scheld 2005:183–93). Such a process employs a range of qualitative and quantitative methods, and triangulates different researchers' observations.

In addition to ethnographic observations, members of the research team conducted visual observations. On multiple field visits to Canarsie, researchers used still photography as a visual method and focused photography on the visual material culture, including smaller objects and signs, and larger visible structures such as the cemetery and building facades (Pauwels 2010). Several members of the team photographed the commercial landscape ("store windows and shop signs that are interpreted by ordinary people as ethnic markers") as well as residential areas of the neighborhood (Krase 2006: 81). Members of the team also conducted formal interviews and analyzed census data.

RACIAL TRANSITION IN CANARSIE

Canarsie's ethnic and racial succession began in the 1960s when black and Puerto Rican families moved into the area surrounding the Breukelen Houses in Canarsie (Rieder 1985). As these families arrived, white families began an exodus. By the mid 1970s as black families moved further south toward Seaview Village and Jamaica Bay, Canarsie residents reacted against the newcomers. White residents resorted to violence and bias attacks on minorities who were trying to buy homes in the area. The "reaction" period stretched all the way into the early nineties when Brian Fining bombed the Fillmore Real estate agency on Flatlands Avenue.

From 1990 to 2000, Jews and Italians started leaving Canarsie in ever-increasing numbers and the black population went from 10 percent to 60 percent in just ten years (Fahim 2009). As blacks became the new majority, a "climax" was reached and the few remaining white residents accepted, gladly or not, that the neighborhood was no longer a white ethnic enclave.

Despite the racial difference between the old Canarsie residents and the new, the two groups did have many similarities. DeSena (2005) points out, "as individuals leave neighborhoods, they are usually replaced by groups of the same general status as the original residents," yet new residents will usually have different social and ethnic characteristics (8). This concept holds true for Canarsians as new black residents were middle- and working-class peoples just as the white ethnics had been. After all, because Canarsie is an area comprised mostly of one-family houses, these new families had to first be in a position to be able to purchase those houses.

White Canarsians recognized that their neighborhood was no longer a white enclave. They also recognized that complaining about that shift in racial terms was not socially sanctioned. Instead, they tried, often unsuccessfully, to articulate their discontent in "colorblind" or nonracial ways (Bonilla-Silva 2009). For instance, Canarsie's public schools had been the site of significant racial violence. One longtime resident was a middle schooler during the rash of school demonstrations protesting new busing initiatives that had begun bringing in new students from East Flatbush, a predominantly black outlying neighborhood, to Canarsie. She sought to deny the role of race in whites' perception of decline: "I had black friends," she said. "As a matter of fact, in my old school photo, I was sandwiched between two black girls. One of my best friends was black." She paused for a few beats then leaned towards one of us with her fingernails planted on her desk. "It wasn't about race. It was that things were changing."

She started tapping her long, well-manicured fingernails to the rhythm of the words that followed for emphasis: "*People* were coming in. People from outside the community." News articles chronicled how perceived threats to schools and, eventually, to the neighborhood were sometimes resolved violently. The justification for angry protests and violent practices seemed grounded in the "right to preserve the community" (Maeroff 1972). Some literature argues that this type of opposition to outsiders is indeed fueled by racial prejudice (Zubrinsky and Bobo 1996). Although she claimed that some of the initial opposition to outsiders "was not about race," she eventually acknowledged that this racially troubled time provided the social conditions for the type of unrest that eventually followed. She qualified her acknowledgement somewhat, though, by explaining that racial conditions were tense throughout all of New York City. She attributed the ensuing chaos to the broader social climate of the time. "It was crazy all around," she said, "And our little Canarsie got caught up in all the stuff [from the 70s], too."

In his article about Canarsie's period of tense race relations and school protests, Gene Maeroff writes, "Preservation of community was, indeed, the prime issue in the minds of Canarsie residents. To them, the children who were being bused into Canarsie symbolized the urban ills they were trying to hold at bay—bad schooling, crime, squalid housing, empty storefronts, drug addiction, and unemployment. They saw the youngsters as the advance guard of an onslaught of blacks who ultimately would transform Canarsie into yet another slum" (Maeroff 1972: np).

For one elderly Canarsie resident who had previously held positions in the local elementary school's PTA, the events surrounding the school protests made the strongest impression on her during that time. She spoke of slurs that had been directed to black schoolchildren. Her facial expressions communicated some of the most brutal vitriol that she kept quiet inside. The racism and hostility of the 1970s continued to set the context in which many white Canarsians saw the neighborhood, though it was less explicitly the frame through which black residents saw the neighborhood.

IMMIGRANT HISTORY

Many black residents in Canarsie were not native African Americans, but rather Afro-Caribbean blacks. Caribbeans had been coming to New York in small but significant numbers for more than a century. The 1965 Hart Celler Immigration Reform Act, which changed the entire focus of American immigration policy, had a great impact on Caribbean immigration. The bill eliminated certain immigration quotas that had limited the number of Caribbean immigrants coming to the United States (Kasinitz 1992: 26).

The Hart-Celler Immigration Reform Act resulted in a tremendous increase in the number of West Indian immigrants coming to the United States. By the early 1980s, almost 60,000 legal immigrants were entering the United States annually and approximately half of them settled in New York City. The immigrants who came to the United States in this cohort were from "virtually every sector of Caribbean society" including the urban elite, children of the middle class, and large numbers of lower class poor people (Kasinitz 1992: 27). High unemployment and lack of economic development in the Caribbean region meant that the majority of these immigrants came to the United States seeking economic security and job opportunities.

Similar to other immigrant groups, West Indians have settled mostly in urban areas, especially New York City (Waters 2001). Brooklyn, in particular, has been the recipient of many Caribbean immigrants, resulting in numerous West Indian neighborhoods including Flatbush, East Flatbush, Crown Heights, and, more recently, Canarsie. As with any group coming to a new country, West Indian immigrants have brought with them a unique and eclectic culture—from food, to clothing, to barber shops, much of which is represented visually in their neighborhoods (Henke 2001: 48).

According to Henke (2001: 52), Caribbean immigrants to the United States are faced with a "fundamental contradiction" surrounding the social construction of race. Peoples of the Caribbean are socialized in societies that do not attach as much significance to race, but rather center cultural identities on ascribed characteristics including hard work, delayed gratification, and personal austerity. Vickerman (1999) echoes this sentiment by stating that West

Indians traditionally interpret race broadly and that being "'black', 'white' or 'colored' was subject to a degree of interpretation and did not predestine individuals to particular outcomes" (p 3).

Upon their arrival in the United States, however, where race is defined much more rigidly, West Indian immigrants have been simply seen as being "black." Henke (2001: 52) points out that being seen as "black" brings with it the prejudices and stigma that whites have attached to that category. This new racial dimension affects the Caribbean community in several ways including how its peoples choose to identify and represent themselves.

While West Indians of different national origins tend to live alongside African Americans, many choose to maintain a distinct ethnic identity separate from the rest of the black population. This separation stems from resistance to the American tendency to use race as a "master status" category combined with long-standing tension between African Americans and first generation West Indian immigrants (Anderson 1990). As Vickerman (1999: 13) and Henke (2001: 53) discuss, West Indians are often conservative and tend to interpret the situation of African Americans in the United States not in terms of structural racism but personal traits. They presume African Americans lack a proper work ethic, personal austerity, and social adeptness. In contrast, African Americans frame their situation around the ways racism affects social, political, and economic outcomes.

This schism between these two groups does not imply that West Indians are oblivious to racial discrimination. Palmer (1995) states that, despite maintaining a separate ethnic identity, West Indians nonetheless "identify with the major civil rights issues that affect blacks in American society" (20). Henke (2001) also points out that West Indians have "stood at the forefront of the struggle against racism and for civil rights since the very beginning" (53). Thus, in our visual study of a commercial strip in Canarsie, researchers noted locations, such as a Haitian restaurant and a tutoring center for children on Avenue L, displaying portraits of Martin Luther King Jr. and President Obama in their windows. Furthermore, how West Indians and their children frame race can shift as the time they spend in United States grows. As a general rule, the more generations West Indian Americans have been in the United States, the more their understanding of racism comports with that of other African Americans.

"THINGS JUST AREN'T THE SAME"

In numerous conversations, white long-term residents described today's Canarsie as "different" and "not the Canarsie I knew." When reflecting upon their experiences growing up in Canarsie, many of these respondents talked about how Old Canarsie "was all I knew." Somehow this statement, said in simple opposition to the previous one, seemed to be addressing something distinctly other. Whereas the first statement seemed to be a subtle allusion to race, the second seemed to be lamenting the progress of advanced modern capitalism and the ways automobiles and privatized living overtook the lifeworld and killed their notions of simple urban village living (Habermas 1984).

Most interviews with longtime and former white Canarsie residents implied racial change was the root of their perceptions of Old Canarsie's deterioration, its broken community and its fallen businesses.

Connecting with former residents of a neighborhood can be challenging. Researchers for this project were able to obtain information about Canarsie when it had been an all-white enclave in two different ways. First, senior citizens who still lived near Canarsie came to the local senior citizen center daily, where we were able to interview them. Second, former residents had compiled photos and recollections of "old" Canarsie on Facebook and other sites.

Some of the more intriguing observations on community came from the ways former Canarsie residents from pre-transition years came together in online forums to remember their old neighborhood. Most interesting was not only the near-fetishistic attachment some residents had to Old Canarsie, but also how these residents thought of Canarsie as "theirs" to the exclusion of the people that actually live there now. For these former Canarsians, present-day residents are still the "outsiders." These attitudes extend to the incoming businesses that replaced some of the longstanding businesses from Old Canarsie. Long Won restaurant, for example, took over the space on Rockaway Parkway that Grabstein's Deli once occupied for decades. Even though Long Won has been in business now for over a decade, some Old Canarsie residents refuse to visit Long Won based on their feelings of resentment that Long Won was the outsider that "took over" (Cole Cross-Reference Directory 2011). Earlier research explains that longtime residents will perceive original business establishments as "better-fits" for the neighborhood (Aitken 1990). Rieder, in a follow-up paper to his book, reflected upon "myth-making" and how Canarsie became "Canarsie" (Rieder 1992). Some social psychological research argues that an overemphasis of bonding within groups can lead to "alienation of outsiders" and create another sort of myth of social capital in community development (Perkins, Hughey and Speera 2002).

THE MORE THINGS CHANGE, THE MORE THEY STAY THE SAME

Despite former residents' conviction that the neighborhood today is utterly different than it was when they lived there, we found striking examples of stability. Comparing former white, Italian, and Jewish residents to predominantly black Caribbean residents of today, many of the more recent residents held the same kinds of jobs, shared the same views on family and homeownership, and even shopped at the same kinds of stores. Even white respondents who sought to show how the neighborhood had changed often unintentionally presented evidence of how consistent the neighborhood has been, as when they described kinds of jobs West Indian residents had, mirroring descriptions of the kinds of jobs Italian and Jewish residents had a few decades earlier.

Much of the current data on Canarsie contradicts the assumptions held by twentieth century residents that the arrival of blacks would trigger the decline of the community. By most quantitative measures, Canarsie is a model of economic stability, ranking twelfth among neighborhoods in median household incomes in New York City (at $62,202) and sixth in the city in homeownership rates. Meanwhile, Canarsie maintains a poverty rate that is comparable to the city average (Furman Center 2011). A 2009 report from the Institute for Children and Poverty even expressed anxiety that Canarsie may have begun the process of gentrification, which the study described as the arrival of new housing investment, cultural, and retail services and improvements in infrastructure by affluent and educated in-movers to the detriment of lower-income residents. In making this assessment, the report cited the marked increase in educational attainment and housing values in Canarsie from 1990–2006, and acknowledged the racial dimensions of a gentrification process in which the gentrifiers are educated blacks (Institute for Children and Poverty 2009). However, in the wake of the financial crisis of 2008, the findings of the ICP may have been premature.[3]

Census data provides a more detailed comparison between 1970, when Canarsie was 98.2 percent white, and 2000, when it was 69.8 percent black and 18.5 percent white (The most recent, detailed employment data currently available comes from the 2000 census. According to the 2010 census, Canarsie was 83.9 percent black, 8.4 percent white, 7.6 percent Hispanic, and 2.9 percent Asian.) Certainly, there are continuities, but differences emerge as well that are attributable to both structural changes in the economic composition of New York City, and to ethnic employment niches.

Residents described Canarsie, then and now, as a neighborhood of teachers, construction workers, and police officers. In 1970, 6.8 percent of Canarsians worked in schools. In 2000, 9.2 percent did. In 1970, 4.8 percent worked in construction. In 2000, 3.5 percent did. In 1970, 607 Canarsians (2 percent) worked in the "protective services" category that included police, firefighters, security guards, and other uniformed services. In 2000, 1,413 people—4.2 percent of residents (and 6.6 percent of men) worked in "protective services." Overall, 17.2 percent worked in the public sector in 1970. By 2000, 25.3 percent did. While the inevitable arbitrariness of employment categories makes exact comparisons difficult (categories are changed over time so that direct comparisons are not always possible), there is evidence in the census data to corroborate qualitative data suggesting continuity in the occupations of Canarsie residents.

Despite some consistency, the fields in which Canarsians worked did change over thirty years. Many differences reflect changes in the economic composition of the city, as New York shifted from a city with many blue-collar manufacturing jobs to one with a larger percentage of financial sector, service sector, and health care jobs. In 1970, 20.3 percent of Canarsians worked in manufacturing, including a heavy concentration in New York's two largest industries: garments (7.7 percent of employed Canarsians) and printing (2.8 percent). Large numbers also worked in various types of retail (17.2 percent), and wholesaling (7.3 percent).

By 2000, many of those industries had declined. The percentage working in manufacturing had shrunk dramatically to 4.5 percent. Only 2 percent worked in wholesaling. Instead, the largest sectors were those that had grown in the city: The FIRE sector (finance, insurance, and real estate) that had come to dominate New York's economy grew from 7.4 percent of the Canarsie workforce in 1970 to 10.3 percent. A solid 26.1 percent worked in health care.

Other differences speak to nationwide shifts in employment. The most dramatic example is the sex ratio of workforce participation. In 1970, there were nearly twice as many employed men as employed women in Canarsie: 19,982 versus 10,272 (a ratio of 1.95 men for every woman in the workforce). By 2000, the ratio had shifted such that there were more women than men (15,248 men and 18,602 women), producing a ratio of 0.82 men for every woman in the workforce.

The largest influence on this ratio is the increase in women's participation in the workforce. The ratio nationwide shifted from 1.64 men to 1.14 men per woman in the workforce. Increases in female-headed households could have shifted the ratio as well. Finally, trends in the employment of black women versus black men could have also influenced the ratio. West Indians, for instance, are highly concentrated in health care and health care has grown considerably in New York's economy (Waters 2001). In 2000, 15.2 percent of women in Canarsie worked in health care, while only 2.0 percent of men did. The field provided far more employment opportunities for Caribbean women than men.

Median household incomes in Canarsie reflected citywide and national economic trends, as well, while remaining above borough-wide, statewide, and nationwide figures. Canarsie incomes dropped after the fiscal crisis of the seventies, as Brooklyn and New York likewise fell more sharply than the rest of the United States during that period. In the 1970s, Canarsie's median income dropped by 22 percent. New York State's median income fell by a similar figure, while Brooklyn's dropped by a staggering 29 percent. Real wages in the United States dropped 13 percent in that decade. From 1980 to 1990, Canarsie incomes rose at a pace shared by Brooklyn and New York State, faster than the rate in the United States. The nineties, when New York suffered a prolonged recession, were also brutal to Brooklyn, which saw incomes drop 5 percent during a time in which incomes nationwide increased by 6 percent. During that same period, Canarsie's income fell by one percent. In contrast, Canarsie in the 2000s experienced faster income growth than the state or the nation, while other parts of Brooklyn registered even sharper rises. Neighborhood and borough data are not adequate for conducting a detailed analysis on the effect of race on wages. However, at the community level, it is clear that while Canarsie has experienced ups and downs since its transition to a predominantly black neighborhood, its income has not been wildly out of range with the fortunes of the borough, state, and nation. Whites' expectations of precipitous declines were defied.[4]

Home values indicate the qualified way in which race shaped economic status in the newly black community. Whites expected home values to drop if blacks moved in. Between 1990 and 2000, Canarsie home values did decline by nearly 3 percent, but they fell by 10.6 percent overall in Brooklyn and dropped by more than 14 percent statewide. During the housing bubble, median prices in Canarsie jumped considerably, from $280,544 in 2000 to $488,715 in 2009. Home prices in the rest of Brooklyn, however, grew 17 percent faster than that. This comparison is complicated by the inflation of home prices during the housing bubble, from which New York housing prices have yet to fully recover. Often, long-term comparisons of black and white communities show poorer real estate appreciation in black neighborhoods than white ones. The tumultuous real estate market of the past decade makes it difficult to identify long-term trends, except to note that while the transition of Canarsie from white to black may have affected home prices, they have tracked borough and statewide prices much more closely for the last twenty years than whites fearful of black in-moving expected.

Beyond the employment and income shifts in the national and regional economy, the differences residents observed in Canarsie before and after the racial transition of the neighborhood were often lateral shifts (representing neither improvement nor deterioration) as one ethnic group replaced another. One Canarsie senior talked about her favorite stores on Avenue L (a main retail corridor in Canarsie) that have long since departed: "We used to have a Reinhardt's. Everybody knew that bakery. Now it's a Jamaican bakery, I think. And next to it is day care, I think. That one next to it . . . That used to be a restaurant. I tell you. We had everything on the Avenue. Bakeries and delis. Now, there's no more."

This speaker experienced the loss of a bakery, even though a bakery is still there. At the corner of Avenue L and 95th Street, the old vertical sign of the long-departed Home (formerly Reinhardt) Bakery remains on the front facade of the building, juxtaposed with the signage for the Jamaican Bakery that has since grown into this space (Schlitchtman and Patch 2008). Likewise, a butcher shop on Avenue L called Country Butcher used to be owned by an Italian man who sold it to a Dominican man. This butcher used to specialize in veal, pork, dried meats, and other essential Italian items.

Changes in the ethnic identities of stores were found to be deeply significant to old time residents, even though they turned out to not necessarily be accurate signs of the ethnic identity of store owners. Some of the newer non-Caribbean businesses that opened up in the past few years have designed storefronts with Caribbean symbols in order to attract more customers. Jono Bagels, which opened up a few doors down from one of Canarsie's oldest retail institutions, Original Pizza, was owned by a Chinese family. The owners said the Caribbean-themed color scheme "seemed right for the neighborhood." In another example, a few streets over from Avenue L on Rockaway Parkway (one of Canarsie's major arteries and commercial corridors), the recently arrived Golden Mango Supermarket inhabited a large lot in a commercial strip mall once dominated by Walgreens. Clearly displayed along the rooftop were a long row of West Indian flags, delivering another strong message of ethnic identity. Combined with the other small ethnic businesses that rounded out the rest of the spaces in the lot, the strip mall broadcast a spirit that was decidedly West Indian. It was a surprise, then, to read that the owner of the Golden Mango was not actually West Indian, but an Asian businessman ("Now It's Official" 2009). In these examples, changes to the retail identity of the neighborhood did not simply reflect changes in store ownership as outsiders often assumed, but, like the comments of white Canarsians themselves, were a commentary on the perceived changes in the neighborhood.

Some literature suggests that increases in ethnic entrepreneurs in an area can expedite the out-migration of those that feel as though their cultural needs and preferences are no longer being served by these ethnic businesses and institutions (Aldrich and Waldinger 1990). Some whites leave integrating black-white neighborhoods because they perceive that African Americans are "taking over" and they do not want to become part of the minority (Bobo and Zubrinsky 1996; Krysan 2002). In the case of Old Canarsie, the perception of Jamaican inflow may have acted as a co-agent of residential out-migration.

The paradoxical way in which sameness was perceived as difference extended from bakeries and butchers to the stereotypes whites use to describe themselves and blacks. White Canarsians described themselves as the descendents of hardworking immigrants, and blacks as fundamentally lacking in that work ethic. In the exchange below, Italian and Haitian work values and work experiences merge as Haitian and Italian employees of a Canarsie cab company discuss the ethnic succession of the business:

> Haitian Driver: There are about 28 drivers in this company . . . the majority of them are West Indian.
>
> Q: Are most of the drivers Haitian Immigrants?
>
> Haitian Driver: Yes, I would say 70 percent or so are Haitian Immigrants.
>
> Q: Is the owner from Haiti also?
>
> Haitian Driver: Yes, he is from Haiti.
>
> Q: How long has this business been here?
>
> Haitian Driver: Oh I don't know . . . (turns to middle-aged Italian cab driver in the room to get answer) . . . 26 years.
>
> Q: Has it always had the same owner?
>
> Italian Driver: No, the current owner purchased the business in the mid 90s from one of my kind of people (laughing).
>
> Q: Are you able to make a good living here in Canarsie?
>
> Haitian and Italian Driver: Yeah we do ok.
>
> Q: If you don't mind, how much does the average driver here make in a year?
>
> Haitian Driver: I know it doesn't look busy now, but in the morning when people need to get to work we are very busy. Some make more than $50,000 a year, some make less.
>
> Q: Do you get a lot of business from West Indians in Canarsie?
>
> Haitian Driver: A lot, yeah, because most of them have city jobs and need to make it to the subway. I think that there's this set notion among Haitians who come to the United States that the goal is to own your own home . . . My one friend he was uneducated when he came here but he got a job as a cab driver and saved up enough money for a down payment. My other friend studied hard and became a doctor.
>
> Q: In your experience do a lot of people who come from Haiti drive cabs?
>
> Haitian Driver: Yes it's a common first job for immigrants from Haiti . . . most have experience with English from customers in Port au Prince; you can make a good living and it doesn't require much education.

In addition to rendering explicit the ethnic succession in occupations, the speakers above also articulate cultural values. While declarations of such values are not, in themselves, evidence that any group actually holds or practices such values, they are indications of how the groups see themselves and wish to present themselves. Particularly during the transitional period, whites ascribed cultural values supporting home, family, and hard work to their own ethnic group while simultaneously claiming that blacks lacked these same values. For instance, a white resident quoted in *Canarsie* argued that "The problems of the blacks are their own fault. It's their ignorance. Jobs are created for everyone, but their own laziness keeps them from going after it. The common black, his problem is laziness and his upbringing" (Rieder 1985:113–14). Even today, Italians and Jews make such invidious distinctions, but by viewing them beside the self-representation of West Indian Canarsians, the underappreciated similarities between the groups becomes more evident.

Several interviews we conducted with white and black Canarsians showed how whites claimed to hold superior work and family values, even as whites and blacks articulated markedly similar sets of values. Thus, a thirty-seven-year-old Italian said that "Italians honor hard work. This [business] is family owned and it's going to be family-owned when the father dies." He suggested that blacks did not value hard work, middle class respectability, and successful business ownership like Italians. In a separate interview, however, a forty-five-year-old Haitian law student described West Indians as strivers in very similar terms: "Haitians are really academic, I mean insanely smart," she said. "Top schools, they're there, top doctors . . . Jamaicans are really good at business . . . There's this set notion among Haitians who come to the United States that the goal is to own your own home."

Suggestively, these two residents also had opposite views of how safety in the neighborhood had changed during Canarsie's forty-year period of racial transition. The Italian American respondent complained that "the neighborhood has gone downhill since they—the black race—has moved in . . . armed guards in schools, metal detectors; they never had any of that when I was here growing up." Contrary to his narrative of increasing crime, fear, and violence in Canarsie, a Haitian American who lived in nearby East Flatbush felt safer in Canarsie than before, noting that crime had dropped citywide over the past twenty years, and had dropped in Canarsie as well. Just as critically, while the Italian American perceived neighborhoods with more blacks as inherently dangerous, the Haitian American remembered white neighborhoods as being more threatening because of the danger whites posed to blacks: "Things have gotten a lot better in New York; now you can go anywhere. But in the seventies—in the seventies Bensonhurst or Bay

Ridge—forget about it. I tried to go to school one time in Bay Ridge and, when the train got to Atlantic Avenue, the train conductor would stop and pull all the blacks off the train. He said it was for our own safety, but I knew who he was working for." Indeed, the sharp decline in crime citywide over the last two decades means that most neighborhoods are considerably safer than they were in the 1970s, the same period about which white Canarsians have such halcyon memories. Just as critically, those white residents never consider the hostility of white neighborhoods towards blacks as examples of criminality. In fact, residents in Rieder's book considered such behavior just the opposite: law and order. Given such disparate framings and definitions of crime, violence, danger, and disorder, it is not surprising that the two groups should have opposing assessments of the changes in safety between white and black Canarsie.

We found other examples in our interviews of respondents speaking, indirectly, across the miscomprehension of the color line. An Italian American who moved from the neighborhood in the mid-nineties but still worked in Canarsie struggled to make sense of how black residents could afford to move into a middle-class neighborhood. "I don't know where they're getting their money but it must be from drugs." In another interview, a forty-nine-year-old Haitian explained that "I came to Canarsie from East Flatbush to try and find a better life for my family. It's safer here . . . I'm a schoolteacher and my daughter goes to Brooklyn College." The assumption of illicit behavior and the reality of civil service respectability highlight the difficulty white Canarsians continue to have imagining a reality for their black neighbors that is as mundane—and familiar—as it really is.

In a similar manifestation of racial blindness, whites were unable to see social structure and social networks if they existed within the black community. Thus one twenty-nine-year-old Italian complained that "there's not a lot of community involvement . . . especially the Caribbean blacks." In contrast, a forty-nine-year-old Haitian high school teacher said that "there is unity in the West-Indian community, we go to school together, we go to the same churches and restaurants, some of us even work together."

The complaint that Canarsie no longer had the vibrant social life of decades past was particularly common among the elderly, or among former residents, who no longer knew many people in the neighborhood. But it was demonstrably not the case for many current residents. On Sunday after church services had finished, the Arch Diner hosted a bustling social scene. Patrons wore their Sunday best. Easter decorations lined the walls and hung from the ceiling. Community social life, constructed around weekly rituals of religion, food, and community, was very much alive. At the same hour, the sidewalk of Avenue L was crowded with groups and families walking or standing in front of church awnings. Church services were important times, and public spaces after services important places, to enact community in Canarsie. Because many whites from Canarsie had virtually no connection to these networks, the community social life embedded in the black community was lost on white residents.

Not all whites were unable to recognize the similarities between white and black residents, or to understand the needs of the black community. One store owner, who had successfully adapted the products he sold to meet the changing ethnic profile of potential customers, could also see the similarities among the jobs of earlier and more recent residents. He attributed the same cultural values to Caribbeans that white Canarsians attributed to themselves. He said, "A lot of West Indians are school teachers and cops. The city likes them because they are hardworking and know how to speak to their community."

Racially homogenous social networks contribute to the propagation of these stereotypes. White residents lived in a network that was white enough to propagate both flattering representations of their own ethnicity as hardworking, family-centered, law abiding, and "respectable," and to repeat racist views of their black neighbors. Similarly, black residents seem to have sufficient ethnic networks to perpetuate self-reinforcing stereotypes of West Indians as hardworking, academic, focused on family unity, valuing home ownership, and striving for higher economic achievement.

RACE AND THE NEOLIBERAL CITY

Independent of racial transformations of particular neighborhoods, New York in the twenty-first century is fundamentally different from New York in the 1970s. In particular, the introduction of the neoliberal order has dramatically altered the landscape of the city and constrained the possibilities for working- and middle-class residents. David Harvey defines neoliberalism as a process beginning in the late-twentieth century that took back the collective gains of middle- and working-class people, gutted social welfare programs, and resecured elite power in economies around the world. In New York City, when the municipal government was unable to balance its budget in 1975, the bankers who held much of the city's debt imposed draconian changes in the city (Harvey 2005: 44–48). The bankers who were appointed to the Municipal Assistance Corporation that was given authority over the city's budget intended to make changes that went beyond what was fiscally necessary to be "punitive" and "painful." The bankers cut wages, hobbled civil service unions, laid off thousands of city workers, cut back public services (such as education, public health, and transportation), and raised taxes and fees for working New Yorkers (Harvey 2005: 45). Their goal was to restructure the city in the short-term interests of financial elites.

Thus while white Canarsians had moved into the neighborhood in a Keynesian era of low unemployment, high wages, and relatively generous public services, blacks moved to Canarsie in the neoliberal era, when wages of city jobs Canarsians had long held were being pinched, public higher education had become more expensive, and city services had been cut. Industrial jobs disappeared, union wages became more rare, and the financial industry, service sector, and health care fields grew in relative size. These employment sector shifts reshaped the labor market for Canarsians. In addition, the neoliberal ideology mandated that New York open far more aspects of society to capitalist markets. Deregulation, privatization, and marketization were key elements to the neoliberal project and reshaped the city.

One example is the changes in retailing options. Until the 1990s, zoning regulations had kept large retail stores out of New York, instead favoring smaller (often locally owned) stores on retail streets. During the Giuliani administration, the large retail chains that characterized much retailing outside of New York gained entrée into the New York market.[5] Retail stores in Canarsie thus faced a very different competitive landscape than they had decades earlier. The lure of "big box" stores like Target, Costco, and Home Depot that had recently opened in New York City was particularly strong in neighborhoods like Canarsie, whose modest home-owning residents had to watch their pennies and lived at the edges of the city where cars were ubiquitous and more frequently used for shopping. Residents began driving to the large stores that had been built on the relatively nearby urban fringes.

One longtime businessman remembered when Avenue L was busier. Families used to line up down the block to buy school supplies. More recently, families conducted their major shopping off of the Avenue. School supplies that were once bought locally were purchased in nationwide chains. Structural changes to retailing in the city diminished Avenue L's economic role.

Given the challenge presented by big-box competition, small business owners in Canarsie needed to find ways of restructuring their businesses to succeed in a neoliberal city. Some research suggests that some small business owners can succeed in niche markets by catering to neighborhood-specific "ethnic consumer tastes" and cultural preferences that produce a "protected market" for the entrepreneur (Aldrich and Waldinger 1990). One young Italian businessman, who spoke nostalgically about the vibrant street life of his section of Avenue L in the early 1990s, adapted his business to meet the changing demographics of the neighborhood. He devoted an entire aisle to African hair care products and sold key chains with flags from Caribbean countries. He reported that he now "loves Caribbean food." Still, business was not booming. "They're cheap," he complained, dissatisfied with the amount of money his Afro-Caribbean customers spent in the community. Instead, he believed residents focused expenditures on home ownership, and sent significant remittances to their countries of origin. His economic outlook for small business in the area was bleak, because of the growth of big-box retailers near Starrett City, the lingering effects of the recession, and the influx of corporate chains stores on nearby Glenwood Road. Although his economic assessment was grounded in nonracial attributions, he nonetheless implied that Canarsie's neighborhood transition from white to black factored into why his business had become stagnant. "The only places that are doing well on this strip are the Caribbean restaurants, the black churches, and the hair salons," he said. He offered a modicum of optimism, but not without an ethnically framed view of the neighborhood, as he wondered if "maybe when the Asians take over, things will get better."

Assumptions about Canarsians' financial capital persisted in responses like those given by one former resident who sought to explain why surveys showed Canarsie as having a high median income, even as the neighborhood seemed financially strained. The former resident said, "That's called inflation and two people working . . . when I grew up there I didn't know many kids I was friendly with whose moms worked . . . it was rare back then to have two income families." Thus, to this former Canarsian, there was something qualitatively different in how contemporary households generated income. In this assessment, Canarsians' relatively high incomes still lacked the social capital that single-income households once possessed. This explanation rolled several macroeconomic and social changes into one explanation: the shift toward more dual income families, falling wages for most workers (represented as "inflation" that seemed to nibble away at income when prices rose faster than salaries), and families that had enough money for mortgage payments, but not enough for some of the other markers of middle-class comfort.

Even though that resident recognized the rise of dual incomes and falling real wages, whites rarely have a solid sense of exactly how inequality is structured and instead attribute shortcomings to race, not racism. Other studies have pointed to how black Americans' lower levels of wealth (which translates into smaller downpayments on homes, and higher monthly mortgage payments, for instance) require greater income to pay for housing. This results in African American home owners being less likely to have as much disposable income when compared to whites with comparable incomes and homes. White neighbors who observe the arrival of blacks may then interpret these manifestations of longstanding racial inequality as evidence that blacks can't maintain homes or neighborhoods to white standards. A current resident lamented the racialized reputation that followed blacks into the neighborhood: "You know what, it's strange to me. The new settlers of Canarsie of African American descent bought the homes here for almost ten times the original cost and people consider the neighborhood quote-unquote 'bad.'"

Indeed, it is not possible to fully disaggregate the effect of neoliberal restructuring from the role of racism, since the damaging effects of neoliberalization have struck people of color harder in the United States. Racism has also aided neoliberal attacks on social welfare policies and even civil service workers, since both could be intertwined with racial stereotypes of the undeserving poor or insufficiently hardworking people. In addition, the pain of neoliberalism was greater for people of color because racism limited their ability to generate support for public policies that would address the threats they faced from neoliberal policies. One such threat was the proliferation of speculative mortgage capital and the resultant real estate bubble and foreclosure crisis.

FORECLOSURE: THE SYSTEMIC ROLE OF RACE AND NEOLIBERALISM ON HOUSING

Despite its many signs of economic health, Canarsie experienced a rapid rise in home foreclosures over the past decade, a trend that accelerated with the housing collapse of 2007. The statistical inconsistency between Canarsie's high median income and its rate of home foreclosure is different than all other New York City neighborhoods with comparable median incomes (Furman Center 2010). Why the disparity? Using a place stratification model of locational attainment, the role of race in exacerbating the effects of the Great Recession in Canarsie is difficult to ignore (Woldoff and Odavia 2009). While racist assumptions and stereotypes helped trigger the flight of white residents from the community at the end of the twentieth century, patterns of institutional racism caught up with the black residents who had replaced them in the twenty-first, intensifying the ways the American financial crisis of 2008 was felt by Canarsians on a local level and complicating perceptions of Canarsie as a middle class neighborhood.

No challenge to Canarsie presented the racially disproportionate damage of neoliberalism more clearly than the foreclosure crisis that struck the nation in 2008.[6] Neoliberal models sought to make capital more mobile, extend the reach of markets, and reduce regulation. The making of the housing crisis was the product of that model: Highly mobile international capital sought profitable investments. Investment banks (in New York in particular) further marketized the home mortgage market by creating mortgage-backed securities and collateralized debt obligations. The rush of capital into what seemed like highly profitable investment vehicles flooded the home mortgage market with capital that ultimately inflated housing prices, increased demands for mortgages to be resold on that secondary market, and induced lenders to make risky loans. Inadequate regulation of mortgage lending, investment vehicles, their rating, and their sale contributed to the bubble and its eventual collapse. The effect of that collapse was particularly evident in Canarsie.

That the foreclosure crisis hit communities of color the hardest is not a new story, nor one that is unique to Canarsie. Beginning in the 1990s, minority homebuyers who had historically faced difficulty getting mortgages due to exclusionary lending policies were brought into a tiered qualification system. Borrowers deemed "sub-prime" were subjected to higher or more adjustable interest rates, steeper penalties or balloon payments (Rugh and Massey 2010). Numerous studies have found that race played a direct role in the kinds of loans sold to home buyers. Compared to whites with similar credit profiles, down payment ratios, personal characteristics, and residential locations, blacks were much more likely to receive subprime loans (Avery, Brevoort, and Canner 2007; Avery, Canner, and Cook 2005; Bocian, Ernst, and Li 2006; Nichols, Pennington-Cross, and Yezer 2005). Residential segregation further compounded the prevalence of subprime lending in that it enabled financial institutions to aggressively target and market sub-prime loans to buyers in black neighborhoods underserved by traditional lending (Rugh and Massey 2010).

From a qualitative standpoint, race played another, more indirect role in the sale of sub-prime mortgages through consumers' use of social networks to buy real estate. A housing counselor who worked with struggling home owners in Canarsie's Community District 18 told one of our researchers that while the overwhelming majority of his clients were black, he didn't believe race was a factor in the kinds of loans his clients received. He simply believed instead that "people trusted the wrong people." Many of his clients were sold mortgages through family and friends, mortgage brokers who were provided with incentives by banks to encourage clients to purchase bad loans or buy property they were unable in actuality to afford. Thus, the counselor believed that the brokers involved in the process (who were black) were not intentionally targeting their clients because of their race. But the kinds of incentives used by banks to motivate brokers to market sub-prime loans to clients within their social network do appear to be influenced by the racial composition of the area in which the transactions were taking place.

As both a cause and consequence of the collapse of the housing market in 2007, homes that had been purchased through sub-prime loans were more likely to enter into foreclosure. According to Sarah Ludwig, executive director of the Neighborhood Economic Development Advocacy Project, "One in five high cost (sub-prime) mortgages is going to end in foreclosure . . . If one in five people with sub-prime loans are expected to lose their homes, it creates an urgent situation" (Buiso 2007: np). The housing crisis would soon expand beyond sub-prime borrowing, however. Michael Hickey, executive director of the foreclosure-prevention clearinghouse group the Center for New York City Neighborhoods, found that while earlier clients were primarily sub-prime borrowers, by 2010 most of the Center's clients had conventional mortgages, but were unable to make their payments because of loss of income.

Canarsie bears witness to the relationship between segregation, subprime borrowing and high rates of foreclosure. Of the eighteen community districts in Brooklyn, Canarsie was ranked in 2006 among the highest in terms of median income (at $58,000), edging out Bay Ridge (which had a median income of $50,000). Yet, in Canarsie, where over half the residents were black, 31.7 percent of all home purchase loans issued that year were issued by a sub-prime lender. In Bay Ridge, where the black population was 0.8 percent (Furman Center 2011), only 3.6 percent of home purchase loans were issued by a subprime lender. By 2010, Bay Ridge was experiencing a foreclosure rate of just 5 per 1,000 1–4 family properties, compared with Canarsie's much higher rate of 26.3 per 1,000 (Furman Center 2011).

The place stratification model helps explain the impact of the foreclosure crisis in the neighborhood. The model views race and ethnicity as more central than economic or educational factors in determining where an individual lives (Logan and Alba 1993; Logan and Molotch 1987). Thus, for a predominantly black neighborhood, quality of life cannot be as accurately determined by the economic or educational status of its residents due to the residential disparities that exist as a result of racial segregation. Furthermore, Rachael Woldoff and Seth Odavia point out that quality of life can be measured in a multitude of ways, from more quantitative criteria of measuring property values to more qualitative approaches of using residents' assessments of neighborhood disorder (Woldoff and Odavia 2009). Both measures demonstrate that racial and ethnic disparities have contributed to a declining quality of life in Canarsie.

In their application of the place stratification model to measure racial and ethnic differences in neighborhood quality, Woldoff and Odavia predicted that differences between black and white neighborhoods would exist even after controlling for disparities in human and financial capital (Woldoff and Odavia 2008). Using property values as a barometer for neighborhood quality, the researchers concluded that, "even if African Americans in the present generation are able to close the racial gaps in college completion and income, our findings suggest that the next generation will still experience racial inequality because of their parents' inability to convert these gains into locational parity with whites" (Woldoff and Odavia 2009). The researchers found that resources such as income not only failed to close the gap in property values between black and white homeowners, but that the value gap grew as incomes increased (Woldoff and Odavia 2009). Indeed, even while Canarsians' median income remained well above that of Brooklyn as a whole, during the mortgage crisis, Canarsians still saw a staggering 20 percent depreciation in the sale prices of their homes, compared to a 4 percent depreciation for Brooklyn home sales overall. Areas like predominantly white Bay Ridge had a lower median income than Canarsie, but only a 4.3 percent depreciation in sale prices.[7]

Distressed homeowners seeking to stave off foreclosure turned to methods of generating income that, on the one hand, enabled them to keep their homes but on the other, invited social instability. Residents subdivided their homes to rent out apartments despite their houses not being zoned as multifamily dwellings. Indeed, one housing counselor who was interviewed promoted this strategy to clients as a way of keeping up with their mortgage payments, particularly when there had been a reduction of employment income. While initially the counselor claimed to be unaware of any of his clients experiencing problems with their tenants, the counselor, in the same conversation, claimed to have received some reports of tenants "on this and that" (different government assistance programs) for whom the supplementary source of income had caused problems. State Senator John Sampson, who represented Canarsie, reported that the problem of renting illicit spaces to tenants was exacerbated by realtors who sold the homes as "two family with rentable basement," even though the basement couldn't be legally rented (Buiso, 2007: np). Said one resident, "The area was zoned for mostly one- and two-family homes, but there are many homes where the garages were closed and turned into basement apartments without DOB [Department of Building] approval." Another fretted, "Most of the new home owners were given bad mortgages; the new home owners cannot afford their mortgages without adding tenants who are not home owners who will overpopulate the neighborhood and bring in a revolving door of residents who create crime and other problems." Although no home owners could be found who had experienced errant tenants to corroborate this pattern, there seemed to be consensus from both official and unofficial sources that the attempts to offset foreclosure may produce other, unintended, negative outcomes for the neighborhood. At the very least, the prevalence of unauthorized apartments in single-family homes taints Canarsie's image as a conventionally middle-class neighborhood.

The effects of the foreclosure crisis in Canarsie can be measured using a qualitative analysis of residents' assessments of neighborhood disorder. Canarsie's status as a middle-class community may be threatened if home foreclosures and the decline of property values continue. Because of its economic precariousness, conflict exists within the community over how exactly to define it. While Jonathan Rieder's subjects shared a collective, albeit romanticized, sense of the neighborhood's identity, current-day Canarsians can't seem to agree on what kind of neighborhood they live in. Competing perspectives of the residents are further complicated by the neighborhood's location in relation to other areas. Middle-class Canarsians live in relatively close proximity to several neighborhoods, such as East New York and Brownsville, in which lower income blacks reside. This is not altogether uncommon for middle-class blacks. The pattern of clustering, partially a product of historic and contemporary patterns of racially discriminatory housing and partially the result of residential preference, tends to place middle-class black neighborhoods in proximity to areas of concentrated poverty (Pattillo-McCoy 2000). In other words, "the worst urban contexts in which whites reside are considerably better than the average context of black communities" (Sampson and Wilson 1995). This spatial distribution affects how black middle-class identities are reinforced and maintained. While Rieder's subjects drew racial boundaries around their community as a way of preserving their precarious class status, modern day Canarsians must rely instead on geographical and class markers to identify "outsiders." In her study of black middle-class neighborhoods, Mary Pattillo cites the ethnographic work of Bruce Haynes and Valerie Johnson to illustrate the "inbetweenness" of the black middle-class experience. Pattillo points out that Haynes' study of Runyon Heights, NY, in which blacks divided along class lines in response to a political redistricting plan, illustrates the vulnerability of black middle-class neighborhoods to the encroachment of black poverty (as well as its growth from within) and the efforts of middle-class black residents to hold the class line (Pattillo 2005).

CONCLUSIONS: PUNCTUATED EQUILIBRIUM

Several decades after white residents aggressively resisted the arrival of black residents, Canarsie has challenged many expectations about racially transitioning neighborhoods. Despite the ongoing challenges facing blacks in the job market, housing market, and mortgage market, black Canarsians have maintained Canarsie as a stable, working- and middle-class community. Contrary to the expectations of white residents, the neighborhood is notable for how similar it is after integration to its earlier demographic profile, community life, and patterns of ethically identified small businesses. Canarsians old and new articulate points of dissatisfaction about their neighborhood, but also continue to work to sustain it.

That notable success not withstanding, this study also identifies several threats facing African American neighborhoods like Canarsie. First, damage from the neoliberal model has had disparate impacts on black communities. In New York as in other U.S. cities, home foreclosures are heavily concentrated in black and Latino neighborhoods.

Second, Canarsie's long period of relative stability, only recently interrupted by the danger accompanying widespread foreclosure, suggests an alternate model to understand the trajectory of black neighborhoods. Studies of blockbusting in the mid-twentieth century concluded that neighborhoods that went from white to black declined quickly and dramatically. This has not been the case in Canarsie, where incomes and home values have remained relatively stable and rising for decades after its racial transition. It would be tempting to conclude that black middle-class families now enjoy the same level of security as their white middle-class counterparts. But the racially disproportionate impact of the foreclosure crisis argues against that conclusion. Instead, in the ecological terminology that has long held sway in urban sociology, Canarsie suggests a pattern of "punctuated equilibrium," or long periods of stability punctuated by periods of crisis (Eldredge and Gould 1972; Gould and Eldredge 1977). It is still too early to tell how the current crisis will shape the neighborhood in the long term.

What does this all mean for the future of Canarsie? The foreclosure crisis, the impact of which was magnified by the racial composition of the neighborhood, has encouraged discussion among residents about what it means to be a middle-class neighborhood and where to place the neighborhood within the urban social landscape. It has also inspired action to correct the damage wrought by economic collapse. More than three hundred residents attended a recent "Homeowners' Assistance and Financial Wellness" event at Holy Family Church hosted by State Senator John Sampson and major housing organizations such as CAMBA and NHS East Flatbush. Small signs of hope can be found in the work of people such as the CAMBA housing counselor who was interviewed for this project, who in the past year helped twelve Canarsie residents modify their mortgages and prevent foreclosure. Much more comprehensive efforts are needed. Yet despite the threats posed to Canarsie by the housing collapse, the community is making a concerted effort to alleviate the crisis and preserve its way of life. In this battle, residents will be confronting large social forces. Canarsians have always fought to defend their homes, their families, their communities, and their sense of class and cultural identity. The battles of the 1970s were misdirected at newcomers who were misperceived as a threat to the community. Canarsians will need to repurpose their neighborhood's storied unity, and resolve to defend their community against the real challenges it faces today.

ACKNOWLEDGMENTS

The authors would like to thank Celeste Roeller and Tisha-Luwana Holdbrooks for their important contributions to this research.

NOTES

1. Throughout much of this article, we use the term "black" as a racial term, and African American and West Indian to connote to ethnic and cultural identifications.

2. For the remainder of this paper the terms West Indian and Caribbean both refer to the peoples of the Islands of the Anglophone Caribbean including but not limited to Anguilla, Antigua, Bahamas, Barbados, Grenada, Guyana, Jamaica, St. Lucia, St. Vincent, Trinidad, and Tobago, and for the purposes of this paper Haiti even though it is part of the Francophone Caribbean. We have included Haitians in this category due to the fact that in Canarsie and throughout the Caribbean neighborhoods of Brooklyn, Haitians tend to identify with and live alongside people of other West Indian nationalities.

3. Furthermore, the study based its assessment on a spatial assimilation model, in which having more resources allows people to live in better communities (Massey 1985). Because of the predominantly black population in Canarsie, this model alone proves insufficient in assessing the quality of the neighborhood.

4. Census data from 1970–2009 (including the 2005–2009 American Community Surveys) comes from reports generated by SocialExplorer.com.

5. Although Giuliani was not initially successful in rewriting the zoning laws, his administration was able to approve an unprecedented number of big-box stores. Terry Pristin. 1999. "Repackaging The Big Box: Despite Zoning Rules and Hostility, Superstores Thrive in Crowded City." *New York Times*, December 20. Retrieved April 10, 2011 (www.nytimes.com/1999/12/20/nyregion/repackaging-big-box-despite-zoning-rules-hostility-superstores-thrive-crowded.html).

6. The bursting of the housing bubble and resultant foreclosure crisis began somewhat later in New York than elsewhere.

7. Neighborhood median income data comes from reports generated from Trulia.com.

REFERENCES

Aitken, Stuart C. 1990. "Local Evaluations of Neighborhood Change." *Annals of the Association of American Geographers* 80(2):247–67.

Alba, Richard D. and John R. Logan. 1993. "Minority Proximity to Whites in Suburbs: An individual-level Analysis Of Segregation." *American Journal Of Sociology* 98(6):1388–427.

Aldrich, Howard E. and Robert Waldinger. 1990. "Ethnicity and Entrepreneurship." *Annual Review of Sociology* 16:111–35.

Anderson, Elijah. 1990. *Streetwise: Race, Class and Change in an Urban Community*. Chicago: University of Chicago Press.

Avery, Robert, Glenn B. Canner, and Robert E. Cook. 2005. "New Information Reported under HMDA and Its Application in Fair Lending Enforcement." *Federal Reserve Bulletin* 91:344–94.

Avery, Robert B., Kenneth P. Brevoort, and Glenn B. Canner. 2007. "The 2006 HDMA Data." *Federal Reserve Bulletin* 93:73–109.

Bobo, Lawrence and Camille L. Zubrinsky. 1996. "Attitudes on Residential Integration: Perceived Status Differences, Mere In-Group Preference, or Racial Prejudice?" *Social Forces* 74(3):883–909.

Bocian, Debbie G., Keith S. Ernst, Wei Li. 2006. "Unfair Lending: The Effect of Race and Ethnicity on the Price of Subprime Mortgages." *Center for Responsible Lending*. Retrieved April 10, 2011 (www.responsiblelending.org/mortgage-lending/research-analysis/rr011-Unfair_Lending-0506.pdf).

Bonilla-Silva, Eduardo. 2009. *Racism without Racists: Color-Blind Racism and the Persistence of Racial Inequality in America*. 3rd ed. New York: Rowman and Littlefield.

Buiso, Gary. 2007. "The American Dream Fizzles Canarsie Suffers from Subprime Mortgages and Foreclosures." *Canarsie Digest,* July 19. Retrieved April 10, 2011 (www.nedap.org/pressroom/documents/2007-July-19_CanarsieDigest.pdf).

Butterfield, Sherri-Ann P. 2004. "'We're Just Black': The Racial and Ethnic Identities of Second Generation West Indian New York." Pp. 288–307 in *Becoming New Yorkers: Ethnographies of the New Second Generation,* edited by P. Kasinitz, J. H. Mollenkopf, and M. C. Waters. New York: Russell Sage.

Cole Cross-Reference Directory, Brooklyn and Vicinity. 2011. *Cole Information*. Retrieved April 14, 2011 (http://coleinformation.com).

DeSena, Judith N. 2005. *Protecting One's Turf.* 2nd ed. Lanham, MD: University Press of America.

Eldredge, Niles and Stephen Jay Gould. 1972, "Punctuated Equilibria: An Alternative to Phyletic Gradualism." Pp. 82–115 in *Models in Paleobiology,* edited by T. J. M. Schopf. San Francisco, CA: Freeman Cooper.

Fahim, Kareem. 2009. "Over Decades, Pizzeria Stays the Same in a Changed Neighborhood." *New York Times*, July 17. Retrieved April 20, 2011 (www.nytimes.com/2009/07/18/nyregion/18metjournal.html).

Furman Center for Real Estate & Urban Policy—New York University. 2011. "State of New York City's Housing and Neighborhoods: 2010." Retrieved April 19, 2011 (http://furmancenter.org/research/sonychan/2010-report/).

Gould, Stephen Jay and Niles Eldredge. 1977. "Punctuated Equilibria: The Tempo and Mode of Evolution Reconsidered." *Paleontology* 3(2):115–51.

Habermas, Jurgen. 1984. *Theory of Communicative Action, Vol. 1*. Boston, MA: Beacon Press.

Harvey, David. 2005. *A Brief History of Neoliberalism*. New York: Oxford University Press.

Henke, Holger. 2001. *The West Indian Americans*. Westport, CT: Greenwood Press.

Institute for Children and Poverty. 2009. *Pushed Out. The Hidden Cost of Gentrification: Displacement and Homelessness*. Retrieved April 20, 2011 (www.icphusa.org/PDF/reports/ICP%20Report_Pushed%20Out.pdf).

Kasinitz, Philip. 1992. *Caribbean New York: Black Immigrants and the Politics of Race*. Ithaca, NY: Cornell University Press.

Krase, Jerome. 2006. "Seeing Ethnic Succession in Little Italy: Change Despite Resistance." *Modern Italy* 11(1): 79–95.

Krysan, Maria. 2002. "Whites Who Say They'd Flee: Who Are They, and Why Would They Leave?" *Demography* 39:675––6.

Kurtz, Josh. 1991. "Suspect Seized In Bias Arson in Canarsie." *New York Times*, August 12. Retrieved April 20, 2011 (www.nytimes.com/1991/08/12/nyregion/suspect-seized-in-bias-arson-in-canarsie.html).

Logan, John, and Harvey Molotch. 1987. *Urban Fortunes: The Political Economy of Place.* Berkeley: University of California Press.

Low, Setha, Dana Taplin and Suzanne Scheld. 2005. *Rethinking Urban Parks: Public Space and Cultural Diversity*. Austin: University of Texas Press.

Maeroff, Gene. 1972. "Right on Both Sides: The Tragedy of Canarsie." *The Nation*, December 4, 550–2.

Massey, Douglas. 1985. "Ethnic Residential Segregation: A Theoretical and Empirical Synthesis." *Sociology and Social Research* 69(3):315–50.

Nichols, Joseph, Anthony Pennington-Cross, and Anthony Yezer. 2005. "Borrower Self-Selection, Underwriting Costs, and Subprime Mortgage Credit Supply." *Journal of Real Estate Finance and Economics* 30(2):197–219.

"Now It's Official," 2009. *Canarsie Courier,* July 2. Retrieved April 20, 2011 (www.canarsiecourier.com/news/2009-07-02/othernews/018.html).

Palmer, Ransford W. 1995. *Pilgrims from the Sun: West Indian Migration to America.* New York: Twayne Publishers.

Pattillo-McCoy, Mary. 2000. *Black Picket Fences: Privilege and Peril Among the Black Middle Class*. Chicago: University of Chicago.

Pattillo, Mary. 2005. "Black Middle-Class Neighborhoods." *Annual Review of Sociology*. 31:305–29.

Pauwels, Luc. 2010. "Visual Sociology Reframed: An Analytical Analysis and Discussion of Visual Methods in Social and Cultural Research." *Sociological Methods and Research* 38(4):545–81.

Perkins, Douglas, Joseph Hughey, and Paul W. Speera. 2002. "Community Psychology Perspectives on Social Capital Theory and Community Development Practice." *Community Development.* 33(1):33–52.

Rieder, Jonathan. 1985. *Canarsie: The Jews and Italians of Brooklyn Against Liberalism.* Cambridge, MA: Harvard Press.

Rieder, Jonathan. 1992. "Placing Canarsie." *Sociological Forum.* 7(2):337–53.

Rugh, Jacob S. and Douglas Massey. 2010. "Racial Segregation and the American Foreclosure Crisis." *American Sociological Review* 75:629.

Sampson, Robert J. and William Julius Wilson. 1995. "Toward a Theory of Race, Crime, and Urban Inequality." Pp. 37–56 in *Crime and Inequality,* edited by J. Hagan and R. Peterson. Stanford, CA: Stanford University Press.

Schlitchtman, Joe and Jason Patch. 2008. "Contextualizing Impressions of Neighborhood Change: Linking Business Directories to Ethnography." *City & Community* 7(3):273–93.

Vickerman, Milton. 1999. *Crosscurrents: West Indian Immigrants and Race.* New York: Oxford University Press.

Waters, Mary. 2001. *Black Identities: West Indian Immigrant Dreams and American Realities.* Cambridge, MA: Harvard University Press.

Woldoff, Racheal A. and Seth Ovadia. 2009. "Not Getting Their Money's Worth: African-American Disadvantages in Converting Income, Wealth and Education into Residential Quality." *Urban Affairs Review* 45:66–90.

Zubrinsky, Camille L. and Lawrence Bobo. 1996. "Prismatic Metropolis: Race and Residential Segregation in the City of the Angels." *Social Science Research* 25(4):335–74.

Index

About the Contributors

Noel S. Anderson, PhD, is associate professor in the Department of Political Science and School of Education (affiliated). Dr. Anderson received his Bachelors *cum laude* from Brooklyn College, Masters from the University of Pennsylvania and his PhD from New York University. His research centers on American politics, urban politics, and youth studies. Dr. Anderson has authored and coauthored numerous scholarly articles and two books titled, *Our Schools Suck: Students Talk Back to a Segregated Nation on the Failures of Public Education* (New York University Press, 2009) and *Education as Freedom: African American Education Thought and Activism* (Lexington Books, 2009). Dr. Anderson is also a frequent contributor to www.politic365.com and www.thegrio.com, an African American news site in conjunction with MSNBC.

Evrick Brown, PhD, of mixed African American and Caribbean parentage, is presently an adjunct assistant professor in the Sociology Department at Brooklyn College. Dr. Brown resides in the East Flatbush section of Brooklyn. His current writing projects include an article *Urban Political Operative in Community Politics* and a book covering the political clash between African Americans and Caribbeans in Brooklyn politics. His areas of interest include race and ethnicity, urban sociology, political sociology, and social movements.

Alessandro Busà, is the chief editor of *The Urban Reinventors* Online Urban Journal, a licensed architect and a doctoral fellow at the Transatlantic Graduate Research Center Berlin/New York. Busà has carried out research in New York City between 2006 and 2010 while on a visiting scholar appointment at the Graduate School of Architecture Planning and Preservation of Columbia University. His writing and research interests explore patterns of socio-spatial restructuring in advanced capitalist cities, with a main focus on entrepreneurial urban policies in New York City under the Administration of Michael Bloomberg. Busà has been awarded the *Erwin Stephan Preis* of the Technical University of Berlin in 2004; has lectured in the United States, Canada, U.K., Germany, Italy, Turkey, and Poland; has published several papers and book chapters in the United States, the Netherlands, Germany and Italy, and cooperated in research projects in several countries.

Jennifer Candipan is a Master's candidate in sociology at Brooklyn College. She earned her BA in English and American literature from the University of Southern California where she received honors for achievements both as a scholar and competing member of the Trojans' NCAA Division I Track & Field team. Professionally, she has worked as a writer, researcher, union organizer, and communications consultant for Los Angeles-based labor associations and advocacy groups. She is also a seasoned musician and performing artist.

Phyllis Conn holds a PhD in history from Indiana University. She is assistant professor at St. John's University in Queens in New York City, where she teaches in the core curriculum. Her recent research has focused on Community District 13 in southeastern Queens, Brighton Beach in Brooklyn, and South Beach in Staten Island. Dr. Conn serves on the executive board of the New York State Political Science Association, where she is the section chair for Gender, Race, and Diversity.

Roberta Cordeau received her Bachelor of Arts degree from Fordham University in 2008. She is currently working on her Master's Thesis entitled "Sharing Strengths and Facing Stigma: An Exploration of Networks of Support for Women Who Have a Loved One Who is Incarcerated." She will be graduating from Brooklyn College with her Master's degree in December 2011.

Judith N. DeSena, PhD, is a professor of Sociology at St. John's University. Her work centers on community, neighborhoods, and gender studies. Her latest research agenda articulates how gentrification affects community relationships in Brooklyn, New York. She has authored *Protecting One's Turf: Social Strategies for Maintaining Urban Neighborhoods* (1990 and 2005), *People Power: Grass Roots Politics and Race Relations* (1999). She has edited readings in sociology and ethnic studies, and is editor of *Gender in an*

Urban World (2008). She has also published various research articles in the area of residential segregation, women's community activism, and gendered space. Her latest book, *Gentrification and Inequality in Brooklyn: The New Kids on the Block* (2009), is a social class analysis of gentrification and the neighborhood dynamics it creates. At St. John's, Dr. DeSena is currently the faculty coordinator of Discover New York, a component of the Core Curriculum, and director of the Interdisciplinary Minor Program in New York Studies.

William DiFazio, PhD, is professor of sociology at St. John's University. He is author of *Ordinary Poverty* and *The Jobless Future*, second edition with Stanley Aronowitz.

Shanna Farrell will complete her Master's degree in the John W. Draper Interdisciplinary Program of Humanities and Social Thought at New York University in the fall of 2011. Also in the fall of 2010, she will be an Oral History Master of Arts at Columbia University. Her research focuses on water quality in contaminated sites and the surrounding community's relationship to this degradation. Currently, she is researching how toxic contaminants emitted by General Electric in Upstate New York have affected the fishing community on the Upper Hudson River.

Kenneth A. Gould, PhD, is professor and chair of sociology at Brooklyn College of the City University of New York, and professor of sociology, and earth and environmental sciences at the CUNY Graduate Center. Gould's work in the political economy of environment, technology, and development examines the responses of communities to environmental problems, environmental social movement coalitions, the role of socioeconomic, and racial inequality in environmental conflicts, and the impacts of economic globalization on efforts to achieve ecologically and socially sustainable development trajectories. He is coauthor of *Environment and Society: The Enduring Conflict* (1994); *Local Environmental Struggles: Citizen Activism in the Treadmill of Production* (1996); *The Treadmill of Production: Injustice and Unsustainability in the Global Economy* (2008); and coeditor of *Twenty Lessons in Environmental Sociology* (2009). His most recent work examines the role of urban environmental amenity restoration and creation as engines of gentrification.

Jerome Krase, PhD, Murray Koppelman and Emeritus Professor at Brooklyn College of The City University of New York, received his BA (Sociology) at Indiana University (1967) and his PhD at New York University (1973). An activist-scholar regarding inter-group relations and other community issues, he has written, photographed, lectured, and conducted research on neighborhoods in the United States and abroad. His "Brooklyn" books include *Self and Community in the City* (1982), and *Ethnicity and Machine Politics* (1992).

Steve Lang has a PhD in sociology and is associate professor at LaGuardia Community College where he teaches urban sociology and environmental sociology. He has done research on the political ecology of urban and suburban coastal environments. At the present time he is doing research on the politics surrounding New York City's updated comprehensive waterfront plan.

Tammy L. Lewis, PhD, is professor of sociology at Brooklyn College of the City University of New York, and professor of sociology, and earth and environmental sciences at the CUNY Graduate Center. She teaches courses on urban sustainability, social movements, environmental sociology, and research methodology. Her research examines the effects of globalization on environmentalism and sustainability, with a focus on Latin America. She is coeditor of *Twenty Lessons in Environmental Sociology* (2009) with Kenneth A. Gould, and coauthor of *Environment, Energy, and Society* (2002) with Craig R. Humphrey and Frederick H. Buttel. She is a council member of the Environment and Technology section of the American Sociological Association. Her recent research looks at the process of urban greening.

Sara Martucci, MA, is a doctoral student in the Sociology program at the CUNY Graduate Center. After graduating summa cum laude from Stony Brook University, Sara moved to Williamsburg, Brooklyn to pursue a Master's degree at Brooklyn College. For the past three years she has combined qualitative and quantitative methods to study consumption, identity, and community in Williamsburg.

Lorna Mason, PhD, is currently the senior research associate at the Center for the Study of Brooklyn at Brooklyn College. Over the last two years, as a senior researcher, Dr. Mason sought to understand and educate the media, politicians, researchers, residents, service providers, and students about the dynamic changes and needs of Brooklynites. Dr. Mason completed her graduate work in 2006 with Frances Fox Piven at the Graduate School and University Center of the City University of New York where she was awarded the Monticciolo Community Studies Fellowship and the CUNY Writing Fellowship, after which she was a visiting professor at Brooklyn College's Sociology Department. She has lived and worked in Brooklyn for over fourteen years and seeks opportunities to research, write, and promote a sustainable and just planet.

Ed Morlock is currently a research associate at the Center for the Study of Brooklyn. Morlock graduated from Brooklyn College, in 2008, with a Bachelor of Arts in American Studies. The interdisciplinary approach of this program allowed Morlock to study the intersection of cultural, social, and economic history in Brooklyn, as well as their implications for those living in Brooklyn today. Researching a broad range of topics, from the folklore of New York to the human, physical, and environmental impacts of urban growth and development in Brooklyn have given Morlock an historical perspective to his current work in the borough. Morlock also has experience in both non- and for-profit construction work, providing him with a pragmatic social and economic justice-inspired lens through which he approaches his work with the Center for the Study of Brooklyn.

Bengisu Peker is a Master's candidate in sociology at Brooklyn College.

Mark Peterson is working towards his MA in sociology at Brooklyn College, where he has developed an interest in the dynamics of riots, anti-authoritarian movements, political identity in multicultural contexts, and the role of communications technology in social movements. He earned a BA in psychology from St. John's University, during which he worked as a canvasser and field director for several local and city-wide political campaigns. He currently lives in Jamaica, NY and works as a research intern at Human Resources Administration.

Christina Pisano is a research associate at the Center for the Study of Brooklyn assisting with data analysis and technical assistance for the Center's various initiatives. Pisano graduated from Brooklyn College with a Bachelor of Arts in history and journalism. She is currently a graduate student in the Department of History at Brooklyn College and a curatorial intern at Fraunces Tavern Museum.

Nicole Riordan is a Master's candidate in sociology at Brooklyn College.

Danielle Shallow is majoring in sociology at Brooklyn College.

Timothy Shortell, PhD, is an associate professor of sociology and director of the MA program in sociology at Brooklyn College of the City University of New York. He earned his doctorate in social psychology from Boston College in 1992. He has published numerous book chapters and journal articles on social semiotics and the public sphere. Since 1997, he has collaborated with Jerome Krase on BrooklynSoc.org, an online photographic archive of urban neighborhoods in global cities.

Gregory Smithsimon, PhD, is a assistant professor of sociology at Brooklyn College of the City University of New York. He is currently working on *Liberty Road*, a book on African American middle-class suburbs. He is the author of *September 12: Community and Neighborhood Recovery at Ground Zero*, and coauthor, with Benjamin Shepard, of *The Beach Beneath the Streets: Contesting New York City's Public Spaces*.

Mark Treskon is a PhD student in the sociology department at New York University. He studies the relationships between advocacy and social movement organizations, private interests, and formal political structures. His dissertation focuses on how advocacy organizations navigated these relationships in their efforts to confront predatory home lending. In Brooklyn, he has studied the intersection of urban planning practices and community formation, paying particular attention to how concerns about affordable housing, gentrification, and displacement are handled by formal political processes.